D1391180

Rare Birds in Britain and Ireland

A Photographic Record

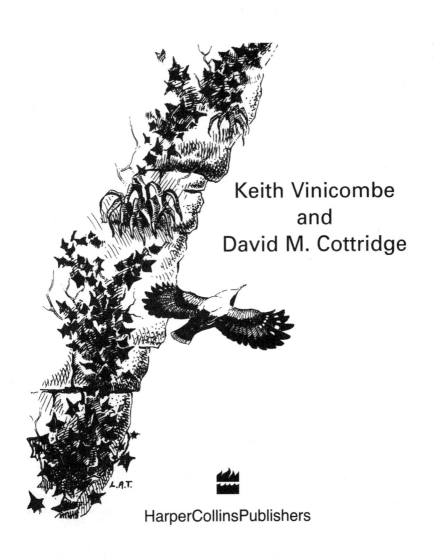

Keith Vinicombe
and
David M. Cottridge

HarperCollinsPublishers

Acknowledgements

I am particularly grateful to all the photographers who so kindly let us use their material. Hopefully this book will stand as a testament to their hard work and expertise. Steve Young in particular was helpful and cooperative. I should also like to make special mention of Lee Evans and Grahame Walbridge with whom I speak on an almost daily basis and whose expert knowledge, both of identification matters and occurrence patterns, I have extensively tapped. I should also like to thank Andy Middleton for the long term loan of his *Birding Worlds* – sorry about the coffee stains! I am also particularly grateful to Pete Fraser for his help and for endless drunken discussions about vagrancy and migration.

Many other people have helped in various ways, often by unwittingly passing on snippets of useful information, sometimes apparently inconsequential. These are Mashuq Ahmad, Ian Andrews, Rick Andrews, Graham Armstrong, Alan Bone, Colin Bradshaw, Phil Bristow, Martin Cade, Geoff Carey, John Clark, Les Cook, Richard Crossley, Mark Darling, Andy Davis, Alan Dean, Jonathan Drew, Phillippe Dubois, Martin Elliott, Tom Ennis, Alan Greensmith, Harold Grenfell, John Harriman, Hugh Harrop, Paul Harvey, Chris Heard, Rupert Higgins, Adrienne Hitchcock, Pete Hopkin, Julian Hough, John Humble, Rob Hume, Chris Janman, Barry Jarvis, Brian Lancastle, Peter Lansdown, Dawn Lawrence, Andy and Margaret Leggatt, Peter and Carole Leigh, Michael McKee, John and Janette Martin, Sid Massey, Cyril Matthews, Sally Middleton, Dominic Mitchell, Andrew Moon, Killian Mullarney, Chris Newman, Phil Palmer, David Parkin, Mark Ponsford, Mike Powell, Dominic Rigby, Mick Rogers, Mike Rogers, Christine Scasbrook, Dick Senior, Tim Sharrock, Ken Shaw, Chris and Theresa Stone, Dave Suddaby, Nigel Tucker and Jack Willmott.

Thanks also to all at D&N Publishing for their hard work in putting this book together.

KEV

Photographic Acknowledgements

Thanks to the following who have provided or helped with photographic material:

Chris Abrams, Steven Addinall, Sam Alexander, Graham Armstrong, David Astins, Dave Atkinson, Mike Barrett, Peter Basterfield, Nigel Bean, Michael Betts, Julian Bhalerao, P. R. Boardman, Greg Brinkley, A. T. Bromby, Tony Broome, Brian Brown, David Burns, Graham Catley, P. B. Chapman, Robin Chittenden, Alan Clark, Peter Clement, Mark Coller, Tony Collinson, Bill Condry, Simon Cook, Dennis Coutts, Dr Simon Cox, Tony Croucher, Mark Cubitt, Larry Dalziel, John Davies, Alan Dean, Jeff Delve, Roy Dennis, Ken Douglas, Andrew Easton, Tom Ennis, David Ferguson, Ian Fisher, Paul Gale, Steve Gantlett, Alan Gibson, David Godfrey, Jason Goodwin, Howard Grenfell, John Hall, John Harriman, Philip Harrison, Paul Harvey, Hugh Harrop, Ren Hathway, Mrs E. Hibbert, Rod Hirst, Paul Hopkins, David Hosking, John Humble, Marian Hunt (for the use of the late David Hunt's pictures), Bill Jackson, Chris Janman, Barry Jarvis, John Johns, Ron Johns, Reston Kilgour, Dave Kjaer, Chris Knights, Gordon Langsbury, Bill Last, Marcus Lawson, Peter and Carole Leigh, Jack Levene, Brian Little, Tim Loseby, Pete Loud, John Lovatt, David MacLeman, Jack Malins, Mike McDonnell, Anthony McGeehan, Mary McIntyre, Michael McKee, Pat McKee, Eleanor McMahon, Harold McSweeney, John Metcalfe, Richard and Hazel Millington, Richard T. Mills, Andrew Moon, Pete Morris, Neil Murphy, Angus Murray, Chris Newman, Howard Nicholls, Eamon O'Donnell, Michael O'Donnell, Kevin Osborn, Phil Palmer, Jim Pattinson, Keith Pellow, Prof. C. M. Perrins, Jeff Pick, Margaret B. Potts, John Raines, George Reszeter, D. C. Richardson, Nick Riddiford, Alan Roberts, Cloe Ross-Smith, Louis Rumis, Michael Sharp, Richard Smith, Dave Stewart, Keith Stone, Graham Sutton, Alan Tate, A. R. Taylor, Don Taylor, Roger Tidman, David Tipling, Nigel Tucker, Vic Tucker, Mick Turton, Will Wagstaff, Alyn Walsh, Peter Walsh, Keith Warmington, David Wheeler, Pete Wheeler, Barrie Wilkinson, Lorrie Williams, Ian Wilson, Rob Wilson, Steve Young and Jeff Youngs.

DMC

Line drawings by the late Laurel Tucker

CollinsNaturalHistory
HarperCollins Publishers
77–85 Fulham Palace Road
London W6 8JB

© Keith Vinicombe & David M. Cottridge 1996

ISBN 0 00 219976 9

The authors assert their moral rights to be identified as the authors of this work
All rights reserved

Edited and designed by D & N Publishing, Ramsbury, Wiltshire

Cartography by Carte Blanche, Basingstoke, Hampshire

Title page: Wallcreeper

Colour reproduction by Colourscan, Singapore

Printed and bound in The Bath Press, UK

CONTENTS

INTRODUCTION

The Photographs and the Photographers

There is something unquestionable about the validity of an image which a photograph portrays. As a historical record it holds a special fascination. Whether it be a famous person or event, the picture is perceived as an accurate record of the way things were, and because of that will hold our attention a little longer. Photographers are naturally drawn to those things which are either unique or extremely rare, and natural history subjects have much to offer in that area, none more so than birds. Bird photographers have been around since 1892 when the Kearton brothers photographed the nest of a Song Thrush *Turdus philomelos*, and it wasn't long before the birds themselves became the subject of the picture. To begin with, they photographed those species in and around Enfield in North London where they lived, but soon they went further afield in search of rarer species. Other photographers quickly came onto the scene, and the likes of Bentley Beetham, Oliver Pike, Alfred Taylor, R.B. Lodge and Francis Heatherley extended the boundaries not only to the far reaches of Britain and Ireland, but into Continental Europe.

The technique of bird photography has come a long way since those pioneering days but the appeal of the rarity has not waned. It has in fact blossomed and come of age in the last twenty years. The late 70s and early 80s saw the growth of the rarity photograph album in which birdwatchers would collect available photographs of the rarities which they had seen. The photograph had to be of the actual individual bird they had seen, and served as a record of a personal contact with an event which was extremely rare, and in some cases unique. A small band of photographers gradually formed who specifically travelled around to get pictures of the individual rarities with a view to selling them on to the birdwatchers. Through the photographs the birdwatchers were able to relive the joy and excitement of seeing birds such as the Golden-winged Warbler *Vermivora chrysoptera* in Kent in 1989 – still the only time that species has ever been seen this side of the Atlantic.

In obtaining these photographs the task of the photographer should not be underestimated, for it is one thing to see a bird but quite another to photograph it. Imagine travelling to somewhere such as the Shetland Isles to photograph an individual bird with no guarantee that it will still be there when you arrive, and even if it is, what are the chances of being able to photograph it? The quality of the pictures taken can vary greatly, but greater effort does not necessarily mean a better picture. A small not-quite-sharp image of a rarity might be the result of a quick eye and hand when the bird revealed itself in a fleeting moment. Such a picture is a greater photographic achievement than a beautiful close-up portrait of an extremely confiding bird. Whatever the quality of the pictures contained within these pages, however, they all have one thing in common: they are the genuine article, every one having been taken in Britain and Ireland.

This book is a collection of the best of the rare bird photographs that could be assembled up to and including the summer of 1996 and, therefore, should be looked upon as the ultimate rarity photograph album. Above all it is a tribute to all those photographers who have travelled thousands of miles and waited many long hours in often extremely difficult conditions for a chance to capture those elusive images. It is thanks to them that we have a lasting record of these rare avian visitors, some of whom may never grace our shores again.

David M. Cottridge, London, July 1996

The Birds and the Birders

Rare birds have always held a fascination for the British, from the Victorian collectors through the notorious 'Hastings Rarities' affair to the pioneering work of W. Eagle Clark on Fair Isle. The modern birding scene can perhaps be traced back to the formation of the bird observatory network in the 1950s, when, as an offshoot of their migration studies, it was discovered that a number of birds formerly considered to be great rarities were in fact occurring here with some regularity. The end of that decade saw the formation of the British Birds Rarities Committee (BBRC), established to cope with the increasing numbers of rarities being reported. With an increase in car ownership, improved communications and a greater general interest in wildlife, the 1960s saw birding start to broaden its appeal. By the 1970s, it had become a young man's hobby, its ranks swollen by a new generation of hippie baby boomers.

With its bird observatory on St Agnes, the Isles of Scilly had always been prominent in the scene – indeed, an astonishing number of rarities had already turned up – but most birders used to pack up and head for home at the end of September. In the late 1960s and early 1970s people began to realize that even though the 'real' migration had started to peter out, the rarities continued to turn up right through October. The year 1975 really marked the watershed for the Scillies, with the discovery in late September of three outstanding rarities: Black-and-white Warbler *Mniotilta varia*, Scarlet Tanager *Piranga olivacea* and Yellow-bellied Sapsucker *Sphyrapicus varius*. Since then, there has been an annual and increasingly popular pilgrimage to the islands, which for many birders is the highlight of their year. The role of the 'Scilly Season' as a catalyst for the twitching scene cannot be underemphasized.

The 1980s and 1990s saw the popularity of birding continue to grow. Several new birding magazines were launched but, most importantly, the advent of bird information telephone lines meant that news could be disseminated more quickly and more widely – it was no longer necessary to rely on the grapevine. Today, things have progressed even further, with the use of pagers and increased media interest.

What makes a twitcher tick? The popular image is of somebody totally obsessed with the pursuit of new birds and increasing his or her list. Yet we all know that the reality is quite different. There can be little doubt that the main reason men go birding is to satisfy a primitive hunting instinct. The principle is no different from fishing, football, rugby or a thousand and one other hunting substitutes. It also explains why there are still so few young women birders. But the idea of the twitcher being a blinkered male monomaniac is, quite clearly, simplistic. Most twitchers are birdwatchers first and foremost, and it is only a small minority who regard twitching as anything other than the icing on the cake of an already extremely rewarding and satisfying hobby.

What of the birds themselves? Surprisingly little interest has been paid to the phenomenon of vagrancy. It is probably true to say that most academics regard it as an irrelevance. At very best, we have had a few papers showing weather charts explaining how these unfortunate waifs have been blown off course by the wind. The study of migration is, of course, difficult and from a scientific point of view the study of vagrancy is infinitely more so. Yet this should not prevent us from theorizing and postulating about its causes. This I have attempted to do in an introductory chapter. In a nutshell, I believe that most vagrants, particularly the ones from further afield, get here as a result of physiological defects and are not simply the victims of inclement weather. Hopefully the ideas put forward will strike a chord and will at least stimulate further discussion of this fascinating subject.

So what of the future? Has twitching gone too far? Ask the average twitcher standing in a crowd of 2,000 and he or she would probably say 'yes'! But there seems to be little sign that interest is subsiding. There are likely to be increasing problems caused by the sheer numbers of people involved, but this may be offset by the fact that, as our lists continue to grow, fewer people will need to go and see most rarities. Whatever the future may hold, surely the main point to make is that the more people who are aware of birds and the world in which they exist, the better the prospects for their conservation.

Hopefully this book will stimulate that appreciation. Whatever your own depth of interest, I am sure that you will marvel at the sheer beauty of the subjects portrayed and wonder at the mind boggling distances that many have travelled to grace our shores.

Keith Vinicombe, Bristol, April 1996

- Fair Isle
- North Ronaldsay
- Flamborough Head
- Seaforth Docks
- Spurn
- Cley
- Bardsey
- Ballycotton
- Skokholm
- Cape Clear Island
- Lundy
- Dungeness
- Marazion Marsh
- Portland Bill
- Isles of Scilly

British and Irish Counties and Some of the Main Rarity Sites

The county boundaries that existed before the 1974 changes are shown, as it was felt that these were generally more familiar. Recent changes have returned many of the boundaries to those indicated.

10	Aberdeenshire
48	Anglesey
13	Angus
91	Antrim
15	Argyllshire
95	Armagh
26	Ayrshire
8	Banffshire
65	Bedfordshire
77	Berkshire
28	Berwickshire
67	Brecknock
66	Buckinghamshire
27	Buteshire
49	Caernarfonshire
3	Caithness
56	Cambridgeshire
71	Cardiganshire
114	Carlow
68	Carmarthenshire
97	Cavan
45	Cheshire
20	Clackmannanshire
110	Clare
119	Cork
86	Cornwall
36	Cumberland
47	Denbighshire
44	Derbyshire
90	Derry
85	Devon
89	Donegal
84	Dorset

94	Down
107	Dublin
33	Dumfries-shire
17	Dunbartonshire
37	Durham
22	East Lothian
70	Essex
93	Fermanagh
18	Fife
46	Flint
106	Galway
75	Glamorgan
73	Gloucestershire
83	Hampshire
63	Herefordshire
71	Hertfordshire
57	Huntingdonshire
11	Inverness-shire
39	Isle of Man
87	Isle of Wight
88	Isles of Scilly
80	Kent
120	Kerry
108	Kildare
115	Kilkenny
12	Kincardineshire
19	Kinrosshire
34	Kirkcudbrightshire
25	Lanarkshire
41	Lancashire
112	Laoighis
54	Leicestershire
98	Leitrim
116	Limerick
42	Lincolnshire
76	London
90	Londonderry
105	Longford
102	Louth
100	Mayo
103	Meath
51	Merionethshire
76	Middlesex
23	Midlothian
96	Monaghan

74	Monmouthshire
52	Montgomeryshire
7	Morayshire
9	Nairn
55	Norfolk
58	Northamptonshire
30	Northumberland
43	Nottinghamshire
109	Offaly
2	Orkney
5	Outer Hebrides
72	Oxfordshire
29	Peebles-shire
69	Pembrokeshire
14	Perthshire
62	Radnorshire
24	Renfrewshire
101	Roscommon
6	Ross-shire
31	Roxburghshire
54	Rutland
32	Selkirk
1	Shetland
53	Shropshire
99	Sligo
79	Somerset
50	Staffordshire
16	Stirlingshire
64	Suffolk
81	Surrey
82	Sussex
4	Sutherland
111	Tipperary
92	Tyrone
59	Warwickshire
118	Waterford
21	West Lothian
104	Westmeath
38	Westmorland
117	Wexford
113	Wicklow
35	Wigtownshire
78	Wiltshire
60	Worcestershire
40	Yorkshire

About this Book

This book is a photographic record of rare birds in Britain and Ireland. It is not intended to be a comprehensive identification guide. It assumes a certain level of expertise and competence and is to be used in conjunction with the better-quality field guides and journals. The text is divided into three sections:

Range This provides an outline of where the bird normally occurs, both in its breeding range, its wintering range and on migration. It must be stressed that this is only an outline and more comprehensive texts should be consulted for further details. Unless otherwise stated, the source of the information is *The Birds of the Western Palearctic* (*BWP*).

Occurrences This section summarizes the numbers of records and their geographical and temporal occurrence patterns. In many cases there is speculation as to how the vagrant(s) got here.

Identification This section largely relates to the features seen on the printed photographs. It is not intended to be a comprehensive identification analysis although, inevitably, the more tricky species are dealt with in more detail than those which are easy to identify. Features not apparent in the photographs, including calls which are relevant to the identification process in Britain and Ireland, may also be given for the sake of completeness. I have also attempted, whenever possible, to age the birds in the photographs. I have based this on standard works such as Svensson (1992), Pyle *et al.* (1987) and *BWP*. Ageing is not always straightforward and I accept full responsibility for any errors.

Information on the species' occurrence patterns have been based mainly on the data contained in the annual 'Report on Rare Birds in Britain and Ireland' published in *British Birds* and also Dymond *et al.* (1989). I have also extensively consulted Lee Evans's *Rare Birds in Britain: 1800–1990* and I have used his figures where it is clear that they are more accurate (this often occurs where he checked and discounted some of the very old records which are still part of the 'official record'). I have included data up to 1995, the last year for which figures are available, although I have also mentioned subsequent significant occurrences where I feel the identification is not in doubt.

With bird names, I have tried to use those which are in contemporary usage, although I have broken with the fine old British tradition of using generic names for species. I have thus adopted some convenient American names, such as Black-legged Kittiwake and Barn Swallow.

With the current débâcle over county names, I have had little alternative but to use the old county names used prior to 1974, particularly since many of these are now back in use (*see* map on page 6).

Since 1958, records of rare birds in Britain have been assessed by the British Birds Rarities Committee (BBRC). First sightings for Britain and 'category changes' have also been assessed by the British Ornithologists' Union Records Committee (BOURC). Irish records are dealt with by the Irish Rare Birds Committee. There are a number of species currently placed in Category D1 of the British and Irish List which I consider likely to have been wild and these have been included, bearing in mind the likelihood of occurrence (*see* pages 10–25) and the age, race, locality, timing and behaviour of the bird(s) involved.

Categories of the British and Irish List

Category A Species that have been recorded in an apparently wild state in Britain or Ireland at least once since 1 January 1958.
Category B Species that were recorded in an apparently wild state in Britain or Ireland at least once up to 31 December 1957 but have not been recorded subsequently.
Category C Species that, although originally introduced by man, have now established a regular feral breeding stock which apparently maintains itself without necessary recourse to further introduction.
Category D Species that would otherwise appear in categories A or B except that:
> **D1** there is reasonable doubt that they have ever occurred in a wild state, or
> **D2** they have certainly arrived with a combination of ship and human assistance, including provision of food and shelter, or
> **D3** they have only ever been found dead on the tideline, or
> **D4** species that would otherwise appear in Category C except that their feral population may or may not be self-supporting.

The Implications of Vagrancy

Little research seems to have been done on vagrancy, and most books and articles concerned with migration mention it only as an afterthought or in passing. Indeed, there is a long tradition of 'serious birdwatchers' pouring scorn on the subject and the people obsessed with it. But are rarities an irrelevance?

Surely the mere fact that some birds get it wrong is of interest in itself.

We can, in fact, learn quite a lot from the occurrence rates and patterns of vagrants. The frequency with which they turn up inevitably reflects population levels in their native range. Indeed, an increase in vagrancy may be the precursor to colonization (one only has to look at Cetti's Warbler *Cettia cetti* to confirm this). Despite a great deal of doom and gloom in the conservation world, a lot of species are clearly on the up. Obvious examples would be recent increases in the numbers of vagrant Great White Egrets *Ardea alba* and Black Kites *Milvus migrans*, these species having clearly increased and expanded their Continental breeding ranges. This happy state of affairs can be linked directly to the introduction of bird protection laws and improved conservation measures.

It seems likely that increases in vagrants from further afield may be telling us other stories. For example, one very striking trend is the increase and westward spread of a number of Eastern European passerines. These include Citrine Wagtail *Motacilla citreola*, Thrush Nightingale *Luscinia luscinia*, River Warbler *Locustella fluviatilis*, Paddyfield Warbler *Acrocephalus agricola*, Blyth's Reed Warbler *A. dumetorum*, Greenish Warbler *Phylloscopus trochiloides*, Penduline Tit *Remiz pendulinus*, Common Rosefinch *Carpodacus erythrinus*, Rustic Bunting *Emberiza rustica* and Little Bunting *E. pusilla*. Why has this been happening? It could be as a result of continuing climatic amelioration since the last Ice Age, or perhaps confirmation of global warming. Could the species be expanding as a consequence of declines in Western European migrants, which in recent years have been hit so hard by sub-Saharan droughts? If the expansion continues, will these species eventually breed in Britain? If we could travel through time 200 years into the future, would the vagrants of today, such as the River Warbler and Penduline Tit, be familiar ingredients of the British avifauna?

Similar questions can be asked of species from even further east. Why have Olive-backed Pipits *Anthus hodgsoni* and Pallas's Warblers *Phylloscopus proregulus* become so numerous in recent years? Sustained observations at places such as Fair Isle, Shetland, surely indicate that the increases are real and not just the result of greater observer awareness. Has forest clearance in Southeast Asia affected these species? Or is it due to changes on their breeding grounds? Do some species, such as Pallas's Warbler, have cyclical population fluctuations in line with their breeding-season food supplies? It seems most likely that some of these species may also be expanding their ranges westwards as any such spread would result in increased vagrancy in Western Europe (*see* Fig 1). If these species begin to survive in Western Europe better than they do in their traditional wintering areas, will they continue to increase

and become regular features of our autumn and winter avifauna?

One of the most intriguing features of vagrancy is that of reversed migration. Although it may be difficult to prove its existence, the circumstantial evidence is surely overwhelming. If 615 Yellow-browed Warblers *Phylloscopus inornatus* are recorded in Britain and Ireland in one autumn, how many *actually* turned up? How many were there in Europe? How many actually left their breeding grounds heading in the wrong direction? One must assume that the answer to the latter is in the thousands. But why? Is it just a peculiar freak of nature or is there a reason for the existence of reversed migration? Could it be some kind of safety valve to ensure the long-term survival of the species? The mere fact that some of these reversed migrants seem to be setting up regular wintering populations in Europe is surely of significance. An important point to make about such vagrants is that, although we regard them as freaks and no-hopers, as far as they are concerned they are migrating normally and Western Europe or north-western Africa are simply at the end of their migration route. Are we even correct to think of them as vagrants in the strict sense of the word?

What about transatlantic vagrancy? If 25 Red-eyed Vireos *Vireo olivaceus* are recorded in one autumn, how many were missed? One must assume that hundreds actually turned up. And if hundreds did turn up, how many more simply perished in the ocean? This may not affect the overall population of a numerous bird like the Red-eyed Vireo, but what happens if a major movement of Buff-breasted Sandpipers *Tryngites subruficollis*, a scarce bird in world terms, is hit by a fast-moving depression? All these questions are surely of interest.

There are many reasons why vagrants turn up. The following are a few ideas which may generate interest and provoke discussion. I firmly believe that, generally speaking, migrating birds 'know' exactly where they are and what they are doing, and that disorientation by inclement weather is usually little more than a temporary phenomenon for which they are usually able to compensate. I believe, therefore, that whilst weather-related vagrancy may account for birds turning up from the near Continent or even for those swept across the Atlantic in depressions, in most cases the vagrants get here because: (1) they intended to get here (as a result, for example, of a food shortage in their usual range); or (2) as the result of a physiological 'flaw' (in other words, by reversed migration or a failure to turn off their migratory urge at the appropriate time). We may have to concede, however, that some individuals may be slightly idiosyncratic and may not necessarily behave as the robotic pre-programmed computers that we would all like to believe!

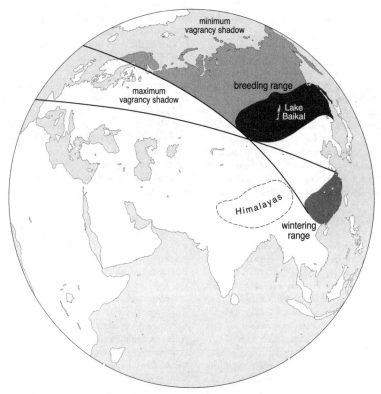

Fig 1 Approximate breeding and wintering ranges of the nominate race of Pallas's Warbler Phylloscopus proregulus, showing the minimum and maximum 'vagrancy shadows' in which birds are likely to occur if they were to reverse migrate. If it is assumed that western breeders may head towards the eastern part of the range, then, if they reverse migrate, they would be likely to reach Britain. It is interesting to note that any westward range expansion would be reflected by more records in western Europe as the 'vagrancy shadow' would shift southwards.

Causes of Short-range Vagrancy

Pre-migratory Dispersal

After fledging, it is well known that young birds, often still in juvenile plumage, may disperse randomly from their breeding areas. Some may even disperse northwards in completely the opposite direction from their eventual southward heading. Usually, such movements are of a relatively short distance. Perhaps the most obvious reason for these movements is that they enable an inexperienced individual to familiarize itself with the geography of the countryside close to its place of birth. This may be particularly beneficial in later life, especially in the following spring when a returning migrant needs to navigate very accurately into its breeding area. Alternatively, if, in subsequent years, an individual needs to move away from the immediate area of its birth, it may be advantageous to have prior knowledge of other good-quality potential nesting areas nearby. Other possible advantages include the relief of pressure on food supplies in the vicinity of its own

nest site, and it may also enable an individual to find a good food supply so that it can fuel up efficiently prior to its main migration.

So far as rarities are concerned, there are few species which owe their occurrence here to such movements. As the movements are of relatively short distance, such vagrants are inevitably limited to those which breed close by on the near Continent. The most obvious examples would be the Melodious Warbler *Hippolais polyglotta*, Woodchat Shrike *Lanius senator*, Ortolan Bunting *Emberiza hortulana* and, from slightly further afield, early autumn Barred Warblers *Sylvia nisoria*. Virtually all such vagrants relate to juveniles or first-winters as, quite clearly, there are few compelling reasons for experienced adults to make such exploratory movements.

Weather Drifting

Ask the average birdwatcher how rarities turn up and many will probably trot out the standard cliché that they are blown off course by the wind or that they are disorientated in bad weather. Weather may have a profound effect on migrating birds but, in most cases, weather-related vagrancy is a relatively short-distance phenomenon. If a bird is disorientated by the weather, it must soon realize this and compensate for it.

In Britain, vagrancy caused by weather disorientation perhaps best manifests itself in periodic east coast falls. In spring, for example, Bluethroats *Luscinia svecica*, Icterine Warblers *Hippolais icterina* and Redbacked Shrikes *Lanius collurio* which are heading for Scandinavia may be deflected across the North Sea by strong easterly winds or by depressions moving the 'wrong way' into Britain from the Continent. A characteristic of such falls, particularly in spring, is that large numbers of vagrants may be involved: for example, the 100 Bluethroats on the Isle of May, Fife, on 14–15 May 1985, or the 32 Ortolan Buntings on Fair Isle, on 3 May 1969. Rarer species may also be involved in the same movements, and examples of such would be Red-throated Pipits *Anthus cervinus* and Rustic Buntings *Emberiza rustica*.

In autumn, southward-moving migrants from Scandinavia may be deflected westwards in the same way and smaller numbers of vagrants may get caught up in these movements. The most classic example of this occurred in September 1965 when a phenomenal fall occurred along the Suffolk and Norfolk coasts as a result of slow-moving weather fronts across the North Sea. The account of the event published in *British Birds* makes compelling reading (Davis, 1966). For example, on 3 September, along a two-mile (3.2-km) stretch of coast south of Walberswick, Suffolk, D.J. Pearson estimated 15,000 Common Redstarts *Phoenicurus phoenicurus*, 8,000 Northern Wheatears *Oenanthe oenanthe*, 4,000 Pied Flycatchers *Ficedula hypoleuca*, 3,000 Garden Warblers *Sylvia borin*, 1,500 Whinchats *Saxicola rubetra*, 1,500 Tree Pipits *Anthus trivialis*, 1,000 Willow Warblers *Phylloscopus trochilus*, 500 Common Whitethroats *Sylvia communis* and smaller numbers of Spotted Flycatchers *Muscicapa striata* and European Robins *Erithacus rubecula*. Along with these phenomenal numbers, small numbers of rarities were seen, including 40 Wrynecks *Jynx torquilla*, 20 Bluethroats, a Great Reed Warbler *Acrocephalus arundinaceus*, an Icterine Warbler *Hippolais icterina* and two Barred Warblers *Sylvia nisoria*, plus three Temminck's Stints *Calidris temminckii* and a Kentish Plover *Charadrius alexandrinus*. Meanwhile, at Minsmere, estimates for the reserve by H.E. Axell included 15,000 Common Redstarts, 10,000 Northern Wheatears and 5,000 Pied Flycatchers, plus 25 Wrynecks, 25 Bluethroats, two Icterine Warblers, a Tawny Pipit *Anthus campestris*, a Red-backed Shrike and three Ortolan Buntings. Although such a fall may affect much of the east coast, in the great scheme of things it is nevertheless a relatively localized event and the birds affected are clearly able to re-orientate once

the problem has passed. This is exemplified by the Rustic Bunting trapped on Fair Isle in June 1963, which had clearly drifted across the North Sea. It was recovered in Greece in October of the same year, presumably on its way back to its wintering grounds (albeit a long way south). One particular characteristic of weather displacement is that it is also likely to affect *adult* birds as well as immatures.

The other main weather-related form of vagrancy involves those North American birds that are swept across the Atlantic in fast-moving depressions. This phenomenon is dealt with below.

Overshooting in Spring

A bird flying 3,000 miles north from Africa may make an error of judgement and overshoot its breeding grounds. This is particularly likely if it hasn't compensated for a strong tail wind. A classic example would be a Hoopoe *Upupa epops* heading for Brittany which overshoots the English Channel and ends up on the south coast. It is probably soon able to re-orientate itself and return to where it should be. Overshoots classically occur during southerly winds and may relate principally to less-experienced first-summer individuals on their first northward migration. As well as overshooting from France, overshooting also occurs from Iberia, leading to classic spring influxes of southern herons, European Bee-eaters *Merops apiaster*, Woodchat Shrikes *Lanius senator* and so on, predominantly into Cornwall and Devon, and southern Ireland. Another characteristic of such movements is that they may occur very early in the year. Some migrants return to Iberia by January or February and, having overshot, they presumably find themselves out over the Bay of Biscay and then simply continue heading north until they hit land. Black-crowned Night Herons *Nycticorax nycticorax*, Squacco Herons *Ardeola ralloides*, Subalpine Warblers *Sylvia cantillans* and Woodchat Shrikes have occurred in March in the Isles of Scilly, Cornwall and southern Ireland, while Great Spotted Cuckoos *Clamator glandarius* and even a Red-rumped Swallow *Hirundo daurica* have turned up in February. Although early spring overshoots tend to occur predominantly in Ireland and the South-west, there is a marked shift later in the spring to the east coast as breeders from south-eastern Europe overshoot across the Continent and the North Sea. This phenomenon is dealt with on page 13 in *Long-range Overshooting*.

Cold Weather Movements

In very cold winters, Britain and Ireland receive cold-weather influxes from Continental Europe. In particular, these involve waterfowl such as Red-necked Grebes *Podiceps grisegena*, geese, Velvet Scoters

Melanitta fusca and Smews *Mergus albellus*. A few vagrants may also arrive here in response to freezing weather, perhaps the best example being the Great Bustard *Otis tarda*.

Altitudinal Migration

As the closest large mountain ranges are as far away as the Alps and the Pyrenees, we do not receive many altitudinal migrants. The only such species which occurs regularly is the Water Pipit *Anthus spinoletta*. Vagrants which fall into this category are the Alpine Accentor *Prunella collaris*, Wallcreeper *Tichodroma muraria* and perhaps Rock Bunting *Emberiza cia*, all of which are extremely rare.

Irruptions

An eruption occurs when a species moves out of its normal breeding area in response to a food shortage. Areas away from the normal range may then receive an irruption. The most obvious eruptive/irruptive species in Britain and Ireland are northern breeders which depend either on the fluctuating crops of conifers or on lemmings and other small rodents. The best known is the Common Crossbill *Loxia curvirostra* which is dependent primarily on the seeds of the spruce, but numbers of other common northern passerines are also linked to variations in food supplies. Populations of northern owls, raptors and Long-tailed Skuas *Stercorarius longicaudus* vary directly in response to the lemming cycle while other Arctic breeders, particularly waders, may fluctuate from year to year in indirect response to their numbers.

A number of vagrants reach our shores mainly or wholly as a result of eruptions and these include the Gyr Falcon *Falco rusticolus*, Snowy Owl *Nyctea scandiaca*, Parrot Crossbill *L. pytyopsittacus*, Arctic Redpoll *Carduelis hornemanni* and real rarities such as Tengmalm's *Aegolius funereus* and Hawk Owls *Surnia ulula*, Spotted Nutcrackers *Nucifraga caryocatactes*, Two-barred Crossbills *L. leucoptera* and Pine Grosbeaks *Pinicola enucleator*. Even some trans-Atlantic vagrants, such as the Red-breasted Nuthatch *Sitta canadensis* and Evening Grosbeak *Hesperiphona vespertina*, have occurred at times when large numbers have been on the move in North America.

Although irruptive vagrants are typically northern, more southerly species may also turn up in response to food shortages. A classic example is Pallas's Sandgrouse *Syrrhaptes paradoxus*, while many summer influxes of Rose-coloured Starlings *Sturnus roseus* are also irruptive and follow large incursions into southeastern Europe where they sometimes breed.

Some species are less obviously irruptive. For example, the movements of some waterbirds may also be related to diminishing food supplies. Periodic influxes of Black-winged Stilts *Himantopus*

himantopus are traditionally put down to overshooting but it seems likely that desiccation of their Mediterranean breeding marshes may sometimes trigger the movements. The influx of White-tailed Plovers *Vanellus leucura* into Europe in the summer of 1975 can be directly related to a severe drought in Kazakhstan. Occasional late summer influxes of Marbled Ducks *Marmaronetta angustirostris* into northern Spain and southern France are prompted by the drying up of wetlands in southern Spain and it is possible that some of our records have stemmed from this source.

Another characteristic of irruptive vagrants is that some may linger and actually breed in Britain. The most remarkable were the Pallas's Sandgrouse which bred in Yorkshire in 1888 and in Morayshire in 1888 and 1889, while others involved the Snowy Owls on Fetlar, Shetland, from 1967–75, and the Parrot Crossbills in Norfolk and probably Suffolk in 1984–85.

Migration from the South

In Britain and Ireland we are so accustomed to birds flying south for the winter that we tend to forget about those regular immigrations which involve birds that breed to the south. Because there is much less land in the southern hemisphere, there are no landbirds which arrive in Europe for our summer, but there are three seabirds which regularly do so: Great *Puffinus gravis* and Sooty Shearwaters *P. griseus* and Wilson's Storm-petrel *Oceanites oceanicus*.

There are, however, birds which breed closer to home in southern Europe and which regularly move north to our area to take advantage of short-lived late summer food supplies. Again, seabirds are well-represented with Mediterranean *P. yelkouan* and Cory's Shearwaters *Calonectris diomedea*, but two rather more terrestrial species are increasingly making similar movements: Little Egret *Egretta garzetta* and Yellow-legged Gull *Larus cachinnans*. As well as birds, it is of course well known that some butterflies and moths also move northwards at this time of year.

Regular northerly movements of Ruddy Shelducks *Tadorna ferruginea* can also be categorized with the foregoing, although the fact that larger movements may be triggered by desiccation makes this species at least partly irruptive.

As these influxes occur principally in July and August, a time that is traditionally poor for vagrancy, many ornithologists have been unable or unwilling to accept that they actually involve wild birds and many have been traditionally dismissed as escapes. The Ruddy Shelduck and the Rose-coloured Starling have long been stigmatized in this way.

Another characteristic of such movements is that, although peak numbers occur in late summer, a minority may actually remain for the entire winter and not move back south until the following spring.

The only trans-Saharan vagrant on the British and Irish list is Allen's Gallinule *Porphyrula alleni*. Reasons for its appearance so far to the north are unclear but rails, crakes and gallinules appear to be prone to erratic long-range vagrancy. The American Purple Gallinule *P. martinica* may also to some extent fall into this category.

Causes of Long-range Vagrancy

Long-range Overshooting

The phenomenon of short-range overshooting in spring is discussed above, but there is another aspect to this phenomenon: that of long-range overshooting. Whilst it is easy to imagine a bird getting caught in a southerly airstream and simply flying just that bit too far, how do we explain spring occurrences of vagrants from much further afield?

Two classic examples would be the Black-headed Bunting *Emberiza melanocephala* and Marmora's Warbler *Sylvia sarda*. In spring, Black-headed Buntings head north-west from the Indian subcontinent towards Asia Minor and south-eastern Europe. The closest they regularly breed to Britain is in the former Yugoslavia, yet they regularly occur here as spring overshoots, at least 900 miles (1,440 km) beyond their normal breeding areas. Marmora's Warbler is a short-range migrant travelling perhaps 400 miles (640 km) from its North African winter range to its northern Mediterranean breeding areas, yet there are now three records in northern Britain, some 900 miles (1,440 km) to the north. Such occurrences cannot be dismissed as simple errors of judgement induced by unusually strong tail winds.

The most plausible solution is that some birds simply fail to 'switch off' their migratory urges at the appropriate time and continue migrating. Such a physiological explanation would neatly explain the huge distances flown by some spring overshoots. A notable phenomenon of spring overshooting is that many of the vagrants are males. Presumably, susceptibility to overshooting is linked to their sexual urges.

Whether or not a species has the potential to occur in Britain as a spring overshoot depends entirely on the orientation of its migration route. For example, if a Woodchat Shrike heading from West Africa to Spain overshoots its breeding area and continues flying north on its normal heading, it may end up in Britain or Ireland. On the other hand, a Masked Shrike *Lanius nubicus* heading from East Africa towards Greece will not end up in Britain if it overshoots. Instead, it is more likely to end up in Scandinavia, where there have indeed been several spring records. This simple fact neatly explains why some relatively numerous close-breeding species, such as the Thrush Nightingale, are so rare in Britain. This species

winters in East and south-eastern Africa and heads practically *due north* to its breeding areas in Eastern Europe. The orientation of migration routes will be discussed further in the section below on reversed migration. Long-range overshooting from the Eastern Palearctic and from North America will also be discussed below.

Abmigration

This term has been given to the phenomenon whereby some individuals, particularly ducks, make atypical migrations as the result of pairing with an alien female and migrating with it. For example, a male Tufted Duck *Aythya fuligula* born in Britain in a population which is fairly sedentary could pair with a female which has migrated here from Russia. The following spring, instead of staying on its local gravel pit, it migrates thousands of miles eastwards with its newly acquired mate. A similar phenomenon may occur with vagrants. For example, a Ferruginous Duck *A. nyroca* which should winter in the eastern Mediterranean may attach itself to a flock of Common Pochards *A. ferina* in late summer and head off west with them to winter in Britain. A Falcated Duck *Anas falcata* could do the same with Eurasian Wigeon *Anas penelope*. Geese are also notoriously prone to this. It is well known that Lesser White-fronts *Anser erythropus* turn up with Russian White-fronts *Anser albifrons albifrons*, Red-breasted Geese *Branta ruficollis* with Brent Geese *B. bernicla* and Snow Geese *Anser caerulescens* with Pink-feet *A. brachyrhynchus*. It may also partly explain the occurrence of Ross's Geese *A. rossii* (*see also* page 23). Although these phenomena are not 'abmigration' in the strict sense of the word, the principle is very similar.

Vagrancy from the Eastern Palearctic

One of the most remarkable aspects of vagrancy is the regular occurrence, every autumn, of hundreds of migrants from the Eastern Palearctic, thousands of miles off course. The tabloid press often picks up on these occurrences and trots out the usual cliché about them being blown here by the wind. Even some of the more learned birding journals have produced papers and weather maps speculating on the routes taken to get here. But just think for a moment: if these birds were being shifted randomly around the globe by the wind, then why are Yellow-browed Warblers from Siberia so much more numerous than Western Bonelli's Warblers *P. bonelli*, which breed as close as France? Why do we get lots of Red-breasted Flycatchers *Ficedula parva* but very few Collared Flycatchers *F. albicollis*? Indeed, why don't Lesser Whitethroats *Sylvia curruca* and Garden Warblers *S. borin* winter in our suburban gardens, as do Blackcaps *S. atricapilla*? It is immediately apparent that vagrancy is not random.

The Importance of Reversed Migration We need initially to understand how Eastern Palearctic vagrants get here, and the first and most fundamental point to make is that these birds are not simply blown off course by the wind. The distances involved are so great that any initial disorientation by adverse weather would be compensated for long before the birds ever reached this country.

The vagrants that arrive here do so because they have deliberately flown in this direction. To understand this, it is probably most helpful to think of a bird's brain as being like a computer. On its first migration, the young bird is 'programmed' to fly in a certain direction for a certain distance, or until its migratory 'urge' subsides. Only on subsequent migrations will the route be deliberately modified as a result of experience.

It seems most likely that the Eastern Palearctic vagrants which reach Britain and Ireland arrive as a result of reversed migration. In other words, they have migrated at 180° in the opposite direction to their normal route. Because the Earth is basically a sphere, those migrants which would normally fly north-west to south-east in autumn from western or central Siberia to south-east Asia may end up in Western Europe if their migration is reversed. To appreciate this it is essential to look at a globe rather than a flat map. It should be noted, however, that the route they take may be 'modified' to some extent by inherent 'migratory turns' or even curved migration routes, and they will also be subjected to the vagaries of the weather, just like any ordinary migrant.

The Migration Itself Our vagrants will have probably set off from their breeding areas in late August or September and will be arriving in Britain and Ireland mainly in October and November, towards the end of their migration (*see* Fig 5). This migration is not completed in 'one hop' but, in common with most autumn migrants, it proceeds at a fairly leisurely pace, moving relatively short distances at any one time, usually with the benefit of a tail wind. Confirmation of this may be obtained by analysing the lengths of time which Eastern Palearctic vagrants linger at migration sites. I have analysed the lengths of stay for Siberian and North American passerine vagrants found in the Isles of Scilly during the month of October from 1975 to 1993. I have chosen this month and locality and this time period because, since the 1970s, the Scillies in October have been very intensively covered. The average length of stay for Eastern Palearctic vagrants was 2.81 days (98 individuals), compared with 7.01 days for Nearctic ones (95 individuals). The stopover period for Nearctic vagrants would have been even longer but for the fact that a number of birds, notably *Catharus* thrushes, are in such a poor state that they probably die soon after arrival. The difference in stopover times is due to the fact that North American vagrants have exhausted most of their fat reserves during a long 'one-hop' trans-Atlantic crossing and will have had to refuel for a longer period, whereas Eastern Palearctic vagrants will, on average, have flown a much shorter distance since their last stopover. Such a stopover is likely to have been on the near Continent. This theory is supported by the record of a male Desert Wheatear *Oenanthe deserti* ringed at Landguard Point, Suffolk, from 20–24 October 1987, and subsequently seen at East Prawle, Devon, from 26–30 October. This bird had moved some 270 miles (430 km) in, presumably, one night and had to spend five days refuelling in each stopover. Incidentally, if one plots its Suffolk to Devon migration route backwards, one can suggest that it originated in Kazakhstan or surrounding regions and that it should really have been heading for India.

Such vagrants will respond to local weather conditions in the same way as more local migrants. Thus Little Buntings and Yellow-browed Warblers crossing the North Sea may appear in falls of commoner species during periods of easterly winds. It is also possible that Eastern Palearctic vagrants on a heading which would take them across western Continental Europe to wintering areas in Iberia or north-west Africa could be drifted to this country during periods of easterly or south-easterly winds.

Because they 'think' they are migrating normally, they will presumably keep flying until their migratory 'urge' subsides or until they find a suitable wintering habitat. This means that they do not stop at what we would regard as major barriers. A Yellow-browed Warbler flying south-west across the North Sea doesn't 'know' that there is land on the other side. Similarly, the same bird heading south-west from Scilly doesn't 'know' that a huge ocean lies before it. We must assume, therefore, that many, if not most of these birds continue on their heading and simply perish in the Atlantic.

Interestingly, there is mounting evidence to suggest that this is precisely what happens. Considering the rarity of the species involved, there have been several records of eastern vagrants landing on boats and islands in the Atlantic. For example, a Paddyfield Warbler *Acrocephalus agricola* was found on a fishing boat 254 miles (409 km) south-west of Ireland in September 1993 (*see* page 129). Similarly, a Yellow-browed Warbler was found on Fuertventura, Canary Islands, in February 1994, a Red-breasted Flycatcher was found on a fishing boat 12 miles (20 km) off Terciera in the Azores in November 1995, and there are four records of Red-breasted Flycatchers in the Canary Islands, including a wintering one on Tenerife from January to March 1995. Even in Britain, there are several records of eastern vagrants (such as

Citrine Wagtail, Blyth's Reed Warbler, Dusky Warbler *Phylloscopus fuscatus* and Rustic Bunting) from the isolated St Kilda off the Outer Hebrides. One can only assume that if these islands didn't exist, the birds would have dropped into the ocean.

What Causes Reversed Migration? For reversed migration to work, we need to postulate that a small minority of migrants 'think' that north is south and vice versa. Presumably, this would have to be linked to their sensitivity to the Earth's magnetic field, and in turn linked to the small particles of magnetite that are found in the brain. Could it simply be that some birds are born with reversed polarity? Hopefully, science will one day come up with the answer.

The Benefits of Reversed Migration Could there be any benefits from reversed migration? A number of possibilities spring to mind. A species could set up an alternative wintering area which may be beneficial should some kind of catastrophe affect the traditional one. Richard's Pipits *Anthus novaeseelandiae* and Yellow-browed Warblers now winter quite regularly in Western Europe. Indeed, there were as many as 16 Richard's Pipits found wintering at the Oued Massa in southern Morocco in January 1995 (Martin Cade, verbally). Were those birds to make it back to Siberia, then there could be survival value in setting up such an alternative. Could it be that the Swiss and German Blackcaps which now so commonly winter in our suburban gardens have stemmed from reversed migrants which originally should have headed south-east to the eastern Mediterranean? This theory has found backing in Scandinavia where Blackcaps recorded in winter are considered to be reversed migrants from further south in Europe (Fransson & Stolt, 1993).

The Vagrancy Shadow If one accepts the theory of reversed migration, one can postulate the potential areas of vagrancy by drawing lines back from the winter range to the breeding range and beyond. If one assumes that birds from the west of the breeding range winter in the west of their winter range, then one can work out a minimum 'vagrancy shadow' in which reversed migrants are likely to occur. If, however, some birds from the west of the breeding range winter in, or at least migrate towards, the east of the winter range, then one can postulate a maximum 'vagrancy shadow' (*see* Fig 1).

The idea that reversed migrants are on a very specific heading is supported by the occurrence patterns of many vagrants. For example, Yellow-breasted Buntings *Emberiza aureola* are known to have a moult stop-over in China (Svensson, 1992), and it seems likely that birds from the western part of their breeding range initially head in a fairly easterly direction in

autumn. This means that the 'vagrancy shadow' of reversed migrants cuts east–west across the north of Britain, but excludes the south (*see* Fig 2), and their rarity in the south is genuine. Similarly, the Pechora Pipit *Anthus gustavi* and the Lanceolated Warbler *Locustella lanceolata* both have rather narrow and northerly breeding ranges and, assuming these birds head south-east in autumn, the 'vagrancy shadow' is quite narrow and again cuts across the northern half of Britain, thus also explaining their rarity in the south. In North America, it is well known that many species of eastern wood-warbler have spread westwards, yet they still follow their inherited migration routes, initially travelling south-east in autumn towards the Atlantic coast before heading south or south-westwards towards their winter quarters in Central America or the West Indies. It seems likely that some north-eastern European and western Siberian breeders – such as Arctic *Phylloscopus borealis* and Greenish Warblers – may also have an inherently easterly orientation in the first stages of their autumn migration before doing a 'dog-leg' turn into southeast Asia.

If one accepts that the Eastern Palearctic vagrants which get here are indeed reversed migrants, then they can get to Britain *only if the orientation of their migration route is such that, if they reverse migrate, the route would pass over Britain*. A very dramatic example to illustrate this can be seen with two species of Eastern European flycatcher. The Collared Flycatcher, although widespread and common in Eastern Europe, is surprisingly rare in Britain (19 records up to 1995). This is because it migrates basically north–south from Eastern Europe to East Africa. Any overshooting spring migrants or reversed autumn migrants are unlikely to hit Britain; they are much more likely to end up in Scandinavia or northern Russia (*see* Fig 3). The Red-breasted Flycatcher, on the other hand, although sharing a similar breeding range (as well as extending into Asia), migrates south-east in autumn towards the Indian subcontinent. Because of the north-west–south-east orientation of its migration route, any reversed migrant is likely to end up in, or pass through, Britain and Ireland (*see* Fig 4). This theory is surely confirmed by the number of records: 2,141 between 1958 and 1985 alone (Dymond *et al.*, 1989).

This has clear repercussions for Eastern Palearctic migrants. For such birds to reach Britain, they will have to breed relatively far to the west in Siberia and migrate north-west to south-east into Southeast Asia. All the non-controversial Eastern Palearctic vagrants that have reached Britain in fact breed west of 100°E and, being a conspicuous feature on a map, it is convenient to use Lake Baikal (105°E) to mark the watershed. To reach Britain, their great circle route would pass over northern Europe (principally the Baltic and Scandinavia),

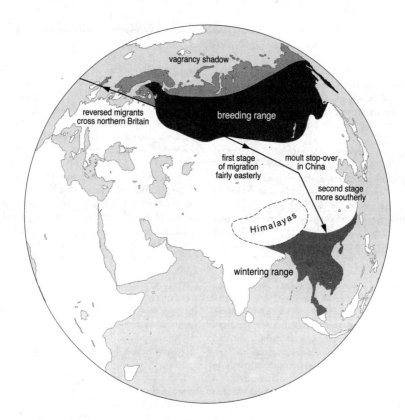

Fig 2.

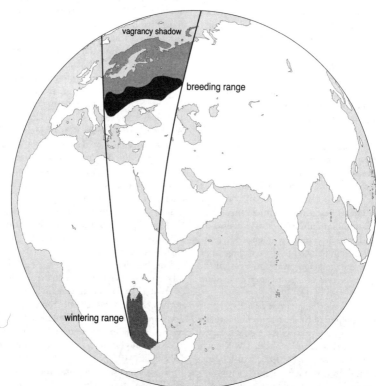

Fig 3.

Fig 2 (Opposite above) Approximate breeding and wintering ranges of Yellow-breasted Bunting Emberiza aureolus. It is known that this species has a moult stop-over in central China and western birds head east from the breeding grounds and then south. This would mean that any reversed migrant is likely to clip the north of Britain, but not the south.

Fig 3 (Opposite below) Breeding and wintering ranges of Collared Flycatcher Ficedula albicollis and the 'vagrancy shadow' in which any overshooting spring birds or reversed autumn migrants would be likely to occur. As this species migrates practically north/south from eastern Europe to East Africa, it is unlikely to reach Britain. This is confirmed by the number of records: only 19 between 1958 and 1995 (cf Fig 4).

and down across the North Sea, the Low Countries and Britain (*see* Fig 5). (Again, to appreciate this fully, it is essential to look at a globe.) Any bird that breeds to the east of the Lake Baikal Watershed is likely to have a much more north–south migration route and, like the Collared Flycatcher in Europe, it would be much less likely to occur as a westerly moving vagrant (*see* Fig 6).

This theory is important for determining what can and cannot turn up in Britain and Ireland. Wallace

(1980) suggested future potential Eastern Palearctic vagrants to Britain but, using the Lake Baikal Watershed, it is possible to be far more specific about what is and what is not likely to occur. The fact of the matter is that the potential for what can turn up is not limitless and the majority of potential Eastern Palearctic vagrants have already occurred. The only long-range migrants breeding in strength to the west of Lake Baikal and not yet recorded in Britain or Ireland are listed in Table 1.

The species listed in Table 2 breed entirely to the east of Lake Baikal and have migration routes that would appear to be too north–south or even north-east–south-west, and/or are not long-range migrants. Whilst one perhaps can never say 'never', these birds should be treated as very unlikely vagrants to Western Europe.

Another important point to make is that, because most Eastern Palearctic migrants probably perish, *their vagrancy is almost entirely a phenomenon associated with immature birds making their first autumn migration.* Very few must survive to make the same 'mistake' twice. Also, as the vagrancy is related to autumnal reversed migration, it follows that direct spring vagrancy is very unlikely.

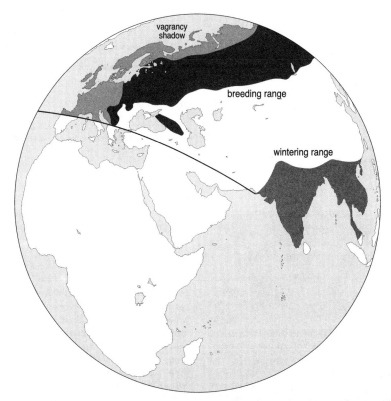

Fig 4 Breeding and wintering ranges of Red-breasted Flycatcher Ficedula parva. Unlike the Collared Flycatcher F. albicollis, this species heads south-east towards the Indian Sub-continent in autumn. This means that any reversed migrants (and spring overshoots) are likely to cross Britain and Ireland. This is confirmed by the number of records: 2,141 between 1958 and 1985 alone.

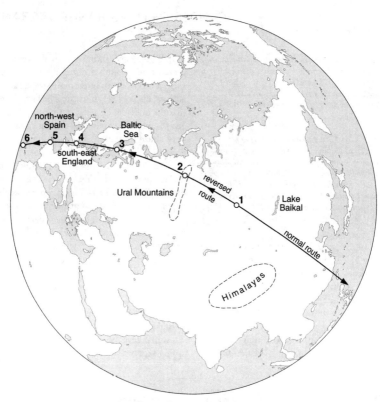

Table 1   Eastern Palearctic passerines considered likely to occur as future vagrants to Britain and Ireland.

Oriental Plover *Charadrius veredus*
Pintail Snipe *Gallinago stenura*
Swinhoe's Snipe *G. megala*
Asiatic Dowitcher *Limnodromus semipalmatus*
Siberian Accentor *Prunella montanella*
Black-throated Accentor *P. atrogularis*
Rufous-tailed Robin *Erithacus sibilans*
Siberian Blue Robin *E. cyane*
Gray's Grasshopper Warbler *Locustella fasciolata*
Sooty Flycatcher *M. sibirica*
Daurian Jackdaw *Corvus dauuricus*
Chestnut Bunting *Emberiza rutila*

The following species, although breeding close to Lake Baikal, are considered unlikely vagrants either because their ranges do not extend significantly to the west of the lake or because they are relatively short-range migrants: Daurian Redstart *Phoenicurus auroreus*, Pallas's Rosefinch *Carpodacus roseus*, Long-tailed Rosefinch *Uragus sibiricus*, Meadow Bunting *Emberiza cioides* and Grey-headed Bunting *E. fucata*. Although the Chestnut Bunting has been recorded in Britain, none of the records involved immatures at 'classic' times of the year.

Fig 5   Hypothetical reversed migration of an Eastern Palearctic migrant, such as a Yellow-browed Warbler Phylloscopus inornatus: *(1) LATE AUGUST sets off from western Siberia heading in a direction 180° to that which it should be taking; (2) MID-SEPTEMBER crosses Urals; (3) EARLY OCTOBER passes through the Baltic; (4) MID-OCTOBER arrives in south-east England; (5) LATE OCTOBER crosses north-west corner of Spain; (6) EARLY NOVEMBER drowns in Atlantic. If it is lucky, it ends up in Morocco, Iberia or France where it spends the winter, before tracing the same route home again in spring. This explains why we get a small spring passage of Eastern Palearctic vagrants, often in early spring.*

Spring Vagrancy of Eastern Palearctic Migrants So, how do we explain the occurrence of Eastern Palearctic vagrants in spring? Three possibilities would seem to exist:

1. It is well known that some Eastern Palearctic vagrants manage to winter successfully in Britain and Ireland. Richard's Pipits and Yellow-browed Warblers are the most frequent, but even rarer species have also wintered: Olive-backed Pipit, Dusky Warbler and Little Bunting, for example. If one follows their autumn great circle route beyond Britain, it curves south-westwards towards Iberia. So why shouldn't some winter in France, Iberia or north-western Africa? There can be little doubt that some in fact do, and there are a handful of records to support this. These include the aforementioned flock of Richard's Pipits in Morocco, a Pallas's Warbler in Spain in April

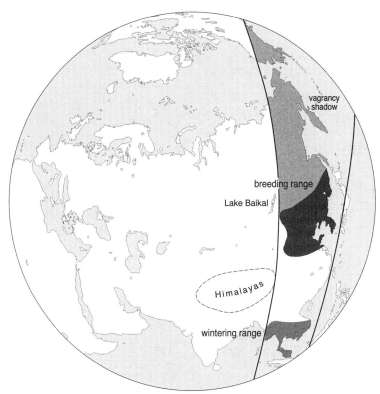

Fig 6 Any bird which breeds east of the 'Lake Baikal Watershed' and which winters in South-east Asia is likely to have a north/south or even north-east/south-west orientation to its migration route. Its 'vagrancy shadow' is such that, if it reverse migrates or overshoots, it will not reach western Europe (in fact it is more likely to reach northern North America). This explains why very far eastern birds, such as the Daurian Starling Sturnus sturninus, *should be regarded as very unlikely potential vagrants to Britain and Ireland.*

Table 2 Eastern Palearctic migrants considered to be extremely unlikely vagrants to Britain and Ireland. All these have either occurred already as escaped cage birds or could be suggested as possible future vagrants.

Forest Wagtail *Dendronanthus indicus*	Narcissus Flycatcher *F. narcissina*
Japanese Waxwing *Bombycilla japonica*	Blue-and-white Flycatcher *Cyanoptila cyanomelana*
Ashy Minivet *Pericrocotus divaricatus*	Grey-streaked Flycatcher *Muscicapa griseisticta*
White-breasted Rock Thrush *Monticola gularis*	Chestnut-flanked White-eye *Zosterops erythropleura*
Grey-backed Thrush *Turdus hortulorum*	
Pale Thrush *T. pallidus*	White-cheeked Starling *Sturnus cineraceus*
Middendorf's Grasshopper Warbler *Locustella ochotensis*	Daurian Starling *S. sturninus*
	Black-naped Oriole *Oriolus chinensis*
Styan's Grasshopper Warbler *L. pleskei*	Yellow-throated Bunting *Emberiza elegans*
Black-browed Reed Warbler *Acrocephalus bistrigiceps*	Tristram's Bunting *E. tristrami*
	Japanese Reed Bunting *E. yessoensis*
Pale-legged Leaf Warbler *Phylloscopus tenellipes*	Oriental Greenfinch *Carduelis sinica*
	Chinese Grosbeak *Eophona migratoria*
Eastern Crowned Warbler *P. occipitalis*	Japanese Grosbeak *E. personata*
Tricolor Flycatcher *Ficedula zanthopygia*	Russet Sparrow *Passer rutilans*

1987 (no doubt on passage from further south), a Pallas's Reed Bunting *Emberiza pallasi* in Spain in April 1996, a Common Rosefinch in Morocco in January 1994, and the aforementioned Red-breasted Flycatcher in Tenerife. Considering that these areas are not heavily covered by birders, it seems inevitable that the small number of vagrants which have been found there in winter represent the tip of an iceberg.

What happens to these birds in the following spring? As far as they are concerned, they have migrated normally and have successfully survived the winter. Just like any other migrant, they start to head for home. It follows, therefore, that many will retrace the same route back towards Siberia. Thus a Richard's Pipit which wintered in Morocco will head north back through Western Europe and eventually swing back towards Siberia. This neatly explains why we have a small spring passage of Eastern Palearctic vagrants. Another important point to make is that, as we are close to their wintering grounds, many of these birds will start to head off in early spring. This explains why some pass through Britain in March (Richard's Pipits, Pallas's Warbler, Little and Rustic Buntings and even Isabelline Shrikes *Lanius isabellinus* have all occurred at this time).

An interesting example can be used to support this theory. On 3 May 1970, a Dusky Warbler was trapped on the Calf of Man, Isle of Man. The following December, it was found dying near Limerick in Ireland. Contemporary commentators suggested that it must have spent the intervening summer in Western Europe. But just think about it. If a Sedge Warbler *Acrocephalus schoenobaenus* was caught in Morocco in May and the same bird was found dead the following December in Senegal, would you conclude that it had spent the intervening summer in Mauritania? Obviously the bird would have headed north (perhaps to Britain) and returned south the following autumn. Why shouldn't that Dusky Warbler have returned to Siberia and then set off west again in the autumn to its previous wintering site in Ireland? The interesting thing is, if one draws a line on a globe from Limerick through the Calf of Man, and if one then projects that line eastwards, it ends up in Siberia.

2. Another more tenuous suggestion is that spring Eastern Palearctic migrants heading north-west from Southeast Asia towards their breeding grounds could overshoot and continue along the same great circle route used by reversed migrants in autumn. This would require the acceptance of the theory that spring overshooting may involve birds which are simply unable to turn off their migratory 'urge', thus travelling huge distances *beyond* those they should travel. Such vagrancy would be likely to occur only in *late* spring. It seems that buntings in particular may be prone to this (think about Black-headed Buntings, *Emberiza melanocephala* and American sparrows), and the theory could explain early July Fair Isle records of Arctic Warbler, Yellow-breasted Bunting and even the 1992 Asian Brown Flycatcher *Muscicapa latirostris*. Direct Eastern Palearctic passerine vagrancy in spring would otherwise appear to be very unlikely.

3. It is also conceivable that some birds head south in autumn, winter in Africa, and then move north into Western Europe in spring. In particular, this may

explain the spring occurrences of White-throated Needletail *Hirundapus caudacutus* and Pacific Swift *Apus pacificus*.

Guidelines for the Evaluation of Eastern Palearctic Passerine Records In recent years, the evaluation of the records of many Eastern Palearctic 'firsts' has been controversial. In my opinion, the following questions need to be addressed when judging such records:

1. Is it a potential vagrant? In other words:
   (a) Does it breed west of Lake Baikal watershed?
   (b) Is it a long-range migrant?
   (c) Is the autumn migration route of at least part of the population likely to be basically north-west–south-east?
2. Has the bird occurred at a predicted time of year (principally late autumn, but possibly also in winter)?
3. Is the bird an immature?
4. Is the bird of the predicted race?
5. Does the bird lack signs of unusual plumage wear?
6. Is the bird unringed?
7. Does the bird lack significantly anomalous plumage?
8. Is the bird's behaviour fully compatible with that of a wild bird?

If the answers to all these questions are 'yes' and the species is not considered to be especially numerous in captivity, then, in my opinion, it should be given the benefit of the doubt and accepted into Category A of the British and Irish List. If any of the answers is 'no', then the record would need to be looked at more critically. For example, a spring occurrence of an otherwise acceptable vagrant may be better placed in Category D until some kind of pattern hopefully evolves.

North American Vagrancy
Direct Transatlantic Vagrancy Vagrancy from North America has traditionally been looked at very simplistically, and two methods are generally recognized:

1. Migrating birds are swept out over the Atlantic and then carried to Britain and Ireland by rapidly moving depressions.

2. Migrant birds are swept out over the Atlantic and then make some or most of the journey on board ship.

Unquestionably, both of these methods are used. Ducks, waders and gulls in particular are prone to the first, especially whilst on their first southward migration or as a response to severe winter weather. Any bird that is capable of making such a crossing, however, *must be capable of accumulating sufficient fat reserves to accomplish the journey in one flight*. Although many species are well capable of this, it is apparent that others are not. For example, according to *BWP*, the Greater Yellowlegs *Tringa melanoleuca* puts on fat reserves sufficient for a maximum journey of only 1,650–1,800 miles (2,650–2,900 km), compared with a maximum of 2,125 miles (3,400 km) for Lesser Yellowlegs *T. flavipes*. Under normal circumstances, this presumably would not facilitate a transatlantic crossing. As for passerines, it is clear that some are more capable of long 'one-hop' migrations than others, and it tends to be the larger, long-winged, long-distance, trans-oceanic migrants that make it on a more regular basis. Grey-cheeked Thrush *Catharus minimus*, Blackpoll Warbler *Dendroica striata*, Red-eyed Vireo *Vireo olivaceus* and Rose-breasted Grosbeak *Pheucticus ludovicianus* are the classic products of late-autumn depressions, and it is clear that most of these have crossed the Atlantic unaided.

Anomalies with Autumnal Occurrence Patterns But is the situation as simple as we would like to believe? It doesn't take much probing to discover some interesting anomalies. Why is it, for example, that 87 per cent of all Red-eyed Vireos have occurred in southern Britain and Ireland (south of Liverpool), despite the northerly track of many autumn depressions? In contrast, why is it that all four British Tennessee Warblers *Vermivora peregrina* plus another in the Faeroes have occurred in the far north? Indeed, the Tennessee Warbler is commoner in Scotland than the Blackpoll Warbler! Several other extremely rare North American wood-warblers have occurred in the north: Yellow *Dendroica petechia* (2), Chestnut-sided *D. pensylvanica*, Blackburnian *D. fusca*, Ovenbird *Seiurus aurocapillus*, Common Yellowthroat *Geothlypis trichas* and Hooded *Wilsonia citrina*. Could it be that many of these trans-Atlantic passerines are on specific headings?

Other anomalies also come to light. First, as one would expect, most of our more regularly-occurring vagrants breed well to the north-east in Canada, and it is not difficult to imagine some of these birds being swept out to sea in depressions. But how do we account for vagrancy by such unlikely southern species as Summer Tanager *Piranga rubra* and Golden-winged Warbler *Vermivora chrysoptera*? Second, why is it that our peak period for many species (late September–early October) is often a month later than the peak migration at many North American east coast migration spots, such as Cape May, New Jersey?

Spring Vagrancy Patterns Another interesting phenomenon already mentioned is that of spring vagrancy. The range of species involved in spring is quite different from that encountered in autumn. In particular, sparrows are found almost exclusively in spring, and there have been very few spring records of the thrushes, warblers, vireos and icterids that are so regular in autumn. In fact, none of the four commonest autumn vagrants

– Grey-cheeked Thrush, Red-eyed Vireo, Blackpoll Warbler and Rose-breasted Grosbeak – have ever occurred in spring. Why is it that 84 per cent of autumn North American passerine vagrants have occurred in southern Britain and Ireland, whereas 60 per cent of spring vagrants have occurred in the north? Why is it that there has never been a spring North American sparrow in Scilly, the autumn Nearctic hotspot?

Spring Overshooting It seems likely that the explanation for both the spring records and many of the more unusual autumn vagrants is tied up with the orientation of the North American eastern seaboard. We tend to think of the American east coast as running north–south but, if one again consults a globe, it is obvious that it in fact runs south-west–north-east. If one draws a line up the eastern seaboard from, say, South Carolina to Newfoundland, and then projects that line out across the Atlantic, *the line bisects Britain and Ireland roughly at the latitude of Glasgow* (*see* Fig 7). If one imagines a passerine moving north-eastwards in spring up the North American eastern seaboard and then *overshooting out into the North Atlantic, then, providing that it has sufficient fat reserves, it would eventually hit northern Britain or northern Ireland*. That this phenomenon occurs is supported by the fact that nearly all our spring North American passerine vagrants breed well to the north-east in Canada. It must be stressed, however, that spring overshooting, as with autumn vagrancy, may be modified by ship assistance, particularly as sparrows may be better suited to survival on board ship than many insectivorous or fruit-eating species.

As well as explaining the numerous spring records of American sparrows in the Northern Isles, and other gross spring rarities such as the Paisley, Renfrewshire, Cape May Warbler (June 1997) and the Islay, Argyllshire, Brown-headed Cowbird *Molothrus ater* (April 1988), the acceptance of the spring overshooting theory would also make the Shetland Cedar Waxwing *Bombycilla cedrorum* (June 1985) likely to be a wild bird, bearing in mind the late date of its occurrence (it is a late-spring migrant in North America). It may also be possible that species which breed further south or west could also occur; the Yellow-headed Blackbird *Xanthocephalus xanthocephalus*, which may migrate from Mexico or the south-western states north-east towards the Great Lakes, would also be a potential spring vagrant. That this species could occur is surely confirmed by other records in Iceland and Greenland.

Autumnal Reversed Migration As for autumn vagrants, it seems likely that, just as we receive reversed migrants from Siberia, so too do we receive reversed migrants from North America. It seems probable that every autumn many North American passerines reverse migrate out into the Atlantic, just as

Fig 7 If a bird flying north in spring up the North American eastern seaboard overshoots out into the North Atlantic, it is likely to hit northern Britain if it continues flying along the same great circle route. Similarly, any bird reverse migrating along the same route in autumn is also likely to turn up in the north. This probably explains why so many of our spring American vagrants and why some of our rarer autumn vagrants have been in Scotland (and others in Iceland).

Siberian vagrants do across Europe but, unless those birds meet extremely favourable conditions (a fast-moving depression and/or a ship), the vast majority must simply drop into the ocean.

If one looks at a globe and imagines a bird migrating south-west from the north-eastern United States towards Central America then, if that bird reverse migrates, it is likely to adopt a heading that could, with a very strong tail wind, bring it to Britain or Ireland. That such birds, like the Siberian vagrants discussed earlier, are on a very specific heading would explain some of the anomalies over their occurrence patterns. The orientation of the eastern seaboard would help to explain some of the extremely rare autumn vagrants that have turned up in northern Scotland (Tennessee and Hooded Warblers, for example). The south-west–north-east orientation of the eastern seaboard would mean than any migrant which normally migrates south-west down the coast or even down the Appalachian Mountains is likely to end up in *northern* Britain if it reverse migrates, following the same route as spring overshoots. Being reversed migrants, it is even possible that some of these birds originate from the North American interior, and this may explain the relative lateness of their arrival in Britain and Ireland.

Transatlantic Cold Weather Movements and Subsequent Spring Migration Another phenomenon to be considered is that of transatlantic vagrancy induced by cold-weather movements. It is often the case that, during periods of severe cold in eastern North America, we receive mid-winter or spring influxes of wildfowl and gulls, as well as other species such as the occasional Killdeer *Charadrius vociferus* and American Robin *Turdus migratorius*. A fundamental point to make is that the US eastern seaboard is at a much lower latitude than Britain and Ireland. For example, New York is on a similar latitude to Barcelona in Spain and the Carolinas are on a similar latitude to northern Morocco. This means that any bird which heads out across the Atlantic to escape the cold is likely to hit southern Europe (France, Spain or Portugal) or north-western Africa (*see* Fig 8). That this theory is true is surely confirmed by the numerous records of Ring-billed Gulls *Larus delawarensis* and other species – such as the Bufflehead *Bucephala albeola* and American Coot *Fulica americana* – in these regions, despite the relative paucity of birdwatchers. What happens then is that these birds may head north in spring and pass through Britain and Ireland from March onwards. This explains why Ring-billed and Bonaparte's Gulls *L. philadelphia* reach a peak in early spring, and why we get so many spring records of Ring-necked Ducks *Aythya collaris* and even rarer wildfowl such as the Bufflehead and Redhead *Aythya americana*.

Other Routes from North America Another important point about North Atlantic vagrancy is that our idea that all these birds come directly across the Atlantic may be false. One particular example makes this glaringly obvious. The Sandhill Crane *Grus canadensis* which was present in Shetland in September 1991, left in a south-easterly direction rather than moving south through Britain, and was rediscovered the following day in the Netherlands. As with all such migrants, this suggests that the bird was on a very specific and innate heading. The Sandhill Crane does not normally occur on the north-eastern coasts of Canada or the USA, and it is in any case difficult to imagine such a large, broad-winged bird making an unaided transatlantic crossing. If one plots the route from Shetland to the Netherlands *backwards*, however, its method of arrival becomes immediately apparent. The route passes through Iceland and Greenland and ends up in north-central Canada, somewhere to the west of Hudson Bay (*see* Fig 9). It becomes clear, therefore, that the bird was probably a reversed migrant

out of northern Canada which 'hopped' its way to the Netherlands via Greenland, Iceland and Shetland. Another similar example involved the Greater Yellowlegs which was present in Cumberland in October–November 1994. This bird was considered to have been the same as that seen subsequently in Belgium and the Netherlands. As has already been noted, this species does not normally put on sufficient fat to enable a transatlantic crossing, but if one plots its Cumberland–Belgium route backwards on a globe, the route again passes through Greenland to northern Canada. This may explain the species' rather eccentric occurrence patterns in this country. If these two species can do it, why not others, such as Ross's Goose *Anser rossii*? By broadening our outlook in these ways, the potential for North American vagrancy becomes much greater.

Vagrancy Potential from Western and Southern North America To broaden our minds even further it is pertinent to have a look at an interesting article in *Winging It*, the monthly newsletter of the American Birding Association. In Vol 6 No. 6 (June 1994), Blake Maybank describes the birds recorded on Seal Island off the southern tip of Nova Scotia. Vagrants

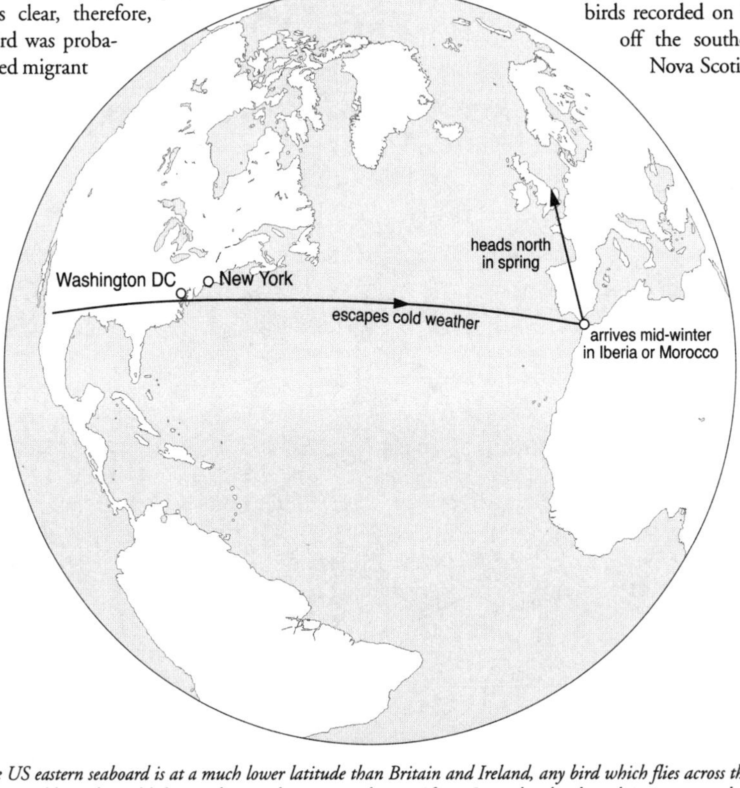

Fig 8 As the US eastern seaboard is at a much lower latitude than Britain and Ireland, any bird which flies across the Atlantic in winter to escape cold weather is likely to end up in Iberia or north-west Africa. Some then head north in spring up through western Europe. Such birds may include Ring-billed Gulls Larus delawarensis *and ducks which may 'abmigrate' north with commoner European species. This probably explains why spring is such a good time in Britain for rare North American ducks.*

Fig 9.

Fig 10.

Fig 9 (Opposite above) Suggested arrival route of the Sandhill Crane Grus canadensis, seen in Shetland and subsequently in the Netherlands in September 1991. If the route is projected backwards, it seems likely that it was a reversed migrant out of northern Canada, having arrived via Greenland and possibly Iceland.

Fig 10 (Opposite below) Suggested route of arrival of the Aleutian Tern Sterna aleutica in Northumberland in May 1979 and possibly the Ancient Murrelet Synthliboramphus antiquus in Devon in 1990–92. Reversed migration from the North Pacific, across northern Canada and through the Davis Strait, would lead to the North Atlantic.

recorded include such unlikely western and southern species as Band-tailed Pigeon *Columba fasciata*, Cave Swallow *Hirundo fulva*, Rock Wren *Salpinctes obsoletus* and Green-tailed Towhee *Pipilo chlorurus*. If these species can make it out over the Atlantic to Seal Island, then there is no reason why they should not make it onto eastward-moving ships! If one accepts this, then the potential for North American vagrancy becomes enormous, and records of Varied Thrush *Zoothera naevia* and Lark Sparrow *Chondestes grammacus* become a lot less difficult to understand. Just imagine the responses to a Band-tailed Pigeon in Cornwall! Yet surely one could not say that such records would be totally impossible. Because of the possibilities of vagrancy provided by ship assistance, I have not prepared a list of potential future North American vagrants. Chandler S. Robbins has already made an excellent, well-thought out attempt at this (Robbins, 1980), but the number of species which have subsequently occurred in Britain and Ireland which were either not on his list or which he considered to have low vagrancy potential must surely prove the unpredictability of vagrancy from the west.

Vagrancy from Further Afield

Two species on the British List have, it is true to say, been received with more incredulity than most. These are the Aleutian Tern *Sterna aleutica* and the Ancient Murrelet *Synthliboramphus antiquus* from the North Pacific. Both are seabirds, and it has been suggested that the Aleutian Tern moved up the 'wrong ocean' having spent the winter in the southern oceans in the company of Arctic Terns *S. paradisaea*. Recent observations from Hong Kong, however, suggest that the species may, after breeding, move south-west to the western Pacific off Southeast Asia and the Philippines (Kennerley *et al.*, 1993). Ancient Murrelets, one assumes, may also disperse south-westwards from the Bering Sea. If one again looks at a globe and retraces those routes backwards, we find that they pass through the Arctic Ocean to the north of Canada, through the Davis Strait

between Greenland and north-eastern Canada, and straight into the North Atlantic (*see* Fig 10). Even these two apparently unlikely vagrants can be explained by reversed migration, although the murrelet is thought more likely to have crossed the North American continent (*see* page 92). Could it be that we can expect even more vagrants from this part of the world?

Ship Assistance

That North American vagrants may hitch a ride on eastbound ships is well known. In 1986 the BOURC decided that ship assistance was no longer a barrier to admission to category A of the British List, providing that the bird concerned had not been artificially maintained by man. One non-American species has occurred here purely as a result of ship assistance: the House Crow *Corvus splendens* (*see* page 151). Another potential addition, the Snowy Sheathbill *Chionis alba*, is not considered to have met the criteria, having been looked after on board ship.

Movements of Escapes

Finally, it may be worth considering what may happen to escapes from captivity. If a bird is captured in, say, China on its autumn migration, transported to Europe and it then escapes, then it would seem probable that, if it resumes its migration, it will continue in the direction that it would have taken had it not been caught. In other words, it will continue to migrate somewhere between south-west and south-east. It is a well-known fact that the largest numbers of Eastern Palearctic cagebirds are brought into mainland Europe, particularly Germany, the Netherlands and Belgium. In theory, therefore, if a bird escapes in autumn there would seem to be little reason why it should then head west or north-west towards Britain. In spring, however, a different situation would arise. A cagebird escaping in the Low Countries is likely to follow its migratory instincts and head off somewhere between north-west and north-east, and such a heading would mean that it is likely to migrate across the North Sea. An eventual landfall on the north-east coast of Britain or in the Northern Isles would then be a strong possibility; several recent such spring records in Orkney and Shetland (for example, Japanese Waxwing *Bombycilla japonica*, Daurian Starling, Pallas's Rosefinch and Japanese Grosbeak *Eophona personata*) are likely to have been escaped cagebirds from the near Continent, as are the Flamborough, Yorkshire, White-cheeked Starling *Sturnus cineraceus* (May 1990) and the Isle of May, East Fife, Daurian Redstart (April 1988). Spring records of some Eastern Palearctic passerines from these areas (particularly those listed in Table 2 on page 19) should, therefore, continue to be treated with suspicion.

The Birds

WHITE-BILLED DIVER
Gavia adamsii

Range Breeds in the Arctic Ocean from Siberia east to Alaska and northern Canada. Most winter in the North Pacific, but a minority travel west to winter off the coasts of Scandinavia.

Occurrences The number of records has increased considerably since 1958 and it can now be regarded as a rare winter visitor, mainly to Scotland and particularly to the Northern Isles. It becomes progressively rarer further south, although there are records from Cornwall and the Isles of Scilly.

Identification Plate 1.1 shows a beautiful summer-plumaged adult which was photographed at Portmahomack Bay, Ross and Cromarty, in June 1984. Unfortunately, it had to be taken into care, where it eventually died of lung disease. After death it was sexed as a female. The plumage is similar to that of a summer-plumaged Great Northern Diver *G. immer*, but its remarkable bill allows for instant recognition. Although feathered down to the nostril, it is otherwise completely ivory (although paler towards the tip) and, unlike the Great Northern, it completely lacks the dark culmen ridge and cutting edges. In shape, the bill is heavy and distinctly uptilted from the gonydeal angle. The bird in Plate 1.3 was a remarkably confiding winter adult which was present in Hartlepool Docks, Co. Durham, in February 1981. Needless to say, such a cooperative bird attracted large numbers of admirers. It is similar in size to the Great Northern but, as in summer, the key difference is the bill. It has a brownish-grey nape and neck sides, distinctly paler in tone than those of the Great Northern. The upperparts are rather uniform (compared with the juvenile) and this, coupled with the white spotting on the wing coverts, shows it to be an adult. Plate 1.2 shows a juvenile which was seen at Holyhead, Anglesey, in February 1991. The birds can easily be aged by the prominent pale scalloping on the scapulars, while the paleness of the head (relieved by a slightly darker smudge at the rear of the ear-coverts) is also typical of a juvenile.

PIED-BILLED GREBE
Podilymbus podiceps

Range Breeds over much of North, Central and South America, with northern populations moving south for the winter.

Occurrences Despite the 17 records between 1963 and 1995, it is still difficult to imagine such an apparently weak-flying bird crossing the Atlantic. Once here, some males have remained for long periods, setting up territory and advertising for mates, giving the low, bellowing song that is a distinctive sound of North American marshes. One particularly pugnacious individual at Kenfig Pool, Glamorgan (1987–88), attacked Whooper Swans *Cygnus cygnus* which encroached on his territory. Even this anti-social behaviour was eclipsed by a long-staying male at Stithians Reservoir, Cornwall, which paired with a Little Grebe *Tachybaptus ruficollis* in 1994 and produced three hybrid young. This was especially remarkable since the two species are not even in the same genus.

Identification Plate 1.4 shows an individual which was present at Radley Gravel Pits, Oxfordshire, in April–May 1992. The photograph illustrates all the distinctive characters of summer plumage: the thick white bill crossed with a black band, the white eye-ring and the black throat, as well as the white under-tail-coverts. It is larger than the Little Grebe, being similar in size to the Black-necked *Podiceps nigricollis*, but it is more thick set with a particularly rounded head. The black bill band is lost in winter, when the plumage is tawnier overall and the throat white. Plate 1.5 shows the infamous Cornish bird in January 1993, when it was at Argal Reservoir, near Falmouth.

BLACK-BROWED ALBATROSS
Diomedea melanophris

Range Circumpolar in the southern oceans.

Occurrences Up to 1996 there were some 44 records of albatrosses around our coasts, 28 of which were acceptable as Black-browed. Some have taken up residence in the North Atlantic and Plate 2.3 shows the most famous of these: the individual that has summered in the Northern Gannet *Morus bassanus* colony at Hermaness, Unst, Shetland, from 1972 to 1995 (although it was strangely absent in 1988 and 1989). This lonely albatross, affectionately nicknamed 'Albert', displayed to the gannets and even built a nest. It seems likely that the same bird spent three summers on the Bass Rock, East Lothian, from 1967 to 1969, and it may even have been the one seen in Iceland in July 1966, in which case it was at least 32 years old, assuming the earliest first attendance at a colony was at the age of three. In a similar case, a Black-browed

Albatross was recorded in a gannet colony in the Faeroes for 35 years from 1860 until 1894, when it was shot (Waterston, 1968).

As an interesting aside, on the night of 19 August 1967 the Bass Rock bird was actually caught by one of the lighthouse keepers, who picked it up without a struggle and carried it to the lighthouse station to remove a piece of fishing net which had become entangled around one of its feet (loc. cit.).

Identification Plates 2.1 & 2 are part of a remarkable set of photographs taken on the Bass Rock in the summer of 1968. Although the Black-browed Albatross is about the same length as a Northern Gannet, it is bulkier and has a 25 per cent longer wingspan. In shape it recalls a giant Northern Fulmar *Fulmarus glacialis*. The bill is mainly orange (redder at the tip), and this alone separates it from the related Yellow-nosed and Grey-headed Albatrosses *D. chlororhynchos* and *D. chrysostoma*, both of which have been predicted as possible future vagrants (indeed, the former was recorded off Norway in April 1994). The dark 'brow', which gives the species its name, is striking. Plate 2.3 shows the blackish upperwings with paler bases to the primaries, and a greyish back and tail. The underwing shows a thick black leading edge and a narrow border to the rear. It glides on bowed wings.

CORY'S SHEARWATER
Calonectris diomedea

Range Breeds in the Mediterranean, the Azores, Madeira, the Canary Islands, the Salvages, the Cape Verde Islands and Portugal. It disperses across the Atlantic (many reaching North America), and most winter off the coasts of Namibia and South Africa. Small numbers reach South America and the western Indian Ocean.

Occurrences It has traditionally been a rare visitor but with periodic late-summer movements in the South-western approaches. There has been a marked upsurge in recent years, with a huge influx of some 17,250 in 1980, including an astonishing 10,940 past Cape Clear Island, Co. Cork, on 16 August. Smaller influxes (generally 1,000–2,000) have occurred in several subsequent years and there are now fairly regular July/August movements off Porthgwarra, Cornwall, and off southern Ireland. These are dependent on the correct weather conditions (generally south-westerly winds, rain and mist), which bring large feeding flocks close to the shore. Smaller numbers are occasionally reported right around the British coast, but the species suffers more than most from misidentification. The most remarkable record was of one picked up exhausted in the heart of the English Midlands at Cannock Chase Reservoir, Staffordshire, on 2 October 1971. Unfortunately it died the following day when an attempt was made to release it back to the sea.

Identification The species has rarely been photographed in Britain; Plates 2.4 & 5 were taken in the South-western Approaches in August 1993. In many ways it is a rather nondescript bird, which has led some to describe it as 'the Garden Warbler *Sylvia borin* of the oceans'. Plate 2.5 shows the brown upperparts (scaled paler at close range), the pale greyish-brown head (which blends into the white underparts), the narrow white horseshoe on the uppertail-coverts (not always obvious) and the black tail. The predominantly pale bill is a good feature, standing out at considerable range in favourable light. Plate 2.4 again shows the head pattern (note the dusky *sides* of the head), as well as the underwing which shows a less obvious transverse bar than the Great Shearwater *Puffinus gravis*. It also lacks the Great's dark belly smudge. Both photographs show the bird's distinctive shape, with the

Great, Cory's, Manx and Mediterranean Shearwaters off Porthgwarra, Cornwall.

wings pushed forwards and the 'hands' angled back and bowed down. The flight, also distinctive, appears slow moving, with a lazy, languid flapping action followed by a long glide close to the surface.

GREAT SHEARWATER
Puffinus gravis

Range Breeds in the South Atlantic, principally in the Tristan da Cunha group and on Gough Island to the south. The birds leave the breeding colonies in April or May, moving north-west towards the Horn of Brazil and reaching the Atlantic coasts of North America in May and early June. During July and August they spread east across the Atlantic, with some reaching British and Irish waters from August to October. Adults begin a rapid return movement to their breeding colonies in August, some reaching their destination by the end of the month.

Occurrences Because of their relative late arrival in British and Irish waters, most are presumed to be non-breeders (*BWP*), which may constitute up to half the world population (Newell, 1968). The numbers recorded here vary considerably from year to year, and obviously depend on food supplies and the weather. For example, 1,693 in 1991 (in Britain only) were followed by only 27 in 1992 (Evans, 1993a). The best-ever year was 1965, when a huge movement included 5,508 off Cape Clear Island, Co. Cork, on 14 September, followed by 5,118 the next day (Newell, 1968).

Identification The one in plate 2.7 was photographed 60 miles (95 km) west of the Isles of Scilly in August 1988. It clearly shows the chocolate-brown cap, which is sharply demarcated from the gleaming white cheeks; this, along with an all-black bill, is an immediate distinction from the similarly sized Cory's Shearwater *Calonectris diomedea*. The upperparts are darker than those of Cory's, with more prominent pale feather fringes. Plate 2.6 shows one in flight. At sea, the white half-collar around the nape is an important feature, as is the white horseshoe on the upper-tail-coverts, this being more prominent than on most Cory's. From below it shows a dark transverse bar across the wing coverts, a small black belly patch and a dark 'bulge' on the sides of the breast. The slim wings are held more stiffly than those of Cory's, and it thus lacks the latter's lazy, languid flight action.

LITTLE SHEARWATER
Puffinus assimilis

Range The race *baroli* breeds in the Azores, Madeira, the Salvages and the Canary Islands, with the race *boydi* in the Cape Verde Islands. Both disperse rela-

tively locally outside the breeding season. Other races breed in the South Atlantic, around Australasia and in the South Pacific.

Occurrences There were 93 records to the end of 1995, and Dymond *et al.* (1989) noted a peak in August–September. The species' true status is, however, hopelessly confused by problems with its identification and subsequent record assessments. Evans (1994) recognized only 59 up to 1990, and it is interesting to note that seven of the nine specimen or trapped records (all of the race *baroli*) were in the period 27 March–29 June.

Identification Plates 3.1 & 2 show an atypically non-controversial individual discovered on Skomer Island, Pembrokeshire, in June–July 1981 and again in 1982 (James, 1986). It frequented a boulder-strewn slope in a European Storm-petrel *Hydrobates pelagicus* colony, away from the usual turf habitat used by Manx Shearwaters *Puffinus puffinus*. It was located by call, which was described as very distinctive, being quicker and higher pitched than that of the Manx. Subsequent sonagram analysis revealed that it was a male. The photographs show a small shearwater (about three-quarters the size of the Manx), with a proportionately large head (with a steep forehead), proportionately larger eyes and a more delicate bill. The most obvious difference from the Manx is the head pattern: it has a predominantly white face (including the ear-coverts) in which the dark eye is isolated. Another difference is its strikingly pale blue legs and feet (pink and black on the Manx). The white undertail-coverts showed it to be of the race *baroli* (*boydi* is mostly dark brown in this area).

At sea, the white face may be apparent in reasonable views and in suitable light, but its identification then relies largely on the proper evaluation of size, shape and flight. Size may be difficult to judge in the absence of direct comparison with the Manx, but the Little has shorter and more rounded wings, and may show more 'front end' and a stumpier 'rear'. It flies low and direct, flapping quickly and stiffly with shallow beats, punctuated by short glides on a horizontal plane, with occasional shallow tilts. Some observers have likened its flight to that of a Common Sandpiper *Actitis hypoleucos*. It has a peculiar habit of sometimes jerking its head upwards (particularly at the end of a glide). The feeding flight seems to be rather petrel-like, foot-paddling with whirring wings and even jumping forwards to feed over new positions. At least in July and August the Little shows a distinctly light silvery-grey area towards the outer secondaries and their coverts, the upperwing thus appearing more two-toned than that of the Manx. At close range, it may even show white tips to the greater coverts. Much of the foregoing is based on McGeehan & Mullarney (1995).

WILSON'S STORM-PETREL
Oceanites oceanicus

Range Breeds in Antarctica and on sub-Antarctic islands. In the southern winter it penetrates into the northern hemisphere, particularly in the Atlantic, where it occurs north to Canada.

Occurrences Prior to 1985 Wilson's Storm-petrel was regarded as an extreme vagrant, with just eight records. Since then, regular pelagic trips into the South-western approaches, both from Ireland and Cornwall, have confirmed that it is a relatively numerous late summer visitor to our waters.

Identification Plate 3.4 is a remarkably good photograph of an individual seen south-west of the Isles of Scilly in August 1988. It is superficially similar to the European Storm-petrel *Hydrobates pelagicus*, but with slightly longer, rather paddle-shaped wings. The large white rump recalls the European, but the upperwing pattern is more reminiscent of Leach's *Oceanodroma leucorhoa*, with a broad grey wing-covert panel. As is sometimes the case, the tail appears to show the effect of a shallow fork, while the long legs projecting beyond the tail are another diagnostic difference from the European. Although not visible in the photograph, it lacks the European's prominent white line on the underwing-coverts. Flight differences from the European are subtle to the inexperienced eye; the Wilson's has a rather butterfly-like flight, skipping over the sea with the wings slightly bowed. It may also fly fast and direct, often well above the surface.

SWINHOE'S STORM-PETREL
Oceanodroma monorhis

Range Breeds in the north-west Pacific, migrating south-west to the Indian Ocean (Harrison, 1983).

Occurrences On 3 August 1988, a Peter Harrison pelagic trip west of the Isles of Scilly discovered and photographed a large, all-dark petrel (Plate 3.5). It was identified as a Matsudaira's Storm-petrel *O. matsudairae*, a Japanese species never before recorded in Britain or Ireland. Its occurrence seemed remarkable, but nobody could have predicted the following events. On 23 July 1989, ringers at Tynemouth, Northumberland, trapped a similar all-dark petrel in mist nets erected to catch tape-lured European Storm-petrels *Hydrobates pelagicus*. Three days later they caught a second and, on 6 July 1990, a third. Incredibly, the latter was retrapped at the same site in July of the four subsequent years. Given that European Storm-petrels do not even breed there, just why this particular bird was so regular in its appearance is a

complete mystery. The identity of the 'Tyne Petrels', as they became known, became a subject of great debate and prompted an investigation to rival the plot of a Sherlock Holmes novel. It was discovered that similar birds had been trapped in the Salvage Islands in 1983, 1988 and 1991, and in Brittany in July 1989, while another was subsequently trapped in Alicante, on the Mediterranean coast of Spain, in July 1994 (King & Minguez, 1994).

The identification was narrowed to Swinhoe's *O. monorhis*, Matsudaira's and the dark-rumped Pacific forms of Leach's Storm-petrels *O. leucorhoa*, but there was also an intriguing fourth option: that it was an undiscovered North Atlantic species unknown to science. In 1992, a blood sample was taken from the trapped bird to facilitate DNA sequencing. This was the final piece in a complicated jigsaw which identified the birds as Swinhoe's Storm-petrels (Cubitt, 1995).

The identities of the original Cornish petrel and several other sight records of dark-rumped petrels have still to be resolved. Although it would seem logical to assume that only one species is involved, the long-winged and long-tailed appearance of the bird in Plate 3.5 may indicate that the initial identification as Matsudaira's was correct.

Identification The bird in Plate 3.3 is the returning individual photographed at Tynemouth in July 1993. Analysis of its call sonagrams showed it to be a female. Swinhoe's is most similar to Leach's, but with a dark rump and white shafts at the base of the primaries. The latter form a patch which is apparently smaller and less prominent than that shown by Matsudaira's. Swinhoe's are longer winged than the dark-rumped forms of Leach's and smaller in all respects than Matsudaira's.

DOUBLE-CRESTED CORMORANT
Phalacrocorax auritus

Range Breeds both coastally and inland over much of North America. It vacates the interior and winters along the coasts south as far as Central America and the West Indies.

Occurrences An individual was found alive in the hold of a cargo ship that arrived at Glasgow from Newfoundland on 22 December 1963 (Evans, 1994), but the first 'proper' record (Plates 3.6 & 7) concerned a 'first-winter' at Charlton's Pond, Yorkshire, from January to April 1989 (Williams, 1996). The only other acceptable record concerns a first-winter at Nimmo's Pier, Co. Galway, from November 1995 to January 1996. That this species should recently make an appearance here is not surprising in view of events in North America. It declined drastically between

World War II and the mid-1970s as a result of contamination from pesticides and from human persecution. Since 1972 the species has been afforded protection under the Migratory Bird Treaty Act and this, coupled with the banning of DDT, has resulted in an extraordinary recovery, so much so that it has become a pest in some areas (Conniff, 1991). In Nova Scotia, for example, it increased from 4,150 pairs in 1971 to over 12,100 by 1982 (Milton & Austin-Smith, 1983). In view of this increase, it seems likely that we can look forward to further occurrences, but the species' similarity to our own Great Cormorant *P. carbo* will no doubt mitigate against its discovery here.

Identification The photographs show the Double-crested Cormorant to be a subtle bird. What would perhaps initially attract attention is its different jizz, produced by a proportionately shorter, deeper bill, a less angular crown/nape juncture, a rather shorter neck and noticeably bright orange-yellow facial skin. It would also appear smaller than the Great Cormorant, being closer in size to the European Shag *P. aristotelis*.

Meticulous observation of the facial pattern would be required to clinch the identification. Immature Great Cormorant can show a bright orange-yellow facial patch, but Double-crested has a distinct band of orange-yellow between the top of the eye and the top of the bill, separated from the chin and throat by a dark line of feathering across the lores. On the Great Cormorant this entire area is usually obscured by dark filoplumes (minute black feathers), but as these can wear off the difference is not absolute. More important is that the rear edge of the gular patch drops *vertically* from the gape line and continues *straight* under the chin and up the other side. On the Great Cormorant, a pointed wedge of feathering projects towards the tip on the underside of the bill.

The brownish upperbreast and (not visible in the photographs) pointed feathers on the upperparts, showed the Yorkshire bird to be a 'first-winter'. Double-crested Cormorants at this age characteristically have a pale upperbreast contrasting with a dark belly and thighs. 'First-winter' Greats tend to be white, mottled white or brownish on the *entire* underparts, right down to the legs. Again this difference is not absolute; some Double-cresteds are much paler (as with the 1995 Irish bird), being basically white on the breast, and some may be entirely white below (Stall-cup, 1982). Conversely, Great Cormorants may show a pale breast and dark belly at certain stages of moult between 'first-year' and 'second-year' plumages.

Only the adults show the double crest, and then only in breeding plumage. On nominate eastern birds the crest is black, while it is mainly white in the western *albociliatus* and *cincinatus*.

AMERICAN BITTERN
Botaurus lentiginosus

Range Breeds across much of North America, and winters in the southern United States, Central America and the West Indies.

Occurrences The first specimen of the American Bittern was identified in Britain (Riegner, 1993), a testimony that it used to occur here much more frequently than now. There were 50 records prior to 1958, but only ten since (up to 1991). The reduction is directly related to the species' decline in North America, due principally to habitat destruction. A 1990 report to the US Congress indicated that the lower 48 states lost an estimated 53 per cent of their original wetlands between colonial times and the 1980s. This translates into the astonishing figure of 60 acres (24 hectares) of wetlands for every hour between the 1780s and the 1980s (loc. cit.). As a habitat specialist, the American Bittern has been badly affected and is now officially considered to be threatened or endangered in several states. Given these depressing statistics, we can perhaps consider ourselves fortunate to have seen this species on a number of occasions in recent years. The bird in Plate 5.1 was a famous well-watched and very confiding individual present at Magor, Monmouthshire, from 29 October 1981 to 3 January 1982. Most have occurred in late autumn and winter.

Identification The American Bittern is superficially similar to the Eurasian Bittern *B. stellaris* but is slightly smaller. The photograph shows the following differences: (1) brown crown (as opposed to black); (2) a thicker dark culmen ridge; (3) a more prominent pale supercilium; (4) a yellow gape line (bordered with blackish plumage); (5) a longer chocolate moustachial line; (6) plain sides to the neck (as opposed to lightly barred); and (7) thick chocolate striping down the breast. The plainer blackish-brown back and scapulars contrast with the relatively plain pale buff wing coverts. In flight, the American has pale wing coverts which contrast with solidly blackish remiges, whilst the secondaries are tipped pale buff, forming a pale trailing edge to the wing. The Eurasian Bittern lacks the trailing edge and has mottled, owl-like primaries.

LITTLE BITTERN
Ixobrychus minutus

Range Breeds across much of southern and mid-latitude Europe and western Asia, as well as in much of tropical Africa, Pakistan and northern India and parts of Australia. Palearctic migrants winter in Africa.

Occurrences Mainly an overshooting spring vagrant between April and June although, surprisingly, there are records from every month of the year. It breeds on the near Continent, where there has been a sharp and worrying decline in recent years. This has been particularly marked in the Netherlands, where there were only one or two breeding pairs in 1992, compared with up to 225 in the 1960s (*Brit. Birds* **86**: 37). This decrease has been reflected in the number of recent British occurrences, but against this trend came the first confirmed breeding record: a pair raised three young at Potteric Carr, Yorkshire, in 1984 (Allport & Carroll, 1989).

Identification The Little Bittern, about the size of a Common Moorhen *Gallinula chloropus*, is our smallest heron. Plate 4.1 shows a male on St Mary's, Isles of Scilly, in April 1987. The large creamy-buff wing covert patch is perhaps the most distinctive feature. The essentially black and buff plumage shows it to be a male, but the slightly streaked, rather dull back and scapulars, as well as brown feathering at the bend of the wing, indicate a first-summer. In full breeding condition, the bill has a deep red base and a bright yellow tip. Plate 4.2 shows an exhausted female found at Ballycotton, Co. Cork, on the remarkably early date of 16 March 1990. Not surprisingly, it subsequently died, presumably having made a long sea crossing from Iberia. Although the pattern is the same as that of the male's, it is much browner, especially on the back and scapulars. Interestingly, it shows a hint of a pale line down the edge of the mantle, mirroring that shown more prominently by the American Least Bittern *I. exilis*. It is a secretive bird, waiting patiently for prey to come within striking distance. Females in particular blend in remarkably well with the reeds, their longitudinal brown neck stripes mimicking the dead reed stems. It can, however, be very lively, jumping and clambering from reed to reed, sometimes practically running, and clasping several stems at a time with its large feet. In flight it looks front-heavy and flies with quick wingbeats. The short, rounded wings show off the prominent buff wing covert patches. On adults, the bright green legs may also stand out, projecting beyond the tail. It tends to fly low over the water and skims the tops of the reeds, dropping abruptly into them. In spring, the male may be detected by its low, rather owl-like call: *o-or, o-or, o-or...*

BLACK-CROWNED NIGHT HERON
Nycticorax nycticorax

Range Has a huge world range, from southern Europe through the Middle East into southern and south-eastern Asia, as well as in Africa and North and South America. Western Palearctic migrants winter in Africa.

Occurrences Mainly an overshooting spring migrant from late March to June. Numbers vary from year to year, but there was a remarkable influx of 59 in 1990. It also occurs in autumn and late arrivals sometimes winter. A first-winter incredibly shot in Lincolnshire in January 1980 had been ringed the previous June along the Russian coast of the Black Sea, proving beyond doubt that wintering birds do not necessarily originate from the free-flying colony at Edinburgh Zoo.

Identification The Black-crowned Night Heron is a small, squat, stocky heron with a thick bill, short legs and a call reminiscent of a Common Raven *Corvus corax*. As its name suggests, it is largely nocturnal – hence the large eyes – and abroad it is usual to see this species leaving its roost as other herons and egrets are arriving. It usually spends the day sitting inconspicuously in a tree or a bush. Plate 4.3 shows an adult photographed on St Mary's, Isles of Scilly, in March 1990. It has the characteristic black crown, back and scapulars offset against the soft grey wings and underparts. The neat and immaculate plumage, together with the long white nape plume, confirm its age. The huge orange eye often stands out like a brightly coloured bead. Plate 4.6 shows a first-winter at Dowdeswell Reservoir, Gloucestershire, in November 1995. The white flecking and spotting on the wings are characteristic of this age but it has already lost its juvenile spotting on the mantle and scapulars. Plate 4.5 shows a more advanced individual: a first-summer on the River Blackwater, near Fermoy, Co. Cork, in June 1988. It has retained the white-tipped juvenile greater coverts but has otherwise acquired a relatively plain brown plumage with a pattern ghosting that of an adult. Plate 4.4 shows the next stage: a second-winter at Briston, Norfolk, in January 1982. Although it appears more adult-like, the back and scapulars are greyish, while the browny wings retain traces of spotting. It has acquired a nape plume which is characteristically rather short at this age.

GREEN HERON
Butorides virescens

Range Breeds in southern Canada, the United States, Central America and the West Indies. Winters mainly from Florida and the Gulf of Mexico to northern South America.

Occurrences The first British record was of an adult nearly caught by a spaniel and subsequently shot at Penrice, near St Austell, Cornwall, on 27 October 1889. In those days leading ornithologists were reluctant to accept the possibility of transatlantic vagrancy for all but the strongest fliers, and it took 83 years for the Green Heron to be admitted to the British List (Hudson, 1972). The next record concerned a heavily twitched adult at Stone Creek, Yorkshire, from 27

November to 6 December 1982 (Plate 5.2). This bird was particularly remarkable for the fact that it shared a drainage ditch with a Great White Egret *Ardea alba*! There have since been records of a first-winter in East Lothian in October 1987 (found dead) and a juvenile on Jersey and Guernsey in August–September 1992.

Identification The Green is a small heron that tends to inhabit ponds and wooded backwaters, often perching in trees. From a distance it appears rather uniformly dark and looks front-heavy, particularly in flight. Plate 5.2 shows dull grey-green upperparts, a black crown and a distinctive chestnut neck (which is divided by white lines down the centre). It often shows a shaggy crest, while the yellow bill and legs contrast with the dark plumage in flight. Juveniles are browner, more heavily streaked below and show buff spotting on the wing coverts. Adult or adult-like plumage is acquired in the late summer or autumn of the second calendar year (Hudson 1972). They are rather noisy and their guttural *kuk-kuk* and piercing *skeow* calls are distinctive sounds around North American marshes. The Green Heron is now once again treated as separate from the almost cosmopolitan Green-backed Heron *B. striatus*.

SQUACCO HERON
Ardeola ralloides

Range Has a patchy distribution from Morocco across southern Europe to south-west Asia. Palearctic migrants winter in Africa, where it also breeds. Further east, it is replaced by three other species of pond heron: the Indian *A. grayii*, the Chinese *A. bacchus* and the Javan *A. speciosa*.

Occurrences It has declined considerably in Europe as a result of habitat destruction, although numbers apparently fluctuate relative to the rainfall in their West African wintering grounds (Hancock & Kushlan, 1984). In the early 20th century, slaughter by plume hunters also caused a serious decline, the Palearctic population crashing from an estimated 16,400 pairs in the late 19th century to 6,000 pairs between the Wars (*BWP*). There has been a recovery since with, for example, about 400 pairs breeding in Spain in 1989 (*Brit. Birds* 84: 227), compared with about 20 in the 19th century (*BWP*). In France, it probably bred as far north as the Lac de Grand Lieu, Loire Atlantique, in 1981 (this site is only 250 miles, or 400 km, from the English south coast).

The population decline has been reflected in the numbers occurring in Britain and Ireland. There were about 90 prior to 1914, and at that time it was actually more numerous than the Little Egret *Egretta garzetta*. Between 1958 and 1995 there were 39 records, and

there has been a distinct upturn since 1970. Its occurrence patterns are typical of an overshooting spring vagrant, with most from April to June in southern England. A preponderance in Cornwall and Devon would suggest that many originate in Iberia.

Identification The individual in Plates 5.3 & 4 was present at Elmley, Kent, in May 1990. With its soft golden plumage tones it is a beautiful and unmistakable bird, but Squacco Herons can be surprisingly inconspicuous when feeding. As Plate 5.4 reveals, there is a complete transformation in flight, when it becomes predominantly white and egret-like. Its short legs allow for easy separation when seen from below. In full breeding condition, the lores and bill base become bright blue, whilst the legs become bright coral red. The bird in Plate 5.5 was found on St Mary's, Isles of Scilly, on the remarkably early date of 20 March 1990. Juveniles and winter adults are browner, less yellow above and are heavily streaked on the head and neck. First-years retain variable amounts of this plumage well into their first-summer. They also show faint traces on brown in their primary tips, although this may be impossible to make out in the field. When not in full breeding condition, most spring birds show a blue-grey bill with a black tip, lime green lores and legs which vary from very dull yellowy-green to a bright deep yellow. Some have a less well-defined bill tip and may show a greeny base. The atypically dark bill of the St Mary's bird is due to mud staining.

CATTLE EGRET
Bubulcus ibis

Range Formerly bred from southern Europe across Africa, the Middle East, southern and Southeast Asia. Since about the 1930s it has spread to South America (having colonized from Africa) and it has since moved into much of North America. A similar range expansion occurred south-eastwards into Australia and New Zealand. The Cattle Egret can be regarded as one of the world's most successful birds.

Occurrences In France, it first bred in the Camargue in 1968, and by 1992 breeding was also taking place in central and northern France, as close to England as the Baie de Somme (*Brit. Birds* 86: 37 and 278–279). It has also shown a large increase in Iberia: in 1989 the Spanish breeding population was estimated at 54,000 pairs, while an Iberian winter census in 1991/92 found between 152,000 and 160,000 (*Brit. Birds* 84: 227; 86: 278). Prior to 1970 there had been just 11 records in Britain (14 birds) but, as it spread north and consolidated in south-western Europe, numbers occurring here showed a contemporaneous upturn which culminated in an influx of 18 in May 1992 (including a group of eight in Hertfordshire). A northerly invasion into France at the same time was thought to have been correlated to drought and population pressure in Spain (*Brit. Birds* **87**: 3). In Britain it occurs mainly as a spring overshoot and as a winter visitor, remaining very rare in Scotland and Ireland. By 1995, there had been 81 records.

Identification Despite its rarity here, the Cattle Egret is a familiar species to most foreign travellers. As its name suggests, it frequents drier situations than other egrets, often in association with cattle. Compared with the Little Egret *Egretta garzetta*, it is stockier, with shorter legs, a thicker neck and a pronounced jowl, but it is most easily separated by the yellow or orange bill (becoming red in breeding condition). It also lacks the Little Egret's yellow or green feet. In summer, it is further separated by the orange crown, nape, back and breast feathers. Most of these features are shown in Plate 6.1: a bird at Hornsea Mere, Yorkshire, in May 1992. Plate 6.2 shows one in winter plumage at East Coker, Somerset, in January 1986. At this time of year the orange is reduced to a pale wash on the forehead and crown. Vagrant Cattle Egrets have to be separated from escaped individuals of the race *coromandus*, which breeds eastwards from Pakistan. *Coromandus* is marginally longer necked and longer billed than the nominate, but it is easily separated in the breeding season by a deep orange coloration covering virtually the whole head, neck, breast and back. In winter, at least some retain a fairly bright orange patch on the forehead.

GREAT WHITE EGRET
Ardea alba

Range Almost cosmopolitan, breeding across much of southern North America, South America, Africa, southern Asia and Australasia. There are isolated colonies in south-eastern Europe, and there has been some recent range expansion (*see* below).

Occurrences In Europe, a widespread decline in the 19th and early 20th centuries was brought about by a combination of plume hunting and habitat destruction. Reflecting this, there were just ten recorded in Britain up to 1951. In recent years, however, it has enjoyed greater success. In Austria, for example, the breeding population increased from 217 pairs in 1987 to 375 in 1988 (*Brit. Birds* **82**: 14), while in the Camargue, France, as many as 98 were counted in January 1991 (*Brit. Birds* **85**: 444). There were two or three nests there in 1994 and, more interestingly, in the same year at least two pairs bred at the Lac de Grand Lieu, Loire Atlantique (this site is only 250 miles, or 400 km, from southern England). Of greatest relevance to Britain, however, was the colonization of the Netherlands in 1978, although the foothold there is still rather tenuous, with only five pairs producing young in 1995 (*Brit. Birds* **89**: 26). It is now annual here, with as many as nine in 1993. Most occur from late April to July, but with some now wintering in the Netherlands and Belgium it seems possible that this pattern will change.

Identification Plate 6.3 was taken at Gibraltar Point, Lincolnshire, in July 1993. About the size of a Grey Heron *Ardea cinerea*, the Great White Egret is a magnificent bird. Immediately apparent in the photograph are the long, pointed, thick-based bill (which merges with the head); the long, thin, snake-like neck; and the long scapular plumes which form a loose train beyond the wings. It has already acquired its non-breeding bare-part coloration, and the predominantly yellow bill and legs immediately distinguish it from the much smaller Little Egret *Egretta garzetta*. Of interest to foreign travellers, the American race *egretta* – or 'Great Egret' – retains an orange bill throughout the breeding season. The flight shot (Plate 6.4), taken at Cley, Norfolk, in April 1993, shows a bird in breeding condition with a black bill, green lores and black legs, with the yellow restricted mainly to the tibia. Separation from Little Egret is less easy in flight, but it has noticeably long legs and slower, less flappy wingbeats which produce a flight action more similar to Grey Heron.

PURPLE HERON
Ardea purpurea

Range Has a wide range across southern Europe through the Middle East to India, Southeast Asia and Indonesia, as well as Africa. Palearctic migrants winter in sub-Saharan Africa.

Occurrences The Purple Heron is an annual overshooting spring visitor mainly from April to June, but with smaller numbers through to October. It breeds as close as France and Spain, but many records, particularly those on the east coast, have been associated with breeding colonies in the Netherlands. During the 1970s, the Purple Heron was occurring here so frequently that at the end of 1982 it was removed from the Rarities List and was even tipped as a potential colonist. Since then, however, the Dutch population has shown a dramatic decline, from 900 pairs in 1977 to only 190 in 1991 (*Brit. Birds* **77**: 233; **85**: 444). Despite this, Fraser and Ryan (1992) could not detect a significant fall in the numbers occurring here – in fact, there were about 40 in 1994 (*Brit. Birds* **88**: 264) – but a decline seems inevitable considering the depressed state of the Dutch population.

Identification Plate 6.5 shows an individual at Ford-wich, Kent, in April 1981. It is easily separated from the Grey Heron *A. cinerea* by its long, dagger-like bill, its black crown, the long, thin, purply-brown neck with prominent black stripes, and the deep chestnut carpal patch and belly. Although ostensibly an adult, its rather browny plumage tones may suggest that it is not fully mature (possibly a second-summer). Plate 7.1 shows a juvenile photographed at Tophill Low Reservoir, York-shire, in August 1994. Its plumage is predominantly sandy-brown, lacking the adult's black crown and neck stripes. The huge bill is particularly apparent in this shot. In flight, the Purple Heron is slightly smaller and markedly scrawnier than Grey Heron, with a 'pouched' effect to the retracted neck and surprisingly prominent feet. When seen from above, adults also show bright orange-yellow legs and feet (duller on first- and second-years). Adults look dark in flight, being slaty-grey across the wing coverts, and show a rich chestnut panel across the underwing-coverts. Many apparently adult Purple Herons, however, show brownish lesser and median coverts and a band of grey across the greater coverts and greater primary coverts. It is unclear whether such birds are fully mature. Juveniles undergo a body moult in their winter quarters (where many remain in their first-summer; *BWP*) but first-summers and apparently also second-summers retain browny feather fringes right across the upperwing-coverts, so lacking a grey panel across the greater coverts. It often feeds inconspicuous-ly amongst the reeds, rather like a Eurasian Bittern *Botaurus stellaris*, swaying its neck from side to side when approaching prey. The neck can look remarkably skinny and, when fully stretched out, it can easily be passed off as a stick or branch growing amongst the reeds. The call is like Grey Heron's but is higher-pitched and shorter.

BLACK STORK
Ciconia nigra

Range An isolated breeding population occurs in Iberia, otherwise it breeds mainly from eastern Europe across Asia to the Pacific. Western Palearctic breeders winter in Africa. Another isolated popula-tion occurs in southern Africa.

Occurrences The Black Stork was formerly more widespread in Western Europe, but a marked decline in the early part of this century was compensated by an increase in adjoining areas to the east (*BWP*). In recent years, however, it has enjoyed an upturn in its fortunes, increasing in Bulgaria, the Czech Republic and eastern Germany, recolonizing Belgium, Den-mark and Sweden, and breeding for the first time in Luxembourg, Italy and France, where there were probably over 200 recorded in 1987 and 19–36

breeding pairs in 1993 (*Brit. Birds* **71**: 255; **77**: 587; **81**: 331; **82**: 322; **83**: 9; **86**: 279; **87**: 3 and 312; **88**: 27 and 265). This welcome increase has been mir-rored in the British records. It was an extreme vagrant here before the late 1960s; indeed, in the first 11 years of the Rarities Committee there were just two records. Since the mid-1970s, however, it has been almost annual, culminating in the remarkable total of 23 in

Black Stork.

1991. One even occurred in Ireland in 1987. Most occur in spring, from late April to mid-June, with fewer in autumn.

Identification Plate 7.2 shows a wing-stretching juvenile at South Walney, Lancashire, in October 1985. This bird had been taken into care by the RSPCA before being ringed and released. Remarkably, it was briefly joined by an adult on 25 October. The dull pinkish bare parts and immaculate, brown-tinged plumage indicate its age. In flight, it looks slightly slimmer and rangier than White Stork *C. ciconia*, with a thinner, scrawnier neck and, on average, slightly more pointed wings. On the face of it, Black Stork would seem to be unmistakable, but some descriptions submitted to the Rarities Committee have been so poor that it has been difficult to eliminate Eurasian Oystercatcher *Haematopus ostralegus!* Then there was the one that was passed off as a golf trolley…

WHITE STORK
Ciconia ciconia

Range Breeds in Iberia and North Africa, much of Eastern Europe, Asia Minor, parts of the Middle East, and in central Asia. Western Palearctic breeders winter in Africa.

Occurrences The White Stork has shown a marked and well-publicized decline over much of its range, although there has been some cause for optimism in recent years. In the Netherlands there was an increase to at least 70 breeding pairs in 1994. In France its numbers reached 315 pairs in 1995, following its nadir in 1973 when there were only ten, while in Spain there has been an impressive increase with 16,463 breeding pairs in 1994, compared with 6,753 ten years earlier (*BWP, Brit. Birds* **88**: 265 and *Dutch Birding* **18**: 91). British records have shown signs of a decrease in recent years (Fraser & Ryan, 1992), although there was a record total of 48 in 1986. This is, however, a conspicuous and mobile species, and wandering individuals can artificially inflate the numbers that apparently turn up. In view of the uncertainty over current trends, the decision of the Rarities Committee to remove the species from its list at the end of 1982 now seems unwise. As with the Black Stork *C. nigra*, most occur in spring, with a secondary peak in September. There are even a few winter records, although the status of these is often confused by the occurrence of escapes.

Identification The bird in Plate 7.4 was photographed at Fordcombe, Kent, in September 1988. The flight shot (Plate 7.3) was taken at Suffield, Suffolk, in July 1982. In a British context, the White Stork is quite unmistakable.

GLOSSY IBIS
Plegadis falcinellus

Range Almost cosmopolitan but a localized breeder in south-eastern Europe, central Asia, through India and Indonesia to Australia, as well as in Africa, the West Indies and the east coast of the USA.

Occurrences The species has suffered a marked decline and range contraction in Europe during the 20th century. Although there were many old British and Irish records, there were only seven between 1958 and 1971 and, at that time, it was considered an extreme vagrant. Since 1972, however, there has been a slow but distinct upturn, culminating in an influx of 18 in 1986, including a party of five in Cornwall. This has reflected a small increase in Italy, higher winter numbers in Morocco and an increase in France, where an influx of 58 in 1991 included three breeding pairs in the Camargue. It also bred in Spain for the first time in 1993, and in Morocco in 1994 (*Brit. Birds* **86**: 279; **87**: 3; **88**: 27). With the spread of the North American population up the eastern seaboard, it would be nice to think that we could also look forward to a sustained recovery on this side of the Atlantic.

The species occurs mainly in spring and autumn, but shows a wide scatter of arrival dates at both seasons (from March to June and from August to December). There are occasional influxes and these have sometimes been correlated with movements of Ruddy Shelducks *Tadorna ferruginea*. In 1994, for example, when there was a widespread Ruddy Shelduck invasion into northern Europe, there were also good numbers of Glossy Ibises, including at least nine in Denmark, and up to 12 individuals and flocks of up to ten in the Netherlands (*Brit. Birds* **88**: 265). Drought conditions in south-western Asia may be the most plausible explanation for these movements.

When discussing this species in Britain, special mention must be made of the well-known long-staying individual which turned up in Kent in December 1975. From the end of October 1979 it was joined by a second, and both roamed the area, frequenting mainly Stodmarsh and Sheppey, until February 1985, when one disappeared. The remaining bird was last seen at the end of 1992: an astonishing 17 years in residence. Inevitably, such a protracted stay raises questions concerning their origins, but a long stay is not unprecedented as an individual was also recorded in Co. Cork from March 1981 to May 1983.

Identification Plate 8.2 is a stunning photograph of a summer-plumaged adult at Fairburn Ings, Yorkshire, in June 1989. With its long, decurved bill, chestnut body and green-glossed upperparts, it is quite unique in a British or Irish context. There have, however, been past problems involving distinction from the South American Puna Ibis *P. ridgwayi*, which has been known to escape from captivity (indeed, one was at large in Hertfordshire and the surrounding areas during much of the 1980s; Webb, 1988). In the breeding season, the Puna Ibis differs from the Glossy in having a crimson iris, a reddish-slate bill and black legs. It is also thicker necked and shorter legged. Plate 8.1 shows a juvenile Glossy on Tresco, Isles of Scilly, in September 1994. It is quite clearly duller and browner than the adult, particularly on the head, and it lacks the adult's white facial lines. In flight, it alternates periods of flapping with spells of gliding, suggesting Great Cormorant *Phalacrocorax carbo* at a distance, but it both flaps and glides on markedly bowed wings. In direct comparison, females may look noticeably smaller and shorter-winged than males.

LESSER WHITE-FRONTED GOOSE
Anser erythropus

Range Breeds in a narrow band from northern Scandinavia eastwards across northern Siberia. Winters in south-eastern Europe eastwards in isolated pockets to China.

Occurrences Traditionally a fairly regular winter visitor in tiny numbers, usually accompanying flocks of Russian White-fronted Geese *A. albifrons albifrons*, mostly at Slimbridge, Gloucestershire. It has become distinctly rarer in recent years, owing to a large decrease in the Scandinavian breeding population and also to the fact that fewer White-fronts now visit this country, most choosing to stop short in the Netherlands. To compensate for the decrease there have been a number of reintroduction schemes in Scandinavia, and a marked influx of at least ten in the winter of 1991/92, mostly to non-traditional areas, involved at least two originating from that source. The schemes are showing signs of success and have led to regular wintering in the Netherlands, where there were 35–40 in 1994/95 (*Brit. Birds* **88**: 266). As a consequence of the reintroductions, and the ever-present problem of escapes, the occurrence patterns in Britain have become clouded. Slimbridge is still the best bet for a 'safe tick', but even there a Finnish neck-ringed individual was present for three winters from 1990/91–1992/3.

Identification Plate 8.3 shows an adult at Slimbridge in February 1995. This species can be frustratingly difficult to locate amongst large flocks of White-fronts, but the photograph shows the main features to look for: (1) its smaller size; (2) the small, rather triangular, bright pink bill; (3) the steep forehead and rather square head; (4) the darker head colour; (5) the short, thick neck; and (6) reduced amounts of black on the belly. The yellow orbital ring is difficult to see at any distance and is not visible in the photograph. The white 'front' extends further towards the crown and, when viewed from the front, it tends to look more pointed than on most White-fronts. First-winter birds soon acquire the white 'front', but lack black on the belly.

SNOW GOOSE
Anser caerulescens

Range Breeds on the tundras of north-eastern Siberia, Alaska and Canada, and in east to north-western areas of Greenland. It winters on the Atlantic coast and in the southern and south-western states of the USA, as well as in northern Mexico (Madge & Burn, 1988).

Occurrences That wild Snow Geese occur in Europe is confirmed by a remarkable observation that took place in the Netherlands in April 1980 when it was discovered that an individual seen amongst a flock of 18 had been ringed in Manitoba, Canada, three years previously (Scott, 1995). The best places to see genuinely wild individuals in Britain and Ireland, are with flocks of Pink-footed Geese *A. brachyrhynchus* in Scotland and northern England, or with Greenland White-fronted Geese *A. albifrons flavirostris* on the Wexford Slobs, where hybrids between the two have also been observed. The possibility also exists of vagrancy from the east, as evidenced by an apparently wild first-winter with Russian White-fronts *A. a. albifrons* at Slimbridge, Gloucestershire, in the winter of 1981/82. Perhaps over a dozen individuals are recorded annually and it is interesting to note that records have increased since 1979, in line with a large increase in North America (loc. cit.). Its status is otherwise confused by escapes and by feral birds, the latter's population estimated to be at least 250 in 1992, with as many as 60 on the islands of Mull and Coll, Argyllshire (Evans, 1993a). The feral populations are not yet considered to be self-sustaining, so the species has been added to Category D4 of the British List, in addition to its wild Category A status.

Identification Two races occur: the nominate Lesser Snow Goose; and the Greater Snow Goose *A. c. atlanticus*, which breeds in north-eastern Canada and north-western Greenland. Both have 'white' and 'blue' phases, although the latter is very rare in the Greater (Madge & Burn, 1988). The Greater is bulkier and closer in size to the Greylag Goose *A. anser*, but is most easily separated by its bill, which is about 12 per cent longer and deeper at the base (Scott, 1995). Plate 9.1 shows an adult white-phase Greater at Marshside, Lancashire, in January 1986. It is both striking and unmistakable. Plate 9.2 shows a blue phase Lesser at Marshside in November 1992. Its plain grey-brown body plumage contrasts with the white head; also of note are the heavy pink bill, the pink legs and the thick white edgings to the blackish tertials and greater coverts. In flight, the upperwing-coverts would appear pale grey. On the face of it, the blue phase may also seem unmistakable but identification problems often occur as a result of hybridization with other species. Hybrids with Canada Geese *Branta canadensis* may be similar to the genuine article, while Harrison & Harrison (1966) described a hybrid between a male Greylag Goose and a female Canada which also showed a white head, thus resembling a blue Snow Goose.

ROSS'S GOOSE
Anser rossii

Range Has a restricted breeding range in the Canadian Arctic, with most in the Perry River region of the Northwest Territories. Formerly wintered entirely in the Sacramento Valley in California, but now known to be more widespread, perhaps as a result of agricultural changes, with wintering in Texas, Louisiana and even a few on the eastern seaboard (Madge & Burn, 1988; Scott, 1995).

Occurrences There have been four adults in Britain which are likely to have been wild. The first individual wintered with Pink-footed Geese *A. brachyrhynchus* in Lancashire in the four winters from 1970/71 to 1973/74, one wintered with Pink-footed Geese in eastern Scotland in 1985 and 1986, another there in 1988, and finally one wintered with Icelandic Greylag Geese *A. anser* at Lossiemouth, Morayshire, in 1991 (Procter, 1991; Scott, 1995). None of these has been accepted by the BOURC owing to the possibility of escape. This caution is perhaps justified in view of the fact that two ringed Ross's Geese which escaped in the early 1960s took up with wild Icelandic Greylags to winter in central Scotland and summer in Iceland, where they attempted to nest in 1963. The last one was found dead at Loch Leven, Kinrossshire, in January 1972. It should be noted, however, that some observers suggested that these individuals might have been Ross's × Snow Goose hybrids (Scott, 1995). Despite this unhappy incident, wild vagrancy is possible if one accepts the theory of displacement within the Arctic and subsequent abmigration with other geese. Indeed, if one projects its California to west Hudson Bay migration route backwards, it crosses Greenland and clips north-east Iceland. To add further support to this theory, the population has increased in North America by 20 per cent in the last 20 years, while three recent individuals in the Netherlands (with Pink-footed and Barnacle Geese *B. leucopsis*) have been

accepted by the Dutch Rarities Committee (Evans, 1994; Scott, 1995).

Identification Plate 9.3 shows the Lossiemouth bird in March 1991. It is a small, compact goose (similar in size to a Lesser White-front *A. erythropus*), with a rounded head and a short, thick neck. The bill is smaller and more triangular than that of a Snow Goose and it shows only a small 'grinning patch' along the cutting edge. It appears to have been 'stuck on' to the head, without the bulge of feathering into the sides, shown by the Snow Goose. In the field it showed the characteristic bluish warty protruberances over the base, most obvious on old males (Madge & Burn, 1988). The bird had a rapid feeding action, recalling the Lesser White-front (Procter 1991).

CANADA GOOSE
Branta canadensis

Range Breeds across northern North America, wintering in milder coastal regions and the southern states into northern Mexico. There are, of course, well-established feral populations in Britain, Ireland and Fenno-Scandia, as well as in New Zealand.

Occurrences With an estimated British feral population in July 1991 of over 63,500, the presence of this familiar species in a book on rarities may seem incongruous. True vagrants are, however, sometimes seen in Ireland, Scotland and northern England, usually with Greenland White-fronted *Anser albifrons flavirostris*, Greylag *A. anser*, Pink-footed *A. brachyrhynchus* or Barnacle Geese *B. leucopsis*. Confirmation that these birds really are genuine vagrants came in December 1992 when one of two discovered in Aberdeenshire was found to be wearing a neck collar. It turned out to be a second-year male ringed in Maryland the previous February; regrettably, this individual and two others were subsequently shot.

Identification Plate 10.3 shows a small Canada Goose (with Pink-footed Geese) at Martin Mere, Lancashire, in January 1994. Since the taxonomy of the Canada Goose is currently the subject of much debate, it would be unwise to assign the wild birds to any particular race.

BLACK BRANT
Branta bernicla nigricans

Range Breeds in eastern Siberia through Alaska to northern Canada. Moves south to winter on the US eastern seaboard and on both sides of the Pacific. Birds of eastern Siberia have sometimes been separated into the separate race of *orientalis*.

Occurrences First recorded in Essex in February 1957, this race is now annual, usually accompanying flocks of dark-bellied Brent Geese *B. b. bernicla* which originate in Siberia. It has been suggested that the recent increase in the dark-bellied Brent Goose population has led to an eastward expansion into the Taymyr Peninsula, causing them to come into contact or extending the range of overlap with the Black Brant and thereby leading to an increased likelihood of their becoming caught up in westward-moving flocks of Brents (van den Berg *et al.*, 1984). The occurrence in 1989 of an individual in Sussex with six apparent hybrid young may add weight to this theory. There have also been records of individuals with Canadian pale-bellied Brents *B. b. hrota*, so it is clear that Black Brants are arriving from both directions.

Identification Plate 9.4 shows an adult at Cley, Norfolk, in February 1988. It is similar to the accompanying dark-bellied Brents but is slightly larger, thicker necked and obviously darker, with less demarcation between the black breast and the dark belly. Most striking is the large white flank patch, which contrasts with the darker plumage. The white neck ring is about twice as thick as that of a Brent and it joins at the front. The so-called *orientalis* is slightly paler than *nigricans* and the neck ring does not necessarily meet at the front.

RED-BREASTED GOOSE
Branta ruficollis

Range Breeds in Siberia, mainly in the Taymyr Peninsula. Winters mostly on the western shores of the Black Sea, and, until recently, also in good numbers around the Aral and Caspian seas.

Occurrences Up to 1969 there were some 25 records and occurrences were traditionally associated with flocks of Russian White-fronted Geese *Anser albifrons albifrons*. An upsurge since 1975 has coincided with a tendency for the birds to occur with dark-bellied Brent Geese *B. bernicla bernicla* instead, which increased six-fold between the mid-1960s and the early 1990s (Cranswick *et al.*, 1992). One even wintered with Barnacle Geese *B. leucopsis* on the Solway in the three winters from 1991/92 to 1993/94. The upturn here reflects the position in the Netherlands, where there were as many as 20 in the early part of 1994. It seems that, as with the dark-bellied Brent, the Red-breasted Goose has enjoyed an increase in recent years. Madge & Burn (1988) stated that the species had declined to about 25,000 by the early 1970s; disturbance and hunting were thought to have been to blame, as was a decline in the population of Peregrines *Falco peregrinus* near to which the geese apparently nest for protection.

In January 1994, however, there was a remarkable count of 75,000 in Bulgaria (Gorman, 1996).

Identification Plate 10.1 shows an adult at Cley, Norfolk, in February 1988. Plate 10.2 shows a first-winter at Holkham, Norfolk, in November 1993. This beautiful goose presents few identification problems! First-winters can be aged by the rather dull upperparts and by the presence of three ill-defined white wing-covert bars. Adults are blacker above and show only two or three prominent bars.

RUDDY SHELDUCK
Tadorna ferruginea

Range The Ruddy Shelduck occurs in three distinct populations: north-western Africa; Ethiopia; and extreme south-eastern Europe across southern Asia to Mongolia and western China. The north-western African population is relatively small and, although up to 200 formerly moved north in late summer to the Guadalquivir delta in southern Spain, it is now rare there. Most of the Asian population moves south to winter in an area stretching east from Turkey through Iran to southern China (Madge & Burn, 1988).

Occurrences The species' occurrences in Britain and Ireland have for many years been fraught with controversy. The first British record was of one killed near Blandford, Dorset, in 1776. Subsequent occurrences during the 19th century culminated in small influxes in 1886 and 1892, the latter producing parties of up to 20. That year, two or three individuals even reached western Greenland. While there can be little doubt that these old influxes were genuine, even as long ago as 1889 it was recognized that some could have escaped from captivity (Rogers, 1982). In recent years all have been treated as escapes, and the species now resides in Category B of the British and Irish List. Rogers concluded that there was no evidence to suggest that wild Ruddy Shelducks were still occurring, despite the fact that they were annual between 1965 and 1979, with a distinct peak from July to September and with most in south-eastern Britain.

Whilst Ruddy Shelducks do escape from captivity, and some of these may occasionally breed in the wild, there is no evidence to suggest that there are viable self-sustaining feral populations, either here or on the Continent. The Ruddy Shelduck is, to a large extent, nomadic and dispersive and, while it is unlikely that significant numbers of North African individuals still disperse northwards, there is still a possibility of vagrancy from the east, particularly since an individual with a Kirghisian ring was found dead in Poland in October 1979 (Lewington *et al.*, 1991).

The argument supporting the continued occurrence of wild Ruddy Shelducks received a boost in the summer of 1994 when there was a large influx into Fenno-Scandia, including about 100 in Finland, at least 50 in Sweden and 75–100 in Denmark (*Brit. Birds* **88**: 28 and 266; **89**: 26). This coincided with a smaller influx into Britain, including at least 12 in Cheshire and the Wirral (Broome, 1995). Another aspect of the 1994 invasion was that, as with previous invasions, there was a contemporaneous influx of Glossy Ibises *Plegadis falcinellus* into north-west Europe (*see* page 35) which, like the Ruddy Shelducks, also occurred in small flocks. It seems likely that wetland desiccation in south-western Asia may provoke such movements. That wild Ruddy Shelducks are occurring in Britain is becoming increasingly difficult to refute.

Identification The flock of six in Plate 10.4 was photographed on the Hayle Estuary, Cornwall, in October 1994. It seems likely that the flock included some of the birds that had earlier been present on the Wirral. As the photograph clearly shows, the birds are striking and virtually unmistakable. The only possibility of confusion would be with Egyptian Geese *Alopochen aegyptiacus*, or with escapes of the closely related Cape Shelduck *T. cana* or Paradise Shelduck *T. variegata* (female only). At rest, male Ruddy Shelducks show traces of a black neck collar, although this is lost in eclipse. Sexing is then more difficult, but males are slightly larger than females, with a larger head and a thicker neck; females also have a better defined area of white around the eyes. Plate 10.5 shows two of the Hayle birds. With its rather bulbous, plain head, the one on the left would appear to be a male. Juveniles are similar to females but duller (Madge & Burn, 1988). They have a loud, deep *a-er* call, reminiscent of a Brent Goose *Branta bernicla*.

AMERICAN WIGEON
Anas americana

Range Breeds across much of northern North America, moving in winter to the coasts of the Atlantic, the Pacific and the Gulf of Mexico, as well as south through Central America into Colombia.

Occurrences Annual in small numbers, usually in winter. Small parties have occurred, with as many as 13 at Lough Akeragh, Co. Kerry, in October 1968. As with most vagrant wildfowl, some have been escapes, but four North American ringing recoveries (including three from New Brunswick) and the predominance of autumn and winter records indicate that most are genuine vagrants.

Identification Plate 11.1 shows an adult male at Aberlady Bay, East Lothian, in January 1996. It is easily separated from the male Eurasian Wigeon *A. penelope* by its cream forehead and crown, the thick green band extending from the eye down the nape, and by its dark-peppered lower face. The body plumage is a purply-brown colour. The only possibility of confusion lies with hybrids between the three species of wigeon (notably American × Eurasian and Eurasian × escaped Chilöe, *A. sibilatrix*; see Harrison & Harrison, 1968 and Carey, 1993). Plate 11.2 shows such a bird, present at Eye Brook Reservoir, Leicestershire, in January–March 1996. It has a yellower forehead and forecrown than the American; in the field this is cut off across the top of the crown rather than extending in a point down the nape. The very strong green head bands meet on the nape, the lower part of the face is rather yellowy, the flanks are too orange, the back and scapulars show dark feather centres and the rump is white. The latter two features reveal the influence of Chilöe Wigeon, and it appears to be a hybrid between that and the Eurasian.

Plates 11.4 & 5 show a juvenile/first-winter which was present on Fair Isle, Shetland, in September 1986. It was ringed in New Brunswick, Canada, on 13 August and shot near Wexford on 30 November. These close shots show the head pattern to good effect: it has a whitish background, peppered with black, giving a greyish effect at any distance. It shows a paler forecrown and a dark area around the eye which extends as a darker shadow back over the crown, ghosting that of a male. Surprisingly, the head colour and pattern usually appear pretty obvious at a distance, the grey head and subdued head stripe contrasting with the orange body plumage. In addition, female and immature Americans usually show thick orange feather fringes to the back and scapulars (contrasting with the dark feather centres) as well as very black tertials with contrasting white fringes. They may appear more bulbous headed and longer tailed than Eurasian. Their identification is often not as problematical as is generally supposed. Plate 11.5 shows well the diagnostic gleaming white axillaries (which extend as a band onto the median underwing-coverts); on Eurasian Wigeon, these are variably speckled with grey, thus appearing grey overall at any distance. At a distance, the white fringes to the upperwing coverts of adult females produce a whiter-looking forewing than on female Eurasian Wigeon, ghosting the white forewing patch of the adult male. The patterned bases of the greater coverts and the dull speculum show it to be a young bird. On adult females, the bases of the greater coverts are completely white, forming a white wing bar (on Eurasian, they are predominantly greyish at all ages). Plate 11.3 shows a similar bird: a juvenile on St Agnes, Isles of Scilly, in October 1985.

FALCATED DUCK
Anas falcata

Range Breeds in eastern Siberia, south to Mongolia, northern China and Japan. It winters in Japan, Korea and eastern China, south to Vietnam, with smaller numbers west into north-eastern India.

Occurrences There were 13 records between 1971 and 1995, possibly relating to just ten individuals. Most were in eastern England in winter and involved drakes associating with Eurasian Wigeon *A. penelope*, a species whose range overlaps that of the Falcated Duck. It seems possible that individuals may occasionally move the 'wrong way' out of Siberia and then become caught up with westward-moving wigeon which migrate to Western Europe. Despite similar records across northern Europe, the BOURC decided that the species should be placed in Category D1 of the British List as there is a significant escape risk.

Falcated Ducks also turn up on the west coast of North America and, intriguingly, a male in Washington in autumn 1992 was also accompanying Eurasian Wigeon (*Birders' World*, April 1993). What are the chances of an escaped Falcated Duck finding and associating with Eurasian Wigeon in a country where that species is itself a rarity? The obvious conclusion is that the American bird was a genuine vagrant, and its association with the Eurasian Wigeon is surely significant from a European point of view. Although the BOURC's decision to place the species in Category D seems inevitable, there is a widespread gut feeling that at least some of our Falcated Ducks have been wild.

Identification The individual in Plate 12.1 was present at Kirkby-on-Bain Gravel Pits, Lincolnshire, in February 1995. The bill is dark grey and rather straight, and the bird has a large head with a steep forehead and a distinctive pointed mane. The head is green in colour, with reddish on the crown and lower cheeks, and there is a small white spot on the forehead. A narrow white neck collar separates the head from the grey body. The rear end is quite remarkable, with long, decurved tertials which overhang the undertail-coverts. These are themselves a rather eye-catching yellow thickly edged with black. The female is rather bland looking, with a narrow grey bill and a greyish head, finely streaked darker. Like the wigeon it is a vegetarian, and it can often be found grazing on bankside vegetation.

BAIKAL TEAL
Anas formosa

Range Breeds in the forest zone of north and north-east Siberia. Winters in Korea, Japan and south-east China (*see also* below).

Occurrences The Baikal Teal was once one of the commonest ducks in north-eastern Asia – described as 'unbelievably abundant' in Japan – but it has undergone a major and worrying decline during the latter half of the 20th century. The total world population is now estimated at around 40,000, with the largest wintering concentration – about 20,000 – on the Chunman Lakes in Korea (Eldridge & Harrop, 1992). Hunting seems to be the culprit.

Although there were some 13 claims in Britain and Ireland between 1906 and 1994, only eight are considered to be fully proven from an identification point of view and even these are officially considered probably to relate to escapes from captivity. It seems that large numbers were imported into the West during the early part of the 20th century and again after World War II, so early records are particularly suspect, while recent ones are tarnished because the species has become so rare in the wild. Following a review in 1993, the BOURC inevitably relegated the Baikal Teal from Category A to Category D of the British List. Despite this, a pattern of winter occurrences still persists, with records from Finland, Germany, Denmark, the Netherlands and Belgium between 1993 and 1995 (*Brit. Birds* **88**: 266; **89**: 28). There can be little doubt that a winter Baikal Teal in Britain would attract a great deal of attention.

Identification Plate 12.2 shows a male which was trapped on Brownsea Island, Dorset, in January 1969. It shows the distinctive head pattern: cream face bisected by a vertical green line and a narrow white supercilium and collar. Also of note are the pinkish breast, the vertical white breast stripe (recalling the Green-winged Teal *A. crecca carolinensis*) and the black undertail-coverts, bordered anteriorly by another vertical white stripe. Also visible is the dark speculum, bordered in front by a dark buff greater covert line and behind by a white trailing edge; in flight, this produces a wing pattern reminiscent of that of the Northern Pintail *A. acuta*.

The female is most similar to a female Garganey *A. querquedula* but shows a white loral spot which is bordered with brown. The facial pattern is otherwise subdued although a pale 'fore-face' contrasts with a darker 'rear-face', often with a dark line of demarcation dropping vertically from the eye.

GREEN-WINGED TEAL
Anas crecca carolinensis

Range Breeds in northern North America, wintering across much of the USA, and south into Central America and the West Indies.

Occurrences An annual visitor in winter and spring, but its occurrence patterns are masked by the fact that eclipse males, females and juveniles cannot be separated from the Common Teal *A. c. crecca*. It was removed from the Rarities List at the end of 1990, at which time it was occurring at the rate of about 25–30 a year but, as with other Nearctic wildfowl, these figures may be inflated by wandering and returning individuals.

Identification Plate 12.5 shows a male at Martin Mere, Lancashire, in January 1992, a bird which wintered at the site discontinuously from 1984 to 1995. The most obvious difference from the nominate race is the vertical white stripe on the sides of the breast which looks as though it has been painted on with a single brush stroke. It lacks the Common Teal's horizontal white scapular line and it has a less well-defined yellow border to the green head stripe. Many individuals are a deeper pink on the breast. In autumn, adult males moult quickly out of eclipse (they may be in full plumage by mid-October), while first-winters acquire their full plumage much more slowly, sometimes retaining brown flank feathering into January. There have been instances of teals showing mixed characteristics of the two races, so a degree of caution is necessary when identifying this race (Vinicombe, 1994).

AMERICAN BLACK DUCK
Anas rubripes

Range Breeds in the eastern halves of Canada and the northern USA. It winters in south-eastern Canada and the eastern half of the USA.

Occurrences There were 21 records between 1954 and 1994, turning up in autumn, winter and early spring. They have been widely scattered but, inevitably, the Isles of Scilly have recorded the most with four. Once here, they have had a tendency to stay for considerable periods and to pair with Mallards *A. platyrhynchos*. The most famous were a female on Tresco, Isles of Scilly, from October 1976 to 1983, and a male at Aber, Gwynedd, from February 1979 to 1985, both of which produced several hybrid young. A male discovered on Tresco in April 1994 seems set to follow suit.

The survival of the Black Duck as a species is currently giving cause for concern. Historically, it has inhabited North American eastern woodlands, whereas the Mallard occurred primarily in the pothole country further west – still the heart of its range. The two species remained largely isolated, but the advance of agriculture changed the landscape of the eastern half of the continent and made it more suitable for Mallards. Consequently, since the 19th century Mallards have been spreading eastwards, and not only have Black Ducks become rarer, but they have

become more Mallard-like due to hybridization. At present, over 80 per cent of Black Ducks show signs of hybridization and there may be only a few thousand pure individuals left (Alison, 1993). It seems surprising, therefore, that we are continuing to receive pure Black Ducks as vagrants to Britain and Ireland.

Identification Plate 12.3 shows the male on Tresco in October 1994. It is slightly smaller, squarer headed and daintier billed than a Mallard, and is easily separated by its oily blackish-brown body which contrasts with the paler greyish-buff head. Of particular importance is that the speculum lacks the white leading and trailing edges shown by the Mallard. In flight, the white underwing-coverts contrast strongly with the dark belly. The individual in Plate 12.4 is the long-staying Tresco female (date unknown). It is similar to the male but slightly browner. It can readily be sexed by the dark bill, which is crossed at the tip by a lime green band; on the male, the entire bill is lime green. Although superficially distinctive, some domesticated forms of the Mallard can appear quite similar to Black Ducks, and these always have to be borne in mind by those fortunate enough to come across the species.

BLUE-WINGED TEAL
Anas discors

Range Breeds over much of North America. It winters from the southern United States through Central America into South America, sometimes as far south as northern Argentina and Chile.

Occurrences This species is very much the North American equivalent of the Garganey *A. querquedula*. Being a 'summer duck' and a long-distance migrant, its occurrence patterns in the British Isles differ from those of other Nearctic ducks in that most occur in spring and autumn (it is especially unusual in winter). Whilst the autumn records no doubt relate mainly to freshly arrived transatlantic vagrants, spring ones may well involve northward-moving individuals that have wintered further south (there have been records down the Atlantic coast as far as Morocco). Although the pattern is inevitably complicated by escapes, ringing recoveries from New Brunswick and Newfoundland suggest that most are genuine vagrants.

There was an interesting case in Cambridgeshire in 1988 of a female pairing with a Northern Shoveler *A. clypeata* and raising three hybrid young, while another female in Somerset in 1993 followed the same path but failed to breed. Remarkably, a pure pair also bred in Denmark in 1986 (*Brit. Birds* **80**: 10), but whether any of these instances involved wild birds is impossible to say.

Identification The full-plumaged male in Plate 12.6 was photographed at Cley, Norfolk, in June 1990. Although very much a record shot, it nevertheless shows the prominent white facial crescent and the distinctive wing pattern: sky-blue wing coverts similar in shade to those of a male Northern Shoveler (and thus bluer than the chalky-grey forewing of a male Garganey), a white greater covert bar and the lack of a white trailing edge to the very dark speculum. It can just be seen that the white underwing-coverts contrast strongly with the dark belly. First-winter males also show a white greater covert bar but females lack this. Instead, the individual feathers are greyish, fringed with white. Plate 12.7 shows an individual that was aged in the field as first-winter female at the Tehidy Country Park, Cornwall, in October 1995. The bill is longer than that of a Common Teal *A. crecca*, being more similar to that of a Garganey. The plumage is coarsely patterned and the tertials are brown (blackish, contrastingly edged white on the Garganey). The key area to look at is the head. Although it has a dark crown and eye-stripe, the head pattern is basically subdued and is closer to the Common Teal than the Garganey. It differs from the teal in its prominent whitish loral spot and eye-ring. Although some individuals are less well marked than others, these features should always be checked carefully. When out of the water, the legs are a pale yellow on males but duller on females.

The Blue-winged Teal also has to be separated from escaped Cinnamon Teal *A. cyanoptera*. This species tends to have a longer and more spatulate bill and a more rounded head (the jizz thus reminiscent of that of the Northern Shoveler). It is browner and has a plainer head, with a less contrasting dark crown and eye-stripe, and the eye-ring and loral spot are much less obvious. The eclipse male Cinnamon retains its red eye and a reddish head and breast.

MARBLED DUCK
Marmaronetta angustirostris

Range Breeds from Morocco and Spain eastwards in isolated pockets through the Middle East to central Asia. Eastern populations move south to winter mainly in Iran and, rarely, east to Pakistan and north-western India. Some western birds may cross the Sahara (Madge & Burn, 1988).

Occurrences Although on the face of it an unlikely visitor, there is in fact a strong case for treating the Marbled Duck as a potential vagrant to Britain. The nearest breeding populations are in Morocco, where winter numbers reached 1,680 in January 1982, and in Spain, where there were 600 in October 1985 (*Brit. Birds* 78: 635; **80**: 10). In 1992, there were 70–100 breeding pairs in southern Spain, and although this

Marbled Duck.

total had dropped to 30–35 two years later (*Brit. Birds* 87: 314; **88**: 266) numbers there traditionally fluctuate in response to droughts. The important point about this population is that it has a history of erratic northerly dispersal. There were 20–25 in the Ebro Delta (north-east Spain) in September 1957, and as many as 80–100 there in September 1968. The species has also been recorded in northern Spain as far as the Bay of Biscay coast. In France, Marbled Ducks sometimes appear in small numbers in the Camargue (for example, at least 11 in September 1957), and there are several records from further north in France, including one in the Baie de Somme in September 1981. Interestingly, the peak time in the Camargue is from late August to September (with a secondary peak in spring). Another point worth making is that the distance from the marshes of the Guadalquivir in south-west Spain north-eastwards to the Camargue is similar to that northwards to Brittany. The species is not commonly held in captivity in France, and most records are treated as genuine by the French rarities committee (Philippe Dubois *in litt*).

There are at least ten British records, the interesting point being that, unlike the Falcated Duck *Anas falcata* and the Baikal Teal *A. formosa*, most have occurred in summer, with peaks of four in May–June and five in August–September, the pattern fitting exactly that found in France. One found at Chew Valley Lake, Somerset, in August 1984, turned up on a southerly airstream which originated in North Africa, and it behaved like a wild bird throughout its four-month stay. The species is, however, relatively common in captivity and the BOURC has placed it in Category D of the British List.

Identification Plate 13.3 shows an individual photographed at the Kingsbury Water Park, Warwickshire, in July 1990. It is a pale, greyish-buff duck, with a longish, dark grey bill, a dark patch extending back from the eye, and with creamy spotting on the back, scapulars and flanks. It has a controversial taxonomic history, and Madge & Burn (1988) placed it with the pochards (Aythyini) rather than with the dabbling ducks (Anatini) in view of its displays and lack of a speculum.

REDHEAD
Aythya americana

Range Although the Redhead breeds in Alaska and in the Great Lakes and St Lawrence region, the main population is centred on the prairies, south to Nevada, New Mexico and northern Texas. It vacates the interior in winter, occurring from British Columbia and the Great Lakes south to Mexico, Guatemala and Cuba (Madge & Burn, 1988; Price *et al.* 1995).

Occurrence The sole record is of a male at Bleasby, Nottinghamshire, from 9–27 March 1996 (Plate 13.4). Occurring at the same time as Britain's second Cedar Waxwing *Bombycilla cedorum* in Nottingham, it provided a remarkable 'purple patch' for the area. Madge & Burn (1988) noted that the Redhead suffered a considerable decline this century through the drainage of prairie marshes, but a stable population estimated at 600,000 was present in the 1970s. It had, however, shown clear signs of an easterly spread, as in the Great Lakes region. In 1995, a second consecutive year of plentiful rains that followed a decade of intensive wetland conservation yielded the highest breeding duck population in North America in 15 years. Numbers of Redheads rose 36 per cent to a record 888,000 (*Birders' World*, October 1995). That the Nottinghamshire bird occurred against this background and following a particularly severe winter in North America is surely significant. As with Ring-billed Gulls *Larus delawarensis*, Bonaparte's Gulls *L. philadelphia*, Ring-necked Ducks *Aythya collaris* and even the occasional Bufflehead *Bucephala albeola*, it seems likely that the Redhead crossed the Atlantic at a much lower latitude and then travelled north in early spring with Common Pochards *A. ferina*. It actually spent some time displaying to female pochards.

Identification The Redhead is similar to a Common Pochard but is slightly bigger and noticeably bulkier, with a slightly higher rear end. Structurally, it has less of a wedge-shaped head/bill profile, with the bill sticking out from a steep forehead, and a noticeably rounded head. When viewed front-on, the cheeks are rather bulbous. In fact, the shape is reminiscent of the Greater Scaup *A. marila*. The body is a noticeably darker grey than that of a pochard, but with slightly paler flanks. The bill is significantly different, being

pale blue-grey with a black 'dipped-in-ink' tip, a narrow, whitish subterminal band and a black line around the nostrils. The other important difference is the eye colour, which is orangey-yellow (most obvious in bright sunlight). When displaying to the pochards it would raise its head, inflate its neck and then jerk it backwards, keeping the head still. The female is a uniformly brown duck (with some grey admixed in winter) but shows a pale eye-ring and a slight capped effect. Some are rather pale on the face. The bill is similar to that of a male but with a greyer base.

RING-NECKED DUCK
Aythya collaris

Range Breeds across northern North America. It winters mainly in coastal states of the USA south into Central America and the West Indies.

Occurrences The species was originally described from a specimen on sale at the Leadenhall Market, London, in 1801. It was apparently taken in the Lincolnshire fens and the examination of the corpse led to the acquisition of its somewhat inappropriate English name. The first accepted record was made as recently as 1955, and even in the mid-1970s it was still considered a major rarity, with only 16 records to the end of 1974. There was a major influx of about 14 in the winter of 1976/77, including the first multiple arrival of four at Chew Valley Lake, Somerset. Since then the species has never returned to its former status and it was removed from the Rarities List at the end of 1993, having amassed a total of 335 records. There can be little doubt, however, that this figure exaggerates its abundance here since individual birds may wander extensively and often return to traditional sites in consecutive years. The upsurge in records has been linked to an eastward expansion in North America (*BWP*).

There is a wide scatter of records, both temporally and geographically, but autumn ones show a distinct cluster in Cornwall and Devon, and in south-western Ireland. Further evidence of genuine transatlantic vagrancy is provided by two interesting ringing recoveries: one ringed in New Brunswick, Canada, in September 1967, was shot in Brecon three months later; and one ringed at Slimbridge, Gloucestershire, in March 1977 (no doubt one of the aforementioned Chew birds) was shot in south-eastern Greenland in May 1977. This latter recovery is clearly indicative of a transatlantic vagrant attempting to return home by the shortest great circle route.

Identification Plate 13.1 shows a male at Strumpshaw Fen, Norfolk, in March 1993. It is a striking bird, with two white bill bands, a peaked crown and rounded grey flanks with the white 'spur' at the front. Even the coppery neck ring can be seen in this photograph. The female in Plate 13.2 was photographed at Marden Quarry, Co. Durham, in February 1990. Although similar in shape to the male it is altogether more subtle. It shows a pale subterminal bill band (often lost in summer), but its head is the most distinctive area: it has a buffish patch on the lores, a brown eye with a whitish ring and a faint 'tear line', while the dark crown contrasts with the paler face. In many ways the female Ring-necked suggests a female Tufted Duck *A. fuligula* with the head of a Common Pochard *A. ferina*. In flight, both sexes show a grey wing stripe.

FERRUGINOUS DUCK
Aythya nyroca

Range Breeds locally in southern Spain, France and Eastern Europe, becoming more widespread eastwards to western China and western Mongolia, the main centre of distribution being the steppe lakes of eastern Europe and the southern republics of the former Soviet Union. It winters in the Black and Caspian Seas, locally in the Mediterranean, from Iran and Iraq eastwards to northern India and in sub-Saharan Africa, chiefly in the Sudan and Ethiopia (Madge & Burn, 1988).

Occurrences Any attempt to analyse the occurrence patterns of this rare and declining species is fraught with difficulty. Regrettably, it was dropped from the Rarities List at the end of 1968 as the Committee was concerned about the 'large number of escapes'. From the point of view of record analysis, however, the real problem is that of separation from Ferruginous × Common Pochard *A. ferina* hybrids, some of which may be very similar to the genuine article. It seems likely that many of the old records would not stand up to modern scrutiny. In recent years its numbers have been low, and Evans (1993a) could trace only ten records in 1990, 13 in 1991 and eight in 1992, and some of those involved returning individuals. Most occur with flocks of pochards, so winter is clearly the peak time, but since pochards return from their breeding grounds as early as late May, late-summer and autumn sightings would not *necessarily* relate to escapes. In view of its current rarity, both here and abroad, it is surely high time that this species was taken more seriously.

Identification Plates 13.5 & 6 show a male at Lea Valley Park, Hertfordshire, in March 1994. It has a distinctive shape with a highly peaked crown. The head and body plumage is a beautiful deep reddish-chestnut, with blacker upperparts, a white belly, and it shows a manic white eye. Unfortunately, the depressed tail largely covers the characteristic large

white undertail-covert patch in Plate 13.5. When identifying Ferruginous Ducks, it is always important to check the bill: any black at the tip should be restricted mainly to the nail, as seen here. Hybrids show more extensive black on the bill and have a more pochard-like head and bill profile. The female shows a dark eye and may show a subdued orangey area on the lores. The black on the bill tip may be slightly more extensive than on the male. In flight, the Ferruginous has a striking white wing bar which extends right across the primaries (and is thus more extensive than that shown by the Tufted Duck *A. fuligula*).

LESSER SCAUP
Aythya affinis

Range Breeds across northern North America. In winters mainly down the west and east coasts of the USA, across the southern states and through Central America to northern South America, as well as in the West Indies.

Occurrences The first British record was made as recently as March/April 1987. This was a first-winter male at Chasewater, Staffordshire (Holian & Fortey, 1992), a satisfying example of a first for Britain found by local patch regulars away from the more traditional coastal hot spots. Remarkably, there have been a further 15 since (to 1996) and, as with the initial British records of Ring-necked Ducks *A. collaris*, all have related to males. There have also been several recent Continental records, and even two on Tenerife, Canary Islands. The species' appearance here may be correlated to its recent spread into Newfoundland.

Identification Plate 14.1 shows a male photographed at Tittenhanger Gravel Pits, Hertfordshire, in April 1996. It is similar to the Greater Scaup *A. marila* but, as its name suggests, it is smaller, being more similar in size to the Tufted Duck *A. fuligula*. The most obvious structural difference is the head shape: whereas the Greater has a smoothly and evenly rounded head, the Lesser has a steeper forehead, a high crown and a sharp angle at the juncture of the crown and nape (often showing a slight indentation at the rear of the crown). It is flatter backed and smaller billed than Greater. Although adult males of both species have black on the bill tip that is largely confined to the nail, on the Lesser this takes the form of a discrete oval patch. This is an important feature in the elimination of most hybrids (note that Greater Scaup × Tufted Duck hybrids may closely resemble Lesser Scaup). The upperparts are more coarsely vermiculated than on Greater and these contrast with the white flanks. A key feature not visible in the photograph is the wing stripe: Lesser has grey primaries and white secondaries, whereas on Greater the white stretches right across the wing. First-winter male may retain traces of brown feathering and variegated flanks until the following spring. The female shows a large white blaze around the base of the bill, a less well-defined black nail, a greyer base and a dull blue-grey area behind the nail. When faced with a potential female Lesser Scaup, the wing stripe should be carefully checked.

KING EIDER
Somateria spectabilis

Range Circumpolar on Arctic coasts. Winters just south of the breeding range, the closest areas being in Iceland and northern Scandinavia.

Occurrences Although there were 62 records prior to 1958, there were very few during the 1960s and, at that time, it was considered a very rare vagrant. Dymond *et al.* (1989) show a dramatic increase after 1969 to a peak of 15 in 1974, but this may have been the result of greater coverage due to organized seaduck monitoring. Another influx appears to have taken place in 1986 but numbers have been distinctly lower since. It is interesting that there have recently been record numbers in Sweden, where there were at least 103 in 1989 (*Brit. Birds* 84: 228). As with the Ring-necked Duck *Aythya collaris*, the exact numbers occurring are difficult to judge as individuals move around and return to favoured sites year after year. The BBRC total stood at 153 from 1958 to 1990, but Suddaby *et al.* (1994) estimated a minimum of 61 in that period. As would be expected of a northern seaduck, most have occurred in Scotland, with 34 per cent in Shetland (loc cit.). Although there have been several occurrences in Ireland, the King Eider remains an extreme rarity in England and Wales; particularly noteworthy was a well-watched female at Portscatho, Cornwall, from January to March 1986.

Identification Plate 14.3 shows an adult male present at Reawick and Tresta Voe, Shetland, in April 1989. This particular individual had been in the area since May 1986 and remained into 1991. The photograph shows a beautiful and stunning duck. It can be aged as an adult (as opposed to a second-winter) by the powder-blue crown, the pale green cheeks, the pink-flushed breast and the large bright bill-shield. A second-winter has a greyer head, whiter cheeks and breast, and shows a smaller, duller shield.

Plate 14.2 shows the Portscatho female. It had rather a fulvous tone to its body plumage and the back and scapulars were thickly edged with rufous. It had a shorter bill, a steeper forehead and a flatter crown than Common Eider *S. mollissima* and the lores were rounded, lacking Common's point of feathering down

the bill (thus leaving the nostril more isolated). Its curved gape line gave it a distinctive grinning expression. The pale eyebrow and line running back from the eye were distinctive, as was the pale buffy loral spot.

STELLER'S EIDER
Polysticta stelleri

Range Breeds along the coasts of Siberia and Alaska. Most winter in the southern Bering Sea. In the late 1950s and early 1960s, up to 200,000 gathered to moult in Izembek Bay, Alaska, but subsequent counts have been much lower, with as few as 30,000 in recent decades. The western population, however, is currently estimated to be 40,000, at least double that previously estimated (*Birding World* 9: 77). This includes increasing numbers which travel west to winter in northern Norway, where there were as many as 5,300 in 1991 (Elmberg, 1992). It has also recently increased in the Baltic.

Occurrences Against this marked increase in Arctic Norway and the Baltic, it is perhaps surprising that the species remains an extremely rare vagrant to Britain. There have been just 13 records, the last new occurrence taking place as long ago as 1976 (although a wing was found on Fetlar, Shetland, in April 1996). The most famous of these records was a long-staying male on South Uist, Outer Hebrides, from May 1972 to August 1984, the object of many a long northern trek. Another male, on Westray and Papa Westray, Orkney, from October 1974 to July 1982, was much less widely twitched. With the increase in numbers on the Continent, it must surely be only a matter of time before there are further records.

Identification Plate 14.4 shows the South Uist male, taken in June 1983. It is a small duck, about the size of a Common Goldeneye *Bucephala clangula*, and only about two-thirds the size of a Common Eider *Somateria mollissima*. The photograph shows the rather square head and the long, triangular 'stuck-on' bill. Like the King Eider *S. spectabilis*, it is a beautiful bird, and the pale green head spots, the black eye patch and the soft, salmon-pink breast are particularly eye-catching. The partially opened wing shows the large white wing covert patch as well as the black speculum with its white trailing edge. Plate 14.5 shows a female which was present on Fair Isle, Shetland, in May–June 1971. The brown plumage and a white-edged blue speculum are distinctly reminiscent of a female Mallard *Anas platyrhynchos*. It is darker and plainer than female Common or King Eiders, showing a small pale patch on the lores and only a narrow eye-ring. The long pointed tail is held cocked when resting, reminiscent of a Common Scoter *Melanitta nigra*.

HARLEQUIN DUCK
Histrionicus histrionicus

Range Breeds along turbulent rivers and streams, its nesting areas frequently coinciding with salmon spawning grounds. It occurs from central Siberia eastwards through Alaska and down the Rockies into the northern USA. There is another population from north-east Canada to southern Greenland and Iceland. In winter, most move south along adjacent coasts.

Occurrences An extremely rare vagrant, with just 12 records (14 birds) to 1996. All of these have been in northern England and Scotland, and this distribution suggests an Icelandic origin. There are, however, a number of records from the Baltic and White seas as well as from inland central Europe, and it is thought likely that these originated in eastern Siberia as that population is more migratory than the Icelandic one (*BWP*). Alternatively, transatlantic vagrancy from north-east Canada or Greenland could be a possibility.

Identification Adult male Harlequins are one of the most beautiful and immaculate of ducks, but females are far less inspiring. Plate 14.6 was taken on Islay, Argyllshire, in October 1987. It shows a small duck with a short rounded body and a short thick neck. The large head shows a steep forehead and an evenly rounded rear crown. The bill is small and predominantly dark grey. It has short wings (about 10 per cent shorter than those of Long-tailed Duck *Clangula hyemalis*) and rather a full tail with a rounded tip. The whole plumage is chocolate brown (with a slightly paler, mottled belly) but the monotony is relieved by a broad swathe of dirty white before the eye and a small neat brilliant white spot behind, the latter being most prominent. The overall effect suggests female Surf Scoter *Melanitta perspicillata*. When visible, the legs are a predominantly dull lime green, with blackish webs. The Islay bird appears to have been a juvenile. It shows noticeable pale fringes to the scapulars and adult female is slightly blacker on the face. Harlequin jumps slightly when diving and it submerges with an open-wing action, like Long-tailed Duck. Prior to diving, it may persistently search below the surface, with the head partially submerged, just like a diver (Gaviidae). They often come ashore to rest on the rocks.

SURF SCOTER
Melanitta perspicillata

Range Breeds in Alaska and northern Canada. Winters down the North American western seaboard from the Aleutians to Baja California, and down the eastern seaboard from Newfoundland to Florida.

Occurrences The Surf Scoter has occurred in all months but is most frequent in winter in Scotland and Ireland. Up to 20–30 have been present in good years, and a marked increase since the mid-1980s led to its removal from the Rarities List at the end of 1990. Small parties often occur, sometimes reappearing for several years in succession. There has recently been a long series of records from the Firth of Forth area, with a maximum of 13 during the winter of 1988/89.

As well as the typical coastal occurrences, there have also been several inland, including two intriguing May–June records from Lower Lough Erne, Co. Fermanagh, this being the main Irish breeding site of the Common Scoter *M. nigra*. Just where they go in summer has been a matter of speculation, but there must be a possibility of occasional breeding on this side of the Atlantic.

Identification Plate 15.1 shows a juvenile which was present on Tresco, Isles of Scilly, in October 1975. It is a stocky duck with a large, wedge-shaped bill and a square head. The brown plumage is enlivened by two pale spots, a large round one before the eye and a smaller one behind. The very dark crown appears as a dark cap and contrasts with the pale face. Adult females are completely brown below but all young scoters have a pale belly. An adult female also usually shows a paler area on the nape, ghosting that of the male. The adult male shows two prominent white head patches and a remarkable multi-coloured bill. Like the Velvet Scoter *M. fusca*, but unlike the Common, the Surf usually dives with an open-wing action and, like Velvet, it may be surprisingly tame.

BUFFLEHEAD
Bucephala albeola

Range Breeds in the coniferous forest zone of North America, mainly across Alaska and Canada but with some occurring south as far as north-east California. It has recently increased and spread in the east. It winters from coastal Alaska south to California and across the whole of the southern USA, with some penetrating south into Mexico (Madge & Burn, 1988).

Occurrences The Bufflehead is an extremely rare vagrant with just nine records, only four of these since 1958 (some of the very old records are currently under review). As with most wildfowl, it is always difficult to eliminate the possibility of escapes, but recent British and Continental records have shown a distinct late-winter peak. It seems probable that they cross the Atlantic in response to severe freezing conditions in North America and then work their way north in spring. A record of a female in Portugal in January–February 1993 (*Brit. Birds* **86**: 280) may support this theory, and it seems more than coincidental that two in 1994 occurred after one of the most severe North American winters on record. The June date of the Yorkshire bird (*see* below) would not mitigate against acceptance as a genuine vagrant since young Buffleheads, like Common Goldeneyes *B. clangula*, may be rather tardy in their spring migration.

Identification Plate 15.2 shows the heavily twitched adult male which was present at Colwick Country Park, Nottinghamshire, in March 1994. It is a small duck, about the size of a Ruddy Duck *Oxyura jamaicensis*, and it recalls a diminutive goldeneye. It has a dumpy body and a rather large head; this is highly domed on adult males and gives the bird its name, which is derived from 'buffalo-head' (Madge & Burn, 1988). Plumage-wise, it is very distinctive, and the large, white, fan-shaped patch over the nape is particularly eye-catching. Plate 15.3 shows a first-summer male at Coatham Marsh, Yorkshire, in June 1994. The dark head with its large white ear-covert patch is similar to that of a female (although the patch is larger), but the white breast, flanks and wing coverts are characteristic of a young male. In flight, both sexes have a white patch on the secondaries and adult males also have extensively white wing coverts. The Bufflehead's short wings and dumpy body produce a rather fast, whirring flight action.

BLACK KITE
Milvus migrans

Range Has a huge range, covering most of the old world. Palearctic breeders are migratory, western birds wintering in tropical Africa.

Occurrences Formerly an extremely rare and highly sought-after vagrant, with just five records between 1866 and 1947, and a further ten between 1966 and 1971. There has since been a dramatic increase, and it is now annual with a total of 238 accumulated by the end of 1995; 1994 was a record year with 30. It has even been tipped as a future colonist. Despite this, it remains difficult to catch up with as many are single-observer fly-overs. The upsurge here is related to a recent increase on the near Continent; for example, it has regularly bred in southern Belgium since 1980 and a survey in France between 1979 and 1981 revealed 5,800–8,000 pairs, and as many as 12,100 passed one site in the Pyrenees in the autumn of 1992 (*Brit. Birds* **75**: 570; **77**: 234; **86**: 280).

Identification Although easily identified, the Black Kite has proven a perpetual bugbear to the Rarities Committee owing to the frequent submission of inadequate and superficial descriptions which often fail to eliminate high-flying Marsh Harriers *Circus aeruginosus*. Plate 15.5 shows the genuine article, photographed on St Mary's, Isles of Scilly, in May 1990. It has long, fingered wings and a long, lightly barred tail. In this shot, the tail is slightly spread and looks square-ended with sharply pointed corners. Subdued pale 'windows' on the inner primaries are also lightly barred, and it otherwise shows a rich brown body, a pale head with a dark patch through the eye, and a yellow cere. In more purposeful flight, the wings are angled back from the carpals and often bowed. The tail is often twisted and it more normally shows a shallow fork, less deep than that of a Red Kite *M. milvus*. Pale fringes to the lesser and median coverts produce a pale panel across the upperwing in flight.

WHITE-TAILED EAGLE
Haliaeetus albicilla

Range Breeds in western Greenland, Iceland, northern, eastern and south-eastern Europe, Asia Minor and across the northern Palearctic to the Bering Sea.

Occurrences The story of the fall and potential rise of the White-tailed Eagle in Britain is well known and represents a considerable conservation success story. It was widespread in the 18th century in Scotland and Ireland, and although it also bred in England and on the Isle of Man, it last bred in Scotland in 1916. It was then reduced to an extreme vagrant, with only two recorded between 1958 and 1972 (both in 1961). Since then, there has been a marked upturn, with four occurrences during the ten-years 1973–82 and 16 during 1983–94. As is to be expected, most of these have been immatures seen in winter on the east coast, but included the well-watched individual in the Brill area of Buckinghamshire/Oxfordshire in the winter of 1983/84. This upturn is related to an increase in numbers wintering in northern France and the Low Countries, and this in turn is correlated to a slow but continuing increase in the breeding populations of Fenno-Scandia and eastern Europe.

Since 1975 the species has been reintroduced into western Scotland and the programme is showing signs of success. It has been added to Category D4, in addition to its wild Category A status, but it is not yet clear whether the reintroduced population is self-sustaining. Winter records north of the border are usually regarded as released or feral birds.

Identification Plate 15.4 shows the immature at Brill in February 1984. It was aged as being in its

Immature White-tailed Eagle with hare.

fourth calendar year. It is a large eagle and the photograph shows its long, broad 'barn-door' wings, as well as its wedge-shaped tail and long neck, this protruding as much in front of the wings as the tail does behind. The whitish patch on the axillaries and the messy whitish mottling on the underwing-coverts are typical of a young bird, as are the pale upperwing-coverts, which are just visible. It also shows a messy pale area on the breast, demarcated from the dark belly. The pale base of the bill (pale yellow in the field) is also noticeable.

BALD EAGLE
Haliaeetus leucocephalus

Range Breeds from north-western Alaska and central Canada south to the southern USA and Baja California. It winters from Alaska and southern Canada southwards to, or beyond, the southern limits of its breeding range (Godfrey, 1966).

Occurrences A record of an adult at Llyn Coron, Anglesey, on 17 October 1978, was placed in Category D of the British List as its origin was considered uncertain. A better candidate for full acceptance was a juvenile at Castleisland, Co. Kerry, from 17 November into December 1988, when it was eventually captured and returned to the USA (Plates 15.6 & 7). A third record, of an immature shot at Garrison, Co. Fermanagh, on 11 January 1973, originally accepted as a White-tailed Eagle *H. albicilla*, has also recently come to light (Killian Mullarney,

verbally). These amazing occurrences must be viewed against a dramatic increase in North America which followed earlier declines caused by habitat loss and pesticides. The Bald Eagle declined to as few as 417 nesting pairs in the continental United States in the 1960s, but has since climbed back to nearly 4,500. In 1995, the United States Fish and Wildlife Service decided to upgrade its status from 'endangered' to 'threatened' in all 48 states (*Birders' World*, October 1995).

Identification The Bald Eagle is similar to the White-tailed Eagle, but the adult is, of course, readily separated by its white head and neck. The juvenile is much more similar to the White-tailed but, as is apparent in the photographs, it has a longer wedge-shaped tail and is generally whiter on the underwing coverts. Plate 15.7 would also indicate that the upperwing-coverts are much more uniform than on a similarly aged White-tailed Eagle, which has the feathers prominently fringed paler.

BLACK VULTURE
Aegypius monachus

Range Breeds from Spain, locally through the northern Mediterranean, the Balkans, Asia Minor and the Caucasus east to Tibet, China and Mongolia. Some winter to the south of the breeding range. It has declined drastically in all areas but has recently shown an increase in Spain, where there were 774 pairs in 1991 (*Brit. Birds* **84**: 229).

Occurrence The only record relates to an adult seen at various localities in mid-Wales from November 1977 to February 1978 (Vinicombe, 1994). Towards the end of its stay, it was heavily twitched and most observers were genuinely impressed by its timidity and apparent wildness. Despite this, the record was rejected by the BOURC as being an escape from captivity, only to be reassigned to category D in 1993. It is not common in captivity and the BOURC was able to trace at least 99 previous records from northern Europe, although the majority were made in summer and date from the 19th century. As can be seen in Plates 16.1 & 2, the Welsh bird showed a certain amount of plumage wear, although the significance of this is debatable. Interestingly, there were six records in Denmark, the Netherlands and Belgium between 1948 and 1990. The first, in the Netherlands in 1948, was accepted as a wild bird, but of the others, two are known to have been escapes and the remainder have been treated as such. Bearing these points in mind, the BOURC decided that the probability of an escaped origin outweighed the possibility of a wild one. Gutiérrez (1995), however, listed a number of examples of erratic, long-range vagrancy by large vultures, and he considered that the behaviour and characteristics of the Welsh bird were compatible with those of a wild individual.

Identification The Black Vulture is the largest vulture in the Western Palearctic. It is essentially dark brown, with pale feet, whitish markings on the head, and a bluish cere and base of the bill (the latter being pink on juveniles). In flight it looks huge, with a wingspan of up to 11 feet (2.95 m). The photographs show the deeply fingered primaries, the relatively parallel-sided wings and the short, wedge-shaped tail.

PALLID HARRIER
Circus macrourus

Range A bird of temperate grassland and steppe, with a breeding range extending from the Black Sea and the Ukraine eastwards across Kazakhstan to Mongolia. It winters in Africa, in a broad band south of the Sahara and southwards through East Africa to eastern Cape Province, as well as in parts of the Middle East and throughout the Indian subcontinent. It migrates south on a broad front but, in spring, there is a greater movement through the central Mediterranean with a considerable passage through North Africa.

Occurrences An extremely rare vagrant, with just three records between 1931 and 1952. It sometimes breeds well to the west of its normal range, and a small invasion in 1952 led to several breeding records in Germany and five to six pairs in Sweden. One of the

offspring of the latter was shot in Yorkshire in October 1952. Another influx occurred in 1993 and, remarkably, there were then five records in Perthshire, Essex, Leicestershire, Shetland and on Humberside. These coincided with small influxes into Germany, Denmark, France (where a male held territory in the Dordogne) and Finland (where a male bred with a female Montagu's Harrier, *C. pygargus*; *Brit. Birds* **87**: 4). In April 1995, a second-summer male took up residence in the Birsay area of Orkney (Plate 16.4) and attempted to breed with a female Hen Harrier *C. cyaneus*. By late June the news had filtered down the grapevine and a large number of people journeyed north to see it. It will be interesting to see if this recent increase continues.

Identification Plate 16.3 shows a juvenile at Exnaboe, Shetland, in September 1993. The identification of 'ringtail' harriers is a complicated subject and the following is based on Forsman (1995) which should be consulted for further details. Pallid and Montagu's Harriers are similar in size and proportions. Many juvenile Montagu's Harriers show dark copper-brown underparts and these are readily identifiable. Those with paler, more yellowish-ochre underparts could be either species and it is then necessary to concentrate on the under primaries and the head pattern. On juvenile Pallid, the under primaries appear rather evenly barred from base to tip and frequently show unbarred primary bases. This leaves a pale 'boomerang' across the base of the primaries, immediately behind the primary coverts. When present, this is probably the single best field character. The 'fingers' are evenly barred and the 'hand' has a fainter trailing edge than on Montagu's. (Montagu's shows all-dark fingers and a dark trailing edge to the hand, producing a wide dark border to the wing tip). The head pattern is also distinctive. The white around the eye is reduced compared with Montagu's and the dark ear-covert patch is more extensive, reaching further towards the tip of the lower mandible. This leaves only a narrow pale throat (Montagu's shows a wide pale throat). The pale collar is clear-cut, distinct and of equal-width (more tapering on Montagu's). It extends from the nape to the throat and may appear to completely encircle the head. Dark lores add to a 'grim-faced' expression, rather than the 'mild-faced' expression of Montagu's. Other features include the under secondaries, which may appear darker at a distance, and the axillaries; some juvenile Montagu's may acquire the diagnostic chequered pattern which is found on adult females.

Plate 16.4 shows the second-summer male in Orkney. Compared with the Hen Harrier, it is smaller and daintier, with slimmer, more pointed wings (like Montagu's). It also appears strikingly pale whitish-grey, indeed pallid, with prominent black wedges in the primaries and no white rump. It differs from adult male in that it has something of a hooded effect, with the throat contrasting with the whiter breast, and it shows brown feathering in several areas, notably the wing coverts and tail (Fairclough, 1995). The photograph shows that it is in primary moult, two of the inners appearing to have been dropped. In the field, there is something about the jizz of males that recalls Black-shouldered Kite *Elanus caeruleus*. In direct comparison, it has shallower, less elastic wing-beats than Montagu's.

LESSER KESTREL
Falco naumanni

Range Breeds from Morocco and Iberia through the Mediterranean, around the Black Sea, in Asia Minor, in parts of the Middle East and discontinuously to eastern China. While some of the Spanish and North African populations are resident, the rest winter over much of sub-Saharan Africa. In 1967, as many as 154,000 were found at regular roosts in South Africa.

Occurrences The Lesser Kestrel is an extremely rare vagrant, with just 17 records. Ten were made between 1867 and 1909, one was in 1926 and there were six between 1968 and 1992. Most have been in May–June. The Lesser Kestrel is very high on most twitchers' 'wanted lists', but its appearances here seem likely to become even less frequent owing to a worrying decline in its breeding populations. In Spain, for example, it decreased from perhaps over 100,000 pairs in the early 1960s to 50,000 pairs in the 1970s, and to only 4,000–5,000 pairs in 1989, mostly in Extremadura and Andalucia. In France, it declined from 50–100 pairs in 1971 to probably fewer than ten in the late 1980s. Similar decreases have been reported over much of its Western Palearctic range, and have been attributed to pesticides and habitat loss (*BWP*, *Brit. Birds* **84**: 5).

Identification Whilst adult males are not difficult to identify, other plumages can be a real nightmare, as evidenced by the infamous 'Blackrock Lesser Kestrel'. This bird, seen in Cornwall in September–October 1979, was eventually abandoned by the Rarities Committee owing mainly to the difficulty of evaluating several conflicting sets of descriptions. Being photographed, the adult male in Plate 16.6 was fortunately spared such controversy; it was present on Fair Isle, Shetland, on 23 June 1987. As its name suggests, the Lesser Kestrel is slightly smaller than the Common Kestrel *F. tinnunculus*, and may show slightly rounder wing tips but, in the absence of direct comparison, such differences are meaningless. Plumage-wise, males are brighter and more colourful

than male Common and the photograph shows some diagnostic features: (1) a plain blue-grey hood, lacking moustachial stripes; (2) a plain chestnut mantle, lacking black spotting; and (3) a broad blue-grey band from the bend of the wing, across the greater coverts and tertials (although this can be frustratingly difficult to make out in flight). Also of note are the long primaries which protrude into the black tail band (shorter on Common, not quite reaching the tail band). If visible, the underparts would be dark cinnamon-orange, variably spotted (mainly on the flanks). They contrast with the silvery-white underwings which show reduced spotting on the wing coverts and contrasting black alula and wing tips. The bright yellow eye-ring and, particularly, the cere, add to the more colourful impression.

A winter body moult means that first-summer male resembles the adult male – with its blue-grey hood and unspotted mantle – but the wings and tail remain juvenile. This means that the wing coverts are barred and lack the blue, the primaries are old and faded and the tail is barred (sometimes with new central feathers). In this plumage it may show faint moustachial stripes and more profuse underpart spotting. Detailed texts should be consulted when faced with a female but longer primaries at rest, a variably greyer face, and whiter underwings may attract attention. On their breeding grounds they are usually gregarious and a distinctive, quick, nasal *chi-chi-chit* call may be heard. Otherwise, behavioural differences are usually difficult to detect, although they are often relatively tame. Contrary to popular belief, they may persistently hover.

AMERICAN KESTREL
Falco sparverius

Range Breeds across most of North America and throughout Central and South America. Northernmost populations are migratory, moving to the southern USA for the winter, with some reaching Mexico.

Occurrences There are two records, both made in 1976: a male on Fair Isle, Shetland, from 25–27 May (Taylor, 1981) and a female at Bearah Tor, Bodmin Moor, Cornwall, from 13–28 June (Mellow & Maker, 1981). That two should turn up within three weeks of each other is quite extraordinary. Other European records have come from the Azores, Denmark and, remarkably, Malta (*BWP*). The latter record may point to ship assistance as their method of arrival.

Identification Plates 16.5 shows the Cornish female. The most distinctive feature is the head pattern, with: (1) its soft grey crown (with a bright rufous rear and centre); (2) its double black vertical

Female American Kestrel.

head stripes, with a large whitish patch between; and (3) a yellowish nape with a black line down the centre. The upperparts were bright rufous, brighter than on female Common Kestrel *F. tinnunculus*, and with heavy black barring. The American Kestrel is about 25 per cent smaller than our bird, with a proportionately shorter tail and, in flight, pale translucent subterminal spots behind a dark trailing edge to the primaries. The male is even more colourful with blue-grey wing coverts which contrast with the bright rufous back and scapulars.

RED-FOOTED FALCON
Falco vespertinus

Range Breeds from the former Czechoslovakia, Hungary and Russia eastwards across southern Siberia. The entire population winters in south-western Africa, mainly in Angola, Namibia, Botswana and Zimbabwe.

Occurrences The Red-footed Falcon is an annual visitor, with most occurring in May and June. It is rare in autumn, but small numbers have been recorded right through to early November. Spring numbers vary considerably. A typical spring would produce somewhere between five and 15, but there have been periodic invasions, including 42 in 1973, 37 in 1989 and a staggering 120 in 1992. The dichotomy between spring and autumn occurrences is obviously related to the species' migration routes. In autumn,

Siberian birds travel west, north of the Caspian and Black Seas, and then move south with European breeders over the Balkans, Turkey and Cyprus, and into Africa over the eastern Mediterranean. In spring, the migration is further west and considerable numbers move through West Africa, with flocks of up to 5,000 recorded in Nigeria. The birds cross the Mediterranean from Algeria eastwards and some penetrate Western Europe, sometimes in numbers. This may lead to sporadic breeding attempts well to the west of the normal range (*BWP*). With easterly winds, small numbers reach Britain and occasionally Ireland; in 1992 a high-pressure area over Scandinavia in late May and early June produced persistent easterly winds (and high temperatures), and this led to the invasion. As many as 450 were also seen in the Netherlands and an amazing 760 in Denmark (Nightingale & Allsopp, 1994).

Identification The photographs show a small falcon, similar in shape to a Eurasian Hobby *F. subbuteo* but in flight it shows proportionately shorter, broader and less pointed wings, a more slender body and a relatively longer, more rounded tail (Small, 1995). At rest, the wing tips fall slightly beyond the tail (unlike the Common Kestrel *F. tinnunculus* which is shorter winged). Although Red-footed Falcons may catch flying insects and will also hover, vagrants are more typically seen feeding from perches, such as roadside wires or fence posts, from which they drop to the ground rather like a shrike (Laniidae). They can also be reminiscent of a cuckoo (Cuculidae), particularly since they tend to droop their wings. Red-footed Falcons can be surprisingly tame.

A number of plumage types are seen here but most vagrants are first-summers. A post-juvenile body moult takes place in the winter quarters and there is then a further protracted moult, from March of its second calendar year throughout the summer, which explains why first-summers are so variable (*see* Small, 1995, for a more detailed discussion). Plates 17.3 & 4 show a first-summer male at Landguard, Suffolk, in May 1992. At rest it appears to be quite an advanced bird (predominantly grey, paler below), but in flight the remiges and most of the larger wing coverts are brown and juvenile. The juvenile tail is also barred, but it has new adult central feathers. The bare parts are a dull orangey and the undertail-covert patch is restricted. Plate 17.6 shows another first-summer male, near Dungeness, Kent, June 1987. This one shows a distinctive orange breast. Plate 17.5 shows an adult male at Studland, Dorset, in May 1987. It can readily be aged by its silvery outer wing and secondaries. Plate 17.1 shows a first-summer female at Shipton Bellinger, Hampshire, in June

1989. Most distinctive is the predominantly whitish head, with a black, shrike-like mask. It can be aged by the fine streaking on the crown, the lightly streaked underparts and by the rather dull and browny upperparts and tail. Note in particular that the tertials are very browny, with just small greyish notches. The bird in Plate 17.2 is an adult female recorded at Filey, Yorkshire, in May 1992. It is greyer on the upperparts and tail, and is much more regularly barred (including the tertials). The unstreaked crown is a rich golden-buff, the mask is more restricted and the cere is brighter.

GYR FALCON
Falco rusticolus

Range Has a circumpolar distribution, mainly in the Arctic and subarctic. It is migratory only in high latitudes, those occurring in the south of its range being resident and dispersive. It is sometimes eruptive and, in some areas, such movements have been linked to population cycles of the Rock Ptarmigan *Lagopus mutus*.

Occurrences The Gyr Falcon is an irregular vagrant, occurring mainly in winter and spring, and, as one would expect, it is most frequently reported in northern Scotland. There have, however, also been a number of records in Ireland and south-west England, particularly in spring; the one seen in Plates 18.1 & 2 was present at Berry Head, Devon, in late March and early April 1986. This magnificent bird was seen and greatly appreciated by hundreds of people, many of whom initially dismissed the claim as an April Fools' joke! The bird itself frequented a small quarry and was readily visible from the ramparts of an adjacent Napoleonic fort. Its prey included a number of Eurasian Jackdaws *Corvus monedula*, and observers on 1 April were treated to the macabre spectacle of a Jackdaw's head rolling down the scree slope as the falcon tore into the body above.

Identification White phase Gyr Falcons are unmistakable, and such birds are assumed to originate in the high Arctic of Greenland. The first-winter in Plate 18.3, photographed on the North Slob, Co. Wexford, in April 1986, is more heavily marked than the Devon bird. Plate 18.4 shows a ship-assisted individual being released in Shetland in March 1973. The photograph clearly shows the size of the bird in comparison to the late Bobby Tulloch. It is heavily patterned and shows the greyish cere of a first-winter. Identification of the darker southern forms is much more problematical and there have been a number of controversies over the years. There is a likelihood of confusion not only

with the Saker Falcon *F. cherrug*, but also with a bewildering and proliferating variety of falconers' hybrids, some of which may be disconcertingly similar to the genuine article. Cynical birders have commented on the fact that the more sedentary dark-phase Gyrs are inevitably single-observer one-day birds, whereas the white ones tend to hang around and be multi-observered. In recent years the Rarities Committee has certainly adopted a tough line with non-white Gyrs.

SORA
Porzana carolina

Range Breeds across much of mid-latitude North America. Winters from the southern United States, through Central America and the West Indies to northern South America.

Occurrences There were five old records between 1864 and 1920, and seven between 1973 and 1991, four of which were made in the Isles of Scilly in September–October. The most appreciated, however, was one at Pagham Lagoon, Sussex, from October to December 1985, last seen on Christmas Eve (Plate 18.5). The most unusual was a juvenile/first-winter male trapped on Bardsey, Caernarfonshire, in 1981 on the extraordinarily early date of 5 August, illustrating just how early some Nearctic vagrants may cross the Atlantic (Roberts, 1984). Other Western Palearctic records have come from France, Spain, Morocco and, amazingly, there have been three in Sweden, including two in June–July 1987 (*Brit. Birds* **82**: 324).

Identification The bird in Plate 18.6 was present on Porthellick Pool, St Mary's, Isles of Scilly, in October–November 1991. Although similar to a Spotted Crake *P. porzana*, it appears more thick set, with a markedly thick-based bill. This is dull yellow but on less-advanced individuals it may be lime-green; it never shows the Spotted Crake's red base. Other differences from Spotted Crake include: (1) it lacks the profuse white head and neck spotting; (2) it has a brown crown with a dark central line; and (3) the outer undertail-coverts are white (like those of the Water Rail *Rallus aquaticus*) and unlike the characteristic dark buff colour shown by the Spotted Crake. As it habitually cocks and flicks its pointed tail, this difference may be obvious. The Pagham bird (Plate 18.5) was more advanced and immaculate, showing an area of black on the lores, chin, throat and upper breast, and it also had a small white fleck immediately behind the eye. The Porthellick bird was mainly in first-winter plumage, whereas the one at Pagham was an adult.

LITTLE CRAKE
Porzana parva

Range Has a fragmented breeding range from Spain and France in the west, across Europe and into Kazakhstan. It winters mainly in Africa, south of the Sahara. In both its summer and winter ranges it is more numerous in the east.

Occurrences The Little Crake is a very rare and irregular vagrant, with 31 records from 1958 to 1994 and 68 before. This no doubt reflects the species' decline in Western Europe, mainly as a result of habitat destruction. Records since 1958 have shown it to be a rather early spring migrant, with several occurring in March and early April. Surprisingly, the autumn peak is in early November. There have even been two January records, suggesting that it may occasionally overwinter. The most famous was an exceptionally tame first-winter female which inhabited a ditch at Cuckmere Haven, Sussex, in March 1985. Visiting birders started to throw it worms and it eventually became so tame that it would stand on people's hands to be fed (Plate 19.2). Two years later, another twitchable individual, this time a male, was present at Shotton Pools, Flintshire, in April 1987 (Plate 19.1).

Identification Although secretive by nature, crakes are often very confiding birds, as the Cuckmere Haven individual so graphically showed. When seen clearly, they are not difficult to identify. In size, the Little Crake is intermediate between Baillon's *P. pusilla* and Spotted Crakes *P. porzana*. Structurally, the Little Crake is rather longer billed, longer necked and longer tailed than Baillon's Crake, but the most important difference is the primary projection. Baillon's has short, bunched primaries, which are about only one quarter of the tertial length and do not project obviously beyond them. The Little Crake on the other hand has a long primary projection, approximately equal to the overlying tertials, and this is shown well in the photographs. The male is uniformly grey below and is striped black and rich brown above, lacking the obvious white spotting and 'scratching' of Baillon's. First-year male Little shows more white than the adult, so the Shotton bird appears to have been an adult (*see* Bradshaw 1993). The female is buff below, with a white throat and a grey supercilium. Retained juvenile white spotting on the wing coverts of the one at Cuckmere showed it to be a first-winter (*see* Becker, 1995). Adult bare-part colours also differ: the Little has green legs and a greenish bill with a small red patch at the base, whereas Baillon's has a completely green bill and legs (although the latter may have a pink component).

BAILLON'S CRAKE
Porzana pusilla

Range Has a fragmented breeding range across Europe, and the limited evidence suggests that it is now rare throughout. It is commoner further east, where its range extends in a narrow band to China and Japan. It also breeds in southern Africa, Madagascar and Australasia. Western Palearctic breeders (race *intermedia*) are thought to winter south of the Sahara, and eastern ones in the Indian subcontinent and Southeast Asia.

Occurrences There were many old records of Baillon's Crake, and it even bred in eastern England in 1858 and 1889 (and probably in 1866). It is now extremely rare and, between 1958 and 1995, there were just 12. There has, however, been something of a recent upsurge, with seven between 1989 and 1995 (May–June and August–September with the exception of one, caught by a cat and released unharmed at Lymington, Hampshire, on the early date of 17 March 1990). The most remarkable of these concerned a very confiding individual which wandered around in full view on a small lake at Mowbray Park, Sunderland, Co. Durham, in May 1989 (Plate 19.4). Two in May 1995 at Stithians Reservoir, Cornwall, and on Lundy, Devon, were equally cooperative.

Identification Plate 19.4 is an excellent shot of the Sunderland bird. Adult Baillon's resembles a male Little Crake *P. parva* (*see* Plate 19.1) but is smaller and more rotund. Its bill is uniformly green, lacking the Little Crake's red spot at the base. The upperparts are more liberally spotted and scratched with white, and the flanks show more extensive black and white barring (extending well in front of the legs). The key feature in their separation is the primary extension: the Little has long primaries which are approximately equal in length to the overlying tertials, whereas Baillon's has short primaries which are only a quarter of the tertial length or less. Unfortunately, this difference fell down on the Sunderland bird as it had lost the tertials on its left wing! This clearly illustrates the need for a degree of caution when interpreting identification features. Plate 19.4 shows the barred undertail-coverts, a feature shared with the Little Crake and differing markedly from the Spotted *P. porzana*. Plate 19.3 shows a juvenile female on Fair Isle, Shetland, in September 1991. Unfortunately, it was eventually found dead (and sexed after death). Unlike the adult, it is buff below and thus more similar to an equivalent-aged Little Crake. It can nevertheless be readily identified by: (1) its overall shape (note in particular the relatively stubby bill); (2) the profuse white 'scratching' on the upperparts; (3) the extensive barring on the flanks, this extending well forward towards the breast sides; and (4) the short primary projection (this bird has a complete set of tertials!).

AMERICAN COOT
Fulica americana

Range Breeds across southern Canada and the USA, south through the West Indies and Central America to the northern and central Andes, as well as in Hawaii. It moves south to winter mainly in the coastal and more southerly states, the Caribbean and Central America as far south as Colombia. It seems that the more southerly breeders move furthest south.

Occurrences Despite the fact that there are many cases of American Coots wandering north-eastward as far as Newfoundland, Labrador and even Greenland in late summer and autumn, and despite two occurrences in Iceland (*BWP*) and one in Portugal (*Brit. Birds* **88**: 270), there are just two records here: one at Ballycotton, Co. Cork, from February to April 1981 (Hutchinson *et al.*, 1984), and another at Stodmarsh, Kent, in April 1996 (Plates 20.1 & 2).

Identification The photographs show the diagnostic differences from Common Coot *F. atra*. The American is smaller and less bulky, squarer headed and flatter backed. The body is much greyer and paler than Common Coot's, but with a blacker head. Most important, the bill has an ill-defined but noticeable dark-grey subterminal band. It lacks the Common Coot's large white frontal shield, and instead shows a small chestnut-red knob at the top of the bill base. White sides to the undertail-coverts recall the Common Moorhen *Gallinula chloropus*, but these are not always obvious and may be concealed when the tail is held flat on the water. Its calls are deeper than those of a Common Coot and the Irish bird was surprisingly vocal.

There have been two published instances of hybrids between the Common Coot and the Common Moorhen (Flower, 1983; Moore & Piotrowski, 1983). One in Suffolk bore a superficial resemblance to an American Coot and was appropriately known as 'The Moot'.

COMMON CRANE
Grus grus

Range Breeds from Scandinavia and north-central Europe across the northern Palearctic to eastern Siberia, with isolated breeding populations in Asia Minor. Winters in France, Iberia, North Africa, Turkey, East Africa and the Middle East, reaching as far east as the Indian subcontinent and China.

Occurrences The species bred in Ireland until the 14th century and in East Anglia until about 1600 (*BWP*). It is now a migrant and winter visitor in small numbers; there were over 1,242 during 1958–87,

with most in October–November and a secondary peak in April–May. This total has, however, been inflated by three notable invasions. The biggest and most famous occurred in 1963, when at least 500 were recorded, and in 1982 and 1985 when there were 200 and 110 respectively. Such movements typically involve flocks which leave northern Europe in response to an abrupt fall in temperature. The birds then drifted across the English Channel in easterly winds and poor visibility. The 1985 total included a single flock of 71 in Kent on 25 October, seen over both Folkestone and Dungeness.

The species was removed from the Rarities List at the end of 1987 owing to a more general upturn that has occurred since the mid-1970s in response to an apparent increase in breeding numbers on the Continent. In the former East Germany, for example, 430–450 pairs recorded in the early 1970s (*BWP*) had increased to at least 1,000 pairs by the late 1980s (*Brit. Birds* **81**: 17), while in France there were record numbers of 25,000 around the Champagne Lakes in March 1988 (*Brit. Birds* **82**: 17). It is salutary to remember that this area is only about 250 miles (400 km) from Kent.

As expected, most cranes are seen along the east and south coasts of England and, since 1979, a small population has been resident in Norfolk, with occasional breeding. This population had increased to nine by the winter of 1993/94, but there have been persistent rumours concerning the origins of the original birds.

Identification Plate 20.3 shows two adults at Kersall, Nottinghamshire, in February 1996. They show the typical shape of flying cranes, with their long necks extended and their legs trailing out behind. The black face and upper foreneck, and the distinctive thick white neck stripe are clearly apparent. Plate 20.4 shows a first-year on Unst, Shetland, in May 1991. Again, the shape is distinctive, with its long neck and messy 'bustle' overhanging the tail. The poorly defined head and neck markings, and the apparent lack of red on its crown show its age, but first-years are variable in their acquisition of adult plumage. Common Cranes may often be located by their loud far-carrying bugling calls: *k-krroo k-krroo, karroo* or *k-roo*.

SANDHILL CRANE
Grus canadensis

Range Breeds from north-east Siberia across North America to Baffin Island and south into the prairies and the western Great Lakes. It winters in the southern USA and Mexico. There are also some resident populations along parts of the Gulf Coast, Florida and in Cuba.

Occurrences Being such a large bird and only a casual visitor to the North American eastern seaboard, it seems remarkable that the Sandhill Crane has crossed the Atlantic. For a long time, a record of one shot in Co. Cork in September 1905 appeared a freak, one-off occurrence, but there have been a further three since 1980. The first was just to the north of Britain, a female shot in the Faeroe Islands in October 1990, followed by a first-summer on Fair Isle, Shetland, in April 1981. The third was in the same neck of the woods and had a remarkable story attached to it. It flew in off the sea near Sumburgh, Shetland, on 17 September 1991 and fed on potatoes at nearby Exnaboe until it left on 27th (Plates 20.5 & 6). It then turned up in Friesland, Netherlands, the following day, a journey of about 510 miles (820 km) at an average speed of about 20 mph (33 kph; Evans, 1994). It left Friesland to the south-east on 30th, never to be seen again. Since the species is unusual on the North American east coast, and since such large birds are not noted for their ability to cross huge expanses of water, it seems probable that the autumn birds at least were reversed migrants out of northern Canada, completing the journey in a series of hops along the great circle route through Greenland and possibly Iceland (*see* Fig 9 and page 23).

Identification The northern nominate race is some 15 per cent smaller than the Common Crane *G. grus* (*BWP*). It is plain grey on the head, neck and body except for a large, bare, red patch on the lores, forehead and forecrown and a whitish area below and behind the eye. In flight, it is grey across the secondaries with only the primaries a blackish colour. Some are stained rufous, apparently due to contamination by iron-rich water. Juveniles lack the red crown, may have a rather tawny head and neck, and have body plumage that is mottled with brownish-red. The retention of brown feathering shows the Shetland bird to be in its second calendar year. The rather messy state of its plumage was due to wet weather conditions when photographed.

LITTLE BUSTARD
Tetrax tetrax

Range Occurs in mid-latitude grasslands from Morocco, Iberia and France eastwards discontinuously to the Russian steppes. Southerly populations are resident but the more northerly ones move south, often wintering in the southern parts of the range.

Occurrences There were some 92 records prior to 1958, but these occurred at a time when the species was much more abundant. A marked decline since the late 19th century has led to the species' extinction over much of its European range, and it now survives mainly in France and Iberia. In the latter, an amazing 170,000 displaying males were recently estimated in southern Meseta and Extremadura (*Brit. Birds* **89**: 31) but in France numbers declined from 6,000 calling males in 1985–89 to only 1,400 in 1995 (*Dutch Birding* **18**: 92). Even in the former Soviet Union, there has been a marked decline and southerly withdrawal, whilst it is now considered extinct in non-Soviet Asia (*BWP, Brit. Birds* **73**: 198–199). Reflecting this depressing state of affairs, there were only 17 records between 1958 and 1996. Four were in spring and summer, but the remainder were in late autumn and winter. There has been a tendency for them to occur in small influxes, and there were three in November–December 1968 and four in December 1987, including a group of three at Sudbourne, Suffolk. Most have occurred in south-eastern England, and *BWP* states that the majority of British specimens are attributable to the eastern population. This was formerly recognized as a separate race, but differences between the two forms are apparently slight.

The most famous record involved the individual in the Christchurch area of Dorset and Hampshire from 30 December 1987 to 5 January 1988. The main twitch occurred on 1 January, a thoroughly miserable affair with a couple of thousand hungover birders spending much of the day wandering around disconsolately in torrential rain.

Identification Plate 21.1 shows an individual which was present on St Agnes and St Mary's, Isles of Scilly, from 29 October to 3 November 1975. The photograph is unfortunately only a record shot, but it shows a stocky bird with a longish neck and broad, rather square wings. These show large areas of white across the remiges, and black wing-tips. It is about the size of a Eurasian Wigeon *Anas penelope* and, with its fast wingbeats, appears almost duck-like in flight.

HOUBARA BUSTARD
Chlamydotis undulata

Range Breeds in the Canary Islands and across North Africa, through parts of the Middle East, Iran, Afghanistan and Pakistan, and into the deserts of Kazakhstan and Mongolia. The central Asian populations move south to winter around the Persian Gulf, Pakistan and north-western India.

Occurrences There were four records in the 19th century between 1847 and 1898, all in October and all on the east coast. The only recent one was at Westleton, Suffolk, from 21 November to 29 December 1962 (Plates 21.2–4). Its rarity here is due to the fact that Arab falconers have senselessly hunted it to extinction over large parts of its range. Even as recently as 1984, more than 250 were killed in eastern and southern Morocco (*Brit. Birds* **78**: 640) and to see Houbaras nowadays most birders have to travel to the Canaries or to the Negev Desert in Israel, where the species is strictly protected. The possibility of future vagrancy seems negligible, although it is interesting to note that one was seen in Lithuania in November 1988 (*Brit. Birds* **84**: 229).

Identification The Suffolk Houbara has achieved near mythical status and the photographs of it will have most birders drooling. It is a smallish bustard, sandy above, mottled darker, with a greyish head and a thick vertical black stripe down the neck sides and onto the breast. It has yellow eyes. The lack of a crest and the virtual absence of black on the crown would presumably indicate that it was a first-winter. In flight, it shows white across the wing coverts and a large white patch across the primaries. Visitors to its Israeli breeding areas usually remember it for its remarkable display, in which the head is sunk into the shoulders, its white breast plumes are raised, its tail is depressed and it trots around the desert like some sort of bizarre animated mop. Western European records are thought to be of the Middle Eastern and Asian race *macqueenii* (*BWP*).

GREAT BUSTARD
Otis tarda

Range It now has a fragmented breeding range that includes northern Morocco, Iberia, parts of eastern Europe, Turkey, the Russian Steppes and eastern China. Eastern populations are migratory but those in the west are largely resident.

Occurrences The Great Bustard's range increased markedly in Western and central Europe with deforestation, and probably reached its maximum extent at the end of the 18th century before beginning to contract with the increase in arable farming (*BWP*). It bred in many parts of Britain but was last recorded doing so in Suffolk in 1832. In recent years it has disappeared from much its range. In the former East Germany, for example, a population of about 3,000 birds in the 1930s declined to about 900 by 1971, 800 in 1975 and only 300 in 1988 (*BWP*, *Brit. Birds* **82**: 325). Only in Spain do large populations persist, and these were estimated at 9,000 birds in 1982 (*Brit. Birds* **77**: 235).

As with the other bustards, the appalling decreases have been reflected in the numbers reaching Britain. There were only five records (involving eight birds) between 1910 and 1963 but, surprisingly, there has been a recent upsurge with 17 between 1970 and 1987, all in eastern England except for one on Fair

Isle, Shetland (this eventually had to be taken into captivity; Plate 21.5). Occurrences are related to severe winter weather in Eastern Europe, and are usually backed up by larger influxes in Germany and the Low Countries. A particularly large influx occurred in 1978/79 when there were about 100 in the Netherlands and considerable numbers in Germany, including 120 in Lower Saxony and 60 in Rhineland (*Brit. Birds* **72**: 277; **73**: 258). Some of these involved ringed individuals which had been released in the former East Germany as part of a captive-breeding project. With numbers apparently still plummeting in Eastern Europe, it seems likely that these periodic influxes will become progressively less frequent.

Identification Plate 21.5 shows the Fair Isle bird of January 1970. Its enormous size is the first thing one notices – and this is an adult female; adult males can be up to 50 per cent larger (*BWP*)! Its grey head and neck, the barred golden-brown upperparts, the white band across the larger wing coverts and the white patch in the primaries combine to make it quite unmistakable. Males are Europe's heaviest birds and they appear huge and majestic in flight, appearing almost swan-like as they lumber slowly into the air.

BLACK-WINGED STILT
Himantopus himantopus

Range Has a huge world range across the southern Palearctic to western China, as well as in Africa, the Indian subcontinent and Southeast Asia, Australasia, southern North America, and Central and South America. Western Palearctic breeders winter mainly in Africa, north of the equator.

Occurrences Mainly an irregular spring overshoot, although it has been annual since 1978. Autumn occurrences are distinctly rarer but, surprisingly, there have even been a few in winter, including a well-watched individual which took up residence at Titchwell, Norfolk, from 1993 to at least 1996.

There are periodic spring invasions, the largest being 18 in 1965, 38 in 1987 and 26 in 1990. These have led to occasional breeding attempts: two pairs bred in Nottinghamshire in 1945, a pair nested in Cambridgeshire in 1983, and a well-watched pair produced three young, two of which fledged, at Holme, Norfolk, in 1987. In 1993, a pair laid eggs at Frodsham, Cheshire, but they were predated. The species has been increasing in Spain and has recently become more widespread in France, although numbers fluctuate considerably with variations in waterlevels. These fluctuations may be responsible for our invasions and there has been irregular breeding in Germany, Denmark, Belgium and the Netherlands in recent years, with as many as 22 breeding attempts in the latter in 1989 (*Brit. Birds* **84**: 5; **88**: 32).

Most spring records have been made from mid-April to early June, but there was a remarkably early influx in March 1990 involving some 15 individuals from 17th onwards. Their westerly distribution, with most in Ireland, suggested that they were early Iberian overshoots.

Identification The bird in Plate 22.2 was a male present at Cogden Beach, Dorset, in April 1990. Plate 22.1 shows the famous breeding pair at Holme in May 1987. The male, with its blacker upperparts, is on the right. They are noisy birds and their *klit, klit, klit …* calls (and variations) are familiar sounds of Mediterranean marshes.

CREAM-COLOURED COURSER
Cursorius cursor

Range Breeds in the Canary and Cape Verde Islands, around the northern and southern fringes of the Sahara and east to western Pakistan. The Saharan and Arabian nominate race makes extensive movements, with most heading across the Sahara or into Arabia, the winter range apparently coinciding with the southern limit of winter frosts (*BWP*). The eastern race *bogolubovi* is partially migratory, moving to southern Iran, Pakistan and north-western India.

Occurrences There were about 26 records prior to 1958 and there have been six since, all in late September–October, the most recent being a first-winter at Hadleigh Marsh, Essex, from 29 September to 2 October 1984 (Plate 22.3), although a first-winter was seen on Jersey in October 1995. *BWP* states that, after the breeding season, flocks form and wander extensively, not infrequently reaching the Mediterranean coasts, and that these are probably the main source of European vagrants. The main trans-Saharan migration, however, occurs in the second half of September and into October, which ties in exactly with the British and Irish appearances. Reversed migration out of North Africa would seem a more plausible explanation. Such birds may find survival here difficult, as evidenced by the well-watched individual in Norfolk in October–November 1969, which was eventually found dead.

Identification With its decurved bill, pale sandy plumage and long pale legs, the Cream-coloured Courser is, in a British context, unmistakable. In flight it is even more striking, with its smartly contrasting black upperwing tips and completely black underwings, relieved by white tips to the secondaries. The rather plain head, with only a faint supercilium

and a diffuse dark line behind the eye, and faint upperpart scalloping show the Essex bird to be a first-winter. In their breeding areas the birds often draw attention to themselves by deep *kik-kik-kik* calls.

COLLARED PRATINCOLE
Glareola pratincola

Range Breeds across southern Europe and North Africa east to Kazakhstan, Iran and Pakistan. These populations winter in tropical Africa, where it is also a widespread breeding species.

Occurrences Being the closest breeding pratincole, the Collared has traditionally been the most frequent to occur here, with 82 records, 51 of which were made between 1958 and 1995. It occurs mainly as a spring overshoot in late May and early June, although there have been records through to early November. In recent years, there have been three April records, including one on St Agnes, Isles of Scilly, as early as 3–4 April 1990, when it was found dead. Numbers occurring increased during the 1970s and early 1980s, but it has since become rare again. This is no doubt related to widespread decreases over much of its Palearctic range, and only in Spain do large numbers persist, estimated at about 3,800 pairs in 1989 (*Brit. Birds* **86**: 40).

Identification Plate 22.4 shows an individual at Girtford Gravel Pits, Bedfordshire, in May 1983. It is easily recognizable as a pratincole by its tern-like shape and sandy plumage, with a characteristic cream throat, bordered with black. It can be identified as a Collared by the prominent white trailing edge to the wing and the rufous underwing-coverts, but both of these may be amazingly difficult to see in the field, even when overhead. The long forked tail is, as the photograph shows, often closed in flight. The length of the tail is a further distinction from the similar Oriental Pratincole *G. maldivarum* (*see* Plate 22.6). It is predominantly an aerial feeder, with a rather nightjar-like feeding technique, often twisting and swooping low over the ground. Its usual call is a loud, but soft, quite deep, somewhat tern-like *kik-kik*, sometimes lengthened to *ki ki ki kik kerru*; also a rolling *kerrrick*, recalling Little Tern *Sterna albifrons*.

ORIENTAL PRATINCOLE
Glareola maldivarum

Range Breeds from India through Southeast Asia to north-eastern China. The more easterly populations winter in Indonesia and northern Australia.

Occurrences Remarkably, there have been at least three British records: a first-summer at Dunwich,

Suffolk, and subsequently at Old Hall Marshes, Essex, from June to October 1981 (Burns, 1993); at Harty, and subsequently at Elmley, Kent, from June to October 1988; and at Gimmingham and other areas in north Norfolk, from May to July 1993. What may conceivably have been the same bird then appeared on Pevensey Levels, Sussex, in August 1993, and at Havergate, Suffolk, in September.

Given its breeding and wintering ranges, this seems an unlikely bird to reach Britain and, at the time of the first occurrence, at least two were known to be present in captivity in this country. The escape possibility seemed to evaporate, however, with the two subsequent occurrences, particularly since they conformed almost exactly with the first, both temporally and geographically. The long stays of all three are particularly noteworthy. How did they get here? It seems unlikely that they were long-range spring overshoots, so it would perhaps seem most likely that they moved north into Western Europe having originally gone astray the previous autumn, perhaps having wintered in Africa. What was particularly extraordinary was that the Kent bird actually appeared with a Black-winged Pratincole *G. nordmanni*, surely an example of fact being stranger than fiction.

Identification The Oriental is very similar to the Collared Pratincole *G. pratincola*, and the original in Suffolk was initially dismissed as that species, not least because, at the time, most British birders had never even heard of the Oriental. Both share the chestnut underwing-coverts but the following are the main differences: (1) the Oriental lacks the white trailing edge to the secondaries and inner primaries; (2) it has a shorter tail, which usually falls well short of the primary tips at rest (on the Collared it usually projects beyond); (3) the tail fork is shallower on the Oriental and the outer tail feathers are not elongated to the same degree; (4) it is slightly darker and thus shows less contrast between the wing coverts and the remiges (more like the Black-winged); and (5) it tends to show an orangey band across the breast, particularly in winter. The bird in Plates 22.5 & 6 was the one present in Norfolk in 1993. Not all the above features are visible, but the wing:tail ratio is clearly apparent in Plate 22.6, while in Plate 22.5 the lack of a prominent white trailing edge to the wing and the short tail are both apparent. The blackness of the lores may indicate that it was a male.

BLACK-WINGED PRATINCOLE
Glareola nordmanni

Range Breeds from Romania and the Ukraine eastwards through the steppes of Kazakhstan. Unlike the Collared Pratincole *G. pratincola* it is mainly a transequatorial migrant. Some winter in Ethiopia and

further west in Chad and Nigeria, but most move south to Botswana, Namibia and South Africa.

Occurrences The Black-winged is about a third as numerous as the Collared, with only 31 records up to 1996. The peak time is from late August to October, and there was a small influx of three in the autumn of 1993. There have also been five May–June records, including three in 1988 (which could conceivably have involved just one wandering individual), and others in July and early August. Most have occurred in south-eastern England, but with an odd cluster of four in Somerset.

Like the Collared, the Black-winged has shown substantial population decreases over much of its range, due mainly to the disappearance of virgin steppe (Tomkovitch, 1992). This decrease, coupled with the apparent north-east–south-west orientation of its autumn migration routes, make its appearances here difficult to explain. For reversed migration to be responsible, one would have to postulate that western populations move south-east from their breeding grounds towards Iran and Iraq before turning south-west towards Africa. In view of its scarcity in the eastern Mediterranean and the Middle East, such a theory may have some merit, and would certainly tie in with the statement in *BWP* that most are believed to enter and leave Africa over the Red Sea.

Identification Plate 23.1 shows an individual at Clevedon, Somerset, in June 1988. It is similar to the Collared but is darker on the upperparts and, in flight, this produces less contrast between the wing coverts and the black remiges. Three other differences are: (1) the wings project well beyond the tip of the tail (on the Collared the tail is equal to or even longer than the wing tips); (2) the red on the bill is smaller and does not reach the nostril; and (3) the black loral line is broader. Plates 23.2 & 3 show one in its scaly juvenile plumage, present at Great Livermere, Suffolk, in September 1993. This plumage is retained only until early autumn as a complete post-juvenile moult commences in August or early September; by early October, most of the scalloping may be lost. Plate 23.2 shows its subdued juvenile facial pattern and necklace of streaking. Plate 23.3 shows the diagnostic black underwings, lacking a white trailing edge. Also, the tail is seen to be shallowly forked, lacking the Collared's elongated outer feathers. The tail shape is, in fact, intermediate between that of the Collared and Oriental *G. maldivarum*.

SEMIPALMATED PLOVER
Charadrius semipalmatus

Range Replaces the Ringed Plover *C. hiaticula* in the Americas, breeding in Alaska and northern Canada and wintering on the coasts of the southern USA, reaching as far south as southern Argentina and Chile.

Occurrence The Semipalmated Plover is a long-range migrant, overflying the western Atlantic *en route* to the West Indies and northern South America, so it is surprising that there has been just one British record: a well-watched juvenile on St Agnes, Isles of Scilly, in October–November 1978 (Plate 23.4). It is particularly surprising that it has not been discovered amongst the large flocks of Ringed Plovers that pass through on their way to and from their breeding grounds in Greenland, where the Semipalmated has also occurred. There can be little doubt that their similarity mitigates against its discovery; the St Agnes bird was found as the result of an astute piece of fieldwork by Paul Dukes, who was attracted by its unusual call (Dukes, 1980). The species has also been recorded in Spain, where there are two recent records (*Brit. Birds* **84**: 229), while an adult in the Azores in September 1972 had been ringed in the Gulf of St Lawrence two months previously (*BWP*).

Identification It is unlikely to be located except by call: a cheerful upslurred *ch-wee* reminiscent of the call of the Spotted Redshank *Tringa erythropus* but not as emphatic or as markedly disyllabic. The call is, however, obviously different from the familiar *poo-eep* of the Ringed Plover. As Plate 23.4 shows, an evaluation of the subtle morphological differences requires close and careful observation. The St Agnes bird differed from accompanying Ringed Plovers in the following respects (it should be noted that many of these are 'on average' features that must be used in combination). It was slightly smaller and more compact, the head was hunched into the body and, at rest, the wing tips were proportionally longer. The bill was quite noticeably short and stubby (many show a somewhat swollen and retroussé effect at the tip). The plumage was very similar to that of the Ringed Plover, although it was slightly darker than the accompanying nominate *hiaticula* and showed a better defined forehead patch and a narrower breast band. More significantly, the eye showed a faint pale yellow orbital ring. Mullarney (1991), noted that the dark loral line meets the bill at the gape on the Ringed but higher up and closer to the culmen on the Semipalmated, and this is apparent in the photograph. As its name implies, Semipalmated shows foot webbing, the web between the middle and inner toes being obvious in certain close-range situations (shown well in Plate 23.4). Both species show a web between the middle and the outer, although it is larger in the Semipalmated. On the open wing, the wing stripe is narrower on the Semipalmated.

Further differences are shown by summer adults, but the first step is to sex them correctly: the male Semi-

palmated has a solid black breast band and ear-coverts, whereas (all?) females are browner in these areas. The Semipalmated shows a more prominent yellow orbital ring (reminiscent of the Little Ringed Plover *C. dubius*) and the male lacks or shows a much reduced white supercilium behind the eye, producing something of a hooded appearance. It should be noted, however, that the male Ringed may occasionally show a yellow orbital ring, while the female Semipalmated shows a much stronger white supercilium (Dunn, 1993).

KILLDEER
Charadrius vociferus

Range Breeds across most of North America, as well as in Central America, the West Indies and in South America from Peru to northern Chile. More northerly breeders move south to winter in the coastal and southern United States southwards to Colombia and western Ecuador. Killdeers from the Great Lakes and north-eastern Canada have been recorded in winter mainly in the south-eastern USA.

Occurrences There were 53 records to October 1996, 44 of which were made since 1958. Unlike other North American waders, most have occurred in winter from late November to late March and it seems likely that many attempt to cross the Atlantic in response to severe freezing weather in North America, rather like the occasional Northern Lapwings *Vanellus vanellus* moving the other way. Records have been widely scattered, but with a distinct westerly bias; there have been 12 in Scilly, including three together in December 1979.

Identification The bird in Plate 23.5 turned up on St Martin's, Isles of Scilly, in October 1982. It is distinctly larger than a Ringed Plover *C. hiaticula*, and is easily identified by the double black breast band and the long tail which projects well beyond the wing tips. Its bill is rather long for a plover and it has a distinctive facial pattern with a red eye. In flight, there is a prominent white wing bar, the rump is orange and the long black tail has white tips to the outer feathers. Although no doubt a first-winter, ageing at this time of year is difficult. It is a noisy species, the call being a rendition of its name, variously transcribed at *kill-dee, dee-dee-dee, pee-eep* and so on. It is a common and familiar bird in North America, and can even be found running around on garden lawns.

GREATER SAND PLOVER
Charadrius leschenaultii

Range Breeds from central Turkey eastwards through Turkestan into China and Mongolia. It has a large winter range from the eastern Mediterranean, South and East Africa eastwards through coastal southern Asia to Indonesia and Australia.

Occurrences The first British record was made as recently as the winter of 1978/79, when an individual was present at Pagham Harbour, Sussex (Kitson *et al.*, 1980). At the time, it seemed an exceptional occurrence but, during the next 14 years, there were another ten. Exactly why it has suddenly started turning up here is a mystery, although it may be more than coincidental that it was first proved to breed in Turkey as recently as 1967 (*BWP*). The third British record was remarkable in that it involved a wintering individual on an inland reservoir – at Chew Valley Lake, Somerset, in 1979/80 – but all the others have been at coastal sites in spring and summer.

Identification Plate 24.2 shows the initial Pagham bird, photographed in December 1978. In winter it recalls a giant Kentish Plover *C. alexandrinus* but, unlike that species, it lacks a white collar around the back of the neck (instead the nape is buff, merging with the crown and the mantle). The bill is long for a plover and, in direct comparison, it is similar in length to that of a Northern Lapwing *Vanellus vanellus*. This is an important difference from the closely-related Mongolian or Lesser Sand Plover *C. mongolicus*. Plate 24.1 shows another, photographed at the Bridge of Don, Aberdeenshire, in August 1991. This bird shows an extensive dull orange breast (bordered above by a faint dark line), and an area of black on the lores, ear-coverts and forehead, all of which indicate a summer-plumaged male. With its rather hunched appearance and extensively orange breast, this individual is in fact rather similar to a Lesser, but that species typically has a broader, darker, more intensely orange breast band, has a shorter, stubbier bill and is noticeably darker above. In addition, it is more similar to the Ringed Plover *C. hiaticula* in size and leg length. The identification of this bird was discussed by Shaw & Webb (1991) who, in the field, considered it to be 10–20 per cent bigger than accompanying Ringed Plovers and to have legs about 25 per cent longer. A number of minor plumage features also pointed towards a Greater. This was no doubt an example of the western race (*columbinus*), which is most similar to the Lesser with a shorter, thicker bill and extensive orange on the underparts. The call of the Greater is a hard, dry trill *trrrr*, apparently similar to some calls of the Lesser.

CASPIAN PLOVER
Charadrius asiaticus

Range Breeds from southern Russia eastwards into Kazakhstan and Turkestan. It migrates south-west to winter from East to South Africa. It forms a super-species with the Oriental Plover *C. veredus*, which, as its name suggests, replaces it to the east.

Occurrences The first British record involved a male which was shot and another seen near Great Yarmouth, Norfolk, on 22 May 1890. Remarkably, it was almost 98 years to the day before the next: a male on Wingletang, St Agnes, Isles of Scilly, on 21 May 1988 (Plate 24.3). Another was then seen later in July of the same year at Aberlady Bay, East Lothian. A female then turned up at Skellberry, Shetland, in June 1996 (Plate 24.4). Unfortunately, none stayed long enough to be seen by many people.

Identification Although it is a record shot, Plate 24.3 shows the salient features of a summer-plumaged male. It is an elegant, long-legged plover with a white face and a large, white, wedge-shaped supercilium. The most striking feature is the bright chestnut breast band, bordered with black on the lower edge. As Plate 24.4 shows, on summer-plumaged females this is earth-brown, lacking the black border of the male. In flight, it is uniformly brown above, lacking an obvious wing bar (this is confined mainly to the inner primaries). The underwing coverts are largely white, a key difference from the Oriental Plover, which has dark underwings. A thin *tchik* flight call may initially attract attention. Unlike the sand plovers, outside the breeding season the Caspian is a bird of dry, inland habitats.

AMERICAN GOLDEN PLOVER
Pluvialis dominicus

Range Breeds from Alaska across northern Canada to Baffin Island. It undergoes a huge migration (*see* below) to winter in South America, in a region stretching from southern Brazil and Bolivia to Argentina.

Occurrences Although it has occurred from April to November and one has wintered, the peak is in late September and early October, with a distinct bias towards the south-west. Occurrences have increased markedly since the mid-1970s, due no doubt to greater observer awareness. Although many juveniles migrate south through the North American interior, other juveniles and all adults cross Canada to the Hudson and James Bays, and then continue on a narrowing front to the north-eastern USA. They then head out over the western North Atlantic on a remarkable great circle route, which means that they next make landfall in the Lesser Antilles or northern South America. Some then continue quickly onwards to Argentina, where the species becomes common from late August. In fine weather few stop in New

England, and it seems that many migrate in one continuous hop from the boreal tundra to South America, an incredible flight estimated to take 37 hours (*BWP*). The spring migration is through the American interior. With such a huge autumnal migratory flight, it is not surprising that this is one of the more frequently occurring American waders on this side of the Atlantic, drifting east in fast-moving Atlantic depressions.

Identification The juvenile in Plate 24.6 was present on St Agnes, Isles of Scilly, in September–October 1991. It is superficially similar to the European Golden Plover *P. apricaria* but smaller and proportionately taller and slimmer. Its immaculate plumage shows it to be a juvenile. Compared with both the European and Pacific Golden Plovers *P. fulva*, it has a prominent white supercilium (which contrasts with a dark cap) and the plumage is cold, lacking the distinctive yellow tones of the two old world species. Its tone is, in fact, more similar to that of a juvenile Grey Plover *P. squatarola*. The photograph shows the relative proportions of the tertials, primaries and tail. Note that the primaries are long, approximately equal in length to the overlying tertials, with four feather tips visible beyond the longest, and that the primaries project, scissor-like, just beyond the end of the tail. The tips of the tertials fall a long way short of the tail tip, whereas on the European and Pacific the tertials are much longer, the tips falling approximately level with or slightly short of it. Consequently, the Pacific's primary projection is much shorter, about a quarter to half the length of the overlying tertials, with usually just two primary tips visible beyond them. In flight, both the American and Pacific have a uniformly grey underwing. Plate 28.7 also shows the above features; it is a remarkable shot of a juvenile with a juvenile Pectoral Sandpiper *Calidris melanotos* at Drift Reservoir, Cornwall, in October 1980.

The bird in Plate 24.5 was seen at the opposite end of the country, on Fair Isle, Shetland, in September 1987. On the face of it, it appears to be an adult moulting out of summer plumage, but careful examination shows that the white blotching on the underparts is caused not by the appearance of winter feathering but by thick white tips to the black feathers. This would suggest that it is in fact a female which has not yet started to moult (the post-breeding moult takes place mainly in the winter quarters). Note that these black feathers extend onto the undertail-coverts (unlike the European). Apart from the structural differences outlined above, it differs from the European in the prominence of the supercilium (contrasting with a darker cap), while the upperparts are more finely spangled with whitish and gold. It is, therefore, much less yellow than both the European and the Pacific.

The American's usual call is distinctly different from the European's, a *t-wee loo*, quite mournful with the emphasis on the central syllable; also sometimes a *t-wee*, rising on the second syllable.

PACIFIC GOLDEN PLOVER
Pluvialis fulva

Range Breeds in northern Siberia, east of the Urals, and also in western Alaska, where it overlaps with the American Golden Plover *P. dominicus*. It winters from north-eastern Africa through southern and south-eastern Asia to Australasia and Polynesia.

Occurrences The two 'Lesser Golden Plovers' were split by the BOURC as recently as 1986 and, prior to that year, there had been only seven records of the Pacific. Since then, a better understanding of its field characters has resulted in a further 26 (to 1995) and it is proving to be a regular visitor. Inevitably, the Northern Isles and the British east coast have produced most records, but there have been adults as far west as Dublin and Co. Wexford. There has been one record in May and four in September–February, but all the others have been post-breeding adults occurring between late June and August.

It is capable of huge trans-oceanic flights and birds sampled on Wake Island (midway between Hawaii and the Philippines) had fat reserves sufficient for an astonishing 6,000-mile (10,000-km) flight, even though it is only 2,500 miles (4,000 km) from there to the Aleutian Islands or Kamchatka (*BWP*). Reversed migration out of Siberia presumably accounts for our vagrants, and some seem to have established a regular migration pattern as there have been a number of cases of individuals reappearing at the same sites in successive years.

An odd plover in Somerset during the winter of 1987/88 was thought most likely to have been a hybrid between a Pacific and a European Golden Plover *P. apricaria*, illustrating the fact that the Pacific has strong affinities to its more familiar western cousin.

Identification In many ways the Pacific is intermediate between the European and American Golden Plovers. It is noticeably smaller and slighter than the European with a proportionately longer bill and legs. The latter project beyond the tail in flight, producing a more attenuated appearance. Like the American it has grey axillaries and underwings. In breeding plumage, it has a tendency to show black mottling on the undertail-coverts. Like the European its plumage is yellower at all times and it has similar tertial, primary and tail ratios (*see* the American Golden Plover above for details). Plate 25.1

shows an individual at Cley, Norfolk, in December 1991. It was accepted as a juvenile but there appears to be one or two dark feathers on its breast and belly. It closely resembles a European, but the supercilium is better marked than most. The bird in Plate 25.2 was present at Elmley, Kent, in August 1995. It is in summer plumage and shows some black in the undertail-coverts; it also shows the characteristic short primary projection, but the overlying tertials are rather worn. Indeed, the amount of wear on the tertials, primaries and, particularly, the wing coverts, would suggest that it is a first-summer. The usual call is an upslurred *chu-wee*, strongly reminiscent of the Semipalmated Plover *Charadrius semipalmatus* (*see* page 58). It can also give a quite shrill *too-lee-oo*, rising on the central syllable.

SOCIABLE PLOVER
Vanellus gregaria

Range Breeds in the steppes of Russia and Kazakhstan, and winters in north-eastern Africa, Iraq, Pakistan and north-western India.

Occurrences Formerly an extremely rare and irregular vagrant, but there has been a distinct increase since the mid-1970s. By the end of 1995, the species had amassed a total of 38 records, virtually all in south-eastern and southern England but with odd birds as far north as Orkney and as far west as Co. Kerry. There is a wide temporal scatter, but most have occurred in September–November. If the occurrences were a result of reversed migration, then one would have to postulate that western breeders heading for India and Pakistan must migrate north-west and end up in Western Europe, but their movements must become complicated by the fact that they regularly tag on to flocks of Northern Lapwings *Vanellus vanellus* and roam around with them. Their increase in Britain and Ireland is at odds with the position on their breeding grounds, where their population has apparently shown a continued gradual decline (Tomkovitch, 1992).

Identification Plate 25.4 shows an adult in summer plumage at Holkham, Norfolk, in April 1993. It is smaller than a Northern Lapwing and is easily identified by its browny-grey plumage, black belly, the smartly contrasting black cap and eye-stripe and prominent white supercilium. The solid black cap and very black belly would suggest that it is a male. Plate 25.3 shows a juvenile at Welney, Norfolk, in October 1990. It has the same basic pattern as the adult but shows noticeable buff scaling over much of the upperparts, a neatly streaked breast, a white belly and a brown cap. Sociable Plovers can be surprisingly

inconspicuous on the ground but once they take flight they are striking. The upperwing pattern recalls that of a Sabine's Gull *Larus sabini*, with black primaries, white secondaries and mainly brown wing coverts and mantle. In flight, the Sociable Plover looks noticeably smaller and slimmer-winged than a lapwing. Unlike White-tailed Plover *V. leucura*, it has a black tail band and dark legs.

WHITE-TAILED PLOVER
Vanellus leucura

Range Breeds mainly in the desert regions of Soviet central Asia and Kazakhstan as well as in Iraq. Winters in the Sudan, Iraq, Pakistan and northern India.

Occurrences The first record concerned an individual at Packington Gravel Pits, Warwickshire, on 12–18 July 1975 (Dean *et al.*, 1977), and it was, at the time, a totally unexpected addition to the British List. It subsequently transpired, however, that there had been eight other records in Europe during 1975 in Sicily, Hungary, Austria (two), Poland, Finland, Sweden and the Netherlands. Six of these occurred in spring, and it is seems probable that they had moved north-west from India and Pakistan and overshot their breeding areas. This movement was undoubtedly provoked by a severe drought in southern Kazakhstan in 1974–75 (Tomkovich, 1992). There has, however, also been a more general northward range expansion in the deserts of central Asia and around the Caspian Sea (loc. cit.), and it bred in Turkey in the early 1970s and in Syria in 1976 (*BWP*). At the time, the 1975 individual seemed to represent a remarkable one-off occurrence but, surprisingly, there have been three subsequent records: in Dorset in July 1979, and in Co. Durham and in Shropshire in May 1984, the latter two conceivably involving the same individual. As with the 1975 records, those in 1984 appeared to be part of a larger movement with one in Germany and two in the Netherlands (Lewington *et al.*, 1991).

Identification Plate 25.5 shows the Warwickshire individual. In a British context, the only similar species is the Sociable Plover *V. gregaria*, but comparison with Plates 25.3 & 4 shows that the White-tailed is distinctive in its own right. Immediately eye-catching are the long, bright-yellow legs which trail beyond the tail in flight and which give it rather a gangly appearance at rest. The bill is also rather long for a plover. Another important difference from the Sociable Plover is the relatively plain head, showing just a slightly paler supercilium and cheeks. In the photograph, the wing pattern is just hinted at, and the sandy-brown breast band and white belly are also just visible. In flight, the white tail is distinctive, as is the brown, white and black wing pattern which, like the Sociable Plover, recalls Sabine's Gull *Larus sabini*. The call is a throaty *thick*.

GREAT KNOT
Calidris tenuirostris

Range Breeds in north-eastern Siberia and it is a long-range migrant, wintering from Pakistan to southern China and south to Australia. In recent years over 1,000 have been discovered wintering in Oman, with smaller numbers in the United Arab Emirates and Saudi Arabia (Ellis, 1992).

Occurrences There are two British records of adults: at Scatness and the Pool of Virkie, Shetland, on 15 September 1989 (Plate 25.6) and on Teesside, Yorkshire, in October–November 1996. There had been previous Western Palearctic records in Spain, Morocco, Israel, Germany and Norway. A juvenile also turned up in the Netherlands in September–October 1991 (loc. cit.).

Identification The Shetland individual was a worn adult. Plate 25.6, although a rather distant shot, is useful as it shows the bird alongside a juvenile Red Knot *C. canutus*. The Great Knot is 10–15 per cent larger, with a distinctly longer bill and a more attenuated rear end. The summer-plumaged adult is basically cold and greyish looking, with essentially blackish upperparts that have white feather fringes. The head and breast are streaked and mottled black on a whitish background, the latter forming a distinct band, with spotting and mottling extending down the flanks. When worn, as on the Shetland individual, the breast band looks more predominantly blackish. The coldness of the plumage is relieved by variable amounts of rufous on the bases of the scapulars. Juveniles show a basically similar pattern, although the upperpart feathers are more neatly and evenly fringed whitish. In flight, the wing bar is weaker than on the Red Knot and the tail is dark (compared to Red Knot's pale grey tail). Lewington *et al.* (1991) describe the call as a muffled *gryt* or *kryt*, although they are usually silent.

SEMIPALMATED SANDPIPER
Calidris pusilla

Range Breeds in northern Alaska and Canada. Winters in coastal South America, as far south as Peru and Uruguay, and north in diminishing numbers to the West Indies and the Pacific coast of Central America as far as Guatemala.

Occurrences The species was first recorded in 1953 but there were only nine records up to 1977. Its rarity was due to our lack of understanding of its field characters in relation to the Little Stint *C. minuta*, a situation that now seems hard to believe. Since 1980 it has been annual, with a peak of nine in 1984. Most records relate to juveniles, which appear mainly in Ireland and south-western England after westerly gales in September and October. These probably stem from the eastern Canadian population, which mostly moves through the Gulf of St Lawrence and the Bay of Fundy before making a huge transoceanic flight direct to the eastern Caribbean, a route that must make the birds vulnerable to displacement by fast-moving depressions. There has also been a wide scatter of spring and late summer adults, presumably either leftovers from previous autumns or individuals that have arrived by a different route.

The best-known 'Semi-p' was the infamous 'Felixstowe Stint', which wintered at Felixstowe, Suffolk, in the winter of 1982/83. It was considered by most observers at the time to be a Western Sandpiper *C. mauri* as it was was not generally appreciated that some eastern female Semipalmateds can have very long bills. An enormous controversy ensued before its identification was finally resolved.

Identification Plate 26.1 shows a juvenile on Porthloo Beach, St Mary's, Isles of Scilly, in October 1986. A number of features separate it from a similarly aged Little Stint: (1) the bill is quite long, thick based and blunt tipped, appearing rather tubular in shape; (2) it has something of a capped effect, lacking the Little Stint's 'split supercilium'; (3) it has a fairly distinct white supercilium; (4) there is a line across the lores, through the eye, and this fans out behind the eye into a fairly solid patch; (5) a thin but clear-cut white eye-ring is totally enclosed within the dark eye patch, this being the final factor contributing to its characteristic facial jizz; (6) it is distinctly brown above (lacking any rufous tones) and is very evenly and regularly patterned; (7) it lacks the Little Stint's prominent white mantle Vs; (8) the lower scapulars have distinctive dark anchor-shaped blotches towards their tips; (9) the primary projection is short, usually with just two primary tips exposed, and finally (10) the breast patches are lightly streaked and diffuse. Juveniles do not moult this plumage until their arrival in their winter quarters. When faced with a potential 'Semi-p', two other features need to be carefully checked. Every effort should be made to see the small webs between the toes and, secondly, the call should be heard and correctly transcribed. The classic call is a low, thin, weak *chreep*, also transcribed as *chirik*, *pir-rik*, or a slightly less disyllabic *turrp* or *chip*. When flushed, it can give thinner *chip-chip* notes, more similar to, but fuller than the classic penetrating *tip* of a Little Stint.

The summer-plumaged adult is similar to a juvenile in general pattern and most of the above criteria apply (the notable exception being point 6). Note in particular that the overall plumage tone is a cold grey-brown, lacking the browner tones of the adult Little Stint. Plate 26.2 shows a worn and moulting adult on Tresco, Isles of Scilly, in August 1993. It is basically in summer plumage, apart from the newly acquired grey winter feathers in its scapulars. An adult's post-breeding moult is started during its southward migration.

WESTERN SANDPIPER
Calidris mauri

Range Breeds mainly in northern and western Alaska, extending into extreme north-eastern Siberia. It winters along the coasts of the southern USA, through the West Indies and Central America to northern South America, and south as far as Peru.

Occurrences An extremely rare vagrant, with only seven records (to 1996). The reason for its rarity lies in its westerly breeding range and migration routes. *BWP* notes that autumn passage is mainly through the Pacific provinces and states, and the weights of Alaskan migrants indicate that they are not capable of an extended movement over water. Some cross North America to move through the eastern USA from about Massachusetts southwards, but the species is very rare in eastern Canada. British and Irish records have been made mainly in August–September and in western localities, suggesting direct Atlantic crossings. Two atypical ones concerned the very first, on Fair Isle, Shetland, in May–June 1956, and one at Rainham, Essex, in July 1973. The most widely appreciated was the juvenile on the North Slob, Co. Wexford, on 3–6 September 1992. It instigated Ireland's largest twitch to date, being seen by some 300 people, about half of whom had crossed the Irish Sea (Mullarney, 1992).

Identification Plate 26.3, photographed by the late David Hunt, shows an adult moulting from summer to winter plumage feeding with a juvenile Dunlin *C. alpina* on the Abbey Pool, Tresco, Isles of Scilly, on 19 August 1969. The fact that it was originally rejected as a Semipalmated Sandpiper *C. pusilla* and was not accepted as a Western until 1984 illustrates how our knowledge progressed during the intervening years. Although the separation of the Western and 'Semi-p' has been the subject of protracted debate, this photograph clearly illustrates a very obvious point: in shape, structure and jizz, the Western Sandpiper is strongly reminiscent of a miniature Dunlin. The bill is long and is gently decurved to a relatively fine tip, and it is rather upright, flat-backed and long-legged. Like the

Dunlin, it has a tendency to wade into the water to feed. Its plumage is undistinguished and this is due to moult: the upperparts are a messy mixture of brown and grey. The moult is, however, of significance in itself. The Western moults much earlier than the Semipalmated, so that adults are largely in winter plumage by late August (compare with the August adult Semipalmated in Plate 26.2). Like the juvenile Dunlin, the juvenile Western moults during its southward migration; most will have moulted at least their scapulars by mid-September. The head pattern of the Tresco adult is fairly distinctive, with a well-marked supercilium and a rather wedge-shaped ear-covert patch. Most significant, however, is the retention of remnants of its diagnostic summer flank streaking. Unlike Semipalmated, in summer plumage Western shows strong rufous tones to the head and scapulars. Juvenile shows a diffuse greyish area behind the eye (weaker than juvenile Semipalmated), two rows of bright rufous-fringed scapulars and often shows rufous fringes to the crown and mantle. The call again shows its affiliations to the Dunlin: it is a shrill, high-pitched somewhat Dunlin-like *chreep*, *treet* or *teet-teet treep* when flushed. The Wexford juvenile gave a thin *jeet*, which was shorter and rather less Dunlin-like.

RED-NECKED STINT
Calidris ruficollis

Range Breeds in eastern Siberia, and winters from India eastwards through Southeast Asia and Indonesia to Australasia.

Occurrences There are four British records (1986–95). These involved three summer plumaged adults on the east coast in late summer and a juvenile found dead on Fair Isle, Shetland, on 31 August 1994. By 1994, there had also been some nine Swedish records (*Brit. Birds* **88**: 271), and it had also occurred in Finland, Germany, Austria, the Netherlands and France. Presumably all these related to reversed migrants out of Siberia. There is evidence that some take a great circle route from eastern Asia 2,000 miles (3,200 km) over the western Pacific direct to New Guinea and Australia (*BWP*). Interestingly, if traced backwards through the western part of the breeding range, this route leads directly to Scandinavia and Britain. It seems highly likely that it has been overlooked in the past and that we are still not picking out juveniles.

Identification Plate 26.4 shows a summer plumaged adult which was present on the River Wansbeck, Northumberland, on 12–13 August 1995. Although not really apparent in the photograph, the Red-necked Stint usually appears shorter legged and stubbier billed than the Little Stint *C. minuta*, and may also look rather long-bodied. The photograph does show the bright rufous face and throat which is offset by a strong white supercilium and a pale area at the base of the bill. Rows of brown streaking on the 'shoulders' below the throat patch are also characteristic. In close views it shows a narrow, pale eye-ring, reminiscent of the Semipalmated Sandpiper *C. pusilla*. It shows a certain amount of chestnut in the scapulars and the mantle Vs are much weaker than on most adult Little Stints. It should be noted that, in spring, some fresh individuals are less bright than others, showing a paler, more cinnamon face and throat. They also tend to be paler above, sometimes lacking rufous in the scapulars. Surprisingly, another species which needs to be eliminated when identifying this species is a rufous plumaged summer Sanderling *C. alba*. It is, therefore, essential to correctly evaluate size and, if in doubt, check the hind claw (lacking on the Sanderling). The juvenile has a plainer head than juvenile Little Stint and lacks that species' split supercilium. It shows weaker mantle Vs while rufous fringed upper scapulars contrast with greyer lower scapulars and wing coverts. The tertials are rather pale greyish, with whitish fringes (Jonsson & Grant, 1984). The call is slightly harder and deeper than that of a Little Stint.

LONG-TOED STINT
Calidris subminuta

Range Has an apparently disjunctive breeding range in the forest zone of Siberia, and thus breeds further south than other Siberian calidrids. It winters from Bangladesh through Southeast Asia and Indonesia to the Philippines, small numbers reaching Australia. It occupies the same niche and forms a superspecies with the Least Sandpiper *C. minutilla* of North America.

Occurrences There are just two accepted records: an adult in summer plumage at Marazion Marsh, Cornwall, on 7–8 June 1970 (Round, 1996); and a juvenile at Saltholme Pools, Co. Durham, from 28 August to 1 September 1982 (Dunnett, 1992). A third was seen at Ballycotton, Co. Cork, in June 1996. The original bird was initially accepted as a Least Sandpiper, but the finder, Phil Round, long maintained that it was Britain's first Long-toed Stint, a fact now accepted after reconsideration of the descriptions and the excellent set of photographs which were fortunately taken at the time. The Saltholme bird was discovered just two days before Britain's first Little Whimbrel *Numenius minutus* and produced a unique purple patch for wader buffs. Both records are likely to have been the result of reversed migration from Siberia, the Cornish and Irish birds presumably heading back towards the breeding grounds after having spent the intervening

winter further south. The species has also been recorded in Sweden (November 1977).

Identification Plate 26.5 is of the Marazion adult. It shows the species' characteristic shape, which has been likened to that of a Wood Sandpiper *Tringa glareola*: rather a square head, long neck, flat back, quite a short rear end, a pot belly and long legs, especially above the 'knee'. Plumage-wise, the species shows a pale supercilium (which in the field is usually obviously split), something of a dark cap, a dark, fan-shaped ear-covert patch, strong pale mantle Vs and a coarsely-streaked breast band which is pointed in the middle (like that of the Pectoral Sandpiper *C. melanotos*). The plumage is coarsely patterned but the tone is variable, although most appear quite a rich brown and rather 'foxy'. The legs are a dull yellow. The call of the Marazion bird was described as a dullish *prrp*, a low-pitched *trrpp*, *chrupp* (not unlike that of a Pectoral Sandpiper), a trilling *preet-preet* or a monosyllabic *prritt* (Round, 1996). Round considered that the following features were most relevant in its separation from the Least Sandpiper: (1) dark forehead (usually a pale narrow area above the base of the bill on an adult summer Least); (2) fairly prominent split supercilium (less pronounced on the Least); (3) loral streak unexceptional (usually more prominent on the Least); (4) prominent broad rufous fringes to tertials, coverts and scapulars (usually duller and narrower on the Least); (5) a call like a Pectoral Sandpiper (thinner and higher-pitched in the Least); and (6) larger in size with long legs and toes. Other features not visible in Plate 26.5 included a hint of a dark 'J' shape on the lores (*see* below) and an underlying tawny-buff background colour to the breast band, both of which indicated a Long-toed. There was some debate about whether it showed the diagnostic greenish coloration at the base of the bill. It also lacked scalloped centres to the greater coverts usually shown by the Least.

The Saltholme juvenile in Plate 27.1 was more straightforward. Many of the features of a summer adult also apply to this bird, particularly the shape, the pale base to the bill, the split supercilium, the coarse, bright, chestnut-fringed upperparts, its larger size and its long toes. Other features of particular note are: (1) the dark forehead, which curves back across the lores to produce a diagnostic 'J' mark; (2) the distinctive facial pattern (caused by the capped effect, white supercilium and dark ear-covert patch); (3) the prominent white mantle Vs; and (4) the profusely streaked breast. The overall effect is reminiscent of a miniature juvenile Sharp-tailed Sandpiper *C. acuminata*. Its calls were a low, liquid *chree* or *chirrup*, similar to those of the Curlew Sandpiper *C. ferruginea* but softer.

LEAST SANDPIPER
Calidris minutilla

Range Breeds in Alaska and northern Canada. Winters in the more southerly coastal states of the USA, the West Indies, and Central and northern South America.

Occurrences Despite more observers and a better understanding of stint plumages, this remains an extreme rarity with 35 records up to 1995. Most have occurred from late July to October, involving both early autumn adults and later juveniles. There were as many as four each in 1966 and 1988. Interestingly, it is mainly a southern bird, being virtually unknown in northern England and Scotland. Although records have been widely scattered, there has been an inevitable south-westerly bias. Records outside the normal period involved one in Hampshire in May 1977 and a surprising winter record in Cornwall at Portscatho from 9 February to 20 April 1986. It was discovered by birders searching for a female King Eider *Somateria spectabilis*, itself a remarkable occurrence in that part of the country. As with the Semipalmated Sandpiper *C. pusilla*, easterly populations use a transoceanic great circle route from north-eastern Canada direct to the West Indies and northern South America. Examination of migrant adults in north-eastern Canada in autumn has shown that they have sufficient fat reserves to fly up to 2,250 miles (3,600 km; *BWP*)

Identification Plate 27.2 shows the Portscatho bird in April 1986, moulting from first-winter to first-summer (most of its plumage is newly acquired fresh summer). It is a small, unobtrusive stint with a short neck (producing a hunched posture), a short, squat body and short legs. It is conventionally 'stint-like' in shape and fails to convey the gangly appearance of the Long-toed Stint *C. subminuta*, which has often been likened to the Wood Sandpiper *Tringa glareola*. Its dull yellowy-green legs are an immediate distinction from all other stints except the Long-toed and Temminck's *C. temminckii*. Its toes are long and spidery, although shorter than those of the Long-toed Stint. The bill is thick-based and gently curved, and tapers to a fine point; it lacks a greenish base. Owing to the moult, the plumage is rather messy. The head and breast are messily streaked, but it shows something of a capped effect (lacking the Long-toed's split supercilium), and has a pale forehead, a whitish supercilium, a noticeable eye-ring and an ear-covert patch.

Plate 27.3 shows a juvenile on the Hayle Estuary, Cornwall, in September 1993. Shape-wise, it is similar to the Portscatho bird but the plumage is very neat. It is particularly interesting to compare this photograph with Plate 27.1, which shows the juvenile Long-toed Stint in Co. Durham in 1982. The Least has more of a capped effect (lacking a split supercilium), it lacks the Long-toed's dark 'J' on the lores and it has a completely dark bill. It lacks strong white mantle Vs and is much duller above, having whitish fringes to the tertials and wing coverts (as opposed to the rich chestnut fringing of the Long-toed). The scapulars are the brightest part of the plumage, being thickly fringed with dull chestnut. The breast band is less coarsely streaked than the Long-toed. It is easily separated from the juvenile Little Stint by its short, dull greeny-yellow legs. It also differs from the Little Stint in that its tertials almost completely cloak the primaries. Its call is a soft, trilling *treep*, *tr-rrrr*, *shreep* or *s-r-eep*, longer when excited: *s-s-s-s-sip*. For further details on its separation from the Long-toed Stint, *see* page 65.

WHITE-RUMPED SANDPIPER
Calidris fuscicollis

Range Breeds mainly on the mainland and islands of arctic Canada. It is a very long-range migrant, wintering in southern South America from Paraguay to Tierra del Fuego.

Occurrences The White-rumped Sandpiper is an annual autumn vagrant in fluctuating numbers. An average year would produce about ten, but as many as 29 were seen in 1984. It shows an interesting split in its occurrence pattern. As to be expected, late-autumn records involve mainly juveniles in western localities, but Dymond *et al.* (1989) noted that 39 per cent in 1958–85 were on the British east coast, mainly adults in July and August. Remarkably, there were as many as four at Breydon Water, Norfolk, in July 1996. It seems possible that these are leftovers from previous autumn influxes. Reversed migration over the poles seems an unlikely explanation as this would dump the birds in eastern Siberia rather than western Europe, but it could be possible that some adults tag onto flocks of Ringed Plovers *Charadrius hiaticula* and Dunlins *Calidris alpina* which regularly cross the Atlantic from Greenland. Another idea is that these are birds which crossed the South Atlantic on their spring migration, rather like Franklin's Gulls *Larus pipixcan* (*see* page 81). They then pass through the North Sea on their way back south

As with many other North American waders, most make a huge transoceanic flight down the western Atlantic from north-eastern Canada to the west Indies and northern South America. Autumn adults examined in north-eastern Canada had sufficient fat reserves to fly up to 2,700 miles (4,200 km), which would enable a comfortable Atlantic crossing, particularly with a strong tail wind. Its migrations in the

Juvenile White-rumped Sandpiper.

New World are strongly elliptical, the spring migration being through the North American interior. This difference ties in with its occurrence patterns here: it is virtually unknown in spring. Interestingly, one was seen at the Goksu Delta in southern Turkey in May 1996 (Sean Browne & Paul Ganney, verbally). Could it be that transatlantic vagrants also perform an elliptical migration (in reverse), thus explaining its rarity in Western Europe in spring?

Identification Plate 27.5 shows an adult at Marazion Marsh, Cornwall, in October 1982. It is moulting into winter plumage, with just a few dark, buff-fringed summer feathers remaining in the scapulars. It is distinctly smaller than a Dunlin, with a short bill and an elongated horizontal appearance with very long primaries that project well beyond the tail. The primary projection is approximately equal to the tertial length, with at least four primary tips visible. This long-winged effect is also apparent in flight, when the narrow, white horseshoe-shaped rump and uppertail-covert patch is readily apparent, contrasting with the blackish tail. As Plate 27.5 shows, its plumage is undistinguished. Like most calidrids, its winter plumage is predominantly grey, the most distinctive feature being a short whitish supercilium from the bill to just behind the eye. A noticeable white eye-ring recalls Temminck's Stint *C. temminckii*. The bill is short, thick-based, blunt and slightly decurved, and it shows a small pale area at the base of the lower mandible. Note also its speckled breast band and the remnants of its summer flank streaking.

Plate 27.4 shows a juvenile on St Mary's, Isles of Scilly, in October 1970. It is similar to the adult but the whole of the upperparts are freshly, evenly and prominently scalloped with whitish feather fringes (chestnut on the upper scapulars). It also shows a faint

mantle V and a stronger white scapular line. The supercilium is more prominent than on the adult (curving down and then up behind the eye), and it is more evenly streaked across the breast, forming a band. Plate 28.4 is a remarkable photograph, showing a juvenile White-rumped (right) with a juvenile Baird's Sandpiper *C. bairdii* at Stithians Reservoir, Cornwall, in October 1989. They are similar in shape, but note that Baird's has a buffer plumage tone, a less strongly marked facial pattern and an all-dark bill. It is finely and evenly scalloped across the back and it lacks the White-rumped's white mantle and scapular Vs as well as its rufous upper scapulars. The White-rumped has already moulted many of its back feathers and its third row of scapulars, which are grey with a dark shaft streak. Its white rump is just visible above the closed tertials. The call is a thin *jeet*.

BAIRD'S SANDPIPER
Calidris bairdii

Range Breeds in the high Arctic of northern Canada and Alaska, as well as in extreme north-east Siberia and in north-western Greenland. Another truly long-range migrant, wintering in South America, south of the equator.

Occurrences Baird's Sandpiper has similar breeding and wintering ranges to the White-rumped Sandpiper *C. fuscicollis* but it is essentially a freshwater species in winter. Its occurrence patterns are similar, except that it is about two and a half times rarer and adults are much rarer in late summer. Most records relate to juveniles in September, and it is most frequent in southern Ireland and south-western England. There have been only five in spring but there was a remarkable wintering record of a first-winter at Staines

Reservoirs, Surrey, from October 1982 to April 1983. It has been suggested that some of our autumn Baird's originate in north-eastern Siberia, but this seems unlikely in view of the restricted nature of its Siberian range and the orientation of the species' migration routes. The main North American route lies through the prairies and then involves a direct 4,000 mile (6,500 km) flight over the eastern Pacific to the South American Andes, which ensures that the species is rare in Central America (*BWP*). The individuals that reach Britain and Ireland presumably stem from a minority which reach South America by a long transoceanic great circle route down the western Atlantic.

Identification Plate 28.1 shows a juvenile on St Agnes, Isles of Scilly, in October 1987. It is similar in size and shape to the White-rumped Sandpiper, being long and slim with primaries which project well beyond the tail. The primary projection is approximately equal to the overlying tertial length. When viewed head-on, it appears peculiarly squat, almost as if it had been trodden on. The overall plumage tone is rather buff and the upperparts are neatly and evenly scalloped, forming a scaly appearance across its back and scapulars. It has a breast band which recalls Pectoral Sandpiper *C. melantos* but this is diffusely streaked and less sharply defined across the lower breast. The head is rather bland, being well-streaked with a whitish supercilium and a narrow white eye-ring. The short, finely tipped bill is completely black, as are the legs. In flight, it shows thick white tips to the greater coverts and an area of whitish across the base of the primaries. Unlike White-rumped Sandpiper, it is dark across the rump. Plate 28.2 shows another juvenile, at Upper Tamar Lake, Devon/Cornwall, in September 1995. This shot shows the upperpart scalloping to good effect. Plate 28.4 shows a juvenile Baird's with a juvenile/first-winter White-rumped (right) at Stithians Reservoir, Cornwall, in October 1989 (*see* page 67).

Plate 28.3 is of a summer plumaged adult at Cantley Beet Factory, Norfolk, in August 1992. Summer adult is rather golden-buff in plumage tone with black centred feathers in the mantle and scapulars. It is otherwise similar to the juvenile. The call is a high-pitched *kreep* or a rolling *prrr prrr*, suggesting a high-pitched Pectoral Sandpiper.

PECTORAL SANDPIPER
Calidris melanotos

Range Breeds in the coastal tundras of Siberia, from the Taymyr Peninsula eastwards across northern Alaska and northern Canada as far as the western shores of Hudson Bay. The majority of birds in the Siberian population are believed to move east through Alaska

and Canada and migrate with North American birds to southern South America. Some must travel huge distances of at least 10,000 miles (16,000 km). Small numbers also migrate through eastern Asia to winter sparingly in Australia and New Zealand.

Occurrences The Pectoral Sandpiper is the most numerous Nearctic wader on this side of the Atlantic, and Dymond *et al.* (1989) noted 1,404 during 1958–85, an average of 52 a year. Numbers increased steadily through the period, due no doubt to the increase in birdwatching. There were as many as 150 recorded in 1984, a particularly good American wader year. As to be expected, most occurrences are juveniles in September and October, with a preponderance in southern Ireland and south-western England. These presumably involve mainly eastern Canadian birds caught in depressions as they migrate down the western Atlantic great circle route direct to the West Indies or South America. There has, however, been a surprising number recorded on the British east coast, these being mostly adults in late summer. It has been suggested that some of these may involve reverse migrating Siberian breeders, but it seems more likely that the bulk are simply North American leftovers from previous years. Occurrences remain rare in spring, but with a wide scatter of records.

Identification As with the Ruff *Philomachus pugnax*, there is considerable size variation, with males averaging up to ten per cent larger than females. Although a male is about the size of a Green Sandpiper *Tringa ochropus*, females can be surprisingly small (some are actually smaller than a Dunlin *C. alpina*). Plate 28.6 shows a juvenile at Davidstow Airfield, Cornwall, in September 1994. It is quite a bulky bird, with a rather oval body, a long primary projection and a medium length, slightly decurved bill. The upperparts are coarsely but immaculately scalloped, richest on the scapulars. In the field, it shows two snipe-like Vs down the sides of the mantle and along the third row of scapulars. It has a brown cap, and a pale supercilium but the head pattern is rather subdued, particularly when compared with the Sharp-tailed Sandpiper *C. acuminata*. The feature which gives the species its name is the clear-cut and delicately streaked breast band. Its legs are a dull ochre-yellow but on others they may appear green, pinkish or even orangey. It is much shorter legged than a Ruff and is more horizontal, feeding with a slow walk on flexed legs, continuously picking with rapid head movements. It is a bird of freshwater habitats. In flight, it appears relatively plain-winged, although narrow whitish tips to the greater coverts form an inconspicuous wing bar. More distinctive are two white oval patches on the sides of the rump. Plate 28.7 shows another juvenile, at Drift Reservoir, Cornwall, in October 1980, keeping company with a juvenile American Golden Plover *Pluvialis dominicus*. Plate 28.5 shows a summer plumaged adult at Minsmere, Suffolk, in May 1985. The upperparts are duller and less neatly fringed and the breast is more coarsely streaked. The call is distinctive: a low, rolling *kreep-kreep* or *t-reep*, reminiscent of a subdued Curlew Sandpiper *C. ferruginea*.

SHARP-TAILED SANDPIPER
Calidris acuminata

Range Breeds in north-eastern Siberia. Interestingly, it breeds further east than the closest Pectoral Sandpipers *C. melanotos*. It winters on islands in the western Pacific and in Australia and New Zealand.

Occurrences It is an extremely rare vagrant, with 23 up to 1996, mainly from late July to September. There is a south-easterly bias but it has been recorded three times in Scotland and once in Ireland. Although most are presumably reversed migrants out of Siberia, the essentially north–south orientation of its normal migration route would perhaps explain its rarity in Western Europe.

One particularly striking feature of the records is that that only four have involved juveniles. Two of these were in North Wales in October 1973, and it is intriguing to note that several reached the eastern seaboard of North America during the same autumn (Smith *et al.*, 1974). In late September 1974, an adult on St Mary's, Isles of Scilly, consorted with three juvenile Pectoral Sandpipers (*Brit. Birds* **68**: Plate 44). These records led to the remarkable yet plausible suggestion that they may have arrived not from the east but from the west, having crossed both North America and the Atlantic!

Identification Plate 29.1 shows a summer plumaged adult at Tacumshin, Co. Wexford, in August 1994. It clearly resembles a Pectoral Sandpiper but its shape is quite distinctive, being short-billed, short-necked and pot-bellied. Its plumage is quite striking, with its rufous cap, whitish supercilium, noticeable white eye-ring and dark patch through the eye. Even more distinctive are the profusely but messily patterned underparts, with mottles and chevrons extending right down to the belly, flanks and undertail-coverts. Plates 29.3 shows a duller summer adult at Scatness, Shetland, in September 1993. Plate 29.2 shows a juvenile at Shotwick Fields, Flintshire, in October 1973. The evenly scalloped upperparts and rounded, not pointed, scapular feathers clearly shows its age

(note that the mantle and scapular Vs are less prominent than on the 'Pec'), and it has the rufous cap, prominent white supercilium and white eye-ring of the adult. Like the Pectoral Sandpiper, the juvenile Sharp-tailed shows fine breast streaking, but this is more diffuse and is not clearly demarcated from the white belly. It is interesting to note that, whereas the juveniles have at least two primaries projecting beyond the tertials, the adult has elongated tertials which practically cover the closed primaries (a similar phenomenon occurs with the Pectoral Sandpiper). It may feed with the rear held up and the legs flexed, appearing almost crake-like at times. The flight pattern is similar to that of the 'Pec' but its call is apparently softer: Lewington *et al.* (1991) describe it as a subdued *ueep* and *ueep-ueep*.

BROAD-BILLED SANDPIPER
Limicola falcinellus

Range The nominate race breeds in Fenno-Scandia east to the White Sea. As its name suggests, the race *sibirica* breeds across Siberia but its distribution is imperfectly known. It winters discontinuously from East Africa (rare), through the Persian Gulf to India, Southeast Asia, the Philippines, Indonesia and parts of Australia.

Occurrences It was very rare prior to 1972, largely due to a poor understanding of its identification features. At that time it was assumed that winter-plumaged birds were occurring and, consequently, there was much confusion with Dunlins *Calidris alpina*. In recent years it has proved to be a regular spring migrant, with as many as 12 per year. Inevitably, spring birds are in summer plumage so the old problem of confusion with Dunlins has largely evaporated. It is most frequent on the British east coast, but there have been a number of records elsewhere, with several in Ireland. It continues to remain very rare inland. Small parties (up to three) have been recorded and a pair was seen displaying at Aberlady Bay, East Lothian, in June 1983, raising some intriguing possibilities. Small numbers have been recorded throughout the summer months and there is a small secondary peak in late August and September, but juveniles are surprisingly rare.

With a basically south-east–north-west spring migration route, our records presumably involve birds which have flown too far to the west and have been deflected by easterly winds across the North Sea. A suggested alternative, however, is that small numbers winter further west in Africa than is generally supposed and that we are simply on their migration route north.

Identification The summer plumaged adult in Plate 29.4 was present at Ballycotton, Co. Cork, in July 1979. Although reminiscent of a small Dunlin in shape, it is distinctive in its own right appearing something like a cross between a Dunlin and a Jack Snipe *Lymnocryptes minimus*. From a distance, the plumage is very dark with a band of mottling across the breast. At closer range, the upperpart feathers are prominently edged with pale buff, although these may largely wear off by late summer. As can be seen in the photograph, narrow buff mantle and scapular Vs are apparent. What really grabs the attention, however, is the stripy head pattern with: (1) a dark area across the lores and through the eye, (2) a prominent broad buff supercilium; and (3) a dark cap with a thin but noticeable buff 'split supercilium'. As its name suggests, the bill is thick at the base, with a distinct downward kink at the tip. Fresh spring adults have prominent whitish feather fringes which may produce a rather frosty appearance, particularly about the neck and breast, but these wear off as the summer progresses. Juveniles are similar to summer adults but are neatly and immaculately patterned at a time when adults are very worn. The call is a hard, dry, trilling *pprrrrrrk*, rather difficult to describe.

STILT SANDPIPER
Micropalama himantopus

Range Breeds in northern Alaska and Canada. Winters mainly in South America, south of the equator.

Occurrences This remains a very rare vagrant, with 26 recorded between 1954 and 1993. The occurrence patterns are unusual, with three in April–May, no less than 16 in July–August and seven in September–October. The late-summer peak suggests that these birds are not direct transatlantic vagrants, and this is further confirmed by the fact that 11 of the 16 occurred along the east and south-east coasts of England, between Yorkshire and Sussex. The bulk of the population migrates through the Canadian prairies and the US interior, with a minority using the Atlantic route. Whilst some of the Irish records indicate that some must make a direct Atlantic crossing, it seems probable that most get here by a different route: perhaps by reversed migration out of Alaska or northern Canada?

Identification The bird in Plate 30.1 was a long-staying first-summer which was present at Frodsham and various other sites in Cheshire from April to October 1984. Its long stay enabled hundreds to see it. It is slightly larger and markedly taller than a Curlew Sandpiper *Calidris ferruginea*, and is slightly longer billed and longer necked, appearing slimmer

and more rakish. The photograph, taken in April, clearly shows all the main features of non-breeding plumage. Note particularly: (1) the long, thick, gently decurved blunt-ended bill, slightly expanded at the tip; (2) the distinct facial pattern with a whitish supercilium and grey patch through the eye; (3) the speckled underparts; and (4) the dirty green legs (which readily distinguish it from the black-legged Curlew Sandpiper). Like many American waders, it has a long primary projection, with two or three generally visible beyond the tertials, but note that this individual has lost two of the overlying tertials.

Plate 30.2 shows a summer-plumaged adult, just starting to moult its scapulars, at Trimley St Mary, Suffolk, in August 1990. This shows even more clearly why the species gets its name: its long legs, with the particularly long tibia, give it a rather gangly appearance. Its head pattern is similar to the Frodsham bird, but the supercilium is whiter. What really makes it distinctive is the profuse black barring which covers the underparts right down to the undertail-coverts. There is a hint of rufous on the rear of the ear-coverts but this is far less extensive than on most. The juvenile is regularly scalloped above and is washed buff and streaked on the breast. Unlike the Curlew Sandpiper, it lacks a wing bar in flight but has a square white rump patch (*see* Plate 30.3, again of the Cheshire bird). It often wades belly-deep into the water, immersing the bill and picking rapidly in the manner of a Dunlin *C. alpina*. It is not particularly vocal, the call being a soft *dju*. Hayman *et al.* (1986) also describe a soft, rattling trill: *kirrr* or *grrrt*.

BUFF-BREASTED SANDPIPER
Tryngites subruficollis

Range Breeds in the high Arctic of northern Alaska and northern Canada, west of Hudson Bay; some also breed in extreme north-eastern Siberia. It winters on the grasslands of Argentina, Uruguay and Paraguay.

Occurrences In former years the Buff-breasted Sandpiper was reduced almost to extinction by shooting in the American Mid-West but, fortunately, it did not go the way of the Eskimo Curlew *Numenius borealis*. Despite this, it has still not made a full recovery and current estimates suggest that only 5,000–15,000 may remain, compared to former estimates of hundreds of thousands or even millions. Indeed, it may still be declining (Lanctot, 1995). In Britain and Ireland, however, there has been a marked upturn in the number recorded. There were only 30 records prior to 1958, compared with 495 during 1958–85 (Dymond *et al.*, 1989). It has been annual since 1960 and there were major influxes in 1975, 1977 and 1980, with peaks of about 67 in both the former two years. As to be expected, it is most frequent in September in southern Ireland and south-western England, and the 1977 influx included an astonishing 15 together on St Mary's, Isles of Scilly. It was considered to be so regular that it was removed from the Rarities List at the end of 1982 but, perversely, its numbers have dipped in recent years, with as few as six in 1987 (Fraser & Ryan, 1992).

Most move south through the prairies, but small numbers diverge in Canada and pass down the western side of Hudson Bay and across the Great Lakes to New England. They then head out to sea to make a huge transoceanic great circle route flight direct to north-eastern South America (*BWP*). These are presumably the source of our vagrants and numbers occurring here obviously depend on the timing and severity of Atlantic depressions during their migration. Interestingly, owing to its migration routes, the species is rare down much of the United States eastern seaboard and there are several stories of American birders actually ticking the species in Britain! It seems likely that some eventually end up in Africa, and an irregular spring passage no doubt relates to those birds heading back north.

Identification Plate 30.4 shows a juvenile at Porthgwarra, Cornwall, in September 1977. Although superficially reminiscent of a small juvenile Ruff *Philomachus pugnax*, it is readily identifiable. It is a small wader, not much bigger than a Dunlin *Calidris alpina*, with a short bill, a small head, a long body, rather a long primary projection and medium-length legs. The vast majority of our vagrants are juveniles which are finely and neatly scalloped across the upperparts. It has a large eye which stands out in a bland face (although there is a narrow, pale eye-ring), and the crown is capped with neat brown streaking. As its name suggests, the whole of the underparts are pale buff, much less orange in tone than the juvenile Ruff, with darker, neat spots on the breast sides. A minority may be whiter on the belly, with the buff demarcated across the lower breast. If in doubt, check the legs: they are ochre yellow (dull green on a juvenile Ruff).

The adult in Plate 30.5, taken at Cliffe Pools, Kent, in August 1994, is moulting into winter plumage. It can be separated by its much thicker buff upperpart fringing and plainer, pointed dark feather centres (rounded on juveniles). The species is readily distinguished in flight, being completely plain across the upperparts and lacking the Ruff's wing bar, oval white rump patches, long projecting legs and languid flight action. Buff-breasts prefer drier habitats, such as airfields and golf courses, and are usually very approachable. When feeding, the stance is horizontal, the legs are flexed, the head is bobbed as the bird walks daintily but erratically, pecking every two or three steps.

They are usually silent in autumn, although they can give a low, rather gruff *chu*. *BWP* also notes a low, rolling *pr-r-r-reet*.

Unfortunately, we do not experience the more extrovert side of the Buff-breast's character, and American birders who have been to its tundra breeding grounds enthuse over the remarkable lekking displays of the males. They raise and lower their wings and perform short flutter-jumps, while the flash of their white underwings can be seen from half a mile away. The male courts the females by spreading his wings into a parabolic shape, stamping his feet, vibrating his wings and emitting a series of soft ticking sounds. As many as four females enter the male's embrace, peck at his dark carpal patches and then rotate so that their backs are against his chest. He then copulates with the closest. Surprisingly, some of these displays may even be performed on the wintering grounds (Lanctot, 1995).

GREAT SNIPE
Gallinago media

Range Breeds in Scandinavia, Poland and in the former Soviet Union, east to the Yenesei. It winters over much of sub-Saharan Africa.

Occurrences Since the 19th century the Great Snipe has suffered a marked decline in the south and west of its European range, becoming extinct in Denmark, Germany and Lithuania (*BWP*). Reasons for the decline are not entirely clear, but habitat loss and hunting are the likely culprits. In recent years there have been some signs of recovery in Norway, and high numbers of migrants in Finland and Sweden in 1987 may give cause for a small degree of optimism (*BWP*, *Brit. Birds* **81**: 333; **82**: 18). The numbers occurring in Britain and Ireland have reflected the European decline: there were 180 prior to 1958, but only 83 since (to the end of 1995), although there has been a slight upturn in recent years. The species has, however, been prone to misidentification and one wonders how many of the old records would stand up to modern scrutiny. The recent trend is for most to occur in late August and September, mainly in the Northern Isles and down the east coast of Britain.

Identification Plates 31.1 & 2 show a remarkably cooperative juvenile which was present at Girton Gravel Pits, Nottinghamshire, in late August and early September 1989. The most obvious feature which distinguishes it from the Common Snipe *G. gallinago* is the heavily scalloped underparts, with chevrons on the flanks, leaving only a tiny unbarred area in the centre of the belly. The photograph shows also: (1) a rounded, pot-bellied appearance; (2) the bill is thicker than the Common Snipe's and thus appears proportionately stubbier; (3) the mantle and scapular stripes tend to appear less well defined; (4) the wing coverts are rather chequered, and there are white tips to the median and greater coverts (forming a double wing bar); and (5) the legs are greyer and thicker than those of the Common.

When feeding, the Great Snipe crouches low to the ground and usually keeps to cover. It also bobs up and down, although this movement is not as exaggerated as that of a Jack Snipe *Lymnocryptes minimus*. In flight, it is very distinctive and, when one sees the genuine article, it is difficult to imagine how it could be confused with a Common Snipe. It is large, bulky and heavy, and flies low and direct for a relatively short distance. It has quite rounded wing tips and the whole feel suggests a Eurasian Woodcock *Scolopax rusticola*. It has a chequered area on the lesser coverts (less obvious on juveniles), and a double white wingbar is formed by the white tips to the median and greater coverts (these continuing across the tips of the median and greater primary coverts). The white trailing edge is less obvious than on the Common Snipe. When dropping into cover it may spread its tail to reveal prominent white corners. The barred underparts may also be obvious in flight. Unlike the Common Snipe, it is usually silent, although it may give a low, throaty *ugh*.

LONG-BILLED DOWITCHER
Limnodromus scolopaceus

Range Breeds in north-eastern Siberia and coastal northern and western Alaska. Its range has expanded both southwards and westwards in Siberia during the present century (Tomkovich, 1992). It winters in the western and southern states of the USA, and south to Guatemala.

Occurrences It has been virtually annual since 1963 with as many as 15 in 1987, although a typical year would produce less than five. It is a late vagrant and most records involve juvenile/first-winters in late September and October. Not surprisingly, most occur in south-western England and Ireland, and there were as many as five at Rahasane, Co. Galway, in October 1963. Given the right conditions such birds sometimes winter; there are also a few spring and late-summer records.

It seems surprising that the Long-billed Dowitcher is so regular here: it breeds far to the west and it apparently does not perform a huge transoceanic great circle route migration down the western Atlantic. In autumn, however, some move south-east right across North America to hit the Atlantic coast from about Massachusetts southwards, and it seems likely that our vagrants involve those which overshoot the coast

and are then swept across the Atlantic in rapidly moving depressions. It seems remarkable that such birds have sufficient fat reserves to get here. Vagrants cross the entire breeding range of the Short-billed Dowitcher *L. griseus*, which has been identified only once (a juvenile at Tacumshin, Co. Wexford, in September–October 1985).

What is particularly baffling is that the Short-billed seems more likely to occur, as some (apparently the nominate race) use the western Atlantic great circle route direct to South America. Indeed, autumn migrants trapped in north-eastern Canada have had sufficient fat reserves to travel up to 2,700 miles (4,300 km) (*BWP*). One explanation for this conundrum is that the Short-billed is an early migrant and so misses most of the autumn depressions, but this seems unlikely to be the whole story and its rarity must be due to fundamental differences in its migration strategies.

Identification Long-billed Dowitcher is only an inch or so bigger than a Common Snipe *Gallinago gallinago* and it is also rather snipe-like in its proportions, particularly in bill-length. It has rather a rhythmic snipe-like feeding action. The bird in Plate 31.4 was present at Lynn Point, Norfolk, in September–October 1990. It is still largely in juvenile plumage. Plate 31.5 shows a buffer juvenile on Fetlar, Shetland, in October 1988. From a distance, juvenile Long-billed looks rather dark sooty-brown. The head pattern, with the whitish supercilium from the bill to the eye, recalls Spotted Redshank *Tringa erythropus*. Also characteristic are the green legs, barred flanks, spotted undertail-coverts, oval white back patch and white secondary tips.

In juvenile plumage, separation from juvenile Short-billed is relatively straightforward. The Short-billed is predominantly buff below and, indeed, is buffer looking overall. The supercilium of Short-billed tends to continue beyond the eye, and this in turn produces more of a capped effect; it therefore fails to convey the 'Spotted Redshank look' to the head. The Short-billed also tends to show more of a dark triangle on the ear-coverts. Most importantly, the juvenile Short-billed shows buff internal markings – so called 'tiger striping'– on the tertials; sub-marginal markings may also be present on the upperpart feathers, such as the scapulars. In contrast, the Long-billed has plain tertials with only a narrow pale fringe. Although there is some overlap, there is an average difference in bill length.

Plate 31.3 shows an adult in fairly fresh summer plumage at Scatness, Shetland, in May 1996. The identification of summer plumaged dowitchers is a complex subject and reference to Jaramillo & Henshaw (1995) is recommended. The subject is complicated by the existence of three races of Short-billed and by problems caused by wear and individual variation.

Adult Long-billed is most distinctive in fresh summer plumage. The entire underparts are orange-red but note that *hendersoni* Short-billed is similar, although the colour is more pinkish-orange (the belly is largely white on the nominate eastern *griseus*). Very fresh summer-plumaged Long-billed shows extensive white feather fringing on the under-parts, imparting a frosty appearance, but this soon wears off, leaving brown-barred breast sides and flanks. The bird in Plate 31.3 can be most easily sep-arated by: (1) the rather barred breast sides (more spotted on *hendersoni*); (2) diagnostic double white tips to the scapular feathers which contrast with large, dark, unbarred subterminal areas (tips buff or greyish on Short-billed); (3) the prominent white lower eye-ring (usually less obvious on Short-billed); and (4) in direct comparison, Long-billed looks longer-billed, taller, bulkier and shorter-winged than Short-billed.

If in doubt, the calls are diagnostic: the Long-billed has a *pit*, *kik* or *keek*, sometimes doubled to *prit-ik*, or trilled *pit-it-it-it-it-it-it-it*. In tone the calls perhaps recall an abrupt Wood Sandpiper *Tringa glareola*. The Short-billed, on the other hand, has a quick, soft *tur-tur-tur*, *tu-tu-tu-tu* or *tur-dur*, more reminiscent of a Ruddy Turnstone *Arenaria interpres*.

HUDSONIAN GODWIT
Limosa haemastica

Range Has a disjunctive breeding range in Alaska and parts of northern Canada, east to Hudson Bay. It winters in South America, mainly in southern Argentina and Tierra del Fuego. It was once thought to be a very rare bird but it is now known to occur in sizeable numbers in favoured places, such as in Bahia San Sebastian in Tierra del Fuego, where over 7,000 winter (Hayman *et al.*, 1986).

Occurrences There are four British records, con-ceivably involving just two individuals: an adult at Blacktoft Sands, Yorkshire, in September–October 1981 (Grieve, 1987), then at Countess Wear, Exeter, Devon, from October–December 1981 (Wright 1987) and back at Blacktoft in April–May 1983; and another was seen in flight near Collieston, Aberdeenshire, on 26 September 1988. After breed-ing, almost the entire population gathers along the southern shore of Hudson Bay and James Bay (over 10,000 in the latter), and they then migrate to South America in one huge flight down the western Atlantic. This means that the species is scarce along the North American eastern seaboard. In spring, the migration passes through Texas and the Great Plains

on a broader front (Hayman *et al.*, 1986). In view of its migration route, it seems odd that there have not been more recorded on this side of the Atlantic. Remarkably, it is almost regular in New Zealand.

Identification Plates 32.1 & 2 show the 1981 indi-vidual, photographed near Exeter. It is similar to the Black-tailed Godwit *L. limosa* but is noticeably smaller and slimmer, with shorter legs, a shorter neck and a long, upcurved bill, features which sug-gest the Bar-tailed Godwit *L. lapponica*. It is largely in winter plumage, which is much darker and browner than that of the Black-tailed, but it is retaining traces of chestnut in the underparts and a few blackish feathers in the upperparts. There is a prominent white supercilium from the eye to the bill, and there is something about its jizz which recalls a Long-billed Dowitcher *Limnodromus scolopaceus*. Plate 32.1 shows one key difference from the Black-tailed: as befitting a long-range migrant, there is a long primary projection. Three or four pri-maries are visible beyond the tertials and these extend about half an inch (1cm) beyond the tail (on the Black-tailed, only about two primaries are visi-ble and these do not project so far beyond the tail). Plate 32.2 shows the diagnostic black underwing-coverts (white on the Black-tailed). In flight, it also shows a narrower white rump and a shorter and narrower wing bar. The call is a soft *kick-kick*, becoming conversational when in a flock.

LITTLE WHIMBREL
Numenius minutus

Range Has a restricted breeding range in eastern Siberia and winters in southern New Guinea and northern Australia. It is thought likely that it prolifer-ated in the tundra steppe which was widespread after the last Ice Age. Until only a few thousand years ago, the area where it breeds was devoid of extensive wood-land, and its currently restricted range and choice of habitat is due to the more recent spread of the larch forest. The species now breeds in open areas that have been affected by fire, and is hence known as the 'fire-wader' by the local Yakut people (Labutin *et al.*, 1982). It has been traditionally regarded as a scarce species, but recent counts in Australia indicate that about a quarter of a million winter there (Lane, 1987). It is the Palearctic equivalent of the North American Eskimo Curlew *N. borealis* which, sadly, may be extinct.

Occurrences Most birders had barely heard of the species at the time of the first British occurrence: an adult at Sker, Glamorgan, from 30 August to 6 September 1982 (Moon, 1983). Remarkably, a sec-ond turned up only three years later: an adult in the

Blakeney, Cley and Salthouse area of Norfolk from 24 August to 3 September 1985 (Plates 32.3 & 4). There are also records from Norway and Finland.

Identification As its name suggests, the Little Whimbrel is the smallest member of its genus, being about two-thirds the size of a Common Whimbrel *N. phaeopus*. In height, the Sker bird only just reached the belly of a Eurasian Curlew *N. arquata*. Its plumage recalls that of a Common Whimbrel, but it is paler and buffer overall and plainer below. The bill is relatively straight and, in flight, the rump is completely dark. Moon (1983) noted the following differences from the Eskimo Curlew: (1) a more distinct crown stripe; (2) plainer underparts (lacking warm rusty tones); and (3) a lack of rich cinnamon on the underwing coverts. It has a *weep-weep* or *weep-weep-weep-weep* call, excitable and far-carrying, and slower than that of a Common Whimbrel. On its breeding grounds it is unusual in that it has a downward drumming display flight, apparently reminiscent of that of a Pintail Snipe *Gallinago stenura* (Labutin *et al.*, 1982).

UPLAND SANDPIPER
Bartramia longicauda

Range Breeds in the prairies and other grassland habitats of North America, from north-west Alaska south to Oklahoma and east to Virginia. It winters mainly on the pampas of southern South America, although there have also been wintering records from Surinam and north-eastern Brazil. Numbers were severely depleted by hunting at the turn of the century but it has since made a good recovery. In fact, despite some alarming declines in North American grassland birds since the 1960s, it has bucked the trend, increasing significantly since then (*Winging It* **6**: No. 2).

Occurrences A rare vagrant, not annual, with 46 recorded up to 1995. The main southward migration takes place through the North American interior although there is evidence to suggest that there is some movement down the western Atlantic (*BWP*). Occurrences have probably increased here in real terms in line with its recovery in North America. There has been one record in spring and five in winter, but most have involved juveniles in late September and October, mainly in western areas. It is very much associated with October in the Isles of Scilly, and almost a quarter of the British and Irish records have come from there. The most famous of these was a remarkably tame and eccentric juvenile which was present in a small field near St Mary's Hospital in October 1983. Birders started to throw it earthworms, and it eventually became so tame that it would feed from the hand

(Plate 33.2). It eventually disgraced itself by taking a worm out of somebody's mouth!

Identification Plate 33.1 is a further shot of the 1983 St Mary's bird and Plate 32.5 shows another juvenile there in October 1993. Although in a genus of its own, it is very reminiscent of a small whimbrel with a short, straight bill. Its plumage is also whimbrel-like, with dark lateral crown stripes and a narrow pale crown stripe. It has a bland face with a large staring eye and there is a strip of yellow down the lower mandible. The most distinctive thing about it, however, is its remarkable shape: it has a small head, a long thin neck, a long barred tail and long lime-yellow legs. It feeds in fields and other dry habitats, bobbing its head back and forth like a chicken. In flight, it is plain across the entire upperparts and looks rakish, with long, slim wings and a long tail. Its call can be variously described as a low, fast, rippling *rip-ip-ip-ip*, *tu-tu-tu* or *lu-lu-lu-lu*, or as a low, soft, melodic *pur-ur-ur*. In quality, it may suggest the song of a Common Quail *Coturnix coturnix*.

MARSH SANDPIPER
Tringa stagnatilis

Range Typically breeds in water meadows that have an abundance of small water bodies, mainly in the steppe and forest-steppe zones of the former Soviet Union (Tomkovich, 1992). It winters mainly in tropical Africa and the Indian subcontinent, with smaller numbers in the Middle East, Southeast Asia and south into Australia.

Occurrences The Marsh Sandpiper was formerly a very rare vagrant, with only 12 records prior to 1958. Even up until the mid-1970s it was rare and irregular, but since then it has been virtually annual, with as many as 11 in 1984 and nine in 1990. Tomkovich (1992) quoted reports of a sharp decline in Europe during the present century, but there has been a marked range extension in recent decades which seems to have been related to forest clearance and a subsequent increase in grazing marshes. This has led to a northward expansion and a marked eastward consolidation of the species' range. Outside the former Soviet Union this has manifested itself with breeding records in Finland and Poland, as well as the first breeding attempt in Sweden in 1992 (*Brit. Birds* **86**: 41). In Denmark, one desperate individual in 1986 actually copulated with a Common Redshank *T. totanus* (*Brit. Birds* **80**: 11). If the range expansion continues, it seems likely that occurrences will continue to be more frequent.

Most records are made in spring from late April to June, and in autumn from July to early October. Most

Adult winter Marsh Sandpiper.

are adults and there have been surprisingly few juveniles. Although the species winters west to Senegal, only a minority cross Europe as the main passage south is thought to take place east of the Black Sea. With a westward range expansion apparently in progress, even small numbers returning directly north-east from West Africa could account for our spring vagrants, which presumably involve birds deflected here by easterly winds.

Identification The Marsh Sandpiper is a small, delicate and dainty wader, its body size smaller than that of a Green Sandpiper *T. ochropus*. Its long, greenish legs and long, needle-like bill give it something of the feel of a miniature Common Greenshank *T. nebularia*. It feeds with a sedate walk, picking from side to side or with a downward dabbing movement. Plate 33.3 shows a summer adult at Bardney, Lincolnshire, in May 1992. Plumage-wise it is unremarkable, being brownish above and heavily mottled and streaked with black. Adults moult out of summer plumage soon after they have finished breeding, and returning migrants are largely grey above and white below, with a white forehead and supercilium and a diffuse grey patch through the eye. Plate 33.4 shows one such bird at Cliffe, Kent, in August 1994. As with many waders, juvenile plumage is something of a half-way house between summer and winter. The upperparts are dark greyish, regularly patterned with pale fringes and notches (the pattern recalls that of a juvenile Common Greenshank), and there is a dark cap, a white supercilium and a dark wedge through the eye. Like the juvenile greenshank, the breast sides are neatly streaked. Plate 33.5 is a remarkable photograph of a group of three juveniles at the Cantley Beet Factory, Norfolk, in August 1995, and it is tempting to suggest that they came from the same brood. The species is very distinctive in flight, all ages showing a white greenshank-like wedge up the rump and long trailing legs beyond the tail. The call is a an abrupt, slightly subdued *teur* or an almost chipping *tyip-tyip*.

GREATER YELLOWLEGS
Tringa melanoleuca

Range Breeds in the boreal zone of Alaska and Canada. Winters in southern coastal areas of the USA and south across the whole of South America.

Occurrences There were 31 records to the end of 1995 (plus one in 1996), compared with 240 Lesser Yellowlegs *T. flavipes*. Considering that both are long-range migrants, this dichotomy is puzzling. Although the 19 post-1958 records show a peak in late August to early October (nine), the others were scattered from late March to late November, suggesting that most are not direct transatlantic vagrants. It seems likely that the species simply does not accumulate sufficient fat reserves to facilitate a transatlantic crossing. Figures given in *BWP* would seem to confirm this: adults in the Gulf of St Lawrence in active moult had low fat deposits, allowing estimated flight ranges averaging only 860 miles (1,380 km). Even the heaviest had enough fat to fly only an estimated 1,650–1,800 miles

(2,650–2,900 km). It seems probable, therefore, that the few we get are either exceptionally heavy individuals or, perhaps more likely given their eccentric occurrence patterns, ones that have arrived by a different route. It is of interest, therefore, that the first-winter at Rockcliffe, Cumberland, in October–November 1994, was thought likely to have been the bird seen subsequently at Zeebrugge, Belgium, in November–December (and later in the Netherlands). If one projects this route backwards, it crosses southern Greenland and Hudson Bay, suggesting a method of arrival similar to that suggested for the 1991 Shetland Sandhill Crane *Grus canadensis* (*see* pages 23 and 54).

Identification Plate 34.1 shows the Rockcliffe bird in October 1994. Unlike the Common Greenshank *T. nebularia*, juveniles of both Greater and Lesser Yellowlegs are neatly and heavily spotted across the upperparts. The Rockcliffe bird had, however, already moulted its mantle and most of its scapular feathers, and these are much greyer. The species is best distinguished from the Lesser by its size and structure: it is very much the American equivalent of the greenshank and, as well as being similar in size, it also has a slightly upturned bill (with a greenish base) and a less attenuated rear end. Plate 34.2 shows a summer adult at Minsmere, Suffolk, in July 1985. In summer plumage it is much less spotted but it instead shows messy blackish mottling and, in particular, stronger barring on the flanks. Both yellowlegs may be easily separated from the greenshank by their bright yellow legs and square white rump. Like the greenshank, it often feeds with an energetic side-to-side sweeping motion. Its call is similar to the *tew-tew-tew* of a Common Greenshank, although it may sound less penetrating and slightly softer – more of a *tip-tip-tip*.

LESSER YELLOWLEGS
Tringa flavipes

Range Breeds in eastern Alaska and across much of Canada east to James Bay. Some winter in southern USA and Central America, but most travel further south to the West Indies and South America, as far south as Chile and Argentina.

Occurrences The Lesser Yellowlegs is an annual vagrant in variable numbers, with a peak of 11 recorded in 1981. Most are juveniles occurring in September and October, and some of these have wintered. There are smaller peaks in spring and late summer, presumably involving leftovers from previous autumns. Records have been widely scattered, although there is the inevitable bias towards southwestern England and southern Ireland. As with many of our transatlantic waders, many fly non-stop down the western Atlantic from north-eastern Canada to the West Indies and South America. Heavier adults in the Gulf of St Lawrence were estimated to have sufficient fat for a flight of 2,125 miles (3,400 km) (*BWP*; *see also* Greater Yellowlegs above).

Identification Plate 34.3 shows a juvenile at Marazion Marsh, Cornwall, in September 1980. It has just started to acquire a few greyer first-winter feathers on its mantle and scapulars. Plumage-wise, it is similar to a juvenile Greater Yellowlegs *T. melanoleuca* (*see* Plate 34.1) and, like that species, it has a square white rump and long yellow legs which project well beyond the tail in flight. It is most easily distinguished by size and structure: whereas the Greater is about the size of a Common Greenshank

Juvenile Lesser Yellowlegs.

T. nebularia, the Lesser is noticeably smaller than a Common Redshank *T. totanus* and is slimmer, longer winged and longer legged. Note in particular the shorter, slimmer and straighter bill, although, like this one, some do show a perceptible upturn; unlike the Greater, the bill lacks a greener base. The birds' calls are readily distinguished from the Greater, being subdued, abrupt and more reminiscent of a Marsh Sandpiper *T. stagnatilis*: a *tiur tiur*, or *tiur-dur*, sometimes lengthened into *ti-ti-tur-tur-tur*, also a scolding *kee-ur*. The juvenile Lesser is also superficially similar to a juvenile Wood Sandpiper *T. glareola*, and Plate 34.4 is a unique photograph of the two together, taken at Stanford Reservoir, Northamptonshire/Leicestershire, in September 1995. Note that the Lesser is taller, has legs that are longer and yellow, has a longer neck and has longer primaries. Also, it is plainer-faced: instead of showing a prominent white supercilium, it has an obvious pale eye-ring.

SOLITARY SANDPIPER
Tringa solitaria

Range Breeds in the coniferous forest belt of northern North America. Winters mostly in South America, as far south as Uruguay and Argentina, but also in Central America and the Caribbean.

Occurrences The Solitary Sandpiper is one of the rarest North American waders in Britain and Ireland, with 27 recorded to the end of 1992. It has occurred from mid-July to mid-October, but September is the peak month.

Identification This is very much the North American equivalent of the Green Sandpiper *T. ochropus*, but is readily identified in flight by its dark rump and tail, the latter showing thick black and white barring at the sides. On the ground it could be passed off as a Green Sandpiper, but there are a number of differences. It is slimmer and rangier, and rather browner above, while the breast patches are more diffuse with a less clear-cut lower border. The white eye-ring is much better defined and more obvious, emphasizing the large, dark eye. The best feature, however, is the wing length: whereas on the Green the primaries project only just beyond the tail (and are largely cloaked by the tertials), on the Solitary there are at least three visible primaries which project scissor-like beyond it. The calls are thinner and quieter than those of the Green Sandpiper, and some are reminiscent of the Coal Tit *Parus ater*: *to-eet to-eet to-eet* or *sweet-weet*. On the ground, it may give a rather metallic alarm – *pink, pink* – or a shrill *pee-eet*. The morphological differences are shown well in Plate 34.5, a bird present on Fair Isle, Shetland, in September 1992. The

immaculate, neatly patterned upperparts show it to be a juvenile.

TEREK SANDPIPER
Xenus cinereus

Range Small numbers breed in Finland, otherwise it breeds from Russia eastwards across Siberia. It winters from the Gulf of Guinea eastwards around the coasts of Africa to the Arabian Peninsula, the Persian Gulf, southern and Southeast Asia through Indonesia and into Australasia.

Occurrences First recorded in 1951, the Terek Sandpiper has shown a marked increase in records since the early 1970s. It has been virtually annual in recent years, with a peak of four in 1986. There were 47 recorded up to 1996, mostly in the period May–June and mostly in eastern and south-eastern England. Ireland's first was in August 1996. There have also been two notable wintering records: on the Plym Estuary, Devon, in 1973/74; and on the Blyth Estuary, Northumberland, in 1989/90 and again in 1990/91. Its increase here coincides with a spread in Europe. It has bred regularly in Finland since 1957 and, since 1967, it has colonized the Kiev and Kanev Reservoirs, south of its main range in the Ukraine. It also bred in Norway in 1967 (*BWP*).

Identification The Terek is not much bigger than a Common Sandpiper *Actitis hypoleucos*, and bears a superficial resemblance to that species in its overall colour and pattern (particularly its breast patches) and in its habit of bobbing its rear end. There the similarity ends and it is easily identified by its long, gently upcurved bill (with an orange base in winter), its white supercilium (most prominent before the eye and recalling that of the Spotted Redshank *Tringa erythropus*) and its orange legs (sometimes greeny-yellow or even dull red in the breeding season). Plate 35.1 shows a summer plumaged adult on Whalsay, Shetland, in June 1975. The individual in Plates 35.2 & 3 was a wintering bird, photographed at North Blyth, Northumberland, in November 1989, and it shows all these features to good effect. The black line down the edge of the mantle shows that it is still largely in juvenile plumage. This feature is also shown by summer adults. In flight, a narrow but prominent white panel across the secondaries recalls a Common Redshank *T. totanus*. Its character is just as distinctive as its plumage, particularly when it lurches forwards and runs after its prey. Its most familiar call is a rather mournful *whit-whit-whit* or *wee-wee-weep*, vaguely suggesting a cross between a Common Whimbrel *Numenius phaeopus* and a Ruddy Turnstone *Arenaria interpres*.

SPOTTED SANDPIPER
Actitis macularia

Range Breeds across much of northern North America. Winters from the southern United States south through Central America, the West Indies and across the northern two-thirds of South America.

Occurrences The Spotted Sandpiper was formerly considered to be conspecific with the Common Sandpiper *A. hypoleucos*. It wasn't until the publication in 1970 of a paper on its identification in non-breeding plumage (Wallace, 1970) that it began to be identified here with regularity. It is now annual, with an average of four or five a year. Most occur in autumn, particularly in September–October, and there is a small spring peak in May–June. A number have wintered and a few have summered. In 1975 a pair attempted to breed in Scotland but the eggs were abandoned (Wilson, 1976). In 1991 an individual in Yorkshire was associating with a Common Sandpiper and three full-grown young, but it is not known whether hybridization took place (Rogers *et al.*, 1992).

Identification The Spotted Sandpiper is very similar to the Common Sandpiper, particularly in juvenile and winter plumages. In direct comparison, it is slightly smaller and stockier, with rather a squarer head and a flatter back, and it appears pot-bellied. Particularly important is the wing:tail ratio at rest. Whereas the Common Sandpiper has a long tail which usually projects well beyond the wing tips, the Spotted's tail is shorter, extending only just beyond the wing tips or even completely cloaked by them. The first-winter in Plate 35.5 shows all these characteristics, and was photographed at Fen Drayton Gravel Pits, Cambridgeshire, in December 1993. It also shows a number of plumage and bare-part differences: (1) the bill is distinctly two-toned with a dark tip and a dull yellowy base; (2) it has a slightly more pronounced white supercilium and a prominent white eye-ring, giving it a 'sharper' facial expression; (3) the breast patches are small and well defined; (4) it shows a large area of cream and dark barring across the wing coverts (this is more contrasting than on an equivalent-aged Common); and (5) the legs are bright ochre-yellow.

Another vital feature is the pattern of the tertials. In the photograph the tertials from the opposite wing are covering those on the near wing but, when seen properly, the edges of the tertials are plain (with perhaps some slight barring at the tip); on a juvenile/first-winter Common they are noticeably notched with buff. In the field, the Spotted usually appears a greyer shade of brown than the Common. Plate 35.5 shows a fairly classic individual but it

should be noted that some are less obvious than this. A minority have a completely dark bill or show only a pale horn or pale flesh base. Similarly, leg colour varies from grey-green through lime-green, pale grey-yellow and dull horn-yellow to classic yellow.

The above structural differences and many of the bare-part and plumage differences also apply to summer-plumaged adults. The bird in Plate 35.4 was present at Worsborough Reservoir, Yorkshire, in August 1984. As well as the name-giving black underpart spotting, it also shows black mottling across the whole of the upperparts. The pinky-orange bill is particularly striking. Note, however, that the tail is much longer on this individual. Adult Spotted Sandpipers do not complete their moult until arrival in the winter quarters, so vagrant autumn adults retain much of their spotting (although their bare-part coloration may be much duller). The birds' calls are more subdued and less ringing than those of the Common, and they seem to be genuinely less vocal. One wintering bird in Somerset was heard to call only twice during several hours of observation, and that was a quiet *tip*, similar to the call of a Little Stint *Calidris minutus*.

GREY-TAILED TATTLER
Heteroscelus brevipes

Range Breeds mainly along stony riverbeds in the mountains of north-eastern Siberia. The first nest was not discovered until 1959 and its breeding range is still poorly known. It winters in the Malay Peninsula, the Philippines, Indonesia and Australasia (Hayman *et al.*, 1986).

Occurrences The first British record was on the Dyfi Estuary, Merioneth/Cardiganshire, in October–November 1981 (Thorpe, 1995). Unfortunately, news of the bird was suppressed at the instruction of the RSPB reserve warden and only a few local observers saw it. The next was at Burghead, Morayshire, in November–December 1994, and this one was seen by an estimated 2,500 birders (Stenning & Hirst, 1994). It seems almost certain that it eventually taken by a Eurasian Sparrow Hawk *Accipiter nisus*. Assuming that both these birds occurred as a result of reversed migration, then one can postulate that the route would have crossed the high Arctic, quite close to the North Pole.

Identification The Grey-tailed Tattler is a rather dumpy, medium-sized, short-legged wader, slightly smaller than a Common Redshank *Tringa totanus* and with a straight, medium-length bill. It may remind one of a giant Common Sandpiper *Actitis hypoleucos*, an impression reinforced by tail bobbing, strong flicking wingbeats and gliding on bowed wings. In non-breeding plumage it is completely grey across the breast and upperparts, this monotony of coloration being relieved by a strong white fore-supercilium (highlighted by a dark sooty-grey loral line), by ochre-yellow legs and by its long primary projection (equal to the overlying tertial length). In flight, it is completely plain across the wings, rump and tail, and the underwings are also grey, with darker axillaries. Plates 36.1 & 2 show the Burghead bird, photographed in December 1994. The whitish fringes and notches on much of the upperparts show it to be a first-winter.

The Grey-tailed Tattler forms a superspecies with the Wandering Tattler *H. incanus*, the latter breeding in Alaska and north-western Canada. In summer plumage the Wandering is variable, but generally speaking its entire underparts are more heavily and darkly barred except for a small area of white in the centre of the belly. On the Grey-tailed the barring is finer and present only on the breast, flanks and sides of the undertail-coverts. In winter the Wandering is associated with rocky shorelines, whereas the Grey-tailed prefers beaches, estuaries and even inland habitats. Distinguishing the species outside the breeding season requires care and the following is based on Stenning & Hirst (1994), Hirst & Proctor (1995), Thorpe (1995) and Kaufman (1995). (1) The Grey-tailed generally has a whiter supercilium, which fades behind the eye, and also a stronger loral line which fades through the eye as an eye-stripe (the supercilium is narrow on the Wandering, extending from the bill to the eye only, and there is a much stronger white eye-ring); (2) the breast sides on the Grey-tailed are suffused with grey, while on the Wandering this area is darker and extends onto the sides of the lower breast and flanks; (3) the upperparts are slightly paler on the Grey-tailed with a slight dust-brown tinge; and (4) the tail is paler than the upperwings and back on the

Grey-tailed (they are concolorous on the Wandering). The best distinguishing feature is the call. The Grey-tailed's usual call is a plaintive, disyllabic upslurred whistle: *chewee*, *choo-woo* or *too-ee*, which is likened variously to the calls of the Grey Plover *Pluvialis squatarola*, European Golden Plover *P. apricaria* or Semipalmated Plover *Charadrius semipalmatus*. The Wandering typically has a single-pitched *tutututututu-tu*. Kaufman (1995) considered differences in wing length to be unreliable.

WILSON'S PHALAROPE
Phalaropus tricolor

Range Breeds in the temperate middle latitudes of North America, centred mainly on the prairies but also extending east to southern Ontario. It winters in southern South America, mainly on the Argentinian pampas.

Occurrences Although first recorded as recently as 1954, the species has been annual since 1961 and has shown signs of a steady increase during that period, with 262 up to 1995. There were as many as 18 in 1987. Like most American waders, it shows a peak from late August to early October, involving mainly juveniles/first-winters. Small numbers have also been recorded in spring and through the summer, while autumn vagrants have lingered as late as early December. In view of the sexual role reversal shown by this species, it is interesting to note that nearly all those in summer have been females (the opposite of most other spring vagrants). Southern Ireland and south-western England have produced most, but there has been a wide scatter of records and it is thought likely that some have reappeared in successive years.

Wilson's Phalaropes migrate south over western USA the main movement then appearing to head

First-winter Wilson's Phalarope.

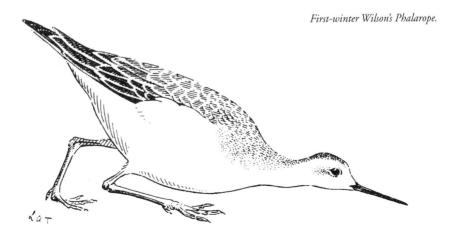

through Mexico and across the eastern Pacific direct to south-west Colombia and Ecuador. From there, the migration moves down the Pacific coast and the Andes before fanning out across southern South America. It is, therefore, uncommon east of the Mississippi and only a straggler to Venezuela and Brazil (*BWP*). In view of its scarcity in the east, why is it so frequent on this side of the Atlantic? It seems that the recent appearance and upsurge correlates with the expansion of a small population in south-eastern Canada, whose movements have not been studied (*BWP*). It may be possible that some of these adopt a more easterly migration route which may render them susceptible to transatlantic vagrancy. Another intriguing possibility is that of reversed migration from the vicinity of the Great Lakes, which could, given a normal south-westerly migration route, put them on a reversed heading that would enable them to reach Europe. The species is, however, a great globe trotter and Hayman *et al.*, (1986) mention records in South Africa, Australia and New Zealand, while one found dead on Alexander Island in Antarctica (immediately south of the southern tip of South America) was the most southerly wader ever recorded.

Identification Most of our vagrants are young birds which have already started to moult out of juvenile plumage. Plate 36.4 shows an individual which was present at Steart, Somerset, in September 1994. Pale-fringed brown upperpart feathering shows it to be a juvenile, but grey first-winter feathers have started to appear on the mantle and scapulars. As the autumn progresses, these feathers will predominate. It has a distinctive capped effect, a whitish supercilium and a brown patch through the eye, which extends as a shadow down the sides of the neck. From any distance, the underparts appear gleaming white. The legs are ochre-yellow, but on some they are greener and on others they are rather orangey. The photograph also shows the bird's characteristic shape, with its needle-fine bill, small head, long neck and rather dumpy body. Plate 36.3 shows an individual which was present on the Hayle Estuary, Cornwall, in August 1990. With its grey upperparts it appears to be a winter adult, but close examination of other photographs appears to show pale-fringed browny wing-coverts and tertials, plus the retention of other juvenile feathers within the mantle and scapulars. It would appear, therefore, that it is a very advanced first-winter, albeit rather worn. The orange on the breast is staining.

Plate 36.5 shows a summer-plumaged female at Porlock Marsh, Somerset, in June 1995. In this plumage it is a stunning bird, with a pale grey crown and nape line, a black band down the neck sides, a beautiful, soft, vinaceous orange wash across the upper breast and deep chestnut patches on the upper-parts. Note also that the legs are black in summer. It usually spends more time on the land than in the water, and it has a distinctive feeding action, leaning forward on flexed legs and picking at the mud from side to side. It will sometimes stalk insects slowly with its head and bill stretched out parallel to the surface, and it will even snap at passing flies. In flight it is plain-winged, its pale grey tail barely contrasting with a square white rump. Vagrants are usually silent, although one individual was heard to give a quiet, whistly *tuu* and a rather quiet croak.

LONG-TAILED SKUA
Stercorarius longicaudus

Range Circumpolar in the Arctic and in sub-Arctic regions. Nearest breeding populations are in Norway. The winter range is poorly known, but is thought to be almost entirely in the southern hemisphere.

Occurrences The Long-tailed is traditionally the rarest of the skuas, but it has shown a significant increase since 1976. During the 1960s there were about 20 a year and it was added to the Rarities List from 1976 to 1979, during which time it averaged about 90 a year. The increase has been due largely to the discovery of a regular spring passage off the Outer Hebrides, although the scale of the passage varies from year to year depending on the prevalent wind direction. There were 1,400 in 1991, 840 in 1992 and 1,350 in 1993, including an astonishing 1,250 past South Uist on 18 May (Evans 1992, 1993a and 1994).

There has also been an increase in autumn, and a clearer understanding of its juvenile plumages is partly responsible for this. As with many Arctic breeders, numbers here fluctuate in relation to the lemming cycle, but the vagaries of the weather also have to be taken into account and, added together, these account for the annual fluctuations. In 1991, as well as the huge spring passage, there was also a massive movement in the autumn following what was obviously a good breeding season. The biggest passage occurred down the British east coast in early September, and the grand total for Britain alone during 1991 was an astonishing 5,324 (Evans, 1993a). During such influxes small numbers appear inland, where they are surprisingly versatile in their choice of food and in their feeding behaviour.

Identification In direct comparison the Long-tailed Skua is about the size of a Black-headed Gull *Larus ridibundus*, but bulkier, more powerful and longer winged. It may even feed with gulls, dropping down to the water's surface to pick up food, and it elicits a far less hostile response than other skuas. It has a continuously flapping flight with little gliding. Plate 37.1 shows a summer plumaged adult inland at Farmoor Reservoir, Oxfordshire, in September 1994. It is, of course, immediately identifiable by its enormously long central tail feathers. Other features of note include its neat black cap, the pale yellow wash to its face and its dark brown belly. In flight, grey-brown wing coverts contrast slightly with the black primaries and secondaries, and the white at the base of the primaries is restricted, being most prominent on the two outer feathers. The dark silvery-grey underwing shows a black border.

Plate 37.2 shows a dark juvenile at King George V Reservoir, London, in September 1990. The identification of juvenile skuas is a complicated subject but this one can be distinguished from an Arctic *S. parasiticus* by the following: (1) a small, slender bill with no gonydeal angle; (2) the basal half of the bill is blue-grey, while the black tip extends back along the cutting edge (the Arctic has only 25–30 per cent black and this is more clear-cut); (3) it has rather a rounded head and this, combined with the small bill, gives it a gentle appearance which is reminiscent of the Common Gull *L. canus*; (4) it has noticeable buff fringes to the upperpart feathers (dark juvenile Arctics do not usually have such obvious edgings); (5) it has plain primaries, lacking the Arctic's pale fringes; (6) there is thick brown and white barring on the undertail-coverts; and (7) it has a whitish area across the lower breast. In flight it should show noticeably protruding but usually blunt central tail feathers, brown and white barring on the rump and uppertail-coverts (forming a whitish horseshoe at the base of the tail), and restricted white bases to the upper-primaries (most prominent on the outer two feathers, but sometimes also on the third and fourth).

LAUGHING GULL
Larus atricilla

Range Breeds from Nova Scotia south along the North American eastern seaboard to the Gulf of Mexico as far as Venezuela and French Guiana, as well as in the West Indies. It moves south to winter from North Carolina to northern South America and on the Pacific coast from southern Mexico to Peru.

Occurrences The Laughing Gull shows very little pattern in its occurrences in Britain and Ireland, the 67 records to 1995 (plus at least eight in 1996) having occurred throughout the year and at a wide scatter of localities, mainly coastal. Unlike the Ring-billed Gull *L. delawarensis*, it fails to show a westerly bias. Sightings have increased markedly since the mid-1970s, mainly due to greater observer awareness.

Identification Plate 38.6 shows a summer plumaged adult at Penzance, Cornwall, in May 1990. It is about the size of a Mediterranean Gull *L. melanocephalus* but with very long primaries. It is easily identified by its jet-black head (with prominent white eye crescents), its dark grey mantle and its black primaries. The bill is heavy like that of a Mediterranean Gull, but it is usually longer; its deep red colour shows it to be in breeding condition (it is reddish-black in winter). It is very worn, particularly across the wing coverts and tertials, and it has lost most of its white primary tips.

Plate 38.4 shows a second-winter at Hull, Yorkshire, in November 1984. At this age and in winter plumage it shows a variable black wedge behind the eye, reminiscent of the Mediterranean Gull, but this is usually fainter, especially when fresh. It is otherwise similar to a winter adult except that it lacks obvious white in the primary tips and shows grey shading on the nape and breast sides. The first-winter in Plate 38.5 was present at Walcott, Norfolk, from December 1991 to January 1992. Perhaps the most distinctive feature is the long, heavy, black bill, and this is emphasised by a heavy black Mediterranean Gull-like wedge behind the eye. Other features to note include the dark grey mantle and scapulars and the long black legs. It is otherwise rather scruffy, with soft greyish mottling on the underparts and heavily abraded wing coverts. Calls include a deep *ger-erk* as well as laughing noises on their breeding grounds.

FRANKLIN'S GULL
Larus pipixcan

Range Breeds in the prairies of North America. Winters mainly on the Pacific coasts of Central and South America from Guatemala to Chile. Small numbers are now known to penetrate the Straits of Magellan and it has also been recorded on the Atlantic coast of Argentina.

Occurrences The species was first recorded in 1970 (two), but since 1977 it has been virtually annual, with a peak of six in 1991. By 1996 it had amassed a total of 31 records. Whilst this upsurge can to some extent be explained by the increase in birdwatching coupled with greater observer awareness, it seems odd that it has occurred against a catastrophic decline in its breeding numbers. Greij (1993) reported that it may well have declined by 90 per cent since the 1960s, and it may now warrant listing as threatened or endangered. At the Salt Plains National Wildlife Refuge in Oklahoma, for example, the breeding population crashed from three million birds in 1950 to 15,000 in 1990. Reasons for the decline are not known, but it correlates with a general decline in North American grassland birds.

The records show a wide scatter, both temporally and geographically. Some have occurred in winter but there is a bigger summer peak, from May to August. The species is rare on the North American eastern seaboard, so direct transatlantic vagrancy seems unlikely to be the main cause of vagrancy, although it seems that a few, mainly immatures, may make a direct Atlantic crossing in autumn and winter. It seems probable that most of our vagrants originate in the Southern Hemisphere, having travelled north up the Atlantic from southern South America. Vagrants recorded in South Africa, the Falklands, Tristan da Cunha, Senegal and the Gambia tie in neatly with this theory. They reach northern Europe from mid-spring onwards when there is a larger proportion of records from Scandinavia and Continental Europe than for other Nearctic gulls. These birds head south again from late summer onwards, explaining the passage records in Britain at this time (see Hoogendoorn & Steinhaus, 1990, for a fuller discussion). All except one of our birds have been first-summer or older, supporting the view that the initial vagrancy takes place when older birds are returning from their winter quarters, rather than from inexperienced first-years going astray on their first journey south.

Identification Franklin's Gull is similar to the Laughing Gull *L. atricilla* but can be distinguished by its size and structure: it is slightly smaller than a Black-headed Gull *L. ridibundus*, with a squat, dumpy body, short legs and a shorter, stubbier bill. The adult is dark grey above (slightly paler than the *graellsii* race of the Lesser Black-backed Gull *L. fuscus*) and it shows large white spots in the closed primaries. In flight it has prominent white tips to the primaries and a band of white separating the grey primary bases from the black subterminal tips (some have very little black). In summer plumage it has a jet-black hood and prominent white eye crescents. Plate 38.1 shows such a bird at Skellister, Shetland, in May 1991. In winter the eye crescents remain, but it then retains a distinctive 'half-hood' over the rear crown.

Plate 38.3 shows what is almost certainly a second-winter at Helston, Cornwall, in March 1987 (there is much individual variation in second-years and adults). It is similar to a classic adult but shows only small white tips to the primaries. It should be noted that some second-years show virtually no white in the primaries and are much more similar to equivalent aged Laughing Gulls (Lehman, 1994). Plate 38.2 shows the only first-winter ever to be recorded in Britain, photographed in Plymouth, Devon, in

February 1982. It resembles a first-winter Laughing Gull but again shows the smaller bill, the black half-hood and the prominent white eye crescents, as well as clean white underparts, and a thicker white trailing edge to the wing. It has a narrower black tail band (with white outer tail feathers), and it lacks any grey across the base of the tail. Franklin's Gull is unique in that it has two complete moults a year, so that a first-summer is appreciably more adult-like than a first-winter (Grant, 1986).

SABINE'S GULL
Larus sabini

Range Has a fragmented but circumpolar breeding range in subarctic regions and the high Arctic. It winters off the Pacific coast of South America and in the South Atlantic off southern Africa.

Occurrences Sabine's Gull is an annual migrant whose numbers depend to a large extent on the incidence of westerly gales in September. Dymond *et al.* (1989) noted 1,869 from 1958 to 1985, or an average of 110 a year. The peak is from late August to mid-October and, although south-western Ireland and Cornwall have proved to be the best areas, they have occurred all around the coast and even inland, where they are surprisingly versatile in their feeding techniques. There have been two particularly large influxes in recent years. A severe gale on the night of 2–3 September 1983 produced a large movement of adults, including over 100 at St Ives, Cornwall, while the infamous 'hurricane' of 15–16 October 1987 produced about 250, of which about 100 were seen inland, mostly in south-eastern England (Hume & Christie, 1989). The unusual track of this depression swept the birds in from the Bay of Biscay. A tiny spring passage occurs in April and May.

Although Sabine's Gulls breed in Spitsbergen, the numbers there are small. Our visitors originate in Greenland and Canada, passing across the North Atlantic towards Iberia and Morocco before turning south into the Canary current (*BWP*). The orientation of this movement explains why occurrences are rarer in the north, particularly in Scotland. Siberian and Alaskan breeders winter in the Pacific.

Identification Although distant birds on seawatches are often misidentified immature Black-legged Kittiwakes *Rissa tridactyla*, Sabine's Gulls are easily identified if seen well. Most are juveniles, such as the bird in Plate 37.4, which was photographed at Ballycotton, Co. Cork, in September 1985. At rest it is grey-brown on the crown, nape and breast sides, as well as across the back, scapulars and wing coverts, the whole area being immaculately scalloped with dark subterminal and pale terminal feather fringes. Plate 37.3 shows a winter plumaged adult which was present at the Queen Mother Reservoir, Berkshire, in October 1987. A yellow tip to the bill is readily apparent, as is the grey, white and black wing patterning. In winter, the black is confined to the nape and this individual has worn away all the small white tips to the primary feathers. Plate 37.5 shows a first-summer in flight at Heysham, Lancashire, in September 1988. It shows the distinctive black, white and grey triangles across the open wing, as well as the forked tail, although the latter can be impossible to make out in the field. The bird in Plate 37.6 is a first-winter, photographed at Goldcliff Pill, Monmouthshire, in April 1994. This plumage is unusual in the northern hemisphere as most first-winters stay behind in their winter quarters. It has lost its juvenile body plumage but retains the brown wing feathers, which are heavily worn (it had just started to moult its inner primaries). The head is largely white, although it shows a brown spot behind the eye and brown mottling on the nape and rear crown, and it has replaced its mantle and scapulars with grey first-winter plumage. In overall appearance, it is reminiscent of a giant first-winter Grey Phalarope *Phalaropus fulicarius*, its short legs giving it a rather similar gait.

BONAPARTE'S GULL
Larus philadelphia

Range Breeds in the North American taiga across Alaska and Canada east to James Bay. It winters on the Great Lakes and coastal USA, south to northern Mexico and the West Indies.

Occurrences As with other Nearctic gulls, Bonaparte's Gull has a wide scatter of records, although in recent years most have occurred in Devon and Cornwall in late winter and spring. By 1995 there had been 87, with a peak of at least 11 in 1990. It seems that small numbers cross the Atlantic in late winter in response to severe weather in North America or simply because they are swept across in fast-moving depressions. It also seems likely that some of our spring birds have wintered further south and have subsequently moved north up the Western European coast (*see also* Ring-billed Gull on page 84). Once here, they may take up residence on this side of the Atlantic, and some of the records have undoubtedly related to individuals returning in subsequent winters.

Identification This species is similar to the Black-headed Gull *L. ridibundus*, but it is smaller (although not always obviously so) and is rounder headed, shorter necked and shorter legged, with a stiff walk. At all ages Bonaparte's shows a slim black bill, tends to be slightly darker above and has noticeably pale pink or orange legs, while winter adults and immatures usually show a well-defined black spot behind the eye. Most of these features are readily apparent in the winter-plumaged adult in Plate 39.1, which also shows characteristic grey shading on the nape and the sides of the neck. It was photographed in Bangor, Co. Down, in February 1980. The first-winters in Plates 39.2 & 4 were present at Radipole Lake, Dorset, in April 1981 and at Marazion Marsh, Cornwall, in March 1990. Both have blacker lesser coverts and tertials than a first-year Black-headed Gull and, in the flight shot (Plate 39.4), the Radipole bird shows a clear-cut black trailing edge to the wing and more extensive black on the leading primaries (resulting in a smaller white primary wedge). The underwing pattern is diagnostic: white with a clear-cut black trailing edge to the primaries. This can just be seen in Plate 39.3, an adult photographed at Seaforth Docks in April 1990.

SLENDER-BILLED GULL
Larus genei

Range Has a disjunctive breeding range extending from Senegal and the Banc d'Arguin in Mauritania to Spain and the south of France, east through the Mediterranean to Turkey, the Black and Caspian Seas, Iraq, Turkestan and Pakistan. Movements are not fully understood, but there is a southward dispersal to the eastern Mediterranean, the Red Sea and the Persian Gulf, east as far as western India.

Occurrences There are just four records: first-summers at Langley Point, Sussex, in June–July 1960 (Harber, 1982) and at Rye Harbour, Sussex, in April 1963; an adult at Dungeness, Kent, in July–September 1971 (also seen at Minsmere, Suffolk, in August; Redshaw, 1972); and, most remarkable of all, a pair at Cley, Norfolk, in May 1987. Whether our vagrants originated from the west or from the east of the range is impossible to know, but the latest record correlated with a significant population increase in the western Mediterranean. In the Camargue, regular breeding began in the early 1970s, with 15–25 pairs from 1970 to 1976, but it increased to 70 pairs in 1986, over 250 in 1988 and 850 in 1995 (*Brit. Birds* **82**: 19; **89**: 35). A similar increase has taken place in the Ebro Delta in Spain, where there were 429 pairs in 1988, the species having first bred in 1975 (*Brit. Birds* **82**: 327). Another increase has been noted in Italy, where there were 32 nests in 1988 and 350 pairs in 1994 (*Brit. Birds* **83**: 12; **89**: 35). In view of this increase and several other extralimital Continental records in recent years, it seems likely that we can look forward to further appearances.

Identification Plate 39.5 shows the pair at Cley. The one threatening the Black-headed Gull *L. ridibundus* is undoubtedly a male by its size, but note that both sexes are slightly larger than the Black-headed. Both show a long, rather thick red bill and a long gape line which produces a grinning effect. Most obvious, however, is the angular pure white head, with a sloping forehead. The eye is pale and at a distance this produces the beady-eyed effect which is apparent in the photograph. The male clearly shows a long, thick neck. The female shows squared-off tertials and a primary projection which is distinctly shorter than that of a Black-headed Gull. When seen out of the water, the legs are long and, in direct comparison, they are noticeably taller than the Black-headed. In breeding condition the bill becomes virtually black. Outside the breeding season the adult acquires a small grey smudge behind the eye, and the bill and the legs become more orangey (on first-years the bill and legs are usually pale orange, the bill often variably darker at the tip). Their brown immature feathering is noticeably paler and more washed out than on the Black-headed, and even first-years show a pale eye. If seen well, the Slender-billed Gull is easily distinguished from the Black-headed Gull, but finders should always bear in mind the possibility of an escaped Silver Gull *L. novaehollandiae* from Australia. The latter species can easily be distinguished in flight by the extensive area of black in its primary tips.

RING-BILLED GULL
Larus delawarensis

Range Breeds in two populations in North America: one based on the prairies and the other based on the Great Lakes and east up the St Lawrence to Labrador and Newfoundland. It winters mainly on the Great Lakes and in the coastal states of the USA, south to Mexico.

Occurrences The story of the appearance and increase of the Ring-billed Gull in Britain and Ireland is well known. The first was an adult discovered at Blackpill, Glamorgan, in March 1973 (Hume, 1973). Blackpill was to maintain a monopoly for three years, by which time 11 had been recorded. The species averaged only five a year, however, until 1981 when there were 55. Even allowing for greater observer awareness and a better understanding of its identification criteria, there can be no doubt that this influx was genuine and it is thought likely to have been caused by an exceptionally cold winter along the eastern seaboard of North America. Since then, the species has continued to be recorded annually in large numbers (often around the 100 mark) and it was removed from the Rarities List at the end of 1982

having become our most numerous North American visitor.

The numbers recorded here fluctuate annually and some years produce larger influxes than others. It seems likely that these depend largely on winter weather in North America combined with the prevalence of westerly gales. Most new arrivals seem to cross the Atlantic in mid- to late winter, but the peak time of occurrence in Britain and Ireland is actually in March and April when there is a regular spring passage through western areas (Vinicombe, 1985). This is thought to involve individuals which have wintered further south (the species has been recorded as far south as Morocco). Where these spring migrants are heading has been the subject of debate. It has been suggested that they could be breeding in northern Scotland or Iceland, but the remarkable recovery a Norwegian-ringed bird *back* in north-eastern Canada would seem to suggest that at least some are actually commuting across the North Atlantic.

Identification The Ring-billed Gull is similar in size to a Common Gull *L. canus* but is usually slightly larger and bulkier, and often looks flatter backed and sleeker, particularly when on the water. Despite statements to the contrary, it often looks round-headed, a fact confirmed by Plate 40.2. The bill is thicker and more 'parallel' looking, often appearing blunter tipped (an effect exaggerated by the bill band). In flight, the wings look longer and, usually, more pointed. Plate 40.1 shows a summer plumaged adult at Rhyl, Flintshire, in March 1994. Adults are most easily located by a combination of the paler mantle (similar in shade to that of the Black-headed Gull *L. ridibundus*) and the squared-off tertials, these showing narrower and less contrasting white tips than on the Common Gull. Closer views reveal that the bill is crossed with a thick black band, and it has pale irides (these produce a beady-eyed look at a distance). As this bird is approaching breeding condition, the bare parts have become yellow and the eye-ring has turned from black to red. In winter it shows pale grey streaking and spotting on the head. In flight, the pattern is distinctly reminiscent of a small Herring Gull *L. argentatus*, with only small white mirrors in the wing tips and very white underwings.

Plate 40.2 shows a second-winter at Copperhouse Creek, Hayle, Cornwall, in August 1987. It is similar to an adult but it still shows a pink-based bill (the acquisition of adult bare-part colours is variable and second-winters usually show a greenish bill base and legs). Other signs of immaturity are the dark eye and the small dark spots on the tertials. Many second-years also show remnants of black in the tail. Note that this bird has not yet finished growing its primaries, hence the truncated rear end.

Plate 40.3 shows a first-winter at Copperhouse Creek in February 1989. Again, it resembles a similarly aged Common Gull, but this particular bird is not very advanced, showing heavy dark streaking and scalloping over much of its body. The very pink bare parts are typical of a first-year, and even at this age it shows a black bill ring (as opposed to a black tip); the bill suggests that of a second-winter Glaucous Gull *L. hyperboreus*. Other differences from a first-winter Common include the following: (1) the back and scapulars are paler, with brown scalloping; (2) the brown centres to many of the wing coverts are pointed (rounded on the Common); (3) the greater coverts show brown subterminal markings (plainer on the Common); and (4) the tertials are darker, with only very narrow fringes. In flight, the tail would show variable dark shading at the base.

KUMLIEN'S GULL
Larus glaucoides kumlieni

Range Despite its name, the nominate race of Iceland Gull breeds in Greenland and is a scarce but regular winter visitor. Across the Davis Strait on Baffin Island and in north-eastern Quebec is the race *kumlieni*, or 'Kumlien's Gull', which winters mainly from Labrador to New England, with small numbers on the Great Lakes, along the St Lawrence River and in Hudson Bay. Further west again is the race *thayeri*, or 'Thayer's Gull' which breeds west to Banks Island and winters mainly down the North American western seaboard.

Occurrences Although the first Kumlien's Gull was recorded as long ago as 1869, only in recent years has it been identified regularly, accumulating at least 41 records up to 1995. Most have occurred in northern and western localities. It seems probable that it is a fairly regular winter visitor in small and variable numbers. The taxonomy of the Iceland Gull group has long been the subject of debate, but it is currently accepted (at least in Britain) that there is a cline between the white-winged nominate *glaucoides* in the east, through *kumlieni* to *thayeri* in the west. The Thayer's is much more similar to a Herring Gull *L. argentatus*, with black in the primary tips. It is difficult if not impossible to separate the darkest *kumlieni* from the palest *thayeri,* and the two forms apparently intergrade, some colonies containing both dark-winged and paler-winged individuals. There have been at least three records in Ireland of dark first-years which have been close to *thayeri*: in Galway in March 1989 and January 1991; and in the Cork area in February–March 1990. A dark individual, resembling an intergrade, was photographed in Ayr Harbour, Ayrshire, in February 1991 (Hogg, 1991).

Identification When faced with one of these races, the first step is to establish that the bird is an Iceland Gull and not a Herring Gull. Structural differences are, therefore, especially important, particularly the small bill and rounded head (which combine to produce a 'gentle' impression), the stocky body, the rather short legs and the long primaries which project well beyond the tail. Note, however, that some *kumlieni*, are longer billed than *glaucoides*. In adults, the presence of a red eye-ring should also be established (yellow or orange-yellow on the Herring). The bird in Plate 40.4 shows all these features, and is an adult Kumlien's photographed at Banff, Banffshire, in March 1991. It wintered in the area from March 1985 to at least February 1995. What distinguishes it from the nominate *glaucoides* is the presence of grey subterminal markings on the primaries. Plate 40.5 shows this to better effect on an adult in flight at Lerwick, Shetland, in February 1983. Plate 40.6 shows another winter adult at Lerwick in April 1995.

Plate 40.7 shows the first-winter at Galway in March 1989. Again the typical Iceland Gull shape is readily apparent, but it differs from the nominate in having brown primaries which are noticeably fringed with cream at the tip. In flight it showed a brown secondary bar and a solidly brown tail band (Kilbane 1989) which are pro-*thayeri* features. In distinguishing it from a pale *argentatus* Herring Gull and *thayeri*, an additional point to note is its pale tertials (concolorous with the wing coverts and paler than the primaries). This bird is perhaps most likely a dark *kumlieni* or a *kumlieni/thayeri* intergrade (Tom Ennis, verbally; *see* Zimmer, 1991, for a more detailed discussion).

ROSS'S GULL
Rhodostethia rosea

Range Breeds in north-eastern Siberia, northern and western Greenland and also in northern Canada, the most famous site being at Churchill, Manitoba. It disperses around the edge of the Arctic ice-cap in winter.

Occurrences Although formerly a great rarity, Ross's Gull has been virtually annual since 1974. By the end of 1995, it had amassed a total of 73 records, with at least eight in 1993. As befitting an Arctic vagrant, it has traditionally been a bird of the Northern Isles, eastern Scotland and north-eastern England, but in recent years there has been a marked tendency for individuals to appear more frequently in western areas. This has led to speculation that we are now receiving vagrants from the new world as well as from the old, perhaps explaining the recent upsurge. Late winter is the peak time but they have been seen in all months; one remarkable occurrence involved a widely appreciated first-summer at Christchurch Harbour, Dorset, in June–August 1974.

Identification Plate 41.1 clearly illustrates why Ross's Gull is so highly sought after, on both sides of the Atlantic. It is only slightly larger than a Little Gull *Larus minutus*, but has a cigar-shaped body, longer, more pointed wings and a longer, wedge-shaped tail. The underwings are dark grey, and the back-lit photograph shows to good advantage the thick white trailing edge, which is confined to the secondaries and inner primaries (not extending around the wing tip as it does on an adult Little Gull). In summer plumage the narrow black neck ring and the pink flush to the breast add the polishing touches to what can only be described as a stunningly beautiful gull. This summer-plumaged adult was present at Cley and Titchwell, Norfolk, in May 1984. Another summer adult, photographed at Greatham, Co. Durham, in June 1995, is less pink (Plate 41.3). Note its very long primaries. Plate 41.2 shows a winter adult at Scalloway, Shetland, in January 1975. In winter it lacks the black neck ring but instead shows a black smudge around the eye and a black spot behind it. This photograph again shows the white trailing edge to the wing, as well as an inconspicuous narrow black line down the outer primary. The tail has lost one or two feathers and it appears shorter and less wedge-shaped than that of the summer adult in Plate 41.1. Plate 41.4 shows another at Fraserburgh, Aberdeenshire, in January 1993.

Plate 41.5 shows a second-winter/second-summer at Drimsdale, South Uist, Outer Hebrides, in May 1994. At rest, it shows a characteristic rounded head, a short bill and attenuated primaries; when standing, its legs are quite short, producing a dove-like walk. Although adult-like, it is peculiarly white-headed, with only a trace of black on the rear neck, and it shows a faint brown bar across the wing coverts, a feature not shown by an equivalent-aged Little Gull. Second-years appear to be rather whiter than adults, particularly on the underwings. Plate 41.6 shows a first-summer at Workington, Cumberland, in June 1994. It shows the diagnostic black summer neck ring but the rest of the plumage resembles that of a first-year Black-legged Kittiwake *Rissa tridactyla*. In flight, this manifests itself as a black 'W' across the upperwings. The underwings are pure white (with black primary tips) and the black band on the tail is restricted to the central feathers (sometimes confined to the projecting central four). Its long wings produce a leisurely, buoyant flight, although direct flight is fast and pigeon-like, with rather deep wingbeats (Grant 1986).

IVORY GULL
Pagophila eburnea

Range Circumpolar in the high Arctic, breeding mainly between 70° and 83° north. It usually remains close to the pack ice all year and ranges further north than any other bird (Haney, 1993).

Occurrences The Ivory Gull remains a rare and highly sought after vagrant, most frequent in winter in the far north, particularly in Shetland. Only 40 were recorded between 1958 and 1995 and, although there were many old reports prior to this, Evans (1994) considered that most would not stand up to modern scrutiny. Occurrences in the south are especially rare, and a first-winter at Chesil Cove, Portland, Dorset, in January–February 1980, was particularly memorable.

Identification The Ivory Gull is slightly larger than a Common Gull *Larus canus* but bulkier. On the ground, noticeably short legs produce a pigeon-like gait. Superficially, it is easily identified but adults can be confused with albino gulls, particularly Black-legged Kittiwake *Rissa tridactyla* which shares a similar combination of a yellowish bill and black legs. When identifying an adult, sensible evaluation of size and structural differences are important, as is close scrutiny of the bill, which should be greyish or grey-green with a variable yellow or yellow and orange tip. Even a first-winter may look all-white at a distance, but at closer range, it is easily distinguished by the black spotting on the wings, the narrow black tail band and the scruffy greyish face. The first-winter in Plate 42.1 was present at Saltburn, Yorkshire, in January–February 1986 and Plate 42.2 shows another at Lerwick, Shetland, in December 1993. In flight it has broad-based, tapering wings and slow, easy wingbeats. It is notably aggressive for its size and can even hold its own against the much larger Glaucous Gull *L. hyperboreus* (loc. cit).

GULL-BILLED TERN
Sterna nilotica

Range Has a fragmented breeding distribution which includes the southern USA, Central America, the West Indies, parts of South America and, in the old world, from the Mediterranean east through Asia into China. It winters in the tropics, eastern birds reaching Australia. The nearest breeding colonies are in Denmark, the Camargue in France, and in Spain.

Occurrences Any attempt at analysing the status of this species is fraught with difficulties. In the 1960s, individuals were regularly reported on seawatches in south-east England, and it was assumed that the birds involved were heading towards Denmark, where there were over 100 pairs, numbers having declined there from about 650 at the turn of the century. That it was then more numerous is reflected by the fact that a pair bred at Abberton Reservoir, Essex, in 1950, having failed the previous year. Ringing recoveries indicated that, in autumn, about 75 per cent of the Danish birds headed south-west towards Iberia, and several recoveries along the English Channel and Bay of Biscay coasts showed that the species did use this route (*BWP*).

In recent years, the Danish population has collapsed (to an estimated 30 pairs in 1979; *BWP*). Despite this, the number of British and Irish claims have only recently shown signs of a decrease. It is likely that this is related to a better understanding of the species' field characteristics, coupled with a tightening of standards by the Rarities Committee. A closer analysis of the records shows some interesting facts: of the 50 recorded between 1973 and 1982, only two stayed more than one day (including a well-watched 1980 individual at Titchwell, Norfolk). Many of the accepted records were one-observer fly-bys seen on seawatches. In hindsight, there can be little doubt that many of these were misidentified and, even at the time, up to 44 per cent were being rejected. In the ten years from 1983 to 1992 there were 27 records, of which six were present for more than one day. All six were in western areas (with two in Ireland), perhaps suggesting a Spanish rather than a Danish origin. The longer-staying individuals have tended to occur on marshes, estuaries and even in ploughed fields, habitats in which they occur abroad.

Identification The summer-plumaged adult in Plate 42.3 was at Penrice, Glamorgan, in July 1993. Plates 42.4 & 5 show another at Llanelli, Carmarthenshire, in July 1996. A faint trace of a secondary bar and less than immaculate wing coverts may suggest that it was in fact a second-summer. The bird is a large, rather gull-like tern with a thick, black, gull-like bill, a rounded head and a thick neck. Long, broad-based wings produce a languid flight action. Notable plumage features include the neat black cap and a thick black trailing edge to the primaries, visible on both surfaces. Some individuals show older and darker outer primaries, but the upperwing is usually plainer than that of the Sandwich Tern *S. sandvicensis*. Most distinctive are the pale grey rump and tail, which are concolorous with the rest of the upperparts. Unlike other terns, moulting adults show a cap which is peppered black and white. In winter and juvenile plumages they show a variable blackish patch behind the eye. Unlike Sandwich Terns, they usually feed over marshes and mudflats, usually picking food from the surface in a sinuous dive. The aforementioned Titchwell bird developed a taste for Little Tern *S. albifrons* chicks! The adult's distinctive call, a low *ger-erk*, may initially attract attention.

CASPIAN TERN
Sterna caspia

Range Has a fragmented breeding range which covers much of Eurasia, Africa, Australasia and North America. The nearest breeding colonies to Britain and Ireland are in the Baltic, where it increased markedly in the second half of the 20th century, although it has recently decreased again in Finland and Sweden (*Brit. Birds* 78: 642; **89**: 36). Baltic breeders winter mainly in West Africa, with some in the Mediterranean.

Occurrences Records occur from the end of March to mid-October, mainly involving dispersing individuals in July and early August. As to be expected, most have been seen in eastern England. There were as many as 20 in 1988, but with such a large, conspicuous bird, there is inevitably a great degree of duplication with wandering individuals. There have been three recoveries of foreign-ringed Caspian Terns in Britain: a Swedish one to Shetland; a Finnish one to Cambridgeshire; and, remarkably, one ringed in Michigan, USA, in July 1927, which was found dead in Yorkshire in August 1939 (Dymond *et al.* 1989).

Identification This, the world's largest tern, is almost the size of a Herring Gull *Larus argentatus* and, as such, it is not difficult to identify. The only real possibility of confusion is with the Royal Tern *S. maxima*, an extremely rare vagrant to Britain and Ireland. The bird in Plate 43.2 was present at Minsmere, Suffolk, in June 1996, and it shows the main identification features which separate it from the smaller Royal Tern: the large red bill and the extensively blackish under-primaries. Plate 43.1 shows a moulting adult with a young bird, already in first-winter plumage, at Ferrybridge, Dorset, in September 1991. The adult's call is a gruff *kraah*, more reminiscent of a Grey Heron *Ardea cinerea* than a tern, and this is a further distinction from the Royal, which has a deep, rolling *ker-r-r-erk*. Juveniles have a pathetic high-pitched, squeaky *wee-ooo* as well as a guttural *wit-ee-oo*.

LESSER CRESTED TERN
Sterna bengalensis

Range Breeds on islands off the coast of Libya, in the Red Sea and the Persian Gulf, and in New Guinea and northern Australia. Libyan breeders disperse through the Straits of Gibraltar to winter in West Africa. Other populations disperse around the coasts of the Indian Ocean, from south-eastern Africa to the Pacific east coast of Australia. It forms a superspecies with the Sandwich Tern *S. sandvicensis*, and probably also with the Elegant Tern *S. elegans* and Chinese Crested Tern *S. bernsteini*.

Occurrences The species was first recorded in 1982 when an individual was seen at Cymyran Bay, Anglesey, on 13 July (Hurford, 1989). Since then it has been annual, due to the recurrence of a single individual which has been seen at many localities between Sussex and Midlothian, but which was pinned down to a Sandwich Tern colony in the Farne Islands, Northumberland, in 1984. This is a female which has been affectionately christened 'Elsie' (from LC for Lesser Crested). It has paired with male Sandwich Terns and fledged hybrid young in at least three years up to 1996 (1989, 1992 and 1996). It is even conceivable that the original Anglesey individual also related to Elsie and the only record not attributable to her (because of an overlap in dates) was at Dawlish Warren, Devon, on 17–20 July 1985 (another was seen in the Isles of Scilly and Co. Cork in August 1996).

Our birds undoubtedly originate from two colonies off the coast of Libya which, remarkably, were rediscovered in July 1993, having been last visited in 1937 (Meininger *et al.* 1994). One colony held 40 pairs, the other 1,700. It seems probable that our vagrants became caught up with Sandwich Terns in their West African winter quarters and that the Farnes bird has obviously been unable to break the attachment. There have been other cases of Lesser Crested Terns hybridizing with Sandwich Terns in various parts of the Mediterranean (loc. cit.). Although at the moment very much taken for granted, it seems likely that the Lesser Crested Tern will revert to its former gross rarity status once Elsie eventually disappears.

Identification Plate 43.4 shows the Farne bird on her nest in May 1990. She is similar to a Sandwich Tern, but is slightly larger and a slightly darker shade of grey. The obvious difference is, of course, the bright orange bill, which appears slightly deeper based. Plate 43.3 shows what was presumably the same bird, moulting into winter plumage, at Blakeney Point, Norfolk, in August 1983. Not visible in the photograph are the grey rump and tail, an obvious difference from the Sandwich Tern in flight. In the field, the tips of the under primaries appear to be darker and broader than on the Sandwich, more similar to those of the Common Tern *S. hirundo*.

ELEGANT TERN
Sterna elegans

Range Breeds in southern California and on the west coast of Mexico. It winters along the Pacific coast of South America, south to Chile (Harrison, 1983).

Occurrence An adult was present in a colony of Sandwich Terns *S. sandvicensis* at Greencastle, Co. Down, from 22 June to 3 July 1982 (Plates 44.1 & 2),

reappearing at Ballymacoda, Co. Cork, on 1 August. On the face of it, this record represents one of the most astonishing additions to the British and Irish List. It is not totally without precedence, however, as one was present in a Sandwich Tern colony at Arcachon, on the Banc d'Arguin, Gironde, south-western France, from 1974 to at least 1987, with a second in 1984 (Lewington *et al.* 1991), and one was seen 190 miles (300 km) north in Loire Atlantique on 22 August 1991 (*Brit. Birds* **85**: 453).

Exactly how a tern from the Pacific coasts of California and Mexico makes it to Western Europe is a complete mystery. The species has occurred in Texas, so it is presumably capable of crossing the Central American isthmus, but to imagine such a bird subsequently being swept across the Atlantic to the old world would stretch credibility. A more likely explanation is that the birds concerned had headed too far south down the west coast of South America, rounded Cape Horn and then moved north up the wrong ocean in a subsequent spring, eventually tagging onto northward-moving Sandwich Terns.

Identification The Elegant Tern is similar in size to the Sandwich and Lesser Crested Terns *S. bengalensis*, and is superficially very similar to the latter. The following differences are based on Dubois (1991): (1) the bill is noticeably longer, apparently rather slimmer and it also appears more decurved or 'sabre-shaped'; (2) in breeding condition, the colour of the bill is a redder shade of orange, particularly towards the base; (3) the rump and tail are white (grey on the Lesser Crested); and (4) it is paler, being fractionally darker than the Sandwich. The Greencastle bird also showed a rosy flush to the underparts, while traces of a dark secondary bar suggested that it may in fact have been a second-summer. The bill was deep vermillion at the base, becoming orange then pale yellow at the tip. The base itself was quite deep (Tom Ennis, *in litt.*). In non-breeding plumage, the black on the head of the Elegant includes the eye, whereas on the Lesser Crested there is a narrow white crescent behind the eye, making the eye more distinct. Its call resembles that of the Sandwich, but is softer and less rasping. *BWP* describes the Lesser Crested's call as similar to that of the Sandwich but 'more scratchy and less ringing in tone'.

ALEUTIAN TERN
Sterna aleutica

Range Breeds on the coasts of Alaska, on some of the Aleutian Islands, and in north-eastern Siberia, Kamchatka and Sakhalin. It is not a numerous species, and Dixey *et al.* (1981) quoted an estimate of 10,000 birds in Alaska. Outside the breeding season, its movements are largely a mystery. The only records away from the breeding grounds were in Japan (about ten, with breeding suspected in 1980) and in the Philippines. To date, it has never been reported from North America south of the Gulf of Alaska or in the central Pacific. In August and September 1992, however, about 190 were discovered south-west of Hong Kong, and it is thought likely that they move south rapidly after breeding to feeding areas somewhere in the western Pacific. After moulting, they probably then continue south to unknown wintering grounds (Kennerley *et al.*, 1993).

Occurrence The sole Western Palearctic record concerns a summer-plumaged adult seen on Inner Farne in the Farne Islands, Northumberland, on 28–29 May 1979 (Dixey *et al.*, 1981; Plates 44.3 & 4). Its appearance was greeted with total astonishment. The most obvious explanation for its arrival is that Aleutian Terns winter much further south than is generally supposed, and that the Farne bird headed north in the wrong ocean, possibly in the company of Arctic Terns *S. paradisaea*, a species with which it nests. There is, however, another very plausible suggestion. If, as suggested by Kennerley *et al.*, they head south-west towards Hong Kong and the Philippines after breeding, then a reversed migrant, travelling at 180° to that route, would travel across the islands of northern Canada and into the North Atlantic (*see* pages 24–25). The distance involved is no greater than a flight from the Aleutians to the Philippines. Once in the Atlantic, it could head south for the winter and return north again in spring, tagging onto other northward-moving terns. The Farne individual's appearance here is not, therefore, as improbable as is so generally supposed.

Identification The following is based on Dixey *et al.* (1981) and Kennerley *et al.* (1993). The Aleutian Tern is slightly larger and longer winged than an Arctic Tern, but with a similarly deeply forked tail. In summer plumage, it is darker, being pale slate-grey above and a gentle shade of grey below. It has a white forehead (recalling the Bridled Tern *S. anaethetus*), a black bill and legs and, unlike the Bridled, a white rump and tail. In flight, the underwing shows a distinctive dark line along the tips of the outer primaries and on the secondaries, while on the upperwing there is a white leading edge to the forewing. Photographs of the Farne bird (Plates 44.3 & 4) show most of the above features, as well as a rather translucent area on the inner primaries. The flight action differs from the Common *S. hirundo* and Arctic in that it has slow wingbeats with the emphasis very much on the downstroke. The Farne bird was very vocal, giving a soft, far-carrying, polysyllabic, staccato wader-like whistle. Those in Hong Kong gave a wader-like *chit* similar to the call of a Red-necked Phalarope *Phalaropus lobatus*.

FORSTER'S TERN
Sterna forsteri

Range Breeds in the North American interior, mainly on the prairies, and also on the east and Gulf coasts from New Jersey to northern Mexico. It winters coastally from California to Guatemala and from Virginia to Mexico.

Occurrences The first Western Palearctic record was made in Iceland in 1959, but our first was 21 years later: a first-winter in Falmouth Bay, Cornwall, in January–March 1980 (Cave 1982). Remarkably, the species has been annual since 1982 and had amassed a total of 25 records by 1995, mainly wintering birds on the coasts of the Irish Sea. Some appear to have returned in successive winters, so it is difficult to be certain of the exact number involved. Forster's Tern winters relatively far north in America, not penetrating as far as South America, so the winter records here are not as surprising as they may at first appear. It has apparently increased and spread in recent years on the North American eastern seaboard, so its regular appearance on this side of the Atlantic is not simply a result of greater observer awareness.

Identification Plate 44.6 shows a winter adult at Abergele, Denbighshire, in October 1986. Plate 44.5 shows a first-winter in flight at Musselburgh, Midlothian, in March 1995 and Plate 44.7 shows another first-winter at Ferrybridge, Dorset, in January 1996. It is structurally similar to the Common Tern *S. hirundo* but slightly larger with a sturdier-looking head and neck. The bill is similar in length to that of a Common but is quite deep-based. Most records have related either to winter-plumaged adults or to first-years, both of which are readily identified by a prominent large black wedge through the eye. Unlike the Common Tern, this wedge does not continue around the nape, but dark bases to the rear crown feathers may produce a greyish area connecting the ear-covert patches, this intensifying with wear. Adults are pale grey across the upperparts, becoming a paler whitish-grey across the primaries. When fresh, they can look very white at any distance. Dark tips to the under primaries produce a trailing edge similar to that of the Common Tern (sometimes less distinct when worn). Prior to their late-summer moult, adults show old dark outer primaries which strongly contrast with the rest of the wings. In non-breeding plumages, the bill is black (orangey with a large black tip in summer adults). The legs are usually bright red or orange (recalling the Atlantic Puffin *Fratercula arctica*!), but on some they are a dull reddish-black.

The first-winter is similar to an adult, but has a shorter tail which is greyish with white outer feathers and shows small dark tips to the inners, best seen from below. The upperwing is similar to that of a winter adult but, by spring, the outer primaries wear darker, contrasting with the whiter primary coverts and inner primaries. The tertials are brown centred. The legs vary from dull orange to bright 'puffin-orange'. Note that, unlike juvenile, first-year and winter adult Common Terns, it does not show a prominent dark carpal bar. Adults' calls are a low, abrupt *kreer-er*, *kyur* and *kyip*, less rasping, drier and softer than those of the Common. They also make an abrupt *kip* or *chik*, again rather softer than the Common's call, as well as a deep, buzzing, descending *peeuwww*.

BRIDLED TERN
Sterna anaethetus

Range Occurs throughout the tropics, the nearest breeding populations being in the Caribbean and on the Banc d'Arguin in Mauritania.

Occurrences A very rare vagrant, with just five dead ones recorded up to 1977 and 16 live ones since (to 1994). There has been a wide geographical and temporal scatter, with records from late April through to the end of November, although most recent ones have occurred in summer. Remarkably, four have been inland. Our birds may relate to individuals swept across the Atlantic from the Caribbean, and also to ones which have travelled north from West Africa (both races have been found dead here).

Identification Plates 45.1–3 show a summer-plumaged adult at Cemlyn Bay, Anglesey, in July 1988. The Bridled Tern is about the size of an Arctic Tern *S. paradisaea* but sturdier, with quite a thick bill. It is readily identified by its dark grey-brown upper-parts, palest on the mantle, and it shows an incon-spicuous narrow white collar between this and the black cap. The grey-brown upperpart coloration includes the rump and tail, the latter with white outer feathers. Also distinctive is the head pattern: the fore-head patch and the supercilium form a narrow white bar, extending back behind the eye (*see also* Sooty Tern *S. fuscata* below). Plate 45.2 shows dusky shading across the under primaries and secondaries; in the field, this is less extensive on the primaries than on the Sooty Tern. In flight, its plumage renders it somewhat skua-like (recalling the Long-tailed Skua *Stercorarius longicaudus* in particular), and the Cemlyn bird fre-quently spooked the other terns in its flights over the colony! The white collar, pale mantle and extensive white in the tail are indicative of the Atlantic race *melanoptera*.

SOOTY TERN
Sterna fuscata

Range Widespread and abundant throughout the tropics. Nearest breeding colonies are in the Caribbean and the South Atlantic.

Occurrences Although there have been some 24 records in total (to 1984), there have been only eight since 1958 and it is currently much rarer than the Bri-dled Tern *S. anaethetus*. Recent sightings have all been made in summer, from late May to mid-August. The most famous was an exhausted first-summer found at Ditchford Gravel Pits, Northamptonshire, on 29–30 May 1980 (Plate 45.4). It was picked up and taken into care, but eventually died on 4 November amidst a sea of mindless bureaucracy over its return to a more hospitable climate.

Identification It is slightly bigger, more robust and heavier than a Bridled Tern, and is longer billed and longer winged but proportionately shorter tailed. The upperparts are uniformly dark chocolate-brown, which may appear black in the field. It thus lacks the contrasting greyer tones to the mantle shown by the Bridled. The black crown joins the black of the man-tle (it thus lacks the white collar of the Bridled). Most significant is that the white forehead appears as a deeper patch, not extending back behind the eye (on the Bridled, the white forehead is narrow and extends back behind the eye to produce an obvious supercili-um). In flight, the Sooty has more extensively dark under-primaries and has white only on the outer tail feather (the Atlantic race of the Bridled *melanoptera* has white on the outer three; Harris, 1988).

WHISKERED TERN
Chlidonias hybridus

Range Breeds from Spain and France through south-ern Europe and discontinuously eastwards to China, as well as in East and southern Africa, northern India and Australia. Western Palearctic breeders winter mainly in Africa.

Occurrences A fairly regular vagrant, with 120 up to 1995. Most occur in May and June, with a secondary peak in September (juveniles are surprisingly rare). Occurrences are usually unrelated to those of the other two marsh terns. There have been signs of a per-ceptible increase in recent years (with a maximum of ten in 1988), this perhaps reflecting recent increases in Poland, the Ukraine and Belorussia (*Brit. Birds* **84**: 7; **89**: 37). There has also been a tendency for increased numbers to winter in the Mediterranean; there were a phenomenal 38,750 on Lake Manzala in the Nile Delta, Egypt, in January 1990 (Meininger & Sorensen, 1993) and 120 were even present as far north as the south of France in February 1993 (*Brit. Birds* **87**: 8). One present at Nimmo's Pier, Co. Galway, from 14 November 1987 into 1988, may reflect this trend.

Identification Plate 45.5 shows a summer-plumaged adult at Abberton Reservoir, Essex, in May 1994, while Plate 45.6 shows a similar bird at Dungeness, Kent, at the same time. The Whiskered Tern is larger and bulkier than the Black Tern *C. niger*, and shows a short neck, longer legs and, in flight, rather broad-based wings and a short tail. The size and plumage combine to produce an appearance which suggests a *Sterna* tern, particularly in winter and immature plumages. Most of our vagrants are in summer plumage, when they are easily identified: the upperparts (including the rump and tail) are pale grey, contrasting with dark grey underparts which in turn contrast with white cheeks. As Plate 45.5 shows, the underwings are silvery-white with dark tips to the primaries, the pattern recalling that of a Common Tern *S. hirundo*. The bill and legs are both blood-red. Interestingly, males have longer bills than females and there is no overlap. One could perhaps suggest, therefore, that the Abberton bird was a male and that the one at Dungeness, with its rather stubby bill, was a female. Although first-summers usually stay behind in their winter quarters they are occasionally observed here as vagrants. These birds virtually lack any dark grey in the underparts and may show a white forehead. Spring adults have a distinctive call: a peculiar, harsh, nasal *ingh* or *kaa*. They may occasionally belly-plunge to catch small fish.

WHITE-WINGED BLACK TERN
Chlidonias leucopterus

Range Breeds in Eastern Europe and eastwards discontinuously to China. Unlike the Black Tern *C. niger*, it winters inland in Africa and in the Far East, from Sri Lanka and Southeast Asia through Indonesia to northern Australia.

Occurrences The White-winged Black Tern is an annual migrant, often with flocks of Black Terns, and mainly occurs in May–June and August–September. During 1958–85, it averaged 17 a year, with 72 per cent in autumn (Dymond *et al.*, 1989), but during the following six years there was a perceptible downturn, with an annual average of only 12. Perversely, 1992 saw record numbers, with 23 in spring and a further 26 in autumn. This westerly spring movement was echoed across northern Europe and coincided with large influxes of other eastern species, such as the

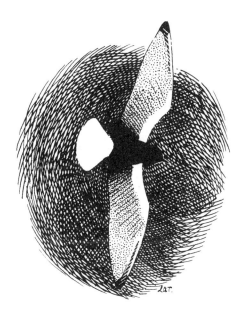

Second-summer White-winged Black Tern.

Red-footed Falcon *Falco vespertinus* (*see* page 51). In Poland, record numbers of about 1,000 pairs stayed to breed, mainly in the north-east (*Brit. Birds* **86**: 42).

Identification Plate 46.1 shows a spring adult, one of three which was present at Kenfig Pool, Glamorgan, on 18 May 1992. Although basically similar to the Black Tern, it is a more striking bird and is easily distinguished by the white leading wing coverts and the red legs. The primaries are also much whiter, but there is contrast with the outer two which are very dark. The bill is typically shorter than the Black Tern's. In flight, the contrasting plumage pattern is heightened further by the white rump, tail and undertail-coverts and by the solidly black underwing-coverts. These features are shown to good effect in Plate 46.2 which was taken at Cattawade, Suffolk, in June 1991. Second-summers are distinguished by their greyer upperwings, with white restricted to the leading coverts, their variably patchy underparts and underwing-coverts, their greyer tail and slightly duller legs. Spring migrants give a harsh, guttural *ghick*, approaching the call of a Whiskered Tern *C. hybridus* in quality.

Plate 46.3 shows a juvenile at Seaforth Docks, Lancashire, in September 1993. In this plumage, it is distinguished by the dark brown 'saddle' (back and scapulars) which contrasts with the white rump and pale whitish-grey wing coverts. It shows less of a carpal bar than a juvenile Black Tern, the black on the head is restricted to a small patch behind the eye and an extension over the rear crown. The legs are red, and again the bill is short (recalling that of a Little Gull *Larus minutus*). When seen from below, it completely lacks the Black Tern's dark shoulder patches. Structural differences between the two are subtle, but it usually appears to have slightly shorter, broader-based and more rounded wings, producing a slightly 'stiffer' flight action. Some juveniles have a less contrasting 'saddle' than others, particularly when the grey first-winter feathers start to show through. First-summer usually remains in the winter quarters and resembles winter adult.

BRÜNNICH'S GUILLEMOT
Uria lomvia

Range Almost circumpolar in the Arctic and near Arctic but, in Newfoundland, a declining population breeds at a latitude equivalent to that of northern France, reflecting the lower sea temperatures on that side of the Atlantic. The nearest breeding colonies to Britain and Ireland are in Iceland, Greenland and northern Norway. In winter it disperses out to sea in northern latitudes, its southerly limit in the eastern Atlantic being well to the north of Scotland.

Occurrences Considering its abundance – almost two million pairs estimated in Iceland alone (*BWP*) – Brünnich's Guillemot is amazingly rare in Britain and Ireland, with just 32 records up to 1995. Of these, only nine were seen alive, the others being picked up as tide-line corpses, mainly in mid-winter in Scotland (particularly in Orkney and Shetland). Significantly, three of the live ones were seen in summer, the best-known being a widely twitched individual in a seabird colony at Sumburgh Head, Shetland, in June–July 1989. The numbers recorded here must surely represent the tip of an iceberg, and one wonders just how many really occur in winter to the north of Scotland.

Identification Plate 46.5 shows a winter-plumaged individual which was picked up at Gulberwick, Shetland, on 4 January 1995. It was kept in care until 1 February when it was released, apparently fully fit. The photograph shows the diagnostic differences from the Common Guillemot *U. aalge*. In particular, Brünnich's has a short, stubby bill with a whitish streak at the base. The dark of the crown extends further down the sides of the head so that the line of demarcation between the brown and the white runs straight back from the bill; it thus lacks the Common Guillemot's prominent invasion of white up behind the eye. Although not visible in the photograph, it also lacks the Common Guillemot's dark streaking on the flanks.

ANCIENT MURRELET
Synthliboramphus antiquus

Range Breeds around the North Pacific from Korea through Kamchatka to the Aleutians, Alaska and British Columbia. It disperses south in winter, as far as Korea and California (Harrison, 1983).

Occurrence One of the most astonishing vagrants ever to have turned up in Britain was the Ancient Murrelet discovered on an RSPB members' group trip to Lundy, Devon, on 27 May 1990 (Campey & Mortimer, 1990; Waldon, 1994). Fortunately, it remained until 26 June and was seen by thousands of visiting birders, although it could be frustratingly elusive at times. Remarkably, it returned in the following two years, and was last seen on 29 April 1992. Towards the end of its stay, it seems that it was largely nocturnal in its visits to the island.

This individual's appearance stunned the twitching fraternity, yet three related North Pacific species are also on the Western Palearctic List. In December 1860, a Parakeet Auklet *Cyclorrhynchus psittacula* was collected inland (!) on Lake Vättern, Sweden, and, in August 1912, a Crested Auklet *Aethia cristatella* was collected in waters to the north of Iceland (*BWP*). Even the Tufted Puffin *Lunda cirrhata* has straggled to the eastern side of North America and one was recorded in Sweden in June 1994 (*Brit. Birds* **88**: 37). On the face of it, these records seem difficult to comprehend, but the Ancient Murrelet has been recorded widely across southern Canada east to Quebec, and across the USA east to New York and, amazingly, south to Louisiana. The related Marbled Murrelet *Brachyramphus marmoratus* has also been recorded more rarely inland but also on the Atlantic coast in Newfoundland, Massachusetts and Florida. Ancient Murrelets occur inland in North America most frequently in October and November, and their appearances have been associated with offshore storms and poor visibility along the Pacific coast. Fewer inland records have been made in spring, but some of the most easterly have occurred at that time. The species is apparently able to survive on fresh water for considerable periods. There were larger-than-usual numbers along the coast from British Columbia to northern California in the winter of 1989/90, and there were four inland records, including ones in Michigan and Idaho.

Unlike the Crested and Parakeet Auklets, the Ancient Murrelet does not occur in the Beaufort Sea or even in the northern Bering Sea, so it seems unlikely that the Lundy individual will have arrived by a northern route around the north of Canada. Instead, it may have crossed North America, found itself in the wrong ocean, then migrated east and north towards

Britain. It may then have followed nesting auks into Lundy, which is at a similar latitude to its British Columbian nesting areas (Waldon, 1994). The possibility of some kind of reversed migration out of the North Pacific should not, however, be completely discounted.

Identification Plate 46.4 was taken about six miles (10 km) east-north-east of Lundy on 28 May 1990 when, quite remarkably, some visiting birders came across the murrelet whilst on their way to the island. The photographs show a small auk, about half the size of the accompanying Razorbill *Alca torda*, with a chunky, neckless appearance and a large, angular, flat-crowned head. It has a black head and throat, a pale bill and a broken white supercilium from the eye back, almost joining at the back of the head. The back and wings are grey, the flanks black (with a small protrusion of black extending onto the breast sides) and the underparts are white, with a large lobe extending up the sides of the neck. In flight, it is grey above with a darker tail. The underwings are pale, contrasting with the black flanks, the wings are rounded and the Lundy bird held up its head in flight. Remarkably, the birders who photographed it even heard it calling, describing a metallic chinking sound, like that made by a distant hammer on an anvil (Palmer, 1990).

PALLAS'S SANDGROUSE
Syrrhaptes paradoxus

Range Breeds from Kazakhstan eastwards to the Gobi Desert of China and Mongolia. It is partially migratory, but the extent of the movements vary, and it is occasionally irruptive (*see* below).

Occurrences The occurrences of this species in Western Europe represent an enigma that is not fully understood. On the face of it, it seems remarkable that an ostensibly short-range migrant from a remote and inaccessible part of central Asia should ever have occurred here, but not only has it occurred, it has even bred.

Pallas's Sandgrouse periodically irrupt into Western Europe, although large movements have not occurred since 1908. Irruptions were noted in 12 years between 1859 and 1909, the largest ones occurring in 1863 and 1888. They bred in Yorkshire in 1888 and in Morayshire in 1888 and 1889, while as many as 180 frequented the Cley area of Norfolk from May 1888 to February 1889 (Dymond *et al.*, 1989).

Reasons for these irruptions are not entirely clear. Deep snow, particularly when there is an ice crust, inhibits feeding and this, rather than high population levels, may cause large-scale autumn and winter

movements. In eastern Asia, irruptive spring wandering seems to develop from abnormal displacement in a preceding cold winter, although irruptions in Soviet central Asia can be preceded by irregular mass movements. The causes of these movements are not known, but food shortages are no doubt the most likely reason (*BWP*). Irruptions are not cyclic and suggested relationships with sunspot activity cannot be upheld. On this latter point, however, the arrival of a Pallas's Sandgrouse out of range in Bedeihe, China, during the autumn of 1989 apparently correlated with an upsurge in sunspot activity (Martin Williams, verbally). The following spring, one turned up in Shetland.

Identification Plate 46.6 shows the Shetland bird, a heavily twitched male present in the Hillwell and Quendale area from 19 May to 4 June 1990. It was only the sixth record (seventh individual) since 1909, and its late spring occurrence corresponded with the old established pattern. The photograph shows what can only be described as a stunning bird. The black belly patch, the long tail and elongated outer primary are all clearly visible, as are the feathered legs and feet which are a feature of the genus *Syrrhaptes*, which it shares with the Tibetan Sandgrouse *S. tibetanus*. The calls are described as a rapid musical chirruping or trilling: *cherrcherrichicherr*, although the number of syllables is not constant. Also, explosive *tchep* or *kep* sounds are interspersed, perhaps suggesting the call of a Common Moorhen *Gallinula chloropus*, while *kok-kerick* calls are heard on take-off and soft *kok-kok* sounds when foraging (*BWP*).

RUFOUS TURTLE DOVE
Streptopelia orientalis

Range Breeds across much of southern Siberia, Turkestan, Afghanistan, the Himalayas, India, China, Japan and Southeast Asia. Northern populations (races *orientalis* and the western *meena*) are migratory, wintering from India through Southeast Asia and China to Japan. The species is much hardier than the Turtle Dove *S. turtur* and winters at much higher and colder latitudes.

Occurrences A very rare vagrant, with just five between 1889 and 1975. One was present on St Agnes, Isles of Scilly, in May 1960, but the other four occurred in late autumn or winter on Fair Isle, Shetland, and on the English east coast from Yorkshire to Norfolk. In Scandinavia, vagrants also traditionally occur in late autumn and winter, and one individual returned to gardens in Öland, Sweden, every year from February 1985 until April 1994. It seems likely that future vagrants may be found amongst winter flocks of Collared Doves *S. decaocto*.

Identification Identification of the Rufous Turtle Dove has always been considered problematical, but when you see the genuine article it is obviously different. This is particularly true of the eastern *orientalis*, and it is interesting to note that both British specimen records were of that race. The most immediate differences from the Turtle Dove are structural: it is some 15 per cent longer and, most importantly, 25–75 per cent heavier. In the field, this means that it looks large and heavy, with a shorter tail and proportionately shorter, more rounded wings. The latter produce a more ponderous flight, lacking the 'whippy' effect of a Turtle Dove. In size, shape and flight it is, therefore, somewhat reminiscent of a Stock Dove *Columba oenas*. In flight, adults appear darker than the Turtle Dove and lack the contrasting whitish belly and undertail-coverts.

Plate 47.1 shows a juvenile moulting to first-winter at Spurn, Yorkshire, in November 1975. A number of plumage features combine to distinguish it from the Turtle Dove. In particular, concentrate on the scapulars, wing coverts and tertials. These show a mixture of juvenile feathers (brown, narrowly fringed buff) and adult feathers (black, thickly fringed rufous). These have rather rounded dark centres and relatively narrow fringes, producing a heavily scalloped effect. On the Turtle Dove, the centres to the adult feathers are narrower and more pointed and the fringes are thicker; on the juvenile feathers, the dark centres are actually diffuse with only a pointed blackish shaft streak. Other differences from the Turtle Dove are: (1) it appears to lack the area of bare skin around the eye (but note that some Rufous Turtle Doves show this feature, albeit reduced); (2) the neck patch consists of narrow black and bluish lines (the Rufous shows four to six lines, the Turtle three to four black and white ones); (3) the nape is brownish and this contrasts with a grey crown on the Rufous (Turtle Dove has a greyer nape, concolorous with the crown); (4) the rump is greyish (browner on the Turtle Dove); (5) the juvenile primaries are dark, contrastingly and sharply fringed with buff (on the Turtle Dove, juvenile primaries are browner, with darker, more diffuse edges); and, finally, (6) the tip of the tail appears to lack white; instead the tips are dull grey. It should be noted, however, that the western race of the Rufous Turtle Dove (*meena*) can show white tips. The western race is, in fact, more like the Turtle Dove in other respects in that it is paler overall, whiter on the belly and undertail-coverts, and can rarely show white bars in the neck patch. For a more detailed discussion, see Hirschfeld (1992), on which much of the foregoing is based.

MOURNING DOVE
Zenaida macroura

Range Breeds from southern Canada south throughout the USA, and into Central America and the West Indies. It winters mainly in the southern part of its breeding range, south to Panama.

Occurrence There is just one record: a first-year male on the Calf of Man, Isle of Man, on 31 October and 1 November 1989 (Plate 47.2; Sapsford, 1996). Although an abundant bird in North America, it was not widely predicted as a vagrant. The Calf of Man individual occurred during severe westerly gales and, in view of the fact that it was regrettably found dead on its second day, an unaided crossing seems likely. A record of one in Iceland in October 1985 confirms its vagrancy potential (*Brit. Birds* **89**: 258).

Identification The Mourning Dove is a small dove, much of its length being accounted for by its long pointed tail. This immediately separates it from both Collared *Streptopelia decaocto* and Turtle Doves *S. turtur*, both of which are larger. Plumage-wise, it is more similar to the Collared, but it is a deeper orangey-brown. It shows prominent white outer tail feathers in flight but, at rest, the most distinctive features are the large, randomly spaced black spots on the tertials, inner wing coverts and rear scapulars. The Calf of Man bird lacked the black neck spot shown by adults. The species has a complete post juvenile moult but the photograph shows that this was suspended during migration: four fresh first-winter inner primaries almost completely cloak the paler, browner, worn juvenile outers. It gets its name from its song: a soft, mournful *ooo-ooo-ooo*.

GREAT SPOTTED CUCKOO
Clamator glandarius

Range Breeds discontinuously through the Mediterranean in Iberia, southern France, western Italy, Asia Minor and parts of the Middle East. Western Palearctic breeders winter in parts of southern Spain, Morocco, Algeria and Egypt, but mainly in tropical Africa. Here its winter range is confused as it is also widespread as a breeding species, with migrant populations south to South Africa.

Occurrences An irregular vagrant, with 39 recorded up to 1995, mainly involving spring overshoots. It has a tendency to occur very early, the most notable being one on Lundy, Devon, on 24 February 1990 (even this was eclipsed by an individual on Alderney, Channel Islands, on 14 February 1982, but this is not included as a British record). Lansdown (1995) found that 87 per cent of spring records were made on the English south coast, with almost half on the South-west Peninsula no doubt involving overshoots from Iberia. In autumn, however, 86 per cent occurred on the English east coast, suggesting a different origin at that time of year.

The species has increased in northern Spain and Italy and, since 1943, it has spread markedly in France (*BWP*). In July 1992, a juvenile was seen being fed by two Carrion Crows *Corvus corone corone* in Vendée, western France, only some 300 miles (480 km) from southern England (*Brit. Birds* **86**: 42). With the continuing increase in the populations of its main host species, the Carrion Crow and the Black-billed Magpie *Pica pica*, it will be interesting to see how future trends develop.

Identification Plates 47.3 & 4 show a first-year at Shoreham Airport, Sussex, in April 1990. With its black head, whispy crest, white underparts, spotted upperparts and long, white-tipped tail, it is quite unique in a British or Irish context. Lansdown (1995) analysed the ages of the British and Irish records up to 1993. In spring, 95 per cent were first-years whilst in autumn, 82 per cent were juveniles. Juveniles can be aged by their inconspicuous crest, glossy black head, a bright red eye-ring and bright rufous-chestnut in the primaries. Spring first-years vary according to when they moulted out of juvenile plumage: early moulters grow more juvenile-like replacement feathers than late moulters which, consequently, are more adult-like. Any spring bird retaining any juvenile features should be aged as a first-year. Thus the Shoreham bird shows some grey in the crown, but the otherwise black head shows it also to be a first-year. In late summer, ageing becomes complicated since juveniles have to be separated from juvenile-like first-years from the previous year; the latter would, however, be much more worn (*see* Lansdown, 1995, for a more detailed discussion).

BLACK-BILLED CUCKOO
Coccyzus erythrophthalmus

Range Breeds in the eastern half of southern Canada and in the more northerly states of the USA. Winters in north-western South America.

Occurrences There have been just 13 records (plus one on a North Sea oil platform) up to 1990, and it is much rarer here than the Yellow-billed Cuckoo *C. americanus*. Most have occurred in the South-west Peninsula, particularly in the Isles of Scilly. In 1982, one was found on St Agnes as early as 29 August, but the others have all occurred in the period 23 September to 8 November. The species' rarity has been attributed to

the fact that, in autumn, it moves south to south-west towards its restricted wintering area and it is uncommon along the Atlantic coast of North America (*BWP*). Like the Yellow-billed Cuckoo, those that arrive here are usually on their last legs and seem unable to find sufficient food to recover. Five of the nine since 1958 have been found dead or dying.

Identification The Black-billed Cuckoo is smaller than a Common Cuckoo *Cuculus canorus*, and is plain olive-brown above and white below. It is slightly smaller than the Yellow-billed Cuckoo and, as its name suggests, it is easily separated by bill colour, which is black with a grey base to the lower mandible. The bill is smaller than that of the Yellow-billed. It lacks the Yellow-billed's rufous area in the primaries (although some young Black-billed's can show a subdued hint of this). It also lacks the Yellow-billed's large white undertail spots, and instead very narrow white tips are visible when viewed from below (with narrow black subterminal bars on adults). Plates 47.5 & 48.1 show an individual which was present on St Mary's, Isles of Scilly, on 21–23 October 1982; unfortunately, it was found dead on 24th. It is sitting in fairly characteristic pose, with its wings drooped. A narrow, dull yellow eye-ring shows it to be a first-winter (this is red on the adult).

YELLOW-BILLED CUCKOO
Coccyzus americanus

Range Has a more southerly distribution than the similarly non-parasitic Black-billed Cuckoo *C. erythrophthalmus*, extending from southern Canada to the Gulf coast and west to British Columbia and California, as well as south into central Mexico and the Caribbean. It is similarly more widespread in winter, from Panama, Colombia and Venezuela south to Argentina.

Occurrences The Yellow-billed is more than four times as common as the Black-billed, with 60 records up to 1995. All have occurred from mid-September to mid-November, except for two surprisingly late ones in December. Most have been found in southern England, with at least 11 in the Isles of Scilly and four on Lundy, Devon. Records away from the South-west Peninsula, including a number on the British east coast, may indicate ship-assistance.

The frequency of the species' occurrence has been attributed to a 2,500-mile (4,000-km) transoceanic migration route from south-east Canada and New England direct to the West Indies and South America. Individuals arriving in the Netherlands Antilles in autumn are often exhausted and at 50 per cent of their normal winter body weight (*BWP*). Some of those that arrive here are probably in a similar state, and an inability to find suitable food inevitably leads to their early demise. Of the 37 recorded between 1958 and 1994, at least 16 were found dead or moribund. Their inability to survive here is legendary; one on St Agnes in 1980, originally nick-named 'Woodstock', was renamed 'Jesus' when it reappeared after a two-day absence.

Identification The Yellow-billed is slightly larger than the Black-billed, with a heavier 'banana-like' bill which is conspicuously yellow on the lower mandible. It also shows a large rusty panel in the primaries and large white patches at the tips of the tail feathers, visible from below. Adults and first-winters are similar but the latter have a less contrasting, less black and white undertail. The individual in Plates 48.2 & 3 was photographed on St Mary's, Isles of Scilly, in October 1985.

EURASIAN SCOPS OWL
Otus scops

Range Breeds from Morocco, Iberia and France east across mid-latitude Europe and North Africa as far as Lake Baikal in Siberia. Small numbers remain in the Mediterranean but most winter in a broad band south of the Sahara. Siberian breeders must travel up to a remarkable 5,000 miles (8,000 km) to their winter quarters (*BWP*).

Occurrences In view of the fact that the species is a long-range migrant, breeding as close as France, it is remarkably rare here. Evans (1994) recognized 72 records up to 1993, although only 21 of these were made since 1958. Most have occurred in southern England from late March to late June, with a secondary peak from late September to late November. Inevitably, the individuals recorded must represent the tip of an iceberg, but it is likely that the species has become genuinely rarer in recent years. This has been associated with a marked northerly range contraction, especially in Switzerland, Austria and the former Czechoslovakia, due mainly to habitat changes and a reduction in the numbers of large insects. Although there are estimated to be a little under 10,000 pairs in France, there too it has retreated southwards, no longer breeding in the extreme north (*BWP*).

The best-known British Scops Owl was a calling male at Dummer, Hampshire, in May–July 1980. This individual was heavily twitched but has since been the subject of controversy, with allegations that it was an escape (Hampshire Ornithological Society, 1993), although the background to this rumour has never been satisfactorily explained. Another twitchable bird was present at Morwenstow, Cornwall, in April 1995 (Plate 48.4).

Identification The bird in Plate 48.5 was picked up injured at Inchydoney, Co. Cork, on 27 April 1993; it subsequently died. Immediately apparent is its small size compared with the hand that is holding it; it is even smaller than a Little Owl *Athene noctua* and not much more than half its weight. The ground colour varies from warm brown to almost grey. It is readily identified by its ear tufts and by its delicately vermiculated and streaked plumage, with a broken whitish line down the edge of the scapulars. Compared with the Little Owl it is long-winged and has deep, elastic wingbeats. It is most easily located by the male's call: a *piu*, repeated rhythmically at two- to three-second intervals. The female's call is more disyllabic and she sometimes duets with the male. The persistent calling of the Dummer bird led local residents to complain to British Telecom!

SNOWY OWL
Nyctea scandiaca

Range Circumpolar on the Arctic tundra. Partially migratory, dispersive and irruptive outside the breeding season.

Occurrences Although we tend to think of the Snowy Owl as a permanent feature of the British avifauna, it is in reality a very rare vagrant, seldom acquiring more than one or two records a year, and these usually in northern Scotland. Records south of the border are particularly rare, and a second-winter male which appeared at several localities in Lincolnshire and Norfolk, from December 1990 to March 1991, was greatly appreciated by southern birders.

Although in Russia most withdraw from northern areas for the winter, the species is otherwise nomadic, dispersing in response to food supplies. In North America and in Greenland, movements are related to numbers of lemmings, which show an abundance cycle of about four years. When lemming numbers crash over a large area, there is then a large-scale Snowy Owl irruption. In Europe, irruptions are less regular, probably because the owls also eat large numbers of voles and are less dependent on the lemmings. It also seems likely that the European movements may to some extent be weather-related (*BWP*). Although it seems possible that our Snowy Owls may originate from either side of the Atlantic, a Norwegian-ringed individual found on North Uist, Outer Hebrides, in May 1992, would no doubt indicate the origin of most.

Tulloch (1968) stated that the species was rare in Shetland during the first half of the 20th century, but there were notable influxes to Britain in 1963–65 (17) and in 1972 (nine). The first irruption led to the famous breeding records on Fetlar from 1967 to

PLATE
01

1 **WHITE-BILLED DIVER** *p.26*
adult female summer

Portmahomack Bay, Ross &
Cromarty ❖ Jun 1984
Roy Dennis

2 **WHITE-BILLED DIVER** *p.26*
(insert above) *juvenile*

Holyhead, Anglesey ❖
Feb 1991   David Tipling

3 **WHITE-BILLED DIVER** *p.26*
adult winter

Hartlepool, Co. Durham ❖
Feb 1981   Simon Cook

4 **PIED-BILLED GREBE** *p.26*
(right) *adult summer*

Radley Gravel Pits, Oxfordshire
❖ Apr 1992   George Reszeter

5 **PIED-BILLED GREBE**
p.26 *winter*

Argal Reservoir, Cornwall ❖
Jan 1993   Paul Hopkins

PLATE
02

1 & *2* **BLACK-BROWED ALBATROSS** *p.26*
(right) *adult summer*

Bass Rock, East Lothian ❖
Jul 1968   Alan Gibson

3 **BLACK-BROWED ALBATROSS** *p.26*
(below) *adult summer*

Hermaness, Unst, Shetland ❖
May 1991   Dennis Coutts

4 & *5* **CORY'S SHEARWATER** *p.27* (left)

South-western Approaches ❖
Aug 1993   Alan Tate

6 & *7* **GREAT SHEARWATER** *p.28*

South-western Approaches
(60 miles west of Scilly) ❖
Aug 1988

David M. Cottridge

PLATE
03

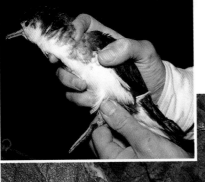

1 & 2 LITTLE SHEARWATER *p.28 male*

Skomer, Pembrokeshire ❖ Jul 1981

Prof. C. M. Perrins

3 SWINHOE'S STORM-PETREL
p.29 (far left) *female*

Tynemouth, Northumberland ❖
Jul 1993   Mark Cubitt

4 WILSON'S STORM-PETREL
p.29 (left)

South-western Approaches
(west of Scilly) ❖
Aug 1988   Brian Little

5 All-dark petrel, possibly MATSUDAIRA'S STORM-PETREL *p.29* (left)

South-western Approaches ❖
Aug 1988   John Hall

6 & 7 DOUBLE-CRESTED CORMORANT
p.29 1st-winter

Charlton's Pond, Yorkshire ❖ Jan 1989

David M. Cottridge

PLATE
04

1 **LITTLE BITTERN** *p.30* (right)
1st-summer male

St Mary's, Isles of Scilly ✤ Apr 1987

Keith Warmington

2 **LITTLE BITTERN** *p.30* (left) *female*

Ballycotton, Co. Cork ✤ Mar 1990 Richard T. Mills

3 **BLACK-CROWNED NIGHT HERON**
p.31 *adult*

St Mary's, Isles of Scilly ✤ Mar 1990

Paul Hopkins

4 **BLACK-CROWNED NIGHT HERON**
p.31 (left) *2nd-winter*

Briston, Norfolk ✤ Jan 1982 Brian Brown

5 **BLACK-CROWNED NIGHT HERON** *p.31*
1st-summer

River Blackwater, nr Fermoy, Co. Cork ✤ Jun 1988

Richard T. Mills

6 **BLACK-CROWNED NIGHT HERON** *p.31*
1st-winter

Dowdeswell Reservoir, Gloucestershire ✤
Nov 1995 Mark Coller

PLATE
05

1 AMERICAN BITTERN *p.30*
Magor, Monmouthshire ❖ Nov 1981
David M. Cottridge

2 GREEN HERON *p.31* (above) *adult*
Stone Creek, Yorkshire ❖ Nov 1982
Graham Catley

3 SQUACCO HERON *p.32* (left)
adult summer
Elmley, Kent ❖ May 1990   David M. Cottridge

4 SQUACCO HERON *p.32*
(right) *adult summer*
Elmley, Kent ❖ May 1990
David Tipling

5 SQUACCO HERON *p.32*
(below) *1st-year*
St Mary's, Isles of Scilly ❖
Mar 1990   John Harriman

PLATE
06

1 **CATTLE EGRET** *p.32* (left)
adult summer

Hornsea Mere, Yorkshire ❖
May 1992   John Harriman

2 **CATTLE EGRET** *p.32*
(above) *winter*

East Coker, Somerset ❖
Jan 1986   David M. Cottridge

3 **GREAT WHITE EGRET** *p.33*
(right) *non-breeding*

Gibraltar Point, Lincolnshire ❖
Jul 1993   John Harriman

4 **GREAT WHITE EGRET** *p.33*
(above) *breeding condition*

Cley, Norfolk ❖ Apr 1993
                    John Humble

5 **PURPLE HERON** *p.33*
(right) *adult type*

Fordwich, Kent ❖ Apr 1981
          David M. Cottridge

PLATE
07

1 PURPLE HERON
p.33 *juvenile*

Tophill Low Reservoir,
Yorkshire ❖ Aug 1994
Tony Collinson

2 BLACK STORK
p.34 (left) *juvenile*

South Walney,
Lancashire ❖ Oct
1985   Andrew Moon

3 WHITE STORK
p.35 (below)

Suffield, Suffolk ❖
Jul 1982
David M. Cottridge

4 WHITE STORK *p.35* (left)
Fordcombe, Kent ❖ Sep 1988

David Tipling

PLATE
08

1 GLOSSY IBIS *p.35* *juvenile*
Tresco, Isles of Scilly ❖ Sep 1994

Ren Hathway

2 GLOSSY IBIS *p.35* (below) *adult summer*
Fairburn Ings, Yorkshire ❖ Jun 1989

Pete Wheeler

3 LESSER WHITE-FRONTED GOOSE *p.36* (below) *adult (centre with White-fronted Geese)*
Slimbridge, Gloucestershire ❖ Feb 1995

Mark Coller

PLATE
09

1 SNOW GOOSE *p.36*
adult white phase (with Pink-footed Geese)
Marshside, Lancashire ❖ Jan 1986   Pete Wheeler

2 SNOW GOOSE *p.36* (below)
adult blue phase (with Pink-footed Goose)
Marshside, Lancashire ❖ Nov 1992
                    Steve Young

3 ROSS'S GOOSE *p.37* (above)
adult (with Greylag Goose)
Lossiemouth, Morayshire ❖ Mar 1991
                    Steve Young

4 BLACK BRANT *p.37* (below)
*adult (3rd from left with Dark-bellied
Brent Geese)*
Cley, Norfolk ❖ Feb 1988   Dave Kjaer

PLATE
10

1 **RED-BREASTED GOOSE**
*p.38 adult (with Dark-bellied
Brent Geese)*

Cley, Norfolk ❖ Feb 1988
Dave Kjaer

2 **RED-BREASTED GOOSE**
p.38 (below) 1st-winter

Holkham, Norfolk ❖ Nov 1993
Pete Wheeler

3 **CANADA GOOSE** *p.37 (right)*
*one of the small races
(with Pink-footed Geese)*

Martin Mere, Lancashire ❖ Jan 1994
Steve Young

4 **RUDDY SHELDUCK** *p.38 (below)*

Six, Hayle Estuary, Cornwall ❖ Oct 1994
Paul Hopkins

5 **RUDDY SHELDUCK** *p.38 two from above flock* Hayle Estuary, Cornwall ❖ Oct 1994   Steve Young

PLATE
11

1 AMERICAN WIGEON *p.39* (above left) *adult male*
Aberlady Bay, East Lothian ❖ Jan 1996
Jim Pattinson

2 HYBRID WIGEON *p.39* (above)
*adult male, probably Eurasian × Chilöe
Wigeon (with Eurasian Wigeon)*
Eye Brook Reservoir, Leicestershire ❖ Jan 1996
Keith Stone

3 AMERICAN WIGEON *p.39*
(above) *juvenile*
St Agnes, Isles of Scilly ❖
Oct 1985
David M. Cottridge

**4 & 5 AMERICAN
WIGEON** *p.39*
juvenile/1st-winter
Fair Isle, Shetland ❖ Sep 1986
(ringed in New Brunswick,
Canada, Aug 1986)
Alan Roberts

PLATE
12

1 **FALCATED DUCK** *p.40 adult male*
Kirkby-on-Bain Gravel Pits, Lincolnshire ❖
Feb 1995   Alan Tate

2 **BAIKAL TEAL** *p.40 adult male*
Brownsea Island, Dorset ❖ Jan 1969
                                    A. T. Bromby

3 **AMERICAN BLACK DUCK** *p.41 adult male*
Tresco, Isles of Scilly ❖ Oct 1994   Rob Wilson

4 **AMERICAN BLACK DUCK** *p.41 adult female*
Tresco, Isles of Scilly ❖ Date unknown (1976–83)
                                    David Hunt

6 **BLUE-WINGED TEAL** *p.41 adult male*
Cley, Norfolk ❖ Jun 1990   Robin Chittenden

5 **GREEN-WINGED TEAL** *p.40*
adult male
Martin Mere, Lancashire ❖
Jan 1992   Steve Young

7 **BLUE-WINGED TEAL**
p.41 juvenile/1st-winter female
Tehidy Country Park, Cornwall
❖ Oct 1995
        Dave Stewart

PLATE
13

1 **RING-NECKED DUCK** *p.43*
(left) *male*

Strumpshaw Fen, Norfolk ❖
Mar 1993   Robin Chittenden

2 **RING-NECKED DUCK** *p.43*
(below) *female*

Marden Quarry, Co. Durham ❖
Feb 1990   Mark Coller

3 **MARBLED DUCK**
p.42 (above)

Kingsbury Water Park,
Warwickshire ❖ Jul 1990
John Harriman

4 **REDHEAD** *p.43* (right) *male*

Bleasby Gravel Pits,
Nottinghamshire ❖ Mar 1996
Steve Young

5 & **6** **FERRUGINOUS DUCK** *p.44* *male*
Lea Valley Park, Hertfordshire ❖ Mar 1994
David M. Cottridge

PLATE
14

1 LESSER SCAUP *p.44* *adult male*
Tittenhanger Gravel Pits, Hertfordshire ❖
Apr 1996
Steve Young

2 KING EIDER *p.45* *female*
Portscatho, Cornwall ❖ Jan 1986
David M. Cottridge

4 STELLER'S EIDER *p.45*
adult male
South Uist, Outer Hebrides ❖
Jun 1983   David M. Cottridge

3 KING EIDER *p.45* *adult male*
Reawick/Tresta Voe, Shetland ❖ Apr 1989
Dennis Coutts

5 STELLER'S EIDER *p.45* *female*
Fair Isle, Shetland ❖ May 1971
Dennis Coutts

6 HARLEQUIN DUCK *p.46* *juvenile*
Islay, Argyllshire ❖ Oct 1987
Gordon Langsbury

PLATE
15

1 SURF SCOTER *p.46* *juvenile*
Tresco, Isles of Scilly ❖ Oct 1975   David Hunt

2 BUFFLEHEAD *p.46* *adult male*
Colwick Country Park, Nottinghamshire ❖
Mar 1994   Robin Chittenden

3 BUFFLEHEAD *p.46* *1st-summer male*
Coatham Marsh, Yorkshire ❖ Jun 1994
                          John Harriman

4 WHITE-TAILED EAGLE *p.47* (below) *immature*
Brill, Buckinghamshire ❖ Feb 1984
                          David M. Cottridge

5 BLACK KITE *p.47* (above)
St Mary's, Isles of Scilly ❖ May 1990
                          Jack Levene

6 & **7**   BALD EAGLE *p.48* *juvenile*
Castle Island, Co. Kerry ❖ Nov 1987
                          Richard T. Mills

PLATE
16

1 & 2 BLACK VULTURE *p.48 adult*
Between Rhulen and Aberedw, Radnorshire ❖ Dec 1977
Harold McSweeney

3 PALLID HARRIER *p.49*
juvenile
Exnaboe, Shetland ❖ Sep 1993
Dennis Coutts

4 PALLID HARRIER *p.49 2nd-summer male*
Birsay, Orkney ❖ Jun 1995
George Reszeter

5 AMERICAN KESTREL *p.50* (above)
female
Sharp Tor, Bodmin Moor, Cornwall ❖ Jun 1976
Nigel Tucker

6 LESSER KESTREL *p.50*
adult male
Fair Isle, Shetland ❖ Jun 1987
Nick Riddiford

PLATE
17

1 RED-FOOTED FALCON *p.51*
1st-summer female
Shipton Bellinger, Hampshire ❖ Jun 1989
David Tipling

2 RED-FOOTED FALCON *p.51* *adult female*
Filey, Yorkshire ❖ May 1992   Tony Collinson

3 & **4** RED-FOOTED FALCON *p.51* (above and
right) *1st-summer male*
Landguard, Suffolk ❖ May 1992   Jack Levene

5 RED-FOOTED FALCON *p.51* *adult male*
Studland Heath, Dorset ❖ May 1987
P. R. Boardman

6 RED-FOOTED FALCON *p.51* *1st-summer male*
Brooklands, nr Dungeness, Kent ❖ Jun 1987
David M. Cottridge

PLATE
18

1 **GYR FALCON** *p.52* (above)   *white phase*
Berry Head, Devon ❖ Apr 1986   Tim Loseby

2 **GYR FALCON** *p.52* (above left)   *white phase*
Berry Head, Devon ❖ Apr 1986   Pete Wheeler

3 **GYR FALCON** *p.52* (left) *1st-winter white phase*
North Slob, Co. Wexford ❖ Apr 1986   Alyn Walsh

4 **GYR FALCON** *p.52* (above)
ship assisted 1st-winter white phase on release
Tingwall, Shetland ❖ Mar 1973   Dennis Coutts

5 **SORA** *p.52* *adult*
Pagham Lagoon, Sussex ❖ Oct 1985
David M. Cottridge

6 **SORA** *p.52* *juvenile/1st-winter*
St Mary's, Isles of Scilly ❖ Oct 1991
David M. Cottridge

PLATE
19

1 **LITTLE CRAKE** *p.53*
adult male
Shotton, Flintshire ❖ Apr 1987
Pete Wheeler

2 **LITTLE CRAKE** *p.53*
(below) *1st-winter female*
Cuckmere Haven, Sussex ❖
Mar 1985
David M. Cottridge

3 **BAILLON'S CRAKE** *p.53* (right) *juvenile female*
Fair Isle, Shetland ❖ Sep 1991   Dennis Coutts

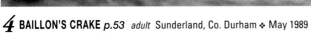

4 **BAILLON'S CRAKE** *p.53* *adult* Sunderland, Co. Durham ❖ May 1989   David Tipling

PLATE
20

1 AMERICAN COOT *p.54*
Stodmarsh, Kent ❖ Apr 1996   George Reszeter

2 AMERICAN COOT *p.54*
Stodmarsh, Kent ❖ Apr 1996   Rob Wilson

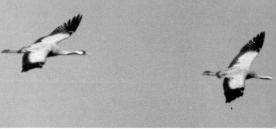

3 COMMON CRANE *p.54 adults*
Kersall, Nottinghamshire ❖ Feb 1996

Steve Young

4 COMMON CRANE *p.54*
1st-year
Baltasound, Unst, Shetland ❖ May 1991

Dennis Coutts

5 SANDHILL CRANE *p.54*
(above) *1st-summer/2nd-winter*
Exnaboe, Shetland ❖ Sep 1991

Rob Wilson

6 SANDHILL CRANE *p.54*
(left) *1st-summer/2nd-winter*
Exnaboe, Shetland ❖ Sep 1991

Dave MacLeman

PLATE
21

_1_ LITTLE BUSTARD _p.55_
St Mary's, Isles of Scilly ❖
Nov 1975   David Hunt

**_2 – 4_ HOUBARA
BUSTARD** _p.55_
probably 1st-winter
Hinton, nr Walberswick,
Suffolk ❖ Nov 1962
                  Eric Hosking

_5_ GREAT BUSTARD _p.56_ _adult female_   Fair Isle, Shetland ❖ Jan 1970   Roy Dennis

PLATE
22

1 BLACK-WINGED STILT *p.56*
(right) *pair, male on right*
Holme, Norfolk ❖ May 1987   David M. Cottridge

2 BLACK-WINGED STILT *p.56* *male*
Cogden Beach, Dorset ❖ Apr 1990   David Tipling

3 CREAM-COLOURED COURSER *p.57*
(above) *1st-winter*
Hadleigh Marsh, Essex ❖ Sep 1984
Tony Croucher

4 COLLARED PRATINCOLE *p.57* (left)
adult, summer
Girtford Gravel Pits, Bedfordshire ❖ May 1983
David M. Cottridge

5 & 6 ORIENTAL PRATINCOLE
p.57 *adult, summer*
Gimmingham, Norfolk, ❖ May 1993
Rob Wilson

· PLATE
23

1 **BLACK-WINGED PRATINCOLE** *p.58*
adult, summer
Clevedon, Somerset ❖ Jun 1988
David M. Cottridge

2 **BLACK-WINGED PRATINCOLE** *p.58*
juvenile
Great Livermere, Suffolk ❖ Sep 1993
Rob Wilson

3 **BLACK-WINGED
PRATINCOLE** *p.58*
(above left) *juvenile*
Great Livermere, Suffolk ❖
Sep 1993
Julian Bhalerao

4 **SEMIPALMATED PLOVER**
p.58 (above) *juvenile*
St Agnes, Isles of Scilly ❖
Oct 1978   David Hunt

5 **KILLDEER** *p.59* (left)
St Martin's, Isles of Scilly ❖
Oct 1982
David M. Cottridge

PLATE
24

1 **GREATER SAND PLOVER** *p.59*
male, summer
Bridge of Don, Aberdeenshire ❖ Aug 1991
Sam Alexander

2 **GREATER SAND PLOVER** *p.59*
probably 1st-winter
Pagham Harbour, Sussex ❖ Dec 1978
Chris Janman

3 **CASPIAN PLOVER** *p.60* *male, summer*
St Agnes, Isles of Scilly ❖ May 1988
Keith Pellow

4 **CASPIAN PLOVER** *p.60* *female*
Skellberry, Shetland ❖ Jun 1996
Reston Kilgour

5 **AMERICAN GOLDEN PLOVER** *p.60*
(above) female, summer
Fair Isle, Shetland ❖ Sep 1987   Tim Loseby

6 **AMERICAN GOLDEN PLOVER** *p.60* *juvenile*
St Agnes, Isles of Scilly ❖ Oct 1991
David M. Cottridge

PLATE
25

1 **PACIFIC GOLDEN PLOVER** *p.61* *winter*
Cley, Norfolk ❖ Dec 1991   Robin Chittenden

2 **PACIFIC GOLDEN PLOVER** *p.61* *1st-summer*
Elmley, Kent ❖ Aug 1995   Alan Clark

3 **SOCIABLE PLOVER** *p.62* *juvenile*
Welney, Norfolk ❖ Oct 1990   Robin Chittenden

4 **SOCIABLE PLOVER** *p.62* *adult, summer*
Holkham, Norfolk ❖ Apr 1993   Steve Young

5 **WHITE-TAILED PLOVER** *p.62* *adult, summer*
Packington Gravel Pits, Warwickshire ❖ Jul 1975
Peter Clement

6 **GREAT KNOT** *p.63* *adult, summer (with juvenile Red Knot, left)*
Pool of Virkie, Shetland ❖ Sep 1989
Dennis Coutts

PLATE
26

1 SEMIPALMATED SANDPIPER *p.63 juvenile*

Porthloo Beach, St Mary's, Isles of Scilly ❖
Oct 1986   Pete Wheeler

2 SEMIPALMATED SANDPIPER *p.63* (above)
adult starting to moult out of summer plumage

Tresco, Isles of Scilly ❖ Aug 1993

Ren Hathway

3 WESTERN SANDPIPER *p.64* (above right)
adult moulting out of summer plumage
(with juvenile Dunlin, left)

Tresco, Isles of Scilly ❖ Aug 1969

David Hunt

4 RED-NECKED STINT
p.64 (above) *adult, summer*

River Wansbeck,
Northumberland ❖ Aug 1995
Jim Pattinson

5 LONG-TOED STINT
p.65 adult, summer

Marazion Marsh, Cornwall ❖
Jun 1970   John Johns

PLATE
27

1 LONG-TOED STINT *p.65* *juvenile*
Saltholme Pools, Co. Durham ✧ Sep 1982

Jeff Delve

2 LEAST SANDPIPER *p.66* (below)
moulting individual mainly in fresh 1st-summer plumage
Portscatho, Cornwall ✧ Apr 1986

David M. Cottridge

3 LEAST SANDPIPER *p.66* (left) *juvenile*
Hayle Estuary, Cornwall ✧ Sep 1993

Rob Wilson

4 WHITE-RUMPED SANDPIPER
p.66 (left) *juvenile*
St Mary's, Isles of Scilly ✧
Oct 1970   John Johns

5 WHITE-RUMPED SANDPIPER
p.66 (right) *adult moulting into winter plumage*
Marazion Marsh, Cornwall ✧
Oct 1982

David M. Cottridge

PLATE
28

1 **BAIRD'S SANDPIPER** *p.67* *juvenile*
St Agnes, Isles of Scilly ❖ Oct 1987
David M. Cottridge

2 **BAIRD'S SANDPIPER** *p.67* *juvenile*
Upper Tamar Lake, Devon/Cornwall ❖ Sep 1995
Peter and Carole Leigh

3 **BAIRD'S SANDPIPER** *p.67* *adult, summer*
Cantley Beet Factory, Norfolk ❖ Aug 1992
Alan Tate

4 **BAIRD'S SANDPIPER** *p.67* *juvenile (with juvenile 1st-winter White-rumped Sandpiper, right)*
Stithians Reservoir, Cornwall ❖ Oct 1989
Paul Hopkins

5 **PECTORAL SANDPIPER**
p.68 *adult, summer*
Minsmere, Suffolk ❖ May 1985
David M. Cottridge

6 **PECTORAL SANDPIPER** *p.68* (above) *juvenile*
Davidstow Airfield, Cornwall ❖ Sep 1994
Peter and Carole Leigh

7 **PECTORAL SANDPIPER** *p.68* *juvenile*
(with juvenile American Golden Plover, right)
Drift Reservoir, Cornwall ❖ Oct 1980
Nigel Tucker

PLATE
29

1 SHARP-TAILED SANDPIPER
p.69 adult, summer
Tacumshin, Co. Wexford ❖
Aug 1994
Rob Wilson

2 SHARP-TAILED SANDPIPER
p.69 (below) *juvenile*
Shotwick Fields, Flintshire ❖
Oct 1973   John Raines

3 SHARP-TAILED SANDPIPER *p.69*
(left) *adult, summer*
Scatness, Shetland ❖ Sep 1993
Dennis Coutts

4 BROAD-BILLED SANDPIPER *p.69 adult, summer*
Ballycotton, Co. Cork ❖ Jul 1979
Richard T. Mills

PLATE
30

1 **STILT SANDPIPER** *p.70* (above)
adult starting to moult out of summer plumage
Trimley St Mary, Suffolk ❖ Aug 1990   Jack Levene

2 **STILT SANDPIPER** *p.70* (above left) *1st-winter*
Frodsham, Cheshire ❖ Apr 1984   Pete Wheeler

3 **STILT SANDPIPER** *p.70*
above) *1st-winter*
Frodsham, Cheshire ❖ Apr 1984
David M. Cottridge

4 **BUFF-BREASTED SANDPIPER**
p.70 (above) *juvenile*
Porthgwarra, Cornwall ❖
Sep 1977   Rod Hirst

5 **BUFF-BREASTED SANDPIPER**
p.70 *adult moulting into
winter plumage*
Cliffe Pools, Kent ❖ Aug 1994
Mike McDonnell

PLATE
31

1 **GREAT SNIPE** *p.71*
(above) *juvenile*

Girton Gravel Pits,
Nottinghamshire ❖ Aug 1989
Alan Tate

2 **GREAT SNIPE** *p.71*
(above right) *juvenile*

Girton Gravel Pits,
Nottinghamshire ❖ Aug 1989
John Harriman

3 **LONG-BILLED DOWITCHER**
p.72 (above) *adult, summer*

Scatness, Shetland ❖
May 1996   Hugh Harrop

4 **LONG-BILLED DOWITCHER**
p.72 (left) *juvenile*

Lynn Point, Norfolk ❖ Oct 1990
Graham Catley

5 **LONG-BILLED DOWITCHER** *p.72* (right) *juvenile*

Fetlar, Shetland ❖ Oct 1988   Larry Dalziel

PLATE
32

1 **HUDSONIAN GODWIT** *p.73*
adult moulting into winter plumage
Countess Weir, Exeter, Devon ❖ Nov 1981
Tony Croucher

2 **HUDSONIAN GODWIT** *p.73*
adult moulting into winter plumage
Countess Weir, Exeter, Devon ❖ Nov 1981
David Burns

3 & *4* **LITTLE WHIMBREL** *p.73 adult*
Cley, Norfolk ❖ Aug 1985   David M. Cottridge

5 **UPLAND SANDPIPER** *p.74 juvenile* St Mary's, Isles of Scilly ❖ Oct 1993   David M. Cottridge

PLATE
33

1 **UPLAND SANDPIPER**
p.74 *juvenile*
St Mary's, Isles of Scilly ❖
Oct 1983
David M. Cottridge

2 **UPLAND SANDPIPER**
p.74 (right) *juvenile*
St Mary's, Isles of Scilly ❖
Oct 1983   Brian Brown

3 **MARSH SANDPIPER** *p.74* (left) *adult, summer*
Bardney, Lincolnshire ❖ May 1992
John Harriman

4 **MARSH SANDPIPER**
p.74 (above) *adult, winter*
Cliffe Pools, Kent ❖ Aug 1994
Mike McDonnell

5 **MARSH SANDPIPER**
p.74 *three juveniles*
Cantley Beet Factory, Norfolk ❖
Aug 1995   Barry Jarvis

PLATE
34

1 GREATER YELLOWLEGS
p.75 1st-winter

Rockcliffe, Cumberland ❖
Oct 1994   Rob Wilson

2 GREATER YELLOWLEGS
p.75 (below) *adult, summer*

Minsmere, Suffolk ❖ Jul 1985
David M. Cottridge

3 LESSER YELLOWLEGS
p.76 (left) *juvenile*

Marazion Marsh, Cornwall ❖
Sep 1980   John Johns

4 LESSER YELLOWLEGS
p.76 (below) *juvenile (with
juvenile Wood Sandpiper, right)*

Stanford Reservoir, Leicester-
shire/Northamptonshire ❖
Sep 1995   Steve Young

5 SOLITARY SANDPIPER
p.77 juvenile

Fair Isle, Shetland ❖ Sep 1992
Dennis Coutts

PLATE
35

1 TEREK SANDPIPER *p.77* (above) *adult, summer*
Whalsay, Shetland ❖ Jun 1975   Dennis Coutts

2 & **3** TEREK SANDPIPER *p.77*
juvenile/1st-winter
North Blyth, Northumberland ❖ Nov 1989
Jeff Youngs

4 SPOTTED SANDPIPER
p.78 adult, summer
Worsborough Reservoir,
Yorkshire ❖ Aug 1984
J. G. and P. M. Hall

5 SPOTTED SANDPIPER *p.78* *1st-winter*
Fen Drayton Gravel Pits, Cambridgeshire ❖ Dec 1993   Rob Wilson

PLATE
36

1 & 2 **GREY-TAILED TATTLER** *p.78* *1st-winter*
Burghead, Morayshire ❖ Dec 1994   Rob Wilson

3 **WILSON'S PHALAROPE**
p.79 (right) *1st-winter (with
breast staining)*
Hayle Estuary, Cornwall ❖
Aug 1990   David Tipling

4 **WILSON'S PHALAROPE**
p.79 (left)
juvenile/1st-winter
Steart, Somerset ❖ Sep 1994
Greg Brinkley

5 **WILSON'S PHALAROPE** *p.79*
(right) *adult female, summer*
Porlock Marsh, Somerset ❖ Jun 1995
Tony Collinson

PLATE
37

1 **LONG-TAILED SKUA** *p.80* (right) *adult, summer*
Farmoor Reservoir, Oxfordshire ❖ Sep 1994
Rob Wilson

2 **LONG-TAILED SKUA** *p.80* (below) *juvenile*
King George V Reservoir, Essex ❖ Sep 1990
David M. Cottridge

3 **SABINE'S GULL** *p.82* (below) *adult, winter*
Queen Mother Reservoir, Berkshire ❖ Oct 1987
Tony Croucher

4 **SABINE'S GULL**
p.82 juvenile
Ballycotton, Co. Cork ❖
Sep 1985   Richard T. Mills

5 **SABINE'S GULL** *p.82 1st-summer*
Heysham, Lancashire ❖ Sep 1988
Steve Young

6 **SABINE'S GULL** *p.82 1st-winter*
Goldcliff Pill, Monmouthshire ❖ Apr 1994
Mark Coller

PLATE
38

1 FRANKLIN'S GULL *p.81* *adult, summer*
Skellister, South Nesting, Shetland ❖ May 1991
Eleanor McMahon

2 FRANKLIN'S GULL *p.81* *1st-winter*
Plymouth, Devon ❖ Jan 1982   Chris Newman

3 FRANKLIN'S GULL *p.81* *2nd-winter*
Helston, Cornwall ❖ March 1987
David M. Cottridge

4 LAUGHING GULL *p.81* *2nd-winter*
Kingston-upon-Hull, Yorkshire ❖ Nov 1984
Graham Catley

5 LAUGHING GULL *p.81* *1st-winter*
Walcott, Norfolk ❖ Jan 1992   Roger Tidman

6 LAUGHING GULL *p.81* *adult, summer*
Penzance, Cornwall ❖ May 1990
Paul Hopkins

PLATE
39

1 **BONAPARTE'S GULL** *p.83* *adult, winter*
Bangor, Co. Down ❖ Feb 1980   Tom Ennis

2 **BONAPARTE'S GULL** *p.83* *1st-winter*
Marazion Marsh, Cornwall ❖ Mar 1990
Rob Wilson

3 **BONAPARTE'S GULL** *p.83*
adult moulting into summer
Seaforth Docks, Lancashire ❖ Apr 1990
Steve Young

4 **BONAPARTE'S GULL** *p.83* (right) *1st-winter*
Radipole Lake, Dorset ❖ Apr 1981
David M. Cottridge

5 **SLENDER-BILLED GULL** *p.83* *pair of summer adults (male on right chasing Black-headed Gull)*
Cley, Norfolk ❖ May 1987   Pete Wheeler

PLATE
40

1 **RING-BILLED GULL** *p.84* *adult, summer*
Rhyl, Flintshire ❖ Mar 1994   Steve Young

2 **RING-BILLED GULL** *p.84*
2nd-winter (primaries still growing)
Copperhouse Creek, Cornwall ❖ Aug 1987
David M. Cottridge

3 **RING-BILLED GULL** *p.84* *1st-winter*
Copperhouse Creek, Cornwall ❖ Feb 1989
Paul Hopkins

4 **KUMLIEN'S GULL** *p.85* *adult, summer*
Banff, Banffshire ❖ Mar 1991   Rob Wilson

5 **KUMLIEN'S GULL** *p.85* *adult, winter*
Lerwick, Shetland ❖ Feb 1983   Dennis Coutts

6 **KUMLIEN'S GULL** *p.85*
adult, winter
Lerwick, Shetland ❖ Apr 1995
Hugh Harrop

7 **KUMLIEN'S GULL**
(kumlieni/thayeri type)
p.85 *1st-winter*
Galway ❖ Mar 1989
Tom Ennis

PLATE
41

1 ROSS'S GULL *p.85 adult, summer*
Titchwell, Norfolk ❖ May 1984   Pete Wheeler

2 ROSS'S GULL *p.85 adult, winter*
Scalloway, Shetland ❖ Jan 1975   Dennis Coutts

3 ROSS'S GULL *p.85 adult, summer*
Greatham, Co. Durham ❖ Jun 1995
                                   Steve Young

4 ROSS'S GULL *p.85 adult, winter*
Fraserburgh, Aberdeenshire ❖ Jan 1993
                                   Steve Young

5 ROSS'S GULL *p.85 2nd-winter/2nd-summer*
Drimsdale, South Uist, Outer Hebrides ❖ May 1994
                                   John Metcalf

6 ROSS'S GULL *p.85 1st-summer*
Workington, Cumberland ❖ Jun 1994
                                   Tony Collinson

PLATE
42

1 IVORY GULL *p.86* *1st-winter* Saltburn, Yorkshire ❖ Feb 1986

Pete Wheeler

2 IVORY GULL *p.86*
1st-winter

Lerwick Harbour, Shetland ❖
Dec 1993   Bill Jackson

3 GULL-BILLED TERN *p.86*
adult, summer

Penrice, Glamorgan ❖
Jul 1993   Rob Wilson

4 & *5* GULL-BILLED TERN
p.86 *adult, summer*

Llanelli, Carmarthenshire ❖
Jul 1995   George Reszeter

PLATE
43

1 CASPIAN TERN *p.87*
(above) *adult moulting to winter plumage (right) and 1st winter*
Ferrybridge, Dorset ❖
Sep 1991   Mark Coller

2 CASPIAN TERN *p.87*
(right) *adult, summer*
Minsmere, Suffolk ❖ Jun 1996
                    Paul Gale

3 LESSER CRESTED TERN *p.87* (left) *adult, winter*
Blakeney Point, Norfolk ❖ Aug 1983   David M. Cottridge

4 LESSER CRESTED TERN *p.87* *adult female, summer, on nest* Inner Farne, Northumberland ❖ May 1990
D. C. Richardson

PLATE
44

1 & 2 ELEGANT TERN *p.88*
adult, summer (with Sandwich and Common Terns)
Greencastle, Co. Down ❖ Jul 1982   Tom Ennis

3 & 4 ALEUTIAN TERN *p.88*
(left and below) adult, summer
Inner Farne, Northumberland ❖ May 1979
A. R. Taylor

5 FORSTER'S TERN *p.89* (left) *1st-winter*
Musselburgh, Midlothian ❖ Mar 1995
Jim Pattinson

6 FORSTER'S TERN *p.89* (above)
adult, winter (with adult, winter Sandwich Tern)
Abergele, Denbighshire ❖ Oct 1986   Steve Young

7 FORSTER'S TERN *p.89* (left) *1st-winter*
Ferrybridge, Dorset ❖ Jan 1996   Keith Stone

PLATE
45

1 **BRIDLED TERN** *p.90* *adult, summer*
Cemlyn Bay, Anglesey ❖ Jul 1988   Steve Young

2 **BRIDLED TERN** *p.90* (right) *adult, summer*
Cemlyn Bay, Anglesey ❖ Jul 1988
David M. Cottridge

3 **BRIDLED TERN** *p.90* (left)
adult, summer (with moulting adult Sandwich Tern)
Cemlyn Bay, Anglesey ❖ Jul 1988   Pete Wheeler

4 **SOOTY TERN** *p.90* (above) *exhausted 1st-summer*
Ditchford Gravel Pits, Northamptonshire ❖ May 1980
Simon Cook

5 **WHISKERED TERN** *p.90* *adult, summer*
Abberton Reservoir, Essex ❖ May 1994
Mike McDonnell

6 **WHISKERED TERN** *p.90* *adult, summer*
Dungeness, Kent ❖ May 1994   John Humble

PLATE
46

1 **WHITE-WINGED BLACK TERN** *p.91*
(left) *adult, summer*

Kenfig Pool, Glamorgan ❖ May 1992

Howard Nicholls

2 **WHITE-WINGED BLACK TERN** *p.91*
(below) *adult, summer*

Cattawade, Suffolk ❖ Jun 1991   Jack Levene

3 **WHITE-WINGED BLACK
TERN** *p.91* *juvenile*

Seaforth Docks, Lancashire ❖
Sep 1993   Steve Young

5 **BRÜNNICH'S GUILLEMOT** *p.92* *winter*
In care, Shetland ❖ Jan 1995   Hugh Harrop

4 **ANCIENT MURRELET** *p.92*
adult, summer (with Razorbill)

6 miles east of Lundy, Devon ❖
May 1990   Dave Atkinson

6 **PALLAS'S SANDGROUSE** *p.93* (below) *male*
nr Quendale, Shetland ❖ May 1990   Larry Dalziel

PLATE
47

1 RUFOUS TURTLE DOVE *p.93* (inset)
juvenile/1st-winter
Spurn, Yorkshire ❖ Nov 1975   Tony Broome

2 MOURNING DOVE *p.94* *1st-winter male*
Calf of Man, Isle of Man ❖ Oct 1989   Ian Fisher

3 GREAT SPOTTED CUCKOO *p.94* *1st-year*
Shoreham Airport, Sussex ❖ Apr 1990
       Alan Tate

4 GREAT SPOTTED CUCKOO
p.94 *1st-year*
Shoreham Airport, Sussex ❖
Apr 1990   Tim Loseby

5 BLACK-BILLED CUCKOO
p.95 *1st-winter*
St Mary's, Isles of Scilly ❖
Oct 1982
       David M. Cottridge

PLATE
48

1 **BLACK-BILLED CUCKOO** *p.95* *1st-winter*

St Mary's, Isles of Scilly ❖ Oct 1982

David M. Cottridge

2 & 3 **YELLOW-BILLED CUCKOO**
p.95 (above and left)

St Mary's, Isles of Scilly ❖
Oct 1985   David M. Cottridge

4 **EURASIAN SCOPS OWL**
p.96 (above) *adult*

Morwenstow, Cornwall ❖
Apr 1995   Julian Bhalerao

5 **EURASIAN SCOPS OWL**
p.96 *adult, injured*

Inchydoney, Co. Cork ❖
Apr 1993   Richard T. Mills

PLATE
49

1* & *2 SNOWY OWL *p.96*
male, probably 2nd-winter
Aranmore Island, Co. Donegal ❖ Oct 1993
Jack Malins

3 — 5 SNOWY OWL *p.96*
female at nest with chicks
Fetlar, Shetland ❖ Jul 1967   Eric Hosking

PLATE
50

1 **HAWK OWL** *p.97 adult*

nr Lerwick, Shetland ❖ Sep 1983   Dennis Coutts

2 **TENGMALM'S OWL** *p.97 adult*

Egilsay, Orkney ❖ May 1986

Mrs E. Hibbert

3 **TENGMALM'S OWL** *p.97*
(above) *adult*

Spurn, Yorkshire ❖ March 1983
Philip Harrison

4 **COMMON NIGHTHAWK**
p.98 (right) *juvenile*

St Agnes, Isles of Scilly ❖
Oct 1971

David Hunt

5 **COMMON NIGHTHAWK**
p.98 (below) *juvenile*

Tresco, Isles of Scilly ❖
Sep 1989

Marcus Lawson

PLATE
51

1 **CHIMNEY SWIFT**
p.98

St Andrews, Fife ❖ Nov 1991

Stephen Addinall

2 **WHITE-THROATED
NEEDLETAIL** *p.98*

Quendale, Shetland ❖
May 1984   Dennis Coutts

3 **WHITE-THROATED
NEEDLETAIL** *p.98*

Hoy, Orkney ❖ Jun 1988

Pete Wheeler

4 **PALLID SWIFT** *p.99*

Stodmarsh, Kent ❖ May 1978   Jeff Pick

5 **PACIFIC SWIFT** *p.99*

Cley, Norfolk ❖ May 1993   Rob Wilson

6 **ALPINE SWIFT** *p.100*

Cromer, Norfolk ❖ Apr 1985

David M. Cottridge

7 **LITTLE SWIFT** *p.100*

Skewjack Pools, Cornwall ❖ May 1981

Rod Hirst

PLATE
52

1 & *2* BELTED KINGFISHER *p.100* *male* Boscathnoe Reservoir, Penzance, Cornwall ✥ Aug 1980

John Johns

3 BLUE-CHEEKED BEE-EATER *p.101*
(above left) *adult*
Cowden, Yorkshire ✥ Jul 1989

Pete Wheeler

4 BLUE-CHEEKED BEE-EATER *p.101*
(above) *adult*
Cowden, Yorkshire ✥ Jul 1989

David M. Cottridge

5 EUROPEAN BEE-EATER *p.101* *adult*
Vidlin, Shetland ✥ Jun 1995   Bill Jackson

PLATE
53

1 EUROPEAN ROLLER *p.102* (left) *adult*
East Budleigh, Devon ❖ Jun 1989

David Tipling

2 YELLOW-BELLIED SAPSUCKER
p.102 (right) *1st-winter female*
Cape Clear Island, Co. Cork ❖ Oct 1988

Anthony McGeehan

3 CALANDRA LARK *p.103*
St Agnes, Isles of Scilly ❖ Apr 1996

Ian Wilson

4 BIMACULATED LARK *p.103*
St Mary's, Isles of Scilly ❖
Oct 1975   David Hunt

5 SHORT-TOED LARK *p.103*
St Mary's, Isles of Scilly ❖
Oct 1992   John Humble

PLATE
54

1 TREE SWALLOW *p.104* *male*

St Mary's, Isles of Scilly ❖ June 1990

Jack Levene

2 TREE SWALLOW *p.104* *male*

St Mary's, Isles of Scilly ❖ June 1990

David M. Cottridge

3 RED-RUMPED SWALLOW *p.104* *adult*

Cley, Norfolk ❖ Apr 1987

David M. Cottridge

5 RED-RUMPED SWALLOW *p.104* *adult*

Gibraltar Point, Lincolnshire ❖ May 1987

Graham Catley

4 RED-RUMPED SWALLOW *p.104* *juvenile*

St Mary's, Isles of Scilly ❖ Oct 1988

David M. Cottridge

PLATE
55

1 **CLIFF SWALLOW** *p.105*
(far left) *juvenile*
St Mary's, Isles of Scilly ❖
Oct 1983   Pete Wheeler

2 **CLIFF SWALLOW** *p.105*
(left) *juvenile*
St Mary's, Isles of Scilly ❖
Oct 1983   David Hunt

3 **RICHARD'S PIPIT** *p.105*
(right) *1st-winter*
St Mary's, Isles of Scilly ❖
Oct 1994   Rob Wilson

4 & *5* **BLYTH'S PIPIT** *p.106* (above and below)
1st-winter
St Mary's, Isles of Scilly ❖ Oct 1993
Jack Levene

6 **BLYTH'S PIPIT** *p.106* *1st-winter*
Skewjack, Cornwall ❖ Oct 1990
Paul Hopkins

7 **BLYTH'S PIPIT** *p.106* *1st-winter*
Landguard Point, Suffolk ❖ Oct 1994
Alan Clark

PLATE
56

1 **TAWNY PIPIT**
p.107 juvenile/1st-winter
Southwold, Suffolk ❖ Nov 1992
Jack Levene

2 **OLIVE-BACKED PIPIT**
p.108 (below)
Bracknell, Berkshire ❖ Feb 1984
David M. Cottridge

3 **OLIVE-BACKED PIPIT**
p.108 (left)
St Agnes, Isles of Scilly ❖
Oct 1989
David M. Cottridge

4 **PECHORA PIPIT** *p.108*
Foula, Shetland ❖ Sep 1993   Michael McKee

5 **PECHORA PIPIT** *p.108*
Foula, Shetland ❖ Sep 1994   Michael McKee

PLATE
57

2 **RED-THROATED PIPIT** *p.109* *male, summer*
Cuckmere Haven, Sussex ❖ Jun 1991
David Tipling

1 **RED-THROATED PIPIT** *p.109* *1st-winter*
St Agnes, Isles of Scilly ❖ Oct 1991
David M. Cottridge

3 & **4** **BUFF-BELLIED PIPIT** *p.109*
St Mary's, Isles of Scilly ❖ Oct 1988
David M. Cottridge

5 **CITRINE WAGTAIL** *p.110*
(above) *1st-winter*
Tresco, Isles of Scilly ❖ Oct 1989
David M. Cottridge

6 **CITRINE WAGTAIL** *p.110*
1st-summer male
Fleet Pond, Hampshire ❖ May 1993
John Humble

PLATE
58

1 BOHEMIAN WAXWING
p.111 *1st-winter*
Holme, Norfolk ❖ Dec 1988
David M. Cottridge

2 CEDAR WAXWING *p.111* *1st-winter*
Nottingham ❖ Mar 1996   Phil Palmer

3 CEDAR WAXWING *p.111* *1st-winter*
Nottingham ❖ Feb 1996   Rob Wilson

4 NORTHERN MOCKINGBIRD *p.111* *1st-summer*
Horsey Island, Hamford Water, Essex ❖
May 1988   Pete Loud

5 NORTHERN MOCKINGBIRD *p.111*
Worm's Head, Glamorgan ❖ July 1978
Harold Grenfell

PLATE
59

1 BROWN THRASHER
p.112 (left)
Durlston Head, Dorset ❖
Nov 1966

David Godfrey

2 ALPINE ACCENTOR
p.112 (below)
The Needles, Isle of Wight ❖
May 1990

David M. Cottridge

3 RUFOUS BUSH CHAT *(syriacus/familiaris)*
p.113 (left) *1st-winter*
Skegness, Lincolnshire ❖ Sep 1963

Barrie Wilkinson

4 THRUSH NIGHTINGALE
p.113 1st-winter
Landguard Point, Suffolk ❖
Sep 1995

Robin Chittenden

5 THRUSH NIGHTINGALE
p.113 1st-winter
Landguard Point, Suffolk ❖
Sep 1995

Rob Wilson

PLATE
60

1 & 2 SIBERIAN RUBYTHROAT
p.114 1st-winter female
Fair Isle, Shetland ❖ Oct 1975   Simon Cook

3 BLUETHROAT (red-spotted *svecica*)
p.114 (left)   *male*
Holme, Norfolk ❖ May 1985
David M. Cottridge

4 BLUETHROAT *p.114*
1st-winter female
Portland, Dorset ❖ Sep 1986
David M. Cottridge

5 BLUETHROAT *p.114*
1st-winter male
St Mary's, Isles of Scilly ❖
Oct 1993   Steve Young

PLATE
61

1 **RED-FLANKED BLUETAIL**
p.115 (left) *probably 1st-winter*
Winspit, Dorset ❖ Oct 1993
Peter and Carole Leigh

2 **RED-FLANKED BLUETAIL**
p.115 (above) *male*
Holy Island, Northumberland ❖
Apr 1995
Michael Sharp

3 **MOUSSIER'S REDSTART** *p.113* (above) *male*
Dinas Head, Pembrokeshire ❖ Apr 1988
Mike Barrett

4 & 5 **WHITE-THROATED ROBIN** *p.115*
female
Skokholm, Pembrokeshire ❖
May 1990
Margaret B. Potts

PLATE
62

_1_ EASTERN STONECHAT *(maura/stejnegeri)*
p.116 *1st-winter*

Salthouse, Norfolk ❖ Sep 1990

Robin Chittenden

_2_ EASTERN STONECHAT *(maura/stejnegeri)*
p.116 (below) *1st-summer male*

Filey, Yorkshire ❖ May 1995   John Harriman

_3_ EASTERN STONECHAT *(variegata)*
p.116 (left) *male*

Porthgwarra, Cornwall ❖ Oct 1985

Graham Armstrong

_4_ ISABELLINE WHEATEAR *p.116* (right)

Gugh, Isles of Scilly ❖ Oct 1991

David M. Cottridge

_5_ PIED WHEATEAR
p.117 *1st-summer male*

Scarborough, Yorkshire ❖
Jun 1991   Steve Young

PLATE
63

1 **PIED WHEATEAR** *p.117* *1st-winter male* Sumburgh, Shetland ❖ Oct 1991   Dennis Coutts

3 **PIED WHEATEAR** *p.117* *female*
Weybourne, Norfolk ❖ Nov 1983   Tony Croucher

2 **PIED WHEATEAR** *p.117*
1st-winter male
Dodman Point, Cornwall ❖
Nov 1991   Paul Hopkins

4 **BLACK-EARED WHEATEAR**
p.118 *1st-winter male*
Stiffkey, Norfolk ❖ Oct 1993
    Rob Wilson

PLATE
64

1 **DESERT WHEATEAR** *p.118* *1st-winter male*
Penclawdd, Glamorgan ❖ Nov 1989
Howard Nicholls

2 **DESERT WHEATEAR** *p.118* *1st-summer male*
Barn Elms Reservoirs, London ❖ Apr 1989
David M. Cottridge

3 **DESERT WHEATEAR** *p.118*
female
Easton Bavents, Suffolk ❖
Dec 1990
David M. Cottridge

4 & 5 **WHITE-CROWNED BLACK WHEATEAR** *p.119* *1st-summer*
Kessingland, Suffolk ❖ Jun 1982
Brian Brown

1 & *2* **ROCK THRUSH** *p.119 male, summer* Holme, Norfolk ❖ May 1995   Robin Chittenden

3 **SIBERIAN THRUSH** *p.120 1st-winter female*
North Ronaldsay, Orkney ❖ Oct 1992
John Harriman

4 **ROCK THRUSH** *p.119 male, winter*
Minster, Isle of Sheppey, Kent ❖ Feb 1983
David M. Cottridge

5 & *6* **WHITE'S THRUSH** *p.120 1st-year*
Rathlin Island, Co. Down ❖ Apr 1993
Pat McKee

PLATE
65

PLATE
66

1 VARIED THRUSH *p.121* *1st-winter, probably male*
Nanquidno, Cornwall ❖ Nov 1982 Tony Croucher

2 HERMIT THRUSH *p.121* *1st-winter*
Tresco, Isles of Scilly ❖ Oct 1993 Rob Wilson

3 HERMIT THRUSH *p.121* *1st-winter*
Tresco, Isles of Scilly ❖ Oct 1993
George Reszeter

4 SWAINSON'S THRUSH *p.121* (right)
St Mary's, Isles of Scilly ❖ Oct 1990
Jack Levene

5 SWAINSON'S THRUSH
p.121
Fair Isle, Shetland ❖ Sep 1990
David Tipling

PLATE
67

1 GREY-CHEEKED THRUSH *p.122* *1st-winter*
St Mary's, Isles of Scilly ❖ Oct 1991
David M. Cottridge

2 BICKNELL'S THRUSH *p.123*
1st-winter, probably this species
Tresco, Isles of Scilly ❖ Oct 1986
David M. Cottridge

3 EYEBROWED THRUSH *p.123* *1st-winter*
St Mary's, Isles of Scilly ❖ Oct 1993
George Reszeter

4 VEERY *p.123* *1st-winter*
Lundy, Devon ❖ Nov 1987   David M. Cottridge

5 DUSKY/NAUMANN'S THRUSH *p.124*
1st-winter intergrade
Firth, Shetland ❖ Nov 1975   Dennis Coutts

6 NAUMANN'S THRUSH *p.124* *1st-winter male*
Woodford Green, Essex ❖ Feb 1990
David M. Cottridge

PLATE
68

1 **RED-THROATED THRUSH** *p.124* *1st-winter male* The Naze, Essex ❖ Oct 1994   Dave Stewart

2 **BLACK-THROATED THRUSH**
p.125 female
Holkham Park, Norfolk ❖ Mar 1996
                Robin Chittenden

3 **BLACK-THROATED THRUSH**
p.125 1st-winter male
Werrington, Cambridgeshire ❖ Feb 1996
                Rob Wilson

4 **BLACK-THROATED THRUSH**
p.125 (above) *1st-winter male*
Webheath, Worcestershire ❖ Jan 1996
                George Reszeter

5 **AMERICAN ROBIN** *p.125* *1st-winter male*
Inverburvie, Kincardineshire ❖ Dec 1988
                David MacLeman

PLATE
69

1 **PALLAS'S GRASSHOPPER WARBLER**
p.126 1st-winter
North Ronaldsay, Orkney ❖ Sep 1992
Robin Chittenden

2 **PALLAS'S GRASSHOPPER WARBLER**
p.126 1st-winter
North Ronaldsay, Orkney ❖ Sep 1992
P. B. Chapman

3 & *4* **LANCEOLATED WARBLER** *p.126 1st-winter* Fair Isle, Shetland ❖ Sep 1990
David Tipling

5 **SAVI'S WARBLER** *p.127 male*
Stanwick Gravel Pits, Northamptonshire ❖
Jul 1991
George Reszeter

6 **RIVER WARBLER** *p.126 male*
Kielder Water, Northumberland ❖ Jun 1996
Tony Collinson

PLATE
70

1 AQUATIC WARBLER
p.128 juvenile
St Agnes, Isles of Scilly ❖
Oct 1990   Rob Wilson

2 AQUATIC WARBLER
p.128 (below) *juvenile behind*
(with juvenile Sedge Warbler)
Chew Valley Lake, Somerset ❖
Aug 1995
                    Keith Vinicombe

3 PADDYFIELD WARBLER
p.128 1st-winter
Quendale, Shetland ❖
Oct 1994   Hugh Harrop

4 & 5 BLYTH'S REED WARBLER
p.129 male
Kergord, Shetland ❖ May 1994   Dennis Coutts

PLATE
71

1 GREAT REED WARBLER
p.130 male
Cley, Norfolk ❖ Jun 1994
Steve Young

2 OLIVACEOUS WARBLER
p.130 (below)
St Mary's, Isles of Scilly ❖
Oct 1985
David M. Cottridge

3 **OLIVACEOUS WARBLER** *(elaeica) p.130*
Fair Isle, Shetland ❖ Jun 1995   Hugh Harrop

4 **BOOTED WARBLER** *(caligata)*
p.131 (above) *male, singing*
Spurn, Yorkshire ❖ Jun 1992   Rob Wilson

5 **BOOTED WARBLER** *(rama)*
p.131 (right)
Seafield, Lerwick, Shetland ❖ Oct 1993
Kevin Osborn

PLATE
72

1 ICTERINE WARBLER *p.132* *1st-winter*
St Mary's, Isles of Scilly ❖ Oct 1990
David M. Cottridge

2 MELODIOUS WARBLER *p.132* *1st-winter*
Tresco, Isles of Scilly ❖ Oct 1989   Paul Hopkins

3 SUBALPINE WARBLER *p.133*
(above) *1st-winter female*
St Agnes, Isles of Scilly ❖ Oct 1987
David M. Cottridge

4 MARMORA'S WARBLER *p.133*
(left) *1st-summer male*
St Abb's Head, Berwickshire ❖ May 1993
Rob Wilson

5 SUBALPINE WARBLER
p.133 (above) *1st-winter male*
The Naze, Essex ❖ Aug 1993
John Humble

6 SUBALPINE WARBLER
p.133 (right) *female*
North Ronaldsay, Orkney ❖
May 1990   Ian Fisher

PLATE
73

_1_ SARDINIAN WARBLER *p.134 1st-summer male*
Holme, Norfolk ❖ May 1994   Rob Wilson

_2_ SARDINIAN WARBLER *p.134 male*
St Mary's, Isles of Scilly ❖ Oct 1985
David M. Cottridge

_3_ RÜPPELL'S WARBLER *p.135 male*
Dunrossness, Shetland ❖ Aug/Sep 1977
Dennis Coutts

_4_ RÜPPELL'S WARBLER *p.135 adult female*
Holme, Norfolk ❖ Sep 1992   John Harriman

_5_ DESERT WARBLER (nana) *p.135*
male, collecting nest material
Blakeney Point, Norfolk ❖ May 1993   Rob Wilson

_6_ DESERT WARBLER (nana) *p.135*
Bembridge, Isle of Wight ❖ Oct 1991
David M. Cottridge

PLATE
74

1 ORPHEAN WARBLER
p.136 1st-winter male

St Mary's, Isles of Scilly ❖
Oct 1981

Gordon Langsbury

2 BARRED WARBLER
p.136 (below) *1st-winter*

St Mary's, Isles of Scilly ❖
Oct 1990   Paul Hopkins

3 BARRED WARBLER *p.136 1st-winter*
Cley, Norfolk ❖ Aug 1985

David M. Cottridge

4 SPECTACLED WARBLER *p.137 male*
Filey, Yorkshire ❖ May 1992

Mark Coller

PLATE
75

1 & **2** **TWO-BARRED GREENISH WARBLER**
(plumbietarsus) p.137 *1st-winter*
Gugh, Isles of Scilly ❖ Oct 1987
David M. Cottridge

3 **GREENISH WARBLER** *(viridanus)*
p.137 (above) *1st-winter*
Wells, Norfolk ❖ Sep 1994   Rob Wilson

4 **GREENISH WARBLER** *(viridanus)*
p.137 (left) *1st-winter*
Quendale, Shetland ❖ Sep 1994   Hugh Harrop

5 **ARCTIC WARBLER** *p.138* (above) *1st-winter*
St Agnes, Isles of Scilly ❖ Oct 1988
David M. Cottridge

6 **ARCTIC WARBLER** *p.138* *probably 1st-winter*
Kenidjack, Cornwall ❖ Oct 1994
Peter and Carole Leigh

PLATE
76

1 **PALLAS'S WARBLER** *p.139*
Felixstowe, Suffolk ❖ Oct 1994

Alan Tate

2 **YELLOW-BROWED WARBLER** *p.139*
St Agnes, Isles of Scilly ❖ Oct 1989

David M. Cottridge

3 **HUME'S YELLOW-BROWED WARBLER** *p.140*
Great Yarmouth, Norfolk ❖ Mar 1995

Rob Wilson

4 **RADDE'S WARBLER** *p.140*
St Mary's, Isles of Scilly ❖ Oct 1994

Steve Young

5 **RADDE'S WARBLER** *p.140* St Agnes, Isles of Scilly ❖ Oct 1986

David M. Cottridge

PLATE
77

1 DUSKY WARBLER *p.141*

Bideford, Devon ❖ Jan 1995

Peter and Carole Leigh

2 WESTERN BONELLI'S WARBLER
p.141 1st-winter

Sumburgh Head, Shetland ❖ Sep 1995

Dennis Coutts

3 EASTERN BONELLI'S
WARBLER *p.142*

Whitley Bay, Northumberland
❖ Sep 1995   Tony Collinson

4 RED-BREASTED FLYCATCHER *p.142 1st-winter*

St Mary's, Isles of Scilly ❖ Oct 1994

Steve Young

5 RED-BREASTED FLYCATCHER *p.142 male*

Spurn, Yorkshire ❖ Oct 1992   John Harriman

6 MUGIMAKI FLYCATCHER
p.143 1st-winter male

Stone Creek, Yorkshire ❖ Nov 1991   Mick Turton

PLATE
78

1 **ASIAN BROWN FLYCATCHER** *p.144*
(above) *1st-summer*
Fair Isle, Shetland ❖ Jul 1992   Dennis Coutts

2 & 3 **COLLARED FLYCATCHER** *p.144*
(right and above right) *1st-summer male*
Lowestoft, Suffolk ❖ May 1985   Brian Brown

4 **RED-BREASTED NUTHATCH** *p.145*
1st-winter male
Holkham Meals, Norfolk ❖ Apr 1990
David M. Cottridge

5 **WALLCREEPER** *p.145* (above)
male, summer
Hastings, Sussex ❖ Apr 1977   Nigel Tucker

6 **SHORT-TOED TREECREEPER** *p.146*
Dungeness, Kent ❖ Dec 1990   Tim Loseby

PLATE
79

1 **PENDULINE TIT** *p.146*
female

Titchwell, Norfolk ❖ Apr 1993
Rob Wilson

2 **PENDULINE TIT** *p.146*
(below) *1st-winter*

St Agnes, Isles of Scilly ❖
Oct 1988
David M. Cottridge

3 **BROWN SHRIKE** *p.148*
(below) *adult, probably male*

Grutness, Sumburgh, Shetland ❖ Oct 1985
Dennis Coutts

4 & *5* **ISABELLINE SHRIKE** *p.148* *1st-winter*
Minehead, Somerset ❖ Sep 1989   David Tipling

PLATE
80

1 **GOLDEN ORIOLE** *p.147* *male, with young*
East Anglia ❖ Jun 1993   Chris Knights

2 **GOLDEN ORIOLE** *p.147* (below) *female, at nest*
East Anglia ❖ Jun 1993   Chris Knights

PLATE
81

1 **LESSER GREY SHRIKE**
p.149 (left) *adult male*
Aberdaron, Caernarfonshire ❖
Nov 1986

David M. Cottridge

2 **LESSER GREY SHRIKE**
p.149 (above) *1st-winter*
Rudston, Yorkshire ❖ Sep 1989
Steve Young

3 **STEPPE GREY SHRIKE** *p.149*
(above) *1st-winter*
Swindon, Wiltshire ❖ Sep 1993
Mark Coller

4 **WOODCHAT SHRIKE** *p.150*
(right) *juvenile/1st-winter*
nr Polgigga, Cornwall ❖ Sep 1992
Nigel Bean

5 **WOODCHAT SHRIKE** *p.150*
(left) *male*
Gugh, Isles of Scilly ❖
May 1989   Paul Hopkins

PLATE
82

1 **SPOTTED NUTCRACKER**
p.150 (right) *1st-winter*

Westleton, Suffolk ❖ Nov 1985
David M. Cottridge

2 **HOUSE CROW** *p.151* (below)

Dunmore East Harbour,
Co. Waterford ❖ Nov 1974
John Lovatt

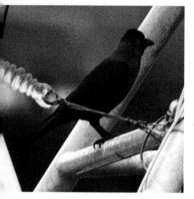

3 **ROSE-COLOURED STARLING**
p.151 (left) *adult*

Bradfield, Essex ❖ Jun 1992
John Humble

4 **ROSE-COLOURED STARLING** *p.151* (right) *juvenile*
St Mary's, Isles of Scilly ❖ Oct 1986

Pete Wheeler

5 **SPANISH SPARROW**
p.152 (left) *male, summer*

Waterside, Cumberland ❖ Jul 1996
Tony Collinson

PLATE
83

1 YELLOW-THROATED VIREO *p.153* (left)

Kenidjack, Cornwall ❖ Sep 1990

David M. Cottridge

2 YELLOW-THROATED VIREO *p.153* (below)

Kenidjack, Cornwall ❖ Sep 1990

Tim Loseby

3 PHILADELPHIA VIREO *p.153* (left)

Tresco, Isles of Scilly ❖ Oct 1987   Pete Wheeler

4 RED-EYED VIREO
p.153 (right)

Trevilley, Cornwall ❖ Oct 1995
Peter and Carole Leigh

PLATE
84

1 & *2* **EUROPEAN SERIN** *p.154* *male*
Southwold, Suffolk ❖ Apr 1994

Robin Chittenden

3 **EUROPEAN SERIN**
p.154 *female*
Ramsgate, Kent ❖ Mar 1994

Nigel Bean

4 **ARCTIC REDPOLL**
p.154 (above) *adult*
Carnoustie, Angus ❖ Jan 1989

David M. Cottridge

5 **ARCTIC REDPOLL**
p.154 *1st-winter*
Langham, Norfolk ❖ Feb 1996

Rob Wilson

PLATE
85

1 **TWO-BARRED CROSSBILL**
p.155 *male*
Fair Isle, Shetland ❖ Jul 1990
Ian Fisher

2 **TWO-BARRED CROSSBILL**
p.155 (below) *female*
Fair Isle, Shetland ❖ Jul 1990
Ian Fisher

3 **PARROT CROSSBILL** *p.156* (above) *male*
Holkham Meals, Norfolk ❖ Apr 1985
David M. Cottridge

4 **PARROT CROSSBILL** *p.156* (right) *female*
Holkham Meals, Norfolk ❖ Apr 1985
David M. Cottridge

5 **PARROT CROSSBILL** *p.156* (below) *juvenile*
Holkham Meals, Norfolk ❖ Apr 1985
David M. Cottridge

PLATE
86

1 **TRUMPETER FINCH** *p.156*
Church Norton, Sussex ❖ May 1984
Tony Croucher

2 **COMMON ROSEFINCH** *p.157*
(below) *male*
North Ronaldsay, Orkney ❖ May 1990   Ian Fisher

3 **COMMON ROSEFINCH**
p.157 (left)
female or 1st-summer male
Fetlar, Shetland ❖ Jun 1995
Paul Gale

4 **PINE GROSBEAK**
p.157 (below) *1st-year male*
Lerwick, Shetland ❖ Apr 1992
Larry Dalziel

PLATE
87

1 **BLACK-AND-WHITE WARBLER**
p.158 1st-winter male
How Hill, Norfolk ❖ Dec 1985

Pete Morris

2 **GOLDEN-WINGED WARBLER**
p.158 (below) *male*
Larkfield, Maidstone, Kent ❖ Feb 1989

David M. Cottridge

3 **TENNESSEE WARBLER** *p.159*
(right) *1st-winter*
Fair Isle, Shetland ❖ Sep 1975   Tony Broome

4 **AMERICAN REDSTART**
p.161 (above) *1st-winter female*
Kenidjack, Cornwall ❖ Oct 1983

David M. Cottridge

PLATE
88

1 & *2* **NORTHERN PARULA** *p.159* *male* St Mary's, Isles of Scilly ❖ Oct 1985   David M. Cottridge

3 **NORTHERN PARULA** *p.159* *female*
Cot Valley, Cornwall ❖ Oct 1988

Peter Walsh

4 **YELLOW-RUMPED WARBLER**
p.160 *probably 1st-winter male*
Ramsey Island, Pembrokeshire ❖ Nov 1994

Steve Young

5 & *6* **YELLOW WARBLER** *p.159* *1st-winter male* Lerwick, Shetland ❖ Nov 1990

Dennis Coutts

PLATE
89

1 **BAY-BREASTED WARBLER** *p.160*
probably 1st-winter female
Land's End, Cornwall ❖ Oct 1995
David Ferguson

2 **BLACKPOLL WARBLER** *p.161*
(below) *probably 1st-winter*
St Mary's, Isles of Scilly ❖ Oct 1990
David M. Cottridge

3 **NORTHERN WATERTHRUSH**
p.162 (above) *1st-winter*
St Agnes, Isles of Scilly ❖ Aug 1989
Marcus Lawson

4 **OVENBIRD** *p.162* (left) *1st-winter*
Dursey Island, Co. Cork ❖ Sep 1990
Michael O'Donnell

5 **COMMON YELLOWTHROAT**
p.163 (above) *male*
Fetlar, Shetland ❖ Jun 1984   Dennis Coutts

6 **WILSON'S WARBLER** *p.163* *male*
Rame Head, Cornwall ❖ Oct 1985   Keith Pellow

0

PLATE
90

1 & 2 **SUMMER TANAGER** *p.163*
1st-winter male
Bardsey, Caernarfonshire ❖ Sep 1957
Bill Condry

3 **SCARLET TANAGER** *p.164*
(right) *1st-winter male*
Tresco, Isles of Scilly ❖ Oct 1975   David Hunt

4 & 5 **LARK SPARROW** *p.164*
Waxham, Norfolk ❖ May 1991   David Tipling

6 **SAVANNAH SPARROW** *p.165*
1st winter (not *princeps*)
Fair Isle, Shetland ❖ Sep 1987   Kevin Osborn

7 **SAVANNAH SPARROW** (race *princeps* or
Ipswich Sparrow) *p.165* *male*
Portland, Dorset ❖ Apr 1982
David M. Cottridge

PLATE
91

1 WHITE-CROWNED SPARROW *p.166* *1st-winter*
Seaforth Docks, Lancashire ❖ Oct 1995
Steve Young

2 SONG SPARROW *p.165*
Fair Isle, Shetland ❖ Apr 1989
Dennis Coutts

3 WHITE-THROATED SPARROW *p.166*
(above left) *'white-striped'*
Trimley St Mary, Suffolk ❖ Jun 1992
George Reszeter

4 WHITE-THROATED SPARROW *p.166*
(above) *1st-winter*
Willingham, Lincolnshire ❖ Dec 1992
Graham Catley

5 DARK-EYED JUNCO *p.167* *1st-winter male*
Portland, Dorset ❖ Dec 1989
David M. Cottridge

6 DARK-EYED JUNCO *p.167* *adult male*
Church Crookham, Hampshire ❖ Jan 1990
George Reszeter

PLATE
92

1 **PINE BUNTING** *p.167* *1st-winter male*
Dagenham Chase, Essex ❖ Feb 1992

David M. Cottridge

2 **ORTOLAN BUNTING** *p.168*
(above) *male*
Minsmere, Suffolk ❖ May 1990
Rob Wilson

3 **ORTOLAN BUNTING** *p.168*
(above) *1st-winter*
Tresco, Isles of Scilly ❖
Oct 1988

David M. Cottridge

4 & 5 **CRETZSCHMAR'S BUNTING**
p.168 *male, probably 1st-summer*
Fair Isle, Shetland ❖ Jun 1967   Roy Dennis

PLATE
93

1 YELLOW-BROWED BUNTING
p.169

St Agnes, Isles of Scilly ❖
Oct 1994   Rob Wilson

2 RUSTIC BUNTING *p.169*
(above right) *male*

Arthog Bog, Caernarfonshire
❖ Apr 1991   George Reszeter

3 RUSTIC BUNTING *p.169*
(right) *1st-winter, probably
male*

Tresco, Isles of Scilly ❖
Oct 1994   Steve Young

4 RUSTIC BUNTING *p.169*
(above) *1st-winter, probably female*

Fair Isle, Shetland ❖ Oct 1987   Tim Loseby

5 LITTLE BUNTING *p.170* (right)

Chippenham, Wiltshire ❖ Apr 1991

Mark Coller

PLATE
94

1 & 2 **YELLOW-BREASTED
BUNTING** *p.170*
1st-winter

Portland, Dorset ❖ Sep 1993
George Reszeter

3 **YELLOW-BREASTED BUNTING**
p.170 (above) *male*
Sumburgh, Shetland ❖ May 1996

Hugh Harrop

4 **BLACK-FACED BUNTING** *p.171*
(above) *1st-winter male*
Pennington Flash, Lancashire ❖ Mar 1994

Steve Young

5 **PALLAS'S REED BUNTING** *p.171* *juvenile*
Fair Isle, Shetland ❖ Sep 1981

Tony Broome

PLATE
95

1 **RED-HEADED BUNTING** *p.172 male*
Belstead, Ipswich, Suffolk ❖ May 1993
Neil Murphy

2 **RED-HEADED BUNTING** *p.172*
(right) *1st-winter, probably this species*
St Mary's, Isles of Scilly ❖ Oct 1994
Andrew Easton

3 **BLACK-HEADED BUNTING**
p.173 (left) *female, probably this species*
Birling Gap, Beachy Head, Sussex ❖ Jun 1994
Alan Clark

4 **BLACK-HEADED BUNTING** *p.173 male*
St Martin's, Isles of Scilly ❖ May 1992
John Humble

5 **BLACK-HEADED BUNTING** *p.173*
1st-summer male
Fishguard, Pembrokeshire ❖ May 1995
David Astins

PLATE
96

1 **ROSE-BREASTED
GROSBEAK** *p.173*
1st-winter male

Tresco, Isles of Scilly ❖
Oct 1986

David M. Cottridge

2 **INDIGO BUNTING** *p.174*
(below) *adult male*

Holkham Meals, Norfolk ❖
Oct 1988

Robin Chittenden

3 **BOBOLINK** *p.174*
1st-winter

East Soar, Devon ❖ Sep 1991
David Tipling

4 **YELLOW-HEADED
BLACKBIRD** *p.175*
1st-summer male

Fair Isle, Shetland ❖
Apr 1990

Kevin Osborn

5 **BALTIMORE ORIOLE**
p.176 *1st-winter female*

Roch, Pembrokeshire ❖
Mar 1989

George Reszeter

1975, during which time 20 young were reared (Plates 49.3–5; Tulloch, 1968; Dymond *et al.*, 1989). Although one lonely female was still surviving in 1994, breeding has proved impossible owing to the lack of a male bird.

Identification At around 2 ft (60 cm) in height, with white plumage, a sloth-like head, piercing yellow eyes and feathered 'carpet slipper' feet, the Snowy Owl is quite unmistakable. Plates 49.3–5 show the female of the Fetlar pair with her chicks, photographed in July 1967. Unlike her mate, her plumage was extensively barred. Plates 49.1 & 2 show an individual at Aranmore Island, Co. Donegal, in October 1993. Reference to *BWP* and Hough (1992) would seem to suggest that this was a second-winter male, mainly because of the lightly spotted plumage and the relative lack of barring on the tertials, primaries and tail.

HAWK OWL
Surnia ulula

Range Has a circumpolar distribution, mainly frequenting the fringes of forest tundra and boreal taiga. It breeds as close to Britain as southern Norway.

Occurrences The Hawk Owl in Plate 50.1 was the eleventh British record and only the fourth this century. It was present on Shetland in 1983, near Lerwick on 12–13 September and on Bressay on 20–21 September.

The species is dispersive and irruptive, leading an essentially nomadic lifestyle within the coniferous taiga zone. Its abundance and its movements are tied in with the local vole populations. In normal years it breeds and winters well to the north but, in abundant vole years, it may temporarily extend its range southwards. Vole populations crash every three to five years and irruptions may then occur but, since vole cycles vary geographically, owl irruptions are unpredictable and large irruptions occur only when prey density falls over very large areas. Hawk Owl movements are thus rather complicated, and owls ringed in Scandinavia have even been recovered in the former Soviet Union, up to 1,160 miles (1,860 km) to the north-east or south-east of their ringing sites. Similarly, while some invasions originate in Scandinavia, others are made up largely of owls from further east (*BWP*).

In recent years, large irruptions occurred in the winters of 1976/77 and 1983/84, with a smaller one in 1989/90. It was the 1983/84 invasion which produced the Shetland individual. There were then large numbers in southern Norway, about 1,000 in southern Sweden, about 200 in Denmark and singles in West Germany and in the Faeroe Islands (*Brit. Birds*

77: 283 and 538; **78**: 343). It is perhaps surprising that more were not seen here, but it seems that they are reluctant to cross large areas of water – even the Baltic presents a formidable barrier (*BWP*). Despite this, there are three 19th-century records of the North American race *caparoch*, which has also occurred on the Canary Islands (*BWP*).

Identification The Hawk Owl is very distinctive, and about the size of a Common Kestrel *Falco tinnunculus*. Its evolution has closely converged with the diurnal birds of prey, and it thus has more compact plumage and rather a hawk-like silhouette. The wings are proportionally shorter and more pointed than those of other owls, and it has a longer tail. It has a flappy flight on bowed wings, with occasional glides. It is partly diurnal and locates its prey more by sight than sound and, unlike most owls, its ears are placed symmetrically. It may be very tame.

Plate 50.1 shows the Shetland bird in classic pose, sitting like a sentinel atop a dead branch. At a distance, its shape recalls a large-headed Common Kestrel. As is usual, the belly feathering completely hides the feet. Plumage-wise, it shows a distinctive greyish-white face, thickly bordered with greyish-black, framing its pale yellow eyes and a pale greeny bill. In the field, heavily barred underparts contrast with the whitish upper breast. From above, there is a large area of white spotting across the scapulars. The North American *caparoch* is usually blacker than the nominate and is best distinguished by broader, tawnier bars on the underparts (*BWP*).

TENGMALM'S OWL
Aegolius funereus

Range Circumpolar in the coniferous forest zone, with populations extending into the mountains of southern Europe. The nearest breeders are in Belgium and it has shown signs of a recent increase in north-western Europe.

Occurrences Dymond *et al.* (1989) mention about 50 records prior to 1958, most of these made before World War I. Since then, there have been just seven, five of which have been made in Orkney, and these have occurred from mid-October to early June. A leg found at Fishburn, Co. Durham, on 10 January 1981, was carrying a ring that had been put on in Norway the previous summer. This recovery no doubt indicates the origins of most of our vagrants.

The species shows three- to four-year cyclical movements in the boreal zone and, inevitably, these are related to prey densities. In Finland, peak production of young in the south is followed by a movement north the following year. Peak breeding in the north is then followed by a poor year when the supply of rodents crashes, this followed in turn by increased breeding in the south as the rodent populations recover. Females tend to be much more nomadic than males and, in years of poor food supply, many are irruptive (*BWP*). Those breeding in central Europe enjoy a more constant food supply and are much more sedentary.

Identification Plate 50.3 shows one at Spurn, Yorkshire, in March 1983, and Plate 50.2 shows another on Egilsay, Orkney, in May 1986; it was found dead a few weeks later. It is a small, large-headed owl, easily identified by its white-streaked forehead and crown, its greyish-white face with a thick blackish border, and its piercing yellow eyes. The underparts are streaked with chocolate-brown (unfortunately very messy in the photograph of the Orkney bird). The upperparts are also chocolate-brown, liberally spotted with white, those on the scapulars coalescing to form a white band. The advertising call of the male is a soft *po-po-po-po-po*, audible for some distance.

COMMON NIGHTHAWK
Chordeiles minor

Range Breeds over much of southern Canada and the USA, south into Central America and the West Indies. It winters over most of South America, south to central Argentina.

Occurrences There have been 13 records up to 1989 involving 14 individuals, nine of which occurred in the Isles of Scilly. All have turned up in September–October. The four mainland records included inland occurrences in Nottinghamshire and London, as well as a widely publicized individual found exhausted at Moreton, Cheshire, on 11 October 1985, and subsequently transported by the RAF to Belize, where it was released. Part of the eastern population apparently uses the transoceanic route direct to South America, and our vagrants no doubt relate mainly to individuals swept across the Atlantic in rapidly moving depressions.

Identification This nightjar has long, pointed wings and a long, cleft tail; it has an almost skua-like jizz in flight. Plate 50.4 is a classic shot taken by the late David Hunt on St Agnes, Isles of Scilly, in October 1971. It shows the large white patch at the base of the primaries, a contrasting pale greyish area across the wing coverts, intricately patterned body plumage and barred sides to the tail. White fringes to the primaries show it to be a juvenile (the post-juvenile moult takes place in the winter quarters). Plate 50.5 shows another juvenile, on Tresco, Isles of Scilly, in September

1989. The species can be immediately separated from the European Nightjar *Caprimulgus europaeus* by the long primaries which extend just beyond the tail (on the European Nightjar, the primary projection is short and the wings fall well short of the tail tip). The plumage is complicated but undistinguished and certainly defies description! It is less nocturnal than the European Nightjar and can sometimes be seen flying around in daylight, particularly towards evening. It has a buoyant flight but it is incredibly erratic, twisting and turning after insects. Vagrants are silent but in the breeding season in North America, they can often be located by a nasal *cu-ip* call, sounding almost like the noise made by a spring.

CHIMNEY SWIFT
Chaetura pelagica

Range Breeds in the eastern half of North America from southern Canada to the Gulf of Mexico. Winters mainly in north-eastern Peru.

Occurrences Remarkably, the first record involved two together at Porthgwarra, Cornwall, in late October 1982 (Williams, 1986). There have since been a further three, in the Isles of Scilly, Cornwall and Fife. All have occurred in late October and early November.

Identification Plate 51.1 shows one at St Andrews, Fife, in November 1991. It is much smaller than a Common Swift *Apus apus*, with a cigar-shaped body, shorter, less pointed wings and a short, blunt, squarish tail. Small spines at the tip are difficult to see in the field. The plumage is dark blackish-brown with quite a large pale throat, this merging into the dark breast. More distinctive are its quick, fluttery bat-like wingbeats, the bird gliding only for short periods on downward-bowed wings. Separation from the slightly smaller Vaux's Swift *C. vauxi* from western North America is difficult, but Vaux's is paler on the breast and rump and shows more contrast in the facial pattern, with slightly darker ear-coverts. Also, Vaux's does very little gliding (Dunn, 1979).

WHITE-THROATED NEEDLETAIL
Hirundapus caudacutus

Range The nominate race breeds in central and eastern Siberia, northern Mongolia and northern China, east to Japan. It is a very long range migrant, wintering in Australia. A resident race (*nudipes*) occurs in the Himalayas.

Occurrences There have been eight records (up to 1991) and, unlike other eastern Siberian vagrants, spring is the peak time: all have occurred in the period 25 May to 27 July. Five have been recorded in the eight years 1983–91, including four in Orkney or Shetland, and it has been suggested that one returning individual may be responsible. In 1991, a record in Kent on 26 May was followed by ones in Staffordshire on 1 June, Derbyshire on the 3rd, and Shetland on 11–14 June, and it does seem likely that these 'four' at least related to one northward-moving bird. Such an unusual occurrence pattern raises the question: how do they get here? Perhaps north-westward-moving spring migrants in Siberia overshoot and, following a great circle route, end up in Britain. The other possibility is that autumn juveniles somehow wind up in Africa and then move north in spring with Common Swifts *Apus apus*. In this respect, the apparently northward-moving 1991 bird and a November record from Malta (*BWP*) may perhaps add credence to this theory.

Identification This is a very spectacular bird and, consequently, it is a highly sought-after vagrant. It is a large swift, about the size of an Alpine *A. melba*, with a wing span of up to 20 in (53 cm). It is one of the world's fastest birds, and authenticated measurements have shown that it is capable of speeds over 100 mph, or 160 kph (Gooders, 1969). When overhead, its presence is sometimes detectable by the 'wooshing' sound of its wings. It is easily distinguished from other European swifts by its square tail (with fine, inconspicuous protruding spines), large white throat, prominent white horseshoe shaped patch on the undertail-coverts, and large whitish patch on the back. These features are shown to good effect in Plates 51.2 & 3, which show those present at Quendale and the Loch of Hilwell, Shetland, in May–June 1984, and on Hoy, Orkney, in June 1988.

PALLID SWIFT
Apus pallidus

Range Breeds from the Banc d'Arguin in Mauritania through the Mediterranean to Pakistan, as well as in isolated localities along the southern edge of the Sahara. Some winter within the breeding range but most move into tropical Africa. They are thought to winter mainly in a broad band across the northern African tropics, but identification problems make the exact extent of their winter range uncertain and it seems likely that, once there, they make extensive intra-seasonal movements (*BWP*).

Occurrences Considering that this is a locally common Mediterranean species, breeding as close to Britain as the Toulouse area of southern France, it is remarkably rare here. The first was an individual recently discovered in the National Museum, Dublin,

which had been collected at St John's Point, Co. Down, in October 1913. The next was a heavily twitched individual at Stodmarsh, Kent, in May 1978 (Harvey, 1981), and this has been followed by another eight (to 1993), including a remarkable influx of four in November 1984, two of which appeared together at Portland, Dorset.

Identification Although the Pallid Swift is probably genuinely rare here, its close similarity to the Common Swift *A. apus* strongly mitigates against its discovery. Plate 51.4 shows the 1978 Stodmarsh bird. It can be distinguished from the Common Swift by its paler, milkier brown plumage, darker outer primaries which contrast with the paler greater coverts and secondaries, slightly darker body (the mantle forming a slight 'saddle' contrasting with the wings), a slightly more extensive pale throat, pale scaling on the flanks (this may be obvious at close range), and a dark eye and 'eye shadow' which contrast with the pale head. Evaluation of these features is, however, dependent on distance and light. A dull, flat light is best, the differences being particularly difficult to detect in bright sunlight. Vagrants have to be separated from the paler eastern race of the Common Swift (*pekinensis*) which could conceivably occur here. *Pekinensis* is very similar to the Pallid in its plumage, but the Pallid differs in having blunter wing tips (the two outer primaries are similar in length) and a slightly shallower tail fork; *pekinensis* is similar in shape to the nominate *apus*, with pointed wings and a long tail with a deep fork. In their breeding areas Pallids give a markedly disyllabic *churr-ic* or *cheeoo-eet* call.

PACIFIC SWIFT
Apus pacificus

Range Breeds from Siberia eastwards to Japan and south through China to Southeast Asia and the Himalayas. The nominate northern race is a long distance migrant, wintering from Southeast Asia to Australia and New Zealand.

Occurrences The first record concerned one which attempted to land on the shoulder of a worker on a gas platform about 28 miles (45 km) off Happisburgh, Norfolk, on 19 June 1981. It was eventually caught and sent ashore by helicopter to Beccles. Fortunately, it was then examined by Mike Parker, a birdwatcher who worked at the heliport. It was eventually released and identified as the Western Palearctic's first Pacific Swift, a species which few British birders had even heard of at the time (Parker, 1990). A second occurred at Cley, Norfolk, on 30 May 1993 (Plate 51.5), and a third at Daventry Reservoir, Northamptonshire, on 16 July 1995.

Identification Similar in size to the Common Swift *A. apus*, the Pacific is most readily distinguished by its prominent, slightly horseshoe-shaped white rump patch (although beware of partially albinistic Common Swifts). It is blacker than the Common with a diffusely paler throat which merges into the breast. It shows delicate pale feather fringes to its underparts and underwing-coverts, although these are invisible at any distance. Structurally, it has longer and proportionately narrower wings with a longer, more deeply forked 'fish-like' tail (this is readily apparent in Plate 51.5).

ALPINE SWIFT
Apus melba

Range Breeds throughout southern Europe and North Africa, east into Kazakhstan and western Pakistan. Other races occur in Arabia, eastern and southern Africa, and in the Indian subcontinent. Palearctic breeders winter in the northern African tropics but its winter range is poorly known, due partly to problems of distinguishing it from the endemic African races.

Occurrences The Alpine Swift is an annual visitor, with as many as 23 in 1988. As to be expected, it is mainly a southern bird, with most occurring in southeastern England. It is one of the earliest spring overshoots (an individual was recorded in 1987 in Pembrokeshire as early as 1 March) but the peak is from April to June. Small numbers may occur right through the summer, with a secondary peak in late September and early October. It sometimes occurs in small parties and there were as many as five at Killiney, Co. Dublin, on 20 March 1992. One found dead on St Agnes, Isles of Scilly, on 24 September 1969 had been ringed as a nestling at Solothurn, Switzerland, two months previously.

Identification Plate 51.6 shows an individual at Cromer, Norfolk, in April 1985. It is a large swift, about 20 per cent larger than the Common Swift *A. apus*. It has noticeably long, scythe-shaped wings but size and shape differences may be surprisingly difficult to evaluate, even when the two species are together. It is easily identified by its white underparts, but the white throat tends to be noticeable only at closer ranges. In bright sunlight the underwings may look very dark, almost blackish, but the upperparts usually appear paler than Common, being similar in shade to those of a Sand Martin *Riparia riparia*. It glides more than the Common and the long wings produce slower wingbeats and a more languid flight action which, at times, can even suggest a Eurasian Hobby *Falco subbuteo*. The only real risk of misidentification lies with partially albino Common Swifts, so it is

always important to clearly establish size and upperpart colour when faced with a vagrant. At its breeding sites it gives quite a loud, slow, fairly high-pitched rippling trill, with a *peee-ut* sometimes tagged on to the end or even used alone.

LITTLE SWIFT
Apus affinis

Range Breeds in Mauritania and in North Africa from Morocco to Tunisia, and also in the Near and Middle East, as well as over much of tropical Africa, east to India, Southeast Asia, Indonesia and Japan. Palearctic breeders are thought to be migratory or partially migratory, although many overwinter in North Africa.

Occurrences The first record was in June 1967 on Cape Clear Island, Co. Cork (Sharrock, 1968), and there have since been a further nine (to 1991) with records in May–June, August and November. Seven have occurred on the western side of the country, perhaps suggesting a Moroccan origin. Only two have stayed more than a single day and, to date, this is a species that has eluded the vast majority of twitchers.

Identification The Little Swift is about three-quarters the size of a Common Swift *A. apus* and is easily identified by its striking broad white rump and square tail. The latter produces a truncated look to the rear end. Its shorter wings produce faster, more fluttery bat-like wingbeats, alternated with short glides and side-to-side banking. High-pitched fast trilling calls may be heard in its breeding areas. Plate 51.7 shows one at Skewjack Pools, Cornwall, on 16 May 1981. The remarkably sharp photograph shows that it was in moult, having lost its secondaries and some of its innermost primaries; the remaining primaries are worn. *BWP* indicates that primary moult can begin as early as late April.

BELTED KINGFISHER
Ceryle alcyon

Range Breeds across much of North America, wintering in the milder coastal and southern areas, and penetrating south to Panama and the West Indies.

Occurrences The Belted Kingfisher has had a chequered history as a British and Irish bird. The first modern record was of a female on the Bunree River, Co. Mayo, from December 1978 to February 1979. On its last date, a small party of birders from Dublin managed to see it, but it was shot that very afternoon by a local man who had an interest in taxidermy. The offender was successfully prosecuted and the specimen now resides in the National Museum in Dublin (Mullarney, 1981). The Irish bird prompted the resurrection of an old British record of a female shot at Sladesbridge, Cornwall, in November 1908, and this was subsequently accepted as the first. Remarkably, the third came from the very same area: a widely twitched juvenile/first-winter male present in the Sladesbridge and other areas of Cornwall from November 1979 to August 1980 (Plates 52.1 & 2). There have been two subsequently in Ireland: in Co. Down in October 1980, and in Co. Clare and Co. Tipperary from October 1984 to March 1985. Incredibly, the former was also shot. There are also old records from the Netherlands and Iceland.

Identification In a British or Irish context, the Belted Kingfisher is simply unmistakable, being about the size of a Eurasian Jackdaw *Corvus monedula*, grey and white in coloration, and with a punk 'hair-do'. In flight, it shows a large white patch at the base of the primaries. It can be sexed by reference to the breast bands, females having a second, chestnut band below the grey one. When it first arrived, the 1979 Sladesbridge bird had a restricted area of chestnut on the sides of the breast and flanks, which is compatible with a juvenile male. By the time the photographs were taken (at Boscathnoe Reservoir, Penzance, in August 1980), this coloration had been moulted out. It was easily located by its distinctive call: a hard, fast, rattling *t-r-r-r-r-r*, frequently likened to the sound of a football rattle, but perhaps more accurately compared to a deepened alarm of a Mistle Thrush *Turdus viscivorus*.

BLUE-CHEEKED BEE-EATER
Merops superciliosus

Range Two races of the Blue-cheeked Bee-eater breed in the Western Palearctic. *Persicus* breeds in Egypt and the Middle East, east to Kazakhstan and north-western India. Further east it is replaced by the closely related Blue-tailed Bee-eater *M. philippinus*. *Chrysocercus* breeds in Morocco and Algeria. Both populations winter mainly in sub-Saharan Africa, where the species breeds south to Namibia, Mozambique and Madagascar. They occur in more arid regions than the European Bee-eater *M. apiaster*, often close to water (*BWP*).

Occurrences The first two recorded in Britain occurred in the Isles of Scilly in 1921 and 1951, and the former, which was shot, can still be seen in the museum on St Mary's. There have been five other records since 1982, including three in 1989, but in view of its extreme rarity here there must be a chance that at least some of the 1989 records related to just one wandering individual. There was, however, also

one in Denmark at the same time, so the possibility of a small influx cannot be entirely ruled out (*Brit. Birds* **83**: 471–472). All but one of the British records have been made in June or July.

Identification This is without doubt one of the most beautiful and exotic birds on the British List. The one in Plates 52.3 & 4 is the only twitchable one to have occurred and was present at Cowden, Yorkshire, in July 1989, in the rather ignominious setting of a caravan site. At rest, it appears longer, slimmer and more attenuated than European Bee-eater, with a longer, less tapered bill and longer projecting central tail feathers. These may be up to 4 in (10 cm) in length but, in direct comparison, the male's projection is about twice as long as the female's. The plumage is almost entirely green, but rather turquoise on the rump in flight. Most distinctive is the facial pattern: it has a clear-cut, jet-black, eye-stripe (appearing almost as if painted on) and this is bordered above and below by brilliant turquoise-blue. In turn, this contrasts with a bright yellow and dull red chin and throat. In flight, it has noticeably copper underwing-coverts and a black trailing edge to the wing (both surfaces). The flight calls are higher-pitched than European, a rolling *prrip, prrreep* or a more disyllabic *pree-up*. It also gives lower, softer calls at rest.

The racial identity of the Cowden bird does not seem to have been firmly established. *BWP* describes *chrysocercus* as having, in general, less or no white on the forehead, a narrower blue supercilium and it shows longer projecting tail streamers than *persicus*. In this respect, it would appear to tie in with *persicus*. *BWP* also states that the Moroccan population is local, with perhaps 40–60 pairs. If that figure is in the right order, then it would seem that *persicus* is far more likely to occur as a vagrant. This is a conclusion also reached by Ebels & van der Laan (1994), who analysed all the European records.

EUROPEAN BEE-EATER
Merops apiaster

Range Breeds through the Mediterranean into the Middle East, northwards into the Ukraine and southern Russia and east into Kazakhstan. It winters in West, East and southern Africa. A separate population breeds in South Africa.

Occurrences The European Bee-eater is a classic spring overshoot, with most records occurring in late May and early June. It has occurred, however, from mid-April right through to November, but it is much more unusual in autumn. The numbers occurring here showed a marked increase in the 1980s, with as many as 36 in 1987 and 32 in 1988. Inevitably, it was dropped from the Rarities List at the end of 1990, just in time to avoid a remarkable influx of 60–72 in 1991 (Evans, 1992). Whilst its appearances here are to a large extent weather-related, there has been a marked increase and northward spread in France since about 1930, with breeding regularly recorded in the Paris region since 1968 (*BWP*). In view of this, it is perhaps surprising that there have been no breeding attempts in Britain since the last in Sussex in 1955, when three pairs nested (two of these raised seven young). Our appallingly wet climate is no doubt to blame.

Identification Little needs to be said about the identification of one of the most brightly coloured and beautiful birds on the British and Irish List. Plate 52.5 is a stunning portrait of an individual which was present at Vidlin, Shetland, in June 1995. In the field, they are most easily located by their distinctive, far-carrying call: a rolling, soft, liquid *prup...prup* or *qulip*. This is often heard long before a flock appears, hawking insects high in the blue summer sky. Their long, pointed wings and protruding central tail feathers are then distinctive. They often alternate periods of gliding with periods of flapping, but prolonged flight is more undulating and purposeful. The male is slightly bigger and brighter than the female.

EUROPEAN ROLLER
Coracias garrulus

Range Breeds from Iberia and Morocco eastwards through the Mediterranean, Asia Minor and the Middle East, north into Eastern Europe and east to the Russian Steppes. It winters in East Africa.

Occurrences The European Roller is a very rare vagrant, with rarely more than two or three a year, mostly in late spring and summer. It has declined considerably over much of north-central Europe and no longer breeds in Sweden or Germany. Climatic change has been blamed, but habitat loss and modern farming practices seem more likely culprits. Despite this sorry state of affairs, the species is still almost annual in Britain and has a wide geographical scatter. English east coast counties provide most, this perhaps suggesting an easterly rather than a southerly origin for the bulk of our vagrants.

Identification The bird in Plate 53.1 was present at East Budleigh Common, Devon, in May–June 1989. Almost the size of a Eurasian Jackdaw *Corvus monedula*, and bright blue with a chestnut back and scapulars, the European Roller is unmistakable. It is often seen sitting in the tops of pine trees or on overhead wires, dropping to the ground for food. From the insect's point of view, the bright blue plumage is presumably good camouflage against a cloudless sky. It has a powerful but flappy flight with quick, deep wingbeats. The wings are long and rounded and the brilliant blue leading upperwing-coverts contrast with the sky blue central area, which in turn contrasts with dark, deep blue primaries and secondaries. On its breeding grounds, it often twists and turns in flight, hence its name. It is surprisingly noisy when nesting, giving a large variety of harsh, throaty, rasping calls.

YELLOW-BELLIED SAPSUCKER
Sphyrapicus varius

Range Breeds across southern Canada and northern USA. Winters in central and southern USA, Central America (south to Panama) and in the West Indies. Females tend to move further south than males.

Occurrences There are two records of juvenile/first-winters: a male on Tresco, Isles of Scilly, from 26 September to 6 October 1975 (Hunt, 1979); and a female on Cape Clear Island, Co. Cork, from 16–19 October 1988. It seems remarkable that a North American woodpecker should cross the Atlantic; the only other species known to have done so was a Northern Flicker *Colaptes auratus*, which flew ashore from the RMS *Mauretania* at Cobh Harbour, Co. Cork, on 13 October 1962. One can only speculate as to whether the sapsuckers were also ship-assisted but, in 1975, the contemporaneous appearance of a Scarlet Tanager *Piranga olivacea* and a Black-and-white Warbler *Mniotilta varia* in Scilly, as well as other North American passerines elsewhere in Britain, would suggest an unaided crossing.

Identification Plate 53.2 shows the Cape Clear bird. It is quite unlike any of our native woodpeckers, with its red crown, suppressed white rear supercilium and a white line running down from the lores. The body plumage messily barred and mottled and it has a large white patch across the inner wing coverts. Although the primaries and tail are moulted prior to autumn migration, much of the juvenile body plumage is retained into the winter, with most of what remains being replaced as late as March–April (*BWP*). The Tresco bird was sexed by the presence of scarlet on the chin; those without red can be either sex (the Irish bird was sexed in the hand).

Sapsuckers get their name from their habit of feeding on sweet sap and on the living tissue of woody plants, called bast, which is found just under the bark. They excavate small holes, or 'sap wells', and wait for droplets of the sweet liquid to accumulate. They make both vertical and horizontal rows of holes and maintain many wells at any one time. The birds palate is sensitive to the sweetness of the sap, and it laps it with a tongue that is abnormally short for a woodpecker but which has barbs at the tip. In spring, rising sap may stop during spells of cold weather and the sugars may then ferment, causing the sapsuckers to get drunk (Jackson, 1992).

CALANDRA LARK
Melanocorypha calandra

Range Breeds from Iberia and Morocco through the Mediterranean to Asia Minor, the Russian Steppes, east into Kazakhstan. It is mainly resident in the Mediterranean, the near East and in North Africa, but more migratory in the former Soviet Union.

Occurrences There are five records: four in April from Portland, Dorset, the Isles of Scilly (two) and Fair Isle, Shetland, and a September one from St Kilda, Outer Hebrides. The April ones at least would suggest a southern origin.

Identification Plate 53.3 shows one on St Agnes, Isles of Scilly, in April 1996. It is a large, bulky, heavy-billed lark, with long wings and a short tail. It has quite long, orange legs and it may show a noticeably crested effect. Most distinctive is a narrow black collar from the sides of the neck to the upper breast, usually just about meeting in the centre. There is variable streaking below this (extensive on some). It tends to be plainer-faced than Bimaculated *M. bimaculata*, with a less obvious supercilium (which sometimes curves around the ear-coverts to form an ear-covert surround). In flight, it has long, broad-based triangular wings which narrow towards the fingered tips. Most distinctively, the underwings are black with a prominent thick white trailing edge. From above, the remiges are contrastingly dark brown. The tail shows narrow white outer feathers. For a comparison with Bimaculated Lark, *see* below. The normal call is a hard, rattling, *t-t trip tip*, suggesting a loud Short-toed Lark *Calandrella brachydactyla* or maybe even a hard Sky Lark *Alauda arvensis*. It has deep wingbeats and often flutters like a Sky Lark. In its breeding areas, it can be seen displaying high in the sky with slow wingbeats and broad triangular wings. Its song is a jumble of soft notes and hard, often recalling quarrelling Common Starlings *Sturnus vulgaris* when heard at a distance.

BIMACULATED LARK
Melanocorypha bimaculata

Range Breeds from Turkey and the Middle East eastwards to Iran and Kazakhstan. Some winter on the southern edge of the breeding range but the majority migrate to north-eastern Africa, the Middle East, and eastwards to Pakistan and north-western India. Where they occur together, Bimaculated tends to occupy broken ground, such as hillsides, whereas Calandra *M. calandra* occurs on lower, flatter areas, such as extensive plains.

Occurrences There are just three British records: on Lundy, Devon, in May 1962; on St Mary's, Isles of Scilly, in October 1975, and on Fair Isle, Shetland, in June 1976.

Identification The Bimaculated Lark is similar to the slightly larger Calandra Lark, and indeed the Lundy bird was originally identified as that species, its true identity coming to light during the record's circulation around the Rarities Committee (Jones, 1965). In an accompanying editorial comment in *British Birds*, the finders were congratulated for producing a description of what they actually saw, even though some of the details seemed 'wrong' at the time. It is larger and plumper than a Sky Lark *Alauda arvensis*, being thick-set, big-headed and thick-necked, with a much stouter bill, and much paler colour. Like the Calandra Lark, it shows a prominent black band from the shoulder, tapering towards the centre of the upper breast. It has a distinct white supercilium from the eye back (more prominent than that of the Calandra and even suggesting that of a Wood Lark *Lullula arborea* at a distance), dark-edged ear-coverts and slight wing bars.

The Bimaculated is most easily separated in flight and Plate 53.4 shows the St Mary's bird from below. It has broad, triangular wings and a short tail but, most distinctively, the underwings are brown, paler towards the rear, with no white trailing edge. The Calandra has longer, broader, more rounded wings and a longer tail. It shows black underwings, with a very conspicuous clear-cut white trailing edge. From above, the Calandra has dark brown primaries and secondaries (the upperwing is more uniformly pale brown on the Bimaculated). Also, whereas the Calandra has white outer tail feathers, the Bimaculated has a shorter, paler tail with a narrow white tip. The call is a hard *chid-ip* but the Lundy bird gave short calls, not unlike those of a Sky Lark: *prrp* or *chrrp*, but occasionally *prrp-cheewit-chewit*; it was also heard singing (loc. cit.).

SHORT-TOED LARK
Calandrella brachydactyla

Range Breeds locally in France, and from Iberia and north-west Africa eastwards through the Mediterranean, the Middle East and the Russian steppes into Mongolia and China. Western Palearctic breeders winter in North Africa and along the southern edge of the Sahara.

Occurrences This is a regular vagrant, occurring mainly in May and again in September–October, although there have been records at other times of the year, including winter. Most have occurred in Shetland and Scilly, as well as along the intervening east and south coasts. The species currently averages about 18 a year and was dropped from the Rarities List at the end of 1993. Our vagrants involve overshooting southern birds in spring (which tend to be redder on the crown) and eastern ones (which tend to be greyer overall). Eastern individuals are thought to predominate in autumn (Dymond *et al.*, 1989).

Identification The Short-toed is a small, pale lark, readily located amongst flocks of Sky Larks *Alauda arvensis* with which it sometimes associates. In flight it has broad-based wings with narrow tips but it lacks that species' prominent white trailing edge. Its hard chirruping calls are more sparrow-like: usually a hard *trip* or *t-t-trip*, but also a soft *wik-wik*.

The bird in Plate 53.5 was present on St Mary's, Isles of Scilly, in October 1992. It is a rather nondescript individual, lacking much in the way of a pale supercilium (which the species usually shows), but it has a creamy eye surround, a faint brown line behind the eye and a very faint curved brown line running from the bill below the eye. This is a rather sandy bird with creamy feather fringes, but individuals vary considerably in plumage tone, from sandy to grey. Note the dark-centred median coverts, which often stand out as a dark bar. Although not really visible in the photograph, the underparts are buffish-white, usually showing two small, rather inconspicuous dark patches on the sides of the breast. Some, like this bird, also show diffuse dark streaking or a brown suffusion across the upper breast, even in spring. The legs are pale, pinky or orangey. The photograph shows to good effect the long tertials, which almost completely cloak the primaries (unlike the Lesser Short-toed Lark *C. rufescens* which shows a long primary projection about half the overlying tertial length). Note that it has its crown feathers raised; it is not always appreciated that it may at times show a distinctly crested effect. It often feeds between short, erratic bursts of running.

TREE SWALLOW
Tachycineta bicolor

Range An abundant species right across North America, breeding in holes in trees and fence posts, in building crevices and in nest boxes. It is particularly common where old dead trees occur alongside fresh water. It is an early and late migrant and may resort to eating berries when available, particularly bayberries. In autumn, huge numbers move down the eastern seaboard and, unlike other North American hirundines, it winters in strength in the southern states, as well as south to Central America and the West Indies.

Occurrence In view of its abundance and distribution in North America, it is not surprising that the Tree Swallow has reached Europe. The individual in Plates 54.1 & 2, is a male that was present at Porthellick Pool, St Mary's, Isles of Scilly, in June 1990. Its five-day stay enabled large numbers of birders to obtain close-range views as it hawked over the pool and adjacent beach, usually with House Martins *Delichon urbica* and Barn Swallows *Hirundo rustica*, often resting on signposts, buildings and boulders on the beach. An old claim of one shot from a flock of Sand Martins *Riparia riparia* in Derby in 1850 is not considered to be acceptable. There is some doubt about the specimen's authenticity and, despite the fact that it was supposed to have been deposited in Norwich Museum, a search there failed to find any trace of it (*Brit. Birds* **86**: 188).

Identification In many respects the Tree Swallow suggests a House Martin without a white rump. It is, however, rather heavier bodied and chunkier, but it is slightly longer winged and has a more swallow-like flight. Unlike the House Martin, the legs and feet are unfeathered, a feature shown well in Plate 54.1. The beautiful metallic blue back, rump and scapulars are very bright in strong sunlight, even giving a greeny tint at some angles. Most females are duller, while juveniles are grey-brown above, with a diffuse grey breast band, but adult plumage starts to show through by their first-autumn. They are quite vocal, giving a soft, sparrow-like *treep* or *trip*.

RED-RUMPED SWALLOW
Hirundo daurica

Range Breeds from Morocco and Iberia, locally in Italy and east through the Balkans, Asia Minor and the Middle East to India, much of China, Mongolia and Japan. It also breeds locally in tropical Africa. Western Palearctic breeders are assumed to winter in the savannah zone of the African tropics, but migrants are inseparable from local African races. Eastern Palearctic breeders winter mainly in the Indian subcontinent, east into parts of Southeast Asia.

Occurrences There were only seven records up to 1958, and it was so rare that three in 1952 in Norfolk, Devon and Co. Wexford were thought possibly to have related to the same bird (Hollom, 1960). It has been annual since 1964 and has shown a large increase, with 13 in both 1977 and 1980. Numbers remained unexceptional during the 1980s until 1987, when there was an astonishing influx of about 64, followed by 18 in 1988, 32 in 1990 and at least 20 in 1994. The 1987 influx occurred mainly during a period of southerly winds in late October and early November, and included parties of up to seven on St Mary's, Isles of Scilly, and five at the Point of Air, Flintshire.

Although unusual weather conditions produced the influx, the general increase here is the result of a northward spread in Iberia. Before 1929 it bred only in the extreme south, but reached central Spain in the early 1950s and the French border by 1960. It first bred in the south of France in 1963, and there have been several breeding records there since (*BWP*). It is of interest, therefore, that a male held territory at Corfe Mullen, Dorset, in the summer of 1988 and even helped to raise a brood of House Martins *Delichon urbica*. It typically occurs here as a spring overshoot in April–June, although in 1994 one arrived on Tresco, Isles of Scilly, on the remarkably early date of 28 February.

Identification The Red-rumped Swallow is superficially similar to the Barn Swallow *H. rustica*, but both the wing shape and flight are more reminiscent of a House Martin, having a stiffer flight action with more gliding. Also, the wings are not swept back like those of a Barn Swallow. The tail streamers are very long and are often held close together, producing a tapered, pointed effect to the rear end (vaguely suggesting a Budgerigar *Melopsittacus undulatus*!). As its name suggests, it has a narrow buffish rump which is markedly duller and smaller than that of a House Martin (although note that juvenile House Martins often show a dull, greyish rump). The other main differences are the blackish 'skull cap' which is isolated from the orangey-red ear-coverts, a pale throat and a narrow neck collar, not always easy to see. The underparts are creamy, it shows a plainer underwing (lacking the Barn Swallow's contrast between the wing coverts and the remiges) and, most importantly, the undertail-coverts are black, giving the impression that the tail has been 'stuck on' to the rear of the body. It has distinctive, soft, sparrow-like calls: *chree-up*, *chur-eet*, *chuwee*, *shreep* and so on.

Plate 54.3 was taken at Cley, Norfolk, in April 1987, this individual showing the distinctive head pattern. Plate 54.5 shows one in flight at Gibraltar Point, Lincolnshire, in the following month. The distinctive rump and long tail are clearly apparent. Plate 54.4 shows a juvenile on St Mary's in October 1988. It is similar to an adult, but is slightly duller with narrow buff fringes to the wing feathers, those on the tertials being most prominent. The tail is surprisingly long and, in the field, it is not strikingly shorter than that of an adult.

CLIFF SWALLOW
Hirundo pyrrhonota

Range Breeds across much of North America, from central Alaska to Nova Scotia and south to central Mexico. It winters mainly in northern Argentina, southern Brazil and Paraguay. It is thus one of the longest range Nearctic passerine migrants

Occurrences There are five records: a juvenile on St Agnes and St Mary's, Isles of Scilly, in October 1983 (Crosby, 1988); one, probably a juvenile, at South Gare, Yorkshire, in October 1988, and, remarkably, three in October–December 1995, at Spurn, Yorkshire, at Dunmore Head, Co. Kerry, and on Tresco, Isles of Scilly (plus one in 1996). A certain amount of confusion following the discovery of the first Scilly individual resulted from the fact that several observers interpreted the CB message as 'Cliff Waller on the Garrison'.

Identification Plates 55.1 & 2 show the 1982 Scilly bird. It is rather bull-necked, with broad-based wings and a stocky body. The photograph shows two important features: the square tail and the dark throat. In good light the latter was blackish with a slight reddish tint, while, below, the breast and flanks were orangey-brown and the belly a whitish coloration. From above, a sandy-grey shawl over the nape and a dull but nevertheless prominent sandy-buff rump were distinctive. The dull plumage and pale tertial fringes showed it to be a juvenile. The collar, tail shape and throat colour allowed instant separation from the more familiar Red-rumped Swallow *H. daurica*. The call is a low-pitched, soft, squeaky *chrrr*.

In North America, the Cliff Swallow has to be distinguished from the similar Cave Swallow *H. fulva*, which is spreading northwards in Texas. The Cave has a pale orangey throat so that the black crown contrasts with the rest of the head. It is more slightly built than the Cliff Swallow with narrower wings, shows a dark forehead and may have a darker rump (Richard Crossley, verbally). The Cave Swallow may seem an unlikely vagrant, but it has occurred as far north as the Maritime Provinces of Canada and several have been recorded in late autumn at Cape May, New Jersey, in recent years.

RICHARD'S PIPIT
Anthus novaeseelandiae

Range Breeds across southern Siberia and eastern China, wintering from Pakistan east through India to southern China and Southeast Asia. Numerous other races occur across much of sub-Saharan Africa, the Indian subcontinent and Southeast Asia, through Indonesia, the Philippines and New Guinea to Australia and New Zealand.

Occurrences Richard's Pipit is an annual visitor, mainly occurring from mid-September to November, with most in the Northern Isles, down the British east coast and along the south coast to the Isles of Scilly. Dymond *et al.,* (1989) noted an average of only seven per year from 1958 to 1965, increasing to 48 per year from 1976 to 1982. In the intervening late 1960s, there were some remarkable influxes, culminating in about 150 in 1968, a total which has never been surpassed. They sometimes occur in small parties, the largest being 11 on North Ronaldsay, Orkney, on 27 September 1992, another big influx year (Evans, 1993a). Small numbers sometimes remain to winter, and a small peak from late March to early May no doubt involves individuals which have wintered further south.

Our birds are undoubtedly reversed migrants. The orientation of a German-ringed vagrant, recovered in the same autumn in south-western France (*BWP*), would appear to conform with a great circle route movement out of central Siberia. It is particularly interesting to note that *BWP* records regular wintering in southern Spain and possibly in the Sahel zone of West Africa, whilst in January 1995 there were as many as 16 at the Oued Massa in southern Morocco (Martin Cade, verbally). This suggests that they have established a regular winter range in the Western Palearctic.

Identification Plate 55.3 shows a first-winter on St Mary's, Isles of Scilly, in October 1994. It can be aged by reference to the median and greater coverts, which are retained juvenile feathers: they are browny-black with narrow and well-marked buffish-white fringes (on the adult these are rather broadly and diffusely fringed brownish-buff; Svensson, 1992). Richard's is a large, bulky pipit, with a hefty, rather thrush-like bill (slightly angled up from the face), rather a wedge-shaped head profile, long pink or orange legs and a long tail. It is rather dark above, variably streaked, it has a large, dark malar patch at the base of the throat, and it shows random dark streaking across the breast. When visible, the hind claw is very long. It usually feeds in longish grass, moving with a jerky walk and often searching in a methodical manner, frequently wagging its tail. It may look bold and upright when alert.

By the time most Richard's arrive, many young Tawny Pipits *A. campestris* will have moulted into an adult-like first-winter plumage, which is basically plain and sandy. Some young Tawnies may, however, retain much juvenile plumage into October and even beyond. Such birds should appear smaller and slighter than Richard's, and should be more neatly streaked on the breast; the retained juvenile upperpart feathers are, in fact, dark-centred with pale

fringes, thus producing a scalloped appearance. If in doubt, check the head. Richard's has rather an 'open' facial expression caused to a large extent by the pale lores; the Tawny has a distinct black line from the bill to the eye, producing a much 'sharper' facial expression (*see* Plate 56.1). On Richard's, the buff supercilium extends around the back of the ear-coverts to produce an ill-defined 'supercilium surround'.

In flight, Richard's Pipit looks rather long-tailed and almost wagtail-like. It has a purposeful, undulating flight and it often hovers before landing, when its white outer tail feathers may be particularly prominent. It is very vocal, the call being a loud, sparrow-like *shreep, chreep* or *chreep-chreep*; several calls are sometimes strung together.

BLYTH'S PIPIT
Anthus godlewskii

Range Breeds in Mongolia and neighbouring parts of China, south to Tibet, and winters in the Indian subcontinent, including Sri Lanka. With the problems of identification, it seems likely that the full details of its wintering range are yet to be discovered.

Occurrences 'There can be few species on the British List quite so enigmatic as Blyth's Pipit'. Colin Bradshaw's opening sentence in his 1994 *British Birds* identification paper hits the nail on the head. The species owes its position on the British List to the late Kenneth Williamson, who in 1963 discovered a specimen in the British Museum which had been obtained at Brighton, Sussex, in October 1862. Since then, it has provided a real identification headache and has generated much discussion in twitching circles. Only in recent years has a clearer understanding of its appearance enabled further confident claims. This has been greatly assisted by the occurrence of trapped individuals in Finland and by the recent increase in European birders visiting China. There are now some top-quality photographs in existence (for example, in Bradshaw, 1994), and a good understanding of its subtle features is rapidly evolving. As a consequence, there have been a number of recent claims, the five best-observed being (to 1994): at Skewjack, Cornwall, in October–November 1990 (Heard, 1990); trapped on Fair Isle, Shetland, in October–November 1993 (Leitch, 1993); on St Mary's, Isles of Scilly, in October 1993 (Evans, 1993b); trapped at Landguard Point, Suffolk, in November 1994 (eventually taken by a Common Kestrel *Falco tinnunculus*; Marsh & Odin, 1994); and at South Swale, Kent, in November-December 1994. There have been several since and it seems likely that it will prove to be tolerably regular here.

Identification Plumage-wise, Blyth's Pipit is very similar to Richard's Pipit *A. novaeseelandiae*, although its size and jizz may suggest a Tawny *A. campestris*. It is heavily streaked and, like Richard's, it can be readily distinguished from the Tawny by its pale lores. Its identification has for a long time been bogged down by the search for a feature or features which can be regarded at 100 per cent diagnostic. Although tail pattern and hind-claw length are particularly good, it has become clear that a holistic approach is required. In other words, it is identifiable by a *combination* of a number of minor and subtle features that produce a distinctive jizz which is quite different from Richard's. It is clear, however, that detailed notes and, preferably, photographs will be required for records of non-trapped individuals.

The following are the main differences from Richard's: (1) **size** It is distinctly smaller, with a more horizontal, wagtail-like posture; (2) **tail** This is comparatively short (because of this the Skewjack bird could be difficult to distinguish from Meadow Pipits, *A. pratensis*, when overhead!); (3) **bill** It has a short, rather delicate, pointed bill, quite unlike the more thrush-like bill and wedge-shaped head profile of a Richard's (compare the head profiles of Plate 55.7 with Plate 55.2); (4) **hind claw** This is comparatively short, more arched and similar in length to the hind toe (Richard's hind claw can best be appreciated when the bird is seen perched on a fence or wires, when it appears ridiculously long);. (5) **supercilium** This is creamy and rather 'squared-off' at the rear; (6) **face** It appears rather pale- and plain-faced; (7) **crown and mantle** These are neatly and boldly streaked; (8) **median coverts** On the adult feathers only (juvenile feathers are similar), the dark centre on Blyth's is more sharply defined and more squarely cut off across the tip (it is more pointed and more diffuse on an adult Richard's); (9) **penultimate tail feather** The white at the tip of this feather tends to be cut off at an angle across the tip of the feather (it extends further up the feather in a point on Richard's); (10) **breast streaking** It shows a gorget of profuse, neat, small, fine streaks; (11) **jizz** It has an overall jizz reminiscent of that of a Tree Pipit *A. trivialis*, (12) **calls** Tends to give a *chup* or *chep* but a shriller *pshreeo* is most distinctive, suggesting a Yellow Wagtail *Motacilla flava* or, with a bit of imagination, even a Red-throated Pipit *A. cervinus* (Alan Dean, verbally).

Plates 55.4–7 show the three Blyth's at Skewjack, St Mary's Golf Course and Landguard Point. What perhaps is initially striking is that they all look different! The Landguard bird (Plate 55.7) is rather brown and well streaked, the Skewjack bird (Plate 55.6) is brown and messy, but the St Mary's bird (Plates 55.4 & 5) is pale with a heavily lined mantle. Careful examination, however, shows that all three are the same species, exhibiting most of the identification features listed above and, quite clearly, their respective 'jizzes' are wrong for a Richard's. The Skewjack bird is more worn than the others and its plumage is dishevelled (hence its messy appearance), whereas the St Mary's bird is fresh and immaculate, with broad, pale creamy feather fringes and well-lined upperparts. This paler appearance ties in with a photograph of a fresh spring bird at Beidaihe, China, in Bradshaw (1994). It seems that, like autumn Tawny Pipits, vagrant Blyth's may be in varying stages of body moult from juvenile to first-winter and that, like most pipits, Blyth's starts pale and wears darker and browner.

TAWNY PIPIT
Anthus campestris

Range Breeds in north-western Africa and right across continental Europe (mainly south of the Baltic), east through Asia Minor to China and Mongolia. It winters in a broad band south of the Sahara, east through the Arabian Peninsula to India.

Occurrences Small numbers occur in spring but the peak time is from late August to mid-October, with most along the English south coast. As it breeds on the near Continent, many of these are best regarded as passage migrants or dispersing first-winters rather than vagrants. Dymond *et al.* (1989) noted 637 from 1958 to 1985, an average of 35 a year, and it was dropped from the Rarities List at the end of 1982. Fraser & Ryan (1994) reported a small increase from 1986 to 1992, with an annual average of 40 and a peak of 55 in 1992. This is surprising in view of a widespread decrease in France, the Netherlands, Germany, Sweden and even regions further east (*BWP*). The decline seems to have been caused mainly by habitat changes.

Identification The Tawny Pipit is smaller, slighter and more wagtail-like than Richard's Pipit *A. novaeseelandiae*, with a finer, more pointed bill. Adults are sandy with faint breast streaking, a buff supercilium, narrow dark moustachial and malar stripes, a dark median covert bar and long orangey legs. Important in its separation from Richard's Pipit is a dark line across the lores, from the bill to the eye.

Juveniles are browner and much more streaky, both above and below, and show a distinct ear-covert patch. Note that the dark centred mantle and scapular feathers are actually scalloped, the feathers being dark with pale fringes. For a further discussion on distinguishing it from Richard's Pipit, *see* page 105.

Plate 56.1 shows an individual at Southwold, Suffolk, in November 1992. Most young birds seem to moult out of juvenile plumage prior to migration, but there is considerable variation. Its plumage is adult-like, but the upperparts show a mixture of dark-centred juvenile feathers and newly moulted plain sandy-brown first-winter ones, while there is some messy spotting on the breast. Retained juvenile greater coverts are narrowly and distinctly fringed buffish-white (they are broadly and diffusely fringed brownish-buff on adults; Svensson, 1992).

It usually feeds in fairly barren or short-grass environments, avoiding long vegetation, and it often moves with a hesitant stop-start action, wagging its tail and rear end. Its calls are softer and less rasping than those of Richard's; a squeaky, sparrow-like *tree-up* or *che-up*, or a musical, sparrow-like *chlup* or softer *schlup*.

OLIVE-BACKED PIPIT
Anthus hodgsoni

Range The race *yunnanensis*, which occurs as a vagrant, breeds from the Urals across Siberia to the Pacific, mainly in the coniferous forest zone. The nominate race breeds further south, from the Himalayas to eastern China and Japan. It winters in India, Southeast Asia and in the Philippines.

Occurrences The first British records were made on Fair Isle, Shetland, in October 1964 and in September 1965 (Dennis, 1967). It subsequently transpired, however, that the species had already occurred here. On 14 April 1948, the late Peter Conder trapped an unusual pipit on Skokholm, Pembrokeshire, and fortunately photographed it. Following the publication of the details of the Fair Isle birds, Conder submitted his photograph to the editors of *British Birds*, who considered that the evidence was not adequate for acceptance as an Olive-backed Pipit. In 1977, however, Dr Tim Sharrock rediscovered the photograph in the *BB* files, and this eventually led to its acceptance as the first for Britain.

Up to the end of 1979, the Olive-backed remained a great rarity, with only 14 recorded, but there has since been a phenomenal upsurge with seven in 1984, 20 in 1987, an astonishing 46 in 1990, 18 in 1992 and 35 in 1993. By the end of 1995 the grand total stood at 195. As the main sites have been Fair Isle and the Isles of Scilly, it seems certain that the increase is genuine and not simply the result of greater observer awareness. Could the increase be related to deforestation in its winter and/or breeding range? Most have occurred in October, but it has also been seen in spring and winter, including the famous individual which wintered on a housing estate in Bracknell, Berkshire, in February–April 1984 (Plate 56.2). Plate 56.3 shows another, presumably a first-winter, on St Agnes, Isles of Scilly, in October 1989.

Identification The Olive-backed Pipit is similar to the Tree Pipit *A. trivialis*, but is plainer and generally greener on the mantle and scapulars and with much more heavily streaked, indeed, lined underparts. Most eye-catching, however, is the head pattern: it has a prominent whitish supercilium from the eye back, and a whitish 'supercilium drop' at the rear of the ear-coverts. Also distinctive is a narrow dark lateral crown stripe above the supercilium, the whole effect reminiscent of a Redwing *Turdus iliacus*. Note also the pale, straw-coloured legs. When photographed, the Bracknell bird had dropped its uppermost tertial. It behaves like a Tree Pipit, walking around slowly and furtively, frequently wagging its tail. Its calls are similar to the Tree Pipit's but are slightly thinner and shriller: *tzzseeep, spzee, skzeee* or *skier*.

PECHORA PIPIT
Anthus gustavi

Range As a breeding bird, it creeps into the Western Palearctic, breeding from the Pechora River eastwards across Siberia in a narrow band along the subarctic, apparently sandwiched between Red-throated *A. cervinus* and Olive-backed Pipits *A. hodgsoni* (*BWP*). It undertakes a huge migration, wintering in the islands of the Philippines, Borneo and Sulawesi. It is thinly distributed, both as a breeding bird and as a migrant, and it is not a familiar species, even to hardened Far Eastern travellers.

Occurrences Although there were some 58 records up to the end of 1995, the Pechora Pipit is very much a Fair Isle speciality, with 36 recorded there, mostly in late September and early October. There has been a recent upsurge, with a peak of ten in 1994. It is extremely rare south of the Northern Isles, with just nine records in England and Wales, including two in spring. Like Pallas's Grasshopper Warbler *Locustella certhiola*, Lanceolated Warbler *L. lanceolata* and Yellow-breasted Bunting *Emberiza aureola*, it would appear that the vagrants we get leave Siberia on a narrow and very precise westward heading which takes them across northern Britain but not the south. Like the two *Locustellas* though, its skulking behaviour mitigates against discovery elsewhere.

Identification The bird in Plate 56.4 was present on Foula, Shetland, in September 1993, and the one in Plate 56.5 was present on the same island in September of the following year. It is a rather small pipit, with quite a long, thin, parallel-looking bill and a rather long neck. It is most likely to be confused with a Red-throated Pipit (*see* Plate 57.1), and Plates 56.4 & 5 show a number of plumage differences to good effect. In particular, the buff mantle braces are prominent, being long and heavily outlined in black (they are much more prominent than on the Red-throated). The median and greater coverts are thickly tipped whitish, forming two solid and conspicuous wing bars, and whitish tertial edgings are also obvious. It has quite a rounded head, with a well-streaked crown, a faint but noticeable supercilium, a narrow white eye-ring and a rather plain face with warm brown ear-coverts (some are quite ginger in this area). The malar stripe is weaker, with a less-prominent triangular base. It is generally a very clean white below (apparent even in flight), with a contrasting, heavily streaked pectoral band which extends in two long lines down the flanks. The legs tend to look rather a bright pink, this being clearly apparent in Plate 56.5. A diagnostic feature of Pechora Pipit is the fact that the tertial tips fall well short of the primary tips, so that there is an obvious primary projection with two or three visible primaries beyond the longest tertial (on the Red-throated and the commoner small pipits, the tertials more or less cloak the primaries). Another important feature is the call. When flushed, Pechoras tend to fly a short distance, dropping quickly and silently back into vegetation, sometimes giving a soft *pwit*, more reminiscent of the call of an Ortolan Bunting *Emberiza hortulana* than the calls of our commoner small pipits.

RED-THROATED PIPIT
Anthus cervinus

Range Has one of the most northerly breeding ranges of any passerine, summering in a narrow belt across the tundra, almost entirely within the Arctic Circle, from northern Scandinavia east to Alaska. It is abundant east of the Urals, but much less numerous in Fenno-Scandia (Ferguson-Lees, 1969). It winters largely in the tropics of Africa (much commoner in the east) and in Southeast Asia, but also in small numbers in parts of the Mediterranean and the Middle East.

Occurrences Despite the fact that the species winters west to the Gambia and even Morocco, it is rare in Western Europe. In Britain, it is an annual vagrant, with most in the Northern Isles, down the east coast and in the Isles of Scilly. Records are fairly evenly distributed between spring (mid-April–early June) and autumn (September–October).

Identification The individual in Plate 57.2 was present at Cuckmere Haven, Sussex, in May–June 1991. It was a singing male and it shows all the distinctive characteristics of summer plumage: the orangey-pink face and throat, heavily streaked sides of the breast and flanks, whitish 'tramlines' down the mantle, and

a yellow base to the bill. Males are generally more highly coloured and less streaked below than females (loc. cit.).

Plate 57.1 shows a first-winter on St Agnes, Isles of Scilly, in October 1991. First-winters lack the pinky-orange colour which is retained by winter adults (although traces of this are occasionally present; Svensson, 1992). They are, therefore, much more similar to the Meadow Pipit *A. pratensis*, particularly the colder, streakier types which are often encountered in western areas. Compared with the Meadow the Red-throated is colder in plumage tone, darker above and whiter below. Its upperpart streaking is blacker, thicker and more lined, it has pale 'tramlines' or 'braces' down the mantle, two obvious whitish wing bars, and whitish tertial and secondary fringes. The malar stripe ends in a heavy blotch and there is heavy breast streaking which extends down the flanks in two thick lines (less lined on this particular individual). Also, the bill has a distinctly yellow base to the lower mandible. If in doubt, check the rump and uppertail-coverts: whereas the Meadow has a plain rump and only faint shaft streaks on the uppertail-coverts, the Red-throated shows obvious streaking with black feather centres on the rump and thick, black, wedge-shaped feather centres to the uppertail-coverts. Most important is the call: a clear, thin, high-pitched, drawn-out *speee* or *pssssssssp*, lacking the 'z's of the more rasping Tree Pipit *A. trivialis*. Once learned, this facilitates the identification of even high-flying individuals and often allows their location amongst flocks of Meadow Pipits. Red-throats often feed with Meadow Pipits, wagging their tail as they do so, but they do not always stand out from the Meadows.

BUFF-BELLIED PIPIT
Anthus rubescens

Range The nominate race of the Buff-bellied Pipit breeds from western Greenland, across northern Canada and down the Rockies into the USA. It winters in the southern USA and Central America. The pale-legged Asian race (*japonicus*) continues westwards into north-eastern Siberia, as far west as Lake Baikal. It winters in Japan and Southeast Asia.

Occurrences Until 1986, the species was treated as conspecific with the Water Pipit *A. spinoletta* and the Rock Pipit *A. petrosus*. Knox (1986), however, explained how the Russians had discovered that the easternmost race of Water Pipit (*blakistoni*) was living alongside *japonicus* and behaving as a different species. The BOURC decided to treat the three forms as a superspecies, and *japonicus* was lumped with the nominate *rubescens* of North America as the 'Buff-bellied Pipit'.

There were four records of *rubescens* in Britain and Ireland between 1910 and 1967, and two since: St Mary's, Isles of Scilly, in October 1988 (Heard, 1988; Plates 57.3 & 4), and in Scilly in September–October 1996.

Identification The photographs show the dark legs which the American race shares with the Water and Rock Pipits, but otherwise it is rather distinctive in its own right. As its new name suggests, the underparts are buff, delicately but profusely streaked with brown across the breast and down the flanks. Unlike Water Pipit, the face is rather plain, with pale lores, and shows a short buff supercilium and eye-ring. The mantle and scapulars are also plain, coloured grey-brown, and the fringes to all the wing feathers are prominently buff. Overall, therefore, it is a distinctly buffer bird than the Water Pipit. Perhaps as important as its plumage is its structure: whereas the Water Pipit is a large, robust pipit with a long, rather hefty bill, the American race of Buff-bellied is smaller, with a round head and a smaller, weaker bill. In this respect it suggests a Meadow *A. pratensis* rather than a Water Pipit and, in flight, it may be difficult to pick out from accompanying Meadow Pipits. Its call, too, is more reminiscent of a Meadow: a quick, shrill *si-sip* or *si-si-sip*. It is a bird of dry habitats and, as the photographs show, the 1988 bird spent most of its time feeding in fields of newly sprouting bulbs.

CITRINE WAGTAIL
Motacilla citreola

Range Has a large distribution over much of northern and central Asia, but extending westwards into Europe in northern Russia (nominate *citreola*), and in Belorussia, central Russia and the Ukraine (race *werae*). It winters mainly in the Indian subcontinent and Southeast Asia.

Occurrences In recent years the species has spread to the west and south-west, and this has led to breeding attempts in Sweden, Finland, the Baltic states, Poland, the former Czechoslovakia and Germany (*BWP* and *Brit. Birds* **84**: 233; **85**: 457; **88**: 40), although some of these have involved mixed pairings with the closely related Yellow Wagtail *M. flava*. There were as many as 42 in Poland in the spring of 1993 (*Brit. Birds* **87**: 320), and 11 pairs bred there in 1995. This spread has led to a marked increase in extralimital records in Western Europe, although the increase has undoubtedly been assisted by a better understanding of the field characteristics of immature birds.

In Britain, the Citrine Wagtail was first recorded in September 1954 on Fair Isle, Shetland, and that island has since acquired the largest number of records. Others have occurred mostly down the east coast, although the Isles of Scilly produced at least eight between 1981 and 1995. The species has been virtually annual since 1960, with a peak of ten in 1995. Like the Yellow-breasted Bunting *Emberiza aureola*, but unlike other eastern vagrants, it tends to be an early visitor in autumn, with records as early as 14 August.

In parallel with the Continental records, in 1976 a male was discovered feeding four young in Essex (Cox and Inskipp, 1978), although the identity of the young was never established. There were no further non-autumn records until 1991, when two occurred in May. In view of the spread in Eastern Europe, we can perhaps look forward to an increase in spring occurrences.

Identification The identification of autumn immatures was, until quite recently, fraught with controversy. The problem is that some eastern races of the Yellow Wagtail (notably *simillima*, *beema* and *taivana*; Svensson, 1992) can lack strong yellow and olive tones in autumn, therefore appearing superficially similar to first-winter Citrine. It is a somewhat sturdier bird than the Yellow Wagtail, rather 'leggy' and with a heftier bill. In general appearance, the first-winter Citrine is pale grey above (reminiscent of the White Wagtail *Motacilla alba alba*) and white below (often with a peachy tint to the throat). Some early autumn vagrants may retain vestiges of juvenile plumage, such as a stronger olive tone to the upperparts, buffer or yellower underparts, and remnants of a throat necklace. At this age, it is more similar to juvenile Yellow Wagtail (loc. cit.).

The first-winter in Plate 57.5, present on Tresco, Isles of Scilly, in October 1989, clearly shows all the classic pro-Citrine features: (1) a prominent whitish supercilium which continues as a 'supercilium surround' right round the back of the ear-coverts (note also the presence of a faint dark lateral crown stripe); (2) a pale 'hollow' centre to the ear-coverts, below the eye; (3) a pale area extending right across the forehead; and (4) really thick, white wing bars and tertial edgings. Also of note in the field are the grey rump and uniformly blackish uppertail-coverts (the rump is olive-tinged and the uppertail-coverts dark-centred on most Yellows). Another characteristic worth remembering is the call, an almost buzzing *dzeep*, *dzzeeup* or *trrrreup*, which is quite different from the familiar *swee-up* of the Yellow Wagtail. It should be noted, however, that some calls of the Citrine are more like those of the Yellow Wagtail (a shrill *ski-up* or a strident *swe-up*), while some eastern Yellows are more rasping. With hybridization occurring between the two species, this is another problem to be borne in mind when faced with a 'non-classic' individual.

Plate 57.6 shows a heavily twitched first-summer male at Fleet Pond, Hampshire, in May 1993. Although superficially similar to a male Yellow Wagtail, it is readily distinguished by its dark grey back and scapulars, black shawl around the nape and by the thick white wing bars. Messy black mottling on the crown and similar markings on the lower throat show it to be a first-summer. The extensive black shawl, bright yellow underparts and the lack of extensive grey on the flanks would indicate that this is the nominate *citreola*.

BOHEMIAN WAXWING
Bombycilla garrulus

Range Breeds in the subarctic and boreal zones, from Scandinavia east through Siberia and into western North America. It winters mainly to the south of the breeding range but it is irruptive.

Occurrences Occurs in winter mainly down the east coasts of Scotland and England, but numbers vary considerably from year to year. In winter it feeds mainly on berries, irruptions occurring when food is short in northern latitudes. The largest invasions in recent times occurred in the winter of 1965/66, when there were an estimated 10,000 in Scotland alone (*BWP*), and in the winter of 1995/96. This latter influx has not been properly analysed at the time of writing but certainly involved thousands of birds, with flocks of up to 500 reaching as far south as Nottingham.

Identification The Bohemian Waxwing is unmistakable in a British and Irish context, and one is always struck by its immaculate beauty and subtlety of plumage tones. Plate 58.1 shows a first-winter in classic pose, taken at Holme, Norfolk, in December 1988. It can be aged by the fact that the yellow lines on the primaries do not hook around the tip of the feather, as they do on adults. The rather diffuse lower border to the small black throat patch would suggest a female. Flocks of waxwings are very vocal, the usual call being a high-pitched, sibilant trill: *sisisisi*.

CEDAR WAXWING
Bombycilla cedrorum

Range Breeds across much of southern Canada and the northern USA. It is a long-range migrant, wintering in the southern part of its breeding range, south into Central America.

Occurrences There are two British records: on Noss, Shetland, on 25–26 June 1985; and a heavily twitched first-winter in Nottingham in February–March 1996. The Noss bird was found by Clive McKay, who also discovered Britain's first Brownheaded Cowbird *Molothrus ater* on Islay, Argyllshire, in April 1988 (McKay, 1994). In North America, the Cedar Waxwing is a late-spring migrant, arriving in Newfoundland and Nova Scotia in June, and so both the location and the date of the Noss bird are compatible with a transatlantic spring overshoot. One recorded in Iceland in April–July 1989 presumably arrived in a similar way. The Nottingham bird was a surprising winter record but occurred after an exceptional autumn for North American passerine vagrancy. It is possible that it was a reversed migrant or was simply swept across the Atlantic in a depression. Finding itself in Scandinavia or northern Britain, it presumably attached itself to a flock of Bohemian Waxwings *B. garrulus* and worked south with them in an exceptional invasion year. Another possibility is that it arrived from the west with Bohemian Waxwings, which were also irrupting in North America at that time. Small numbers of Cedar Waxwings are also kept in captivity, and one found entangled in netting in Oxfordshire in May 1985 was traced to a captive source near by.

Identification The Cedar is noticeably smaller and slighter than the Bohemian and has a shorter crest. There are a number of plumage differences: (1) the black mask kinks upwards more strongly and shows a white border above as well as below; (2) it lacks the Bohemian's large black throat patch, instead showing a more restricted area of black that is confined largely to the chin (more extensive on males); (3) the wings are plain, except for the waxy red tips to the secondaries, although these are reduced or even absent on first-winters; (4) there is a white border to the upper edge of the tertials (this stands out at any distance); (5) the belly is suffused with yellow; and (6), perhaps most obvious of all, the undertail-coverts are whitish instead of reddish-brown. Plates 58.2 & 3 show the Nottingham bird. It lacked the waxy red tips on the wing and also showed fairly pointed, as opposed to truncated, tips to the tail feathers, a further indication that it was a first-winter. The call is high-pitched and sibilant, slightly trilling at times, sounding almost like a dog whistle.

NORTHERN MOCKINGBIRD
Mimus polyglottos

Range Breeds over much of the USA, just creeping into southern Canada, and south to southern Mexico, Jamaica and the Virgin Islands. In recent years it has gradually expanded its range northwards, and these populations have tended to be more migratory than those further south.

Occurrences There are four British records but only two have been accepted on to Category A of the British List. The first was an individual at Blakeney Point, Norfolk, on 20–28 August 1971, but at that time the species was available in captivity. Also, its wings and tail were heavily abraded and it had a bald patch above its bill. It was, therefore, treated as an escape. The second occurred at Worm's Head, Glamorgan, from 24 July to 11 August 1978. The west coast location was ideal but the date was odd, although there is evidence from the USA that the species does move this early. This one was placed in Category D1, but it seems likely that it was an early ship-assisted vagrant. The two records accepted on to Category A were one at Saltash, Cornwall, on 30 August 1982, and one at Horsey Island, Hamford Water, Essex, on 17–23 May 1988. The first of these occurred after a violent westerly gale, which also produced a first-winter Black-billed Cuckoo *Coccyzus erythrophthalmus* on St Agnes, Isles of Scilly, and a Black-and-white Warbler *Mniotilta varia* near Penryn, Cornwall. It seems likely, however, that both of these were ship-assisted.

Identification The Northern Mockingbird is a distinctive bird, with grey upperparts, white underparts, a long black tail (with white outer feathers), and black wings with a double white wing bar and a white patch at the base of the primaries. When adult, it shows a white eye. The one in Plate 58.4 is the Essex bird. It could be aged as a first-summer by its rather dark eye, by traces of flank streaking, and by the contrast between old and new greater coverts. The white patch at the base of the primaries immediately distinguishes it from the Tropical Mockingbird *M. gilvus*, which has been mooted as a possible escape. Plate 58.5 shows the one at Worm's Head, apparently an adult. It America it is frequently encountered in urban environments, often feeding on the ground with half-opened wings. It is revered as a superb singer and a strong mimic, singing by night as well as by day.

BROWN THRASHER
Toxostoma rufum

Range Breeds in eastern North America, from southern Canada to the Gulf of Mexico. In winter it withdraws into the southern part of its breeding range.

Occurrence The sole Western Palearctic record concerned an individual at Durlston Head, Dorset, from 18 November 1966 to 5 February 1967 (Incledon, 1968), which was trapped on 23 November (Plate 59.1). This seems an unlikely species to cross the Atlantic unaided, and its south coast location would add weight to the theory that it was ship-assisted.

Identification Plate 59.1 shows a bird that is unique in a British or Irish context. It most resembles a thrush and is similar in size to a Song Thrush *Turdus philomelos* but with a strikingly long tail (lacking any white). Its upperparts are rich chestnut, with a prominent double black and white wing bar, and it has a manic yellow eye set in a grey face. The underparts are heavily but neatly streaked with brown. As can be seen in the photograph, the dark bill appears fairly straight (although it appeared slightly curved in the field). It feeds on the ground, usually in cover, and it often holds its tail slightly cocked. The Durlston bird fed mainly on acorns, 'which it hammered with much vigour, throwing its head back with each stroke and bringing its bill down vertically' (loc. cit.). The call is a distinctive, abrupt *thik*, and it was this that initially drew attention to the Durlston bird.

ALPINE ACCENTOR
Prunella collaris

Range Breeds from Morocco and Spain in the west, through the mountain ranges of southern Europe and Asia Minor, and eastwards through the Himalayas, central and eastern Asia to Japan. It is exclusively a montane species, occurring from 6,000–6,500 ft (1,800-2,000 m) up to the snowline. On Mt Everest, it occurs up to 26,000 ft (8,000 m; *BWP*). In winter, it descends below the snowline and is widespread but sparsely distributed in lowland southern Europe.

Occurrences Despite the relative closeness of its breeding range, the Alpine Accentor is an extremely rare and highly sought-after vagrant. There were 29 records prior to 1958, but have been only ten since (to 1994). It seems likely that it is largely overlooked here, particularly since it may occur in montane areas infrequently visited by birdwatchers. It is quite salutary to compare its breeding range with that of the Water Pipit *Anthus spinoletta*: the two are extremely similar, yet the latter is a widespread if thinly distributed winter visitor to southern Britain. Most recent records have been made along the south coast of England in spring, where the birds may eke out a clifftop existence in a habitat which must resemble a microcosm of an Alpine mountain top. The individual in Plate 59.2 conformed to this pattern: it was present at The Needles, Isle of Wight, from 27 May to 6 June 1990.

Identification The Alpine Accentor creeps along the ground rather like a Dunnock *P. modularis*, although it can appear rather more pipit-like. It is distinctly larger and bulkier than the Dunnock, and Plate 59.2 shows it to be rather nondescript except for: (1) messy orangey streaking on the sides of the breast; (2) black greater coverts (narrowly tipped white), forming a black wing panel; (3) a pale yellow base to the bill; and (4) the black-spotted white throat patch, although this can be inconspicuous. It has a stronger flight than Dunnock and appears bulkier, with rather rounded wings. A white tip to the tail is prominent in flight, as are the black greater coverts.

RUFOUS BUSH CHAT
Cercotrichas galactotes

Range Breeds in Iberia and North Africa east to Jordan, Syria and Israel (nominate race), and from south-eastern Europe through Turkey (race *syriacus*), and east through Iraq and Iran to Kazakhstan (race *familiaris*). Other races occur south of the Sahara. Palearctic migrants winter in the northern African tropics alongside the resident African races, eastern birds reaching Kenya.

Occurrences This is an extremely rare vagrant with 11 records, just five of them since 1958 (to 1980). All except two have occurred in September–October. So far, it has eluded the top twitchers, and Ron Johns described an abortive attempt to see one at the Butlin's Holiday Camp in Skegness, Lincolnshire, in September 1963, when his carload represented the only birders present (Johns, 1991)!

Identification It is a small chat with a long rounded tail. It feeds on the ground when the tail is frequently cocked (sometimes quickly) and is even raised right over the back with a two- or three-actioned jerk. The tail is also flashed and the wings held open and these movements show off the rufous colour of the tail as well as its black subterminal band and prominent white tips to the outer feathers. It has a dark eye-stripe, a whitish supercilium, a slightly darker lateral crown-stripe and a faint black moustachial stripe, the whole effect recalling Bluethroat *Luscinia svecica*. The colour of the plumage varies according to race. The western nominate is rufous-brown above (more rufous on the rump) and has a brighter chestnut-red tail with a narrow black subterminal band. The underparts are sandy-white. The eastern races are much less rufous (*familiaris* being the paler), and pale tawny-brown upperparts contrast more with the rufous rump and tail. Also, they have a more contrasting head pattern and a broader black tail band. At rest, all the wing feathers are edged pale, the secondary fringing forming a prominent buff panel. The long, finely pointed bill is pale and the rather long legs are pale orangey-yellow. It has a fast, dashing flight, swooping low over the ground but perching up on low vegetation. The tail is frequently spread in flight, particularly when alighting, again emphasizing the rufous coloration. Plate 59.3 shows the 1963 Skegness bird which, on plumage tone and tail pattern, is clearly one of the eastern races. The fresh remiges and neat pale fringes, and tips to the greater coverts show it to be a first-winter.

MOUSSIER'S REDSTART
Phoenicurus moussieri

Range Has a restricted world range, being confined to northern Morocco, Algeria and Tunisia. It is resident, dispersive and perhaps migratory over relatively short distances within North Africa. In Morocco, there is a general movement out of the Atlas Mountains in winter.

Occurrence There is just one British record: a male at Dinas Head, Pembrokeshire, on 24 April 1988 (Barrett, 1992; Plate 61.3). In view of its relatively sedentary nature, its occurrence here is quite remarkable, although there have been two similar records of spring overshoots in Western Europe: a male at the Ebro Delta, Spain, in April 1985; and a female on Ouessant, Brittany, France, in May 1993 (*Brit. Birds* **88**: 40; **89**: 39). It has also been recorded in Italy, Malta and Greece.

Identification As Plate 61.3 shows, the male is a really beautiful bird. It is noticeably smaller than a Common Redstart *P. phoenicurus*, dumpier, more rotund and with a shorter tail. The whole of the upperparts are black except for a broad white stripe that runs from the forehead back over the eye, widening down the sides of the neck. It also has a conspicuous white patch at the base of the inner primaries and secondaries. The underparts are orange and the tail is orangey-red with darker central feathers. The female is dark grey-brown above, shows a faint buff eye-ring, and has uniform deep, dark orange underparts right down to the under-tail-coverts. It lacks the male's white wing patch but shows pale fringes to the tertials and secondaries, sometimes forming a slight wing panel. Its structural differences from the Common Redstart are obvious. It has a soft alarm call as well as a rasping, nasal, almost buzzing *preee*, rising at the end and sounding almost like the fast scraping of a washboard.

THRUSH NIGHTINGALE
Luscinia luscinia

Range Breeds from southern Norway and Denmark eastwards across Eastern Europe to western Mongolia. It winters in East Africa.

Occurrences Surprisingly, there were only two records prior to 1958, both made on Fair Isle, Shetland.

There has been a dramatic increase since 1970, with 116 recorded by the end of 1995. There were as many as ten in 1989, although numbers still fluctuate from year to year. Its relative rarity here is related to the orientation of its north–south migration route from East Africa. The upsurge is related to marked increases throughout the north-western part of its range. For example, in Finland it increased from about 200 pairs in the 1950s to about 8,000 pairs in the early 1980s (*BWP*). It bred for the first time in the Netherlands in 1995 (*Brit. Birds* **89**: 38) and it has even been tipped as a potential colonist in Britain. Most records have occurred in the Northern Isles and down the east coast in May and early June, and there is a small secondary peak from August through to early October. The only Irish record was an individual on Cape Clear Island, Co. Cork, from 29 October to 1 November 1989, 26 days later than the latest British occurrence.

Identification Plates 59.4 & 5 show a very confiding first-winter which attracted large crowds at Landguard Point, Suffolk, in September 1995. It is similar to the Common Nightingale *L. megarhynchos* but is much browner and lacks the Common's contrastingly rufous rump and tail, these areas being only slightly more orangey than the upperparts. The head is rather rounded, it has an obvious eye-ring, the bill is shorter and stubbier than the Common's and shows a noticeable yellow gape line, rather like that on a baby bird. Most importantly, it has a mottled breast although, as Plate 59.5 shows, this is rather faint. Plate 59.5 fails to show the first primary, which is much shorter on the Thrush Nightingale, rarely projecting beyond the primary coverts; the Common Nightingale's first primary is often visible in photographs. It would appear not to show any pale tips to the greater coverts, but small buff tips to the tertials are indicative of a first-winter. When identifying autumn birds, the possibility should be borne in mind of vagrancy from the paler eastern *hafizi* race of Common Nightingale. *Hafizi* is greyer above than the nominate, sandy-buff on the breast and virtually white below. The lores are whitish and it shows a rather distinct supercilium. The edges of the flight feathers are sandy-grey (*BWP*). It is also longer tailed. The race *africana* from the Caucasus and Iran is intermediate between the nominate and *hafizi*.

Spring Thrush Nightingales are often detected by song. This is loud and powerful, higher-pitched than Common's, with harder notes interspersed. Whilst some phrases recall a mellow Song Thrush *Turdus philomelos*, some of the grating phrases may suggest a Sedge Warbler *Acrocephalus schoenobaenus*. It lacks the *lu lu lu…* phrase of Common but includes a distinctive deep *choc choc choc choc*.

SIBERIAN RUBYTHROAT
Luscinia calliope

Range Breeds across Siberia from the Urals to the Pacific, its range approximately replacing that of the European Robin *Erithacus rubecula* (*BWP*). It winters from eastern India through Southeast Asia to the Philippines.

Occurrence The only British record was a first-winter female trapped on Fair Isle, Shetland, on 9–11 October 1975 (Lowe, 1979; Plates 60.1 & 2). It occurred in a classic 'Sibe' autumn which also produced a Yellow-browed Bunting *Emberiza chrysophrys* in Norfolk and a Siberian Blue Robin *Luscinia cyane* in the Channel Islands. Since 1985, there have been others recorded in Finland, Sweden, Denmark and Germany (*Brit. Birds* **84**: 233; **85**: 11).

Identification The Siberian Rubythroat is a slim bird, in many ways rather nightingale-like. Also like a nightingale, it feeds on the ground, often with the wings drooped and with the tail half-cocked. In colour, it is a robin-like mid-brown above, but the underparts are creamy-buff, paler on the belly and vent. Plate 60.2 shows the pale eye-ring and the distinctive pale supercilium from the bill to the eye. Also of note is the pale throat, which contrasts with the buff upper breast. This showed it to be a female, but in the hand it was seen to have faint, smudgy traces of red. A first-winter male is a stunning bird and, by October, it would have already acquired the vivid and intense ruby throat.

BLUETHROAT
Luscinia svecica

Range Breeds right across the Palearctic, from Spain and the Atlantic coast of France to the Pacific, with small numbers penetrating into Alaska. It winters in the Mediterranean, through the Sahel zone south of the Sahara, and east through the Middle East to India and Southeast Asia.

Occurrences The Bluethroat is a spring and autumn migrant, occurring mainly in May and September. Dymond *et al.*, (1989) noted that 62 per cent of those recorded from 1958 to 1985 occurred in spring. The bulk of those are of the red-spotted nominate race, which occurs as a May drift migrant mainly in the Northern Isles and down the British east coast. In some years there are substantial arrivals, the largest being 590 in 1985, including a remarkable 100 on the Isle of May, Fife, on 14–15 May (*Brit. Birds* **78**: 415). Despite these occasional influxes, nesting has been recorded on only one occasion: in the Moray Basin, Scotland, in 1968, although the male, if present, was never seen (Greenwood, 1968). The southerly white-spotted forms *cyanecula* or the smaller '*namnetum*' appear rarely as spring overshoots, sometimes as early as mid-March (but there was a large influx of up to 11 between 23 March and 20 April 1996 with subsequent breeding in eastern England). There has been a perceptible decrease in autumn, and this may be linked to recent declines in the Netherlands, Germany and Poland.

There have been two intriguing ringing recoveries at Slapton Ley, Devon: an adult male ringed on 17 May 1958 was retrapped there on 5 May 1963; and a first-winter male ringed on 21 September 1966 was retrapped there on 14 September 1968 (*BWP*). Not only do these incidents illustrate that migrants may use the same stopover sites year after year, but they also show that so-called vagrants are not necessarily doomed to failure.

Identification The male in Plate 60.3 was present at Holme, Norfolk, in May 1985. It clearly illustrates why the species is so popular with birders and non-birders alike. Plate 60.4 shows a first-winter female at Portland, Dorset, in September 1986. It is similar to the male except that it completely lacks any colour in the underparts. All it shows are black malar stripes and a narrow gorget of black across the lower throat. Plate 60.5 shows a first-winter male on St Mary's, Isles of Scilly, in October 1993. Wedge-shaped rufous-buff tips to the greater coverts show it to be a first-winter, and the blue and rufous bands across the breast show it to be a male. When flushed, Bluethroats fly low across the ground, and the initial view is usually of a small dark chat with obvious reddish patches at the base of the rather broad tail. The supercilium is prominent even in flight. They feed on the ground, half running and half hopping, sometimes nervously cocking and flicking open the tail. The usual call is a hard *tchak*.

RED-FLANKED BLUETAIL
Tarsiger cyanurus

Range Breeds across the Siberian taiga from western Russia to Japan. Another race occurs from Afghanistan to north-eastern China. It winters mainly in Southeast Asia.

Occurrences There have been recent signs of a westward spread from the Urals, the species first being recorded in Finland in 1949. A recent estimate has put the Finnish population as high as 200–300 pairs (Rajasärkkä, 1996). It also bred in Estonia in 1980 (*BWP*) and singing males have recently been discovered in Sweden. With just 11 untwitchable records up to 1992, traditionally this has been a highly sought-after species. All that changed on 30 October 1993, however, when a confiding individual was discovered at Winspit, Dorset. It remained until 8 November, and its protracted stay, enforced by a long period of anticyclonic gloom, enabled a couple of thousand people to see it. The initial crush was so great that at least one observer actually feared for his life as he was swept off his feet during a surge in the crowd! By the end of 1994 the total had risen to 15 with a second twitchable individual at Great Yarmouth, Norfolk, during the autumn of that year. Rajasärkkä correlated the European autumn records with high summer totals.

There are two spring records: a male on Fetlar, Shetland, on 31 May and 1 June 1971; and another male on Holy Island, Northumberland, on 23 April 1995. It seems likely that the Shetland bird was a spring overshoot from Russia, but the one in Northumberland may well have been on its way back east after having wintered in Western Europe (the species moves early in spring). All the others have occurred in late September and October in the Northern Isles or down the east coast. The Winspit individual was the first to be recorded on the south coast but, coincidentally, there was also one on Ouessant, Brittany, on 27 October 1993 (*Brit. Birds* **87**: 321).

Identification It is its attractiveness as well as its rarity which has made the Red-flanked Bluetail so highly prized. It is superficially similar to a European Robin *Erithacus rubecula* but, as its name suggests, it is readily distinguished by its dull blue rump and tail. Females and first-winters have a prominent whitish eye-ring, a well-defined whitish throat patch (which contrasts with a grey-brown breast) and orange flanks. Plate 61.1 shows the Winspit bird which was considered probably to be a first-winter. Plate 61.2 shows the Holy Island male. It can readily be sexed by the blue on the head, mantle and scapulars, and it also shows a whitish supercilium. The predominantly brown crown, nape and ear-coverts would suggest that it was a first-summer, although there is currently some debate as to whether brown upperpart feathering is age-related (Rajasärkkä, 1996). As Plate 61.1 shows, bluetails look very robin-like in jizz and posture, often feeding on the ground with drooped wings and a raised tail, which is often flicked.

WHITE-THROATED ROBIN
Irania gutturalis

Range Breeds from Turkey eastwards to Kirgizia. It winters in East Africa.

Occurrences There are just two records: a male on the Calf of Man, Isle of Man, on 22 June 1983 (del

Nevo, 1994); and a female on Skokholm, Pembrokeshire, on 27–30 May 1990. In view of the apparently north–south orientation of its migration route, it is surprising that the species has occurred here at all, particularly at two west coast localities. It has, however, also been recorded in France, the Netherlands, Norway and in Sweden, where there were five records between 1971 and 1989. The spring occurrences tie in with the pattern on the Continent, although the first Dutch record involved a male in November 1986.

Identification Plates 61.4 & 5 show the Skokholm female. In many ways it is reminiscent of a female Red-flanked Bluetail *Tarsiger cyanurus* but it is readily separable by size and shape. It is a larger bird (about the size of Common Nightingale *Luscinia megarhynchos*) and always looks long and sleek, with a sturdier bill. It has a uniform grey-brown head, breast and upperparts (relieved only by a whitish eye-ring and a paler fore-supercilium and throat), and it shows dull orange-coloured flanks. Where it differs most obviously from the bluetail is in its tail colour, which is black, contrasting with the upperparts in flight. Males are stunning birds, with a whitish supercilium, a black face mask, a white throat, orange underparts and dark grey upperparts. It feeds on the ground with the wings drooped and the long black tail is habitually flicked quickly and nervously upwards. It is lively and energetic in character, flying off fast and low between bushes. The call is a *chur*, like Common Nightingale but higher pitched.

EASTERN STONECHATS
Saxicola torquata maura/stejnegeri and *variegata*

Range The Common Stonechat is a widespread species, breeding throughout much of temperate Europe as well as over a large part of Africa. In Asia it is strongly migratory, breeding over a huge area in the northern two-thirds of the continent and wintering in the Middle East, the Indian subcontinent and Southeast Asia.

Occurrences There are about 25 races of Common Stonechats, the majority occurring outside the Western Palearctic. Two or three from Asia have occurred here as vagrants. *Maura* breeds across much of Siberia but is replaced in the Far East by the similar *stejnegeri*. *Maura* is the only race that has been proved to occur here and, on geographical grounds, it is likely that all our vagrants have been of this race. Most occur on the Northern Isles and down the east coast in October and November, with occasional wintering and spring birds. The first British record was made as long ago as

October 1913, but that was the only one prior to 1960. In 1977, a paper in *British Birds* by Iain Robertson helped to clarify the identification features and, since then, it has proved to be a regular vagrant. By the end of 1995 there had been 238 records, with a peak of 29 in 1991. There are also two records of *variegata*, which breeds in the area between the Black and Caspian seas. These were males at Porthgwarra, Cornwall, in October 1985, and at Stiffkey, Norfolk, in October 1990.

Identification In autumn *maura* is similar to our race of Common Stonechat (*hibernans*) but is obviously paler, being rather peachy below and much paler grey-buff on the upperparts (although some are darker), with contrasting pale buff fringes to the wing feathers which form a pronounced pale panel on the closed wing. The throat is whiter and there may be a weak, buffish supercilium. Plate 62.1 shows these features well on a first-winter at Salthouse, Norfolk, in September 1990. Some first-winter males start to show black on the face, and males of all ages can be sexed by their black underwing-coverts and axillaries. Plate 62.2 shows a first-summer male at Filey, Yorkshire, in May 1995. It is similar to an autumn bird in general coloration except that it has acquired a large area of black on the face. The key feature in identifying these races is the rump and uppertail-coverts, these being unstreaked and varying from whitish to pale orangey-buff on less-worn individuals (some may show streaking on the uppertail-coverts). The race *variegata* can be distinguished by the large white patches at the base of its tail (taking up at least a third to half the tail length). Also, it is paler above than *maura/stejnegeri*, and has a larger and whiter rump patch. First-winter males also show more black on the face and throat. Plate 62.3 shows the male at Porthgwarra in 1985. Much of the above is based on Stoddart (1992).

ISABELLINE WHEATEAR
Oenanthe isabellina

Range Breeds from Greece eastwards through Asia Minor to the Gobi Desert. It winters in the Sahel zone of Africa from Senegal to East Africa, and through the Arabian Peninsula to Pakistan and western India.

Occurrences First recorded in Cumbria in November 1887, it was almost 90 years before the second, in Norfolk in May 1977. Since then, there have been a further eight (to 1994), all between mid-September and early November, with three records involving well-watched individuals in the Isles of Scilly. The one in Plate 62.4 was present on Gugh in October 1991.

Identification One of the reasons for the species rarity here is its similarity to the Northern Wheatear *O. oenanthe*, some examples of which may be disconcertingly pale in autumn. Plate 62.4 shows most of the diagnostic features to good effect. Firstly, it is a very pale, sandy looking bird, with no hint of grey in the upperparts. Although dark before the eye when viewed front-on (as one is looking down the forward-pointing feathers), in side-on views it is much plainer faced and shows less of a dark smudge behind the eye than the Northern. There is a faint supercilium, of fairly even width, and a narrow, pale eye-ring. The main feature to concentrate on, however, is wing colour. Note that the bases of all the wing feathers are brown, forming relatively little contrast with the sandy feather fringes. On an equivalent-plumaged Northern, the feather bases are black, contrasting sharply with more richly coloured orangey-buff fringes. Because the wings of the Isabelline are so pale, there is little contrast between them and the scapulars and mantle. Also, the black alula stands out as it contrasts strongly with the pale adjacent feathering; this feature is shown well in the photograph.

Structural differences between the two species are often quoted, but they are at best subtle and must be evaluated sensibly. Plate 62.4 perhaps shows the rather pear-shaped body and the shorter tail, as well as the slightly shorter primary projection. On the wing, the wider gap between the tips of the fourth and fifth primaries is clearly visible; on the Northern, all the primaries are more evenly, if increasingly, spaced. The Isabelline has a wider dark tail band but, surprisingly, this is not always easy to judge in the field, particularly when the bird is at rest. The underwings are obviously pale whitish or silvery-white, best seen as the bird glides towards the observer when picking up prey. In direct comparison, the underwing of the Northern Wheatear is obviously darker. The ageing of autumn Isabelline Wheatears is difficult, although it is highly likely that all of our autumn vagrants have been first-winters. On its breeding grounds it is surprisingly loud and remarkably extrovert in character, the male's song containing some bizarre sweet whitling noises, including a distinctive loud *WEE-oo*.

PIED WHEATEAR
Oenanthe pleschanka

Range Breeds from the Black Sea eastwards across mid-latitude Asia to Mongolia and China. The whole population winters in East Africa and the south-western part of the Arabian Peninsula.

Occurrences This was formerly an extremely rare vagrant, with just four British records between 1909 and 1968. Since 1976, however, it has been much more regular, with a total of 34 recorded by the end of 1994. It was annual between 1985 and 1994, with as many as five in 1991. The British east coast has produced most, but it has occurred widely, with three records from southern Ireland. It typically occurs in October and November, but there are single records in May, June and July. The reason for the upsurge is uncertain, but the increase in the numbers of birders and a better understanding of the species' distinction from the Black-eared Wheatear *O. hispanica* are perhaps most significant.

Identification The Pied Wheatear forms a superspecies with the Black-eared Wheatear, and the separation of the two in autumn requires care. Indeed, Clement (1987) states that some are inseparable, while the existence of hybrids further complicates the matter. Compared with the Northern Wheatear *O. oenanthe*, the Pied is smaller, slighter and distinctly more chat-like. The latter effect is caused to some extent by its rather rounded head and small bill, while a narrow eye-ring on females and first-winters contributes to a rather open-faced appearance. As on the Black-eared, the tail band is narrower than that of the Northern and it often lacks the black bar altogether; instead, the black is confined to the central feathers and small amounts on the outers. Also like the Black-eared, it has dark brown or black underwing-coverts.

The bird in Plate 63.1 is a first-winter male which was present at Sumburgh, Shetland, in October 1991. First-winter males may be sexed by the varying amounts of black on the face and throat, this appearing as pale feather tips gradually wear off during the course of the autumn. The prominent buff fringes to the primary coverts of this individual indicate a first-winter (on the adult these feathers are either all black or only finely tipped/fringed with white; Svensson, 1992). Note that the upperparts are a rather cold shade of brown or grey-brown compared with the Black-eared, which is typically a warmer orange-brown in plumage tone (*see* Plate 63.4). Note also the particularly pale creamy-buff fringes and tips to most of the wing feathers (browner on the Black-eared). Plate 63.2 shows another male, presumably a more advanced first-winter, at Dodman Point, Cornwall, in November 1991. Two rather more concrete differences from the Black-eared are visible in Plate 63.3, which shows a female in the Weybourne and Sheringham area of Norfolk in October–November 1983. These differences are the darker centres to the feathers of the mantle and scapulars (the paler fringes producing a subdued scaly pattern), and a rather contrasting orangey-buff wash across the breast.

Finally, Plate 62.5 shows a first-summer male at Scarborough, Yorkshire, in June 1991. It is a distinctive bird with its black face and throat and black upperparts, these contrasting with a greyish-white crown and white underparts. The retained brown wing feathers show it to be a first-summer. The similar Mourning Wheatear *O. lugens*, which could conceivably occur as a vagrant, usually shows a buff wash to the undertail-coverts and, in flight, white inner webs to the primaries and secondaries, which form a broad white wing bar (perhaps suggesting that of a Tufted Duck *Aythya fuligula*!). This wing bar is more restricted and is largely confined to the secondaries on the North African race *halophila*.

BLACK-EARED WHEATEAR
Oenanthe hispanica

Range Breeds from Morocco and Iberia east through the Mediterranean and Asia Minor to Iran and Turkestan. It winters in semi-desert and in the acacia savannah belt immediately south of the Sahara.

Occurrences Considering that it breeds as close to Britain as southern France, the species is inexplicably rare here, with only 54 records up to 1993. It is interesting to note that 20 recorded in the 12 years 1983–94 compared with 26 Pied Wheatears *O. pleschanka*, which breed much further away. Most of the Black-eareds occurred as spring overshoots in late May, with a secondary peak in late September and early October. As would be expected, most have occurred on the south and east coasts.

Identification The Black-eared Wheatear forms a species pair with the Pied Wheatear, and some individuals are inseparable, not least because hybridization may occur between the two. The bird in Plate 63.4 was a heavily twitched individual present at Stiffkey, Norfolk, in October–November 1993. The blackish area across the lores and ear-coverts indicates that it is a male, presumably a first-winter. Structurally, it is very similar to the Pied Wheatears shown in Plates 63.1–3, being a slimmer, longer-tailed bird than the Northern Wheatear *O. oenanthe*. It tends to perch up on vegetation much more than the Northern, and the bird in the photograph is in a classic pose. Plumage-wise, it is very similar to a Pied except that it shows very obvious orange tones to virtually the whole plumage. Also, it shows little trace of a supercilium compared to a male Pied. This particular individual is white-throated, although black-throated morphs also occur and are more frequent towards the east (Clement, 1987, and *contra BWP*). Although not visible in the photograph, the black tail band is typically narrower than on the Northern, and on some males it may be completely broken between the central and outer feathers. Like the Pied, the Black-eared shows blackish underwing-coverts and axillaries.

DESERT WHEATEAR
Oenanthe deserti

Range Breeds across North Africa (race *homochroa*) through the Middle East (race *deserti*) to the Caspian Sea and Iran, and then east to Mongolia (race *atrogularis*), with another race (*oreophila*) in central Asia east to Inner Mongolia. It winters in the Sahara, east through Saudi Arabia to Pakistan and north-western India.

Occurrences There were 49 records up to 1994, with a distinct increase in recent years and peaks of five each in 1989, 1991 and 1994. It is a late vagrant, with most in late October and November; four have attempted to overwinter (one in Cornwall to 20 March 1995). There is a distinct south-easterly bias to the records, although Orkney and Shetland have produced eight. Surprisingly, there have also been six in spring and, just as it is a late-autumn vagrant, it is an early spring one with all but one occurring between 23 March and 17 April.

One of the most remarkable occurrences involved a male trapped at Landguard, Suffolk, on 20–24 October 1987, which subsequently moved about 270 miles (430 km) south-west to East Prawle, Devon, where it was seen from 26–30 October. Although interesting in itself, this bird clearly illustrated that apparently unrelated vagrants may in fact involve the same birds moving around the country, and confirms an old suspicion that autumn vagrants arriving on the east coast tend to filter south-westwards. It also illustrates the kind of distances that many migrants may fly in one night, and says a lot about modern day observer coverage!

Identification The birds in Plates 64.1–3 were photographed at different times of the year. The one in Plate 64.2 is a male which was found feeding in some dried-out filter beds at, of all places, Barn Elms Reservoir, London, on 13–14 April 1989. Its occurrence, only 6 miles (10 km) from the very centre of London, is another glowing example of how rare birds can turn up just about anywhere. This photograph shows to excellent effect the main features of a male Desert Wheatear: its sandy crown, back and scapulars contrasting with its black face and throat, these connected at the shoulder to the black wings. It also shows the species' diagnostic black tail, lacking any significant white. Fully adult males at this time of year are immaculate, with smartly contrasting jet-black wings. This one shows browner, pale-fringed primary coverts, primaries, secondaries and tertials, and note how the older, paler outer five greater coverts contrast with the newer, blacker inner two. This shows it to be a first-summer (Svensson, 1992). The male in Plate

64.1 was a first-winter present at Penclawdd, Glamorgan, in November 1989. It is in much fresher plumage, and note the buff feather edgings to the throat patch and wings.

The individual in Plate 64.3 was present at Easton Bavents, Suffolk, in November–December 1990. The lack of any black in the throat probably indicates that it was a female. This one shows the rather long but fine, delicate bill, the rounded head and the species' more diminutive 'chat-like' character compared with the Northern Wheatear *O. oenanthe*. It also just shows how the rump and uppertail-coverts may be strongly suffused with buff.

Old British specimens have been assigned to both the Middle Eastern *deserti* and the North African *homochroa* races (Hollom, 1960). It would seem possible that the spring records, such as the Barn Elms bird, relate to North African overshoots, particularly since some of them appeared with falls of Northern Wheatears. Autumn individuals may, perhaps, come from either source, but an easterly origin would seem more likely at this time. Indeed, if one follows the route of the 1987 Devon bird back through Suffolk, an origin somewhere in the deserts of south-western Asia can be suggested.

WHITE-CROWNED BLACK WHEATEAR
Oenanthe leucopyga

Range Largely sedentary across the Sahara and east into the Arabian Peninsula.

Occurrence The only British record concerns a first-summer at Kessingland, Suffolk, from 1 or 2–5 June 1982 (Plates 64.4 & 5). It occurred during a warm, southerly airflow at a time when temperatures in Suffolk were at their highest for 35 years (Brown, 1986). That it should have occurred here seems extraordinary given its apparently sedentary nature, but in May 1986 its vagrancy potential was confirmed by another which turned up in Bayern, Germany (*Brit.Birds* **85**: 458). There have also been four claims of Black Wheatear *O. leucura* in Britain (the best being one at Greatstone-on-Sea, Kent, on 17 October 1954), but all have recently been reviewed and rejected by the BOURC. There is also a record of a Black or White-crowned Black in Co. Donegal in June 1964.

Identification Although not sharp, Plates 64.4 & 5 show the salient features of the species, most important of which is the tail pattern. Whereas the Black Wheatear has a thick tail bar like the Northern Wheatear *O. oenanthe*, the outer feathers of the White-crowned Black are more or less completely white, with only the central ones black. Although slightly smaller than the Black, the White-crowned Black is otherwise similar although, as its name suggests, many show a diagnostic white crown. Whilst all juveniles and first-years lack a white crown, so do some adults, so it is not possible to deduce an individual's age by the lack of this feature. The fact that the Suffolk bird had one white crown feather does indicate, however, that it was a first-summer, and this diagnosis is confirmed by the retention of faded brown juvenile primaries (contrasting paler than the body) and the lack of any bluish gloss to the body plumage. The former feature at least is readily apparent in Plate 64.4.

ROCK THRUSH
Monticola saxatilis

Range Breeds in mountains from Morocco and Iberia through southern Europe and Asia Minor east to the Himalayas. It winters mainly in Africa, from the west coast through the Sahel and into East Africa. Migrants from eastern China therefore travel a remarkable 4,700 miles (7,500 km) to their winter quarters (*BWP*).

Occurrences Despite being a widespread and numerous long-range migrant, breeding as close as Spain and southern France, the Rock Thrush is remarkably rare in Britain, with just 27 records up to 1996. *BWP* notes that its migration routes and timing are obscured by the infrequency with which passage is detected, so it seems likely that most complete the trans-Saharan crossing in one flight, with little room for error. Virtually all the British records have related to spring overshoots, but there have also been five in late autumn. Given this predictable occurrence pattern, the bird in Plate 65.4 was remarkable as it was present at Minster, Kent, from 5 February to at least 1 April 1983. The more cynical suggested that it was an escape and quoted its missing left hind claw as evidence for this. It seems likely, however, that it had arrived the previous autumn; an old (1931) November record from Fair Isle, Shetland, and a December 1983 one from Heligoland, Germany (*Brit. Birds* **85**: 458), may support the idea that wintering is possible.

Identification It is a small thrush, best identified by its orange tail. It recalls a large-headed wheatear in shape, with an upright posture and a rounded, rather pear-shaped body. It has a long, fine bill and the long wings nearly reach the tip of its short tail. The latter is occasionally shimmied like a redstart's. Summer plumaged males are distinctive, with a grey-blue head and upperparts, dark orange underparts and a white patch in the middle of the back. Plates 65.1 & 2 show such a bird at Holme, Norfolk, in May 1995. This one was attacked by a Eurasian Sparrow Hawk *Accipiter nisus* but was rescued by birders, kept overnight and then released the following day, apparently none the worse for its experience. Plate 65.4 shows the male at Minster, in February 1983. Winter plumage reflects the pattern of a summer adult, but the colours are subdued by brown and buff feather tips, which produce a barred effect to much of the body plumage. The predominantly grey-blue upperparts indicate that it was a male, a fact confirmed when it moulted into summer plumage prior to its departure. Rock Thrushes feed on the ground, digging around amongst rocks and gravel like a typical thrush, although their movements are distinctly wheatear-like.

WHITE'S THRUSH
Zoothera dauma

Range Although it breeds as far west as the Urals, the main range (which involves the races *aurea* and *toratugumi*) is across eastern Siberia, through Japan to Korea. These winter mainly in India, Southeast Asia and the Philippines. Further races occur in the Himalayas, peninsular India, Indonesia, New Guinea and the Solomon Islands.

Occurrences Although there were 29 records prior to 1958, there have been only 19 since (to 1993). This appears to be a species whose east–west reverse migration route is well to the north, as 16 of those recorded since 1958 have occurred in Scotland, northern England or northern Ireland. As such, it is still highly sought after. Most have occurred from late September to November, with a few in winter, and two since 1958 have occurred in spring, including a twitchable one on Rathlin Island, Co. Down, on 16–20 April 1993 (Plates 65.5 & 6). The spring records no doubt involved birds which wintered in Western Europe.

Identification White's Thrush is a large thrush, about the size of a Mistle Thrush *Turdus viscivorus* and, like that species, it shows white tips to the outer tail feathers. It can be easily distinguished by its remarkably scalloped plumage. The proportionately rather small head is speckled, but with white lores and a faint supercilium, and the large dark eye stands out, surrounded by a narrow white eye-ring. The mantle is dark with pale mottling, and there are two buff wing bars and pale bases to the primaries. The breast is prominently scalloped, but rather more spotted on the flanks. It also has a striking black and white striped underwing (shown well in Plate 65.5). Its legs

are a rather pale bubble-gum pink. The Rathlin bird was aged as a first-winter by its pointed tail feathers and by the fact that the white tips were neither pure white nor clear-cut (McKee, 1993). Unlike the Mistle Thrush, it is a shy and secretive bird, feeding slowly and unobtrusively on the woodland floor and flying up into the canopy when flushed. Direct flight is strong and purposeful.

SIBERIAN THRUSH
Zoothera sibirica

Range Breeds from Siberia east to Japan, mainly in the boreal coniferous taiga. It winters in India, Southeast Asia, Indonesia, and in the Andaman Islands.

Occurrences There have been six records (to 1994), with one in September, three in October and singles in November and December. The female in Plate 65.3 was the first twitchable one, present on North Ronaldsay, Orkney, on 1–8 October 1992. Until then, the species was one of the most sought after of vagrants, the North Ronaldsay bird inducing a large number of twitchers to dig deep into their pockets to make the long journey north. This individual was found in a mist net at the end of a very exciting day which also produced five Richard's Pipits *Anthus novaeseelandiae*, four Yellow-browed Warblers *Phylloscopus inornatus*, two Red-breasted Flycatchers *Ficedula parva*, a Great Grey Shrike *Lanius excubitor* and a Little Bunting *Emberiza pusilla*, as well as 201 birds ringed (Woodbridge, 1992). It was the high spot of a remarkable autumn on the island, which also produced a Pallas's Grasshopper Warbler *Locustella certhiola*, a Yellow Warbler *Dendroica petechia* and a Yellow-browed Bunting *E. chrysophrys*.

Identification The adult male Siberian Thrush is a stunning bird, being basically black (although greyer below with white crescents on the undertail-coverts) with a striking white supercilium. Both sexes share white tips to the outer tail feathers, two striking white bands down the underwing and distinctively pale legs (yellow on adult males, but pinker on the North Ronaldsay bird). The female's plumage is much less distinctive, but the photograph shows brown-grey upperparts, browner wings (with paler bases to the primaries), a messy golden-buff supercilium and ear-covert surround, a broken buff eye-ring and, most distinctive of all, neat brown scalloping right across the underparts. It was aged as a first-winter by the small pale orange wedge-shaped tips to the greater coverts and by the pointed tail feathers; it was sexed as a female by the pattern and coloration of the underparts (loc. cit.). The pale rufous-yellow outer webs of the primary coverts, contrasting with the darker tips, also indicate a first-winter female (Svensson, 1992). A first-winter male, although rather subdued compared with an adult, would nevertheless show more definite male characteristics.

Like White's Thrush, the Siberian Thrush prefers to feed on the forest floor, frustratingly spooking into the canopy when flushed. Vagrants, like the North Ronaldsay bird, may of course be far more cooperative! When feeding on the ground, it may lower its head and move with rather a lurching, kangaroo-like hop. The call of migrants is a soft *sic*.

VARIED THRUSH
Zoothera naevia

Range Breeds from Alaska south through the Rockies to northern California. It winters mainly from southern British Columbia to southern California.

Occurrence There is one Western Palearctic record: at Nanquidno, Cornwall, on 9–24 November 1982. Of all the birds on the British and Irish List, this is perhaps the most astonishing. Being seabirds, even the Ancient Murrelet *Synthliboramphus antiquus* and the Aleutian *Sterna aleutica* and Elegant Terns *S. elegans* somehow pale into insignificance in comparison. What was particularly remarkable was that the Nanquidno individual had a rarely observed plumage type which lacks the normal orange pigmentation (Madge *et al.*, 1990).

So just how does a passerine from Alaska and the Rockies cross the whole of North America and the North Atlantic to reach Cornwall? Since the early 1960s it has become apparent that unknown numbers of Varied Thrushes penetrate eastwards in late autumn, into southern Canada and northern USA. Such records date back to 1848 but, probably as a result of increased observer coverage, the species is now known to be a scarce but regular winter visitor to bird-feeders along the eastern seaboard, chiefly from Maine to New York. It is, in fact, probably present right across the region, but is forced into gardens mainly during cold weather (loc. cit.) in the manner of Blackcaps *Sylvia atricapilla* in Britain. During the winter of 1982/83, Varied Thrushes were reported more frequently than usual through the northern Great Plains to the east coast, although the mildness of the winter resulted in a paucity of records from backyard feeders. It seems that the Cornish individual was one such bird which continued eastwards, over-shooting the coast and crossing the Atlantic during a spell of severe westerly weather. Its occurrence coincided with that of two American Robins *Turdus migratorius*, two American Redstarts *Setophaga ruticilla* and a Green Heron *Butorides virescens* (Madge *et al.*, 1990). Given that the species winters almost

entirely within Canada and the USA, which do not allow the export of their native birds, the escape potential was considered to be very low.

Identification Plate 66.1 shows a beautifully and uniquely patterned thrush. The apparently pointed tail feathers would indicate a first-winter, while the well-defined breast band would suggest that it was a male. In normal individuals, the whites are orange.

HERMIT THRUSH
Catharus guttatus

Range Breeds across much of northern North America and down the Rockies. It is an early spring and late-autumn migrant, and it winters mainly in the milder western and southern states, south to El Salvador.

Occurrences The first British record occurred in spring: on Fair Isle, Shetland, on 2 June 1975 (Broad, 1979). The three subsequent occurrences were all October records in the Isles of Scilly: St Mary's in 1984, St Agnes in 1987 and Tresco in 1993. Fair Isle then hit back with a second in October 1995. The first Fair Isle individual fed all day in a small ploughed field, but those in Scilly have been altogether less cooperative. As well as occurring in Iceland, remarkably there are also records from Luxembourg, Germany and Sweden (Lewington *et al.*, 1991).

Identification Plates 66.2 & 3 show the 1993 Tresco individual. It is perhaps most similar to Swainson's Thrush *C. ustulatus*, particularly since it shows a fairly obvious pale eye-ring, but, unlike that species, it lacks a noticeable pale supra-loral line. The breast is more heavily blotched, but perhaps the most obvious difference is the contrastingly reddish-brown rump and tail, shown particularly well in Plate 66.2. As if to exaggerate this, it often slowly raises its tail. The obvious buff tips to the greater coverts show it to be a first-winter (Pyle *et al.*, 1987), and it is interesting to note that it also has pale tips to the median coverts, forming a second wing bar. Its call is a low *chuck*.

SWAINSON'S THRUSH
Catharus ustulatus

Range Breeds across much of northern North America, mainly in the coniferous forest zone. It winters from Mexico to north-western Argentina.

Occurrences As with the Hermit Thrush *C. guttatus*, the first record occurred in spring: one found dead at Blackrock Lighthouse, Co. Mayo, on 26 May 1956. The 19 subsequent records (up to 1995) have all been made in autumn, from 30 September through October. As to be expected, the lion's share has occurred in the south-west, with eight recorded in the Isles of Scilly. The only east coast record was of one trapped at Sandwich Bay, Kent, on 27 October 1976.

Identification Swainson's Thrush is a small thrush, about the size of a Northern Wheatear *Oenanthe oenanthe*, appearing rather neckless and long-winged with a rather short tail. Autumn vagrants are often to be found feeding on blackberries. Unlike the Song Thrush *Turdus philomelos*, prominent spotting is confined to the throat and upper breast, and it is more diffusely mottled across the lower breast. Compared with the more regularly occurring *aliciae* race of the Grey-cheeked Thrush *C. minimus*, it is a warmer, more olivey-brown above, similar in shade to a Song Thrush, this coloration including the ear-coverts. The throat is strongly tinged buff. The most obvious difference is a prominent buff eye-ring and a pale supraloral line which connects the eye to the bill (although the latter can be less obvious or even lacking on some). The bill appears stubbier than the average Grey-cheeked's, and a pale yellowy base to the lower mandible ends abruptly half-way down. Some, however, appear to have an all-dark bill. Its call is a liquid *quilp* or *klip*, reminiscent of a tap dripping into water. Plate 66.4 shows an individual on St Mary's, Isles of Scilly, in October 1990, which was one of two seen together at the north end of the island. Plate 66.5 shows another on Fair Isle, Shetland, in September 1990. Pale tips to the greater coverts indicate a first-winter but those which lack them, like this bird, can be either first-winter or adult.

for granted in the south-west. There have even been multiple arrivals, with five in 1976 and at least 12 in 1986. Many are clearly at the end of their tether, and eight in Scilly in 1986 included the famous one that was killed by a cat in front of a crowd of horrified birders, and the even more pathetic individual which was washed off a rock by a wave. For every one that gets here, one wonders just how many must drop into the ocean.

Identification Plate 67.1 shows a typical *aliciae* present on St Mary's, Isles of Scilly, in October 1991. Prominent buff tips to the greater coverts show it to be a first-winter (although not all first-winters show these). It is a small, wheatear-sized thrush with a very round body. Unlike the Song Thrush *Turdus philomelos*, prominent spotting is confined to the throat and upper breast. It is much colder-looking than Swainson's Thrush *C. ustulatus*, being grey-brown above and silvery-grey below, and lacking any warm olive or buff tones. As its name suggests, it has greyish ear-coverts. The most obvious difference from Swainson's is its facial pattern: it is rather plain-faced, lacking a prominent pale supra-loral line and, most importantly, it shows only the faintest of pale eye-rings. The bill looks more pointed and there is a tendency for the pale base to the lower mandible (flesh or yellowish-flesh in colour) to extend further towards the tip in a point. The call is a high-pitched *whe-err*. The Newfoundland race *minimus* is browner and some may not be distinguishable in the field from Bicknell's Thrush *C. bicknelli* (*see* below).

GREY-CHEEKED THRUSH
Catharus minimus

Range Breeds from north-eastern Siberia through northern North America, the bulk of its range being further north than those of the other four *Catharus* thrushes. It is a long-range migrant, wintering in northern South America.

Occurrences There are two races of Grey-cheeked Thrush: *aliciae* is the more widespread, whilst the nominate *minimus* breeds only in Newfoundland. A south-eastern race (*bicknelli*) has recently been split as Bicknell's Thrush (*see* page 123). Grey-cheeked Thrush is one of the more regular transatlantic passerine vagrants, and 42 records between 1953 and 1993, about half of which were in the Isles of Scilly, no doubt referred mainly to *aliciae*. It is now virtually annual and, given the right weather conditions, it is to some extent taken

Grey-cheeked Thrush.

BICKNELL'S THRUSH
Catharus bicknelli

Range Breeds in the mountains of New England, in upstate New York, and in southern Quebec and the Maritime Provinces. It winters in the West Indies.

Occurrence Bicknell's Thrush was split from the Grey-cheeked Thrush *C. minimus* by the BOURC in 1995 (Knox, 1996) following the work of Dr Henri Ouellet, who measured a large number of specimens, examined plumage and bare-part colours and recorded their songs. He found that Bicknell's in southern Quebec did not respond to tapes of Grey-cheeked songs (Ouellet, 1993). Also, whereas the Grey-cheeked winters in northern South America, Bicknell's winters in the West Indies. There are no accepted British or Irish records, but a thrush seen well and photographed at Abbey Farm, Tresco, Isles of Scilly, on 20 October 1986, is thought probably to have been this species (Plate 67.2).

Identification The Tresco thrush was clearly exhausted and appeared largely oblivious to its crowd of admirers, some of whom threw it earthworms in an attempt to revive it. The fact that it could not be found the following day suggests that it did not survive the night. Whilst it can be notoriously difficult to judge plumage tones from photographs, it was immediately apparent in the field that this was no ordinary Grey-cheeked Thrush. In fact, several observers commented on its superficial similarity to a Hermit Thrush *C. guttatus* and suggested at the time that it was probably *bicknelli*, although it was then treated as a race of Grey-cheeked.

Bicknell's is smaller than *aliciae* Grey-cheeked Thrush, its tail is chestnut, more warmly coloured than the upperparts, and the base of the lower mandible is bright yellow and more extensive. It is considered, however, that Bicknell's is not safely distinguishable in the field from some examples of the *minimus* race of Grey-cheeked, which breeds in Newfoundland. That said, it seems that virtually all Bicknell's and no Grey-cheeked should show a combination of a brighter chestnut tail and a half-yellow lower mandible. On most *minimus* the tail is concolorous with the upperparts and the base of the bill is flesh or yellowish-flesh in colour (McLaren, 1995). North American birders are looking into their field separation, so it is possible that the Tresco bird will one day be considered identifiable.

In the field, the Tresco bird showed a domed head and a fine, pointed bill with yellow on the base of the lower mandible extending half-way towards the tip. The upperparts were quite a warm brown, especially on the rump and tail. The flanks were dark buff and the legs appeared orange. The lack of pale tips to the greater coverts may suggest that it was an adult, but sharply tapered tail feather tips clearly show that it was a first-winter.

VEERY
Catharus fuscescens

Range Breeds from eastern Canada and north-eastern USA, west to British Columbia and Colorado. It winters in northern South America.

Occurrences There are three British records: a first-winter trapped at Porthgwarra, Cornwall, on 6 October 1970 (Allsopp, 1972); another first-winter trapped on Lundy, Devon, from 10 October to 11 November 1987 (King, 1990); and an individual on North Uist, Western Isles, on 20–28 October 1995. Towards the end of its stay, the Lundy bird (Plate 67.4) became readily visible at the top of Millcombe Valley, enabling crowds of birders to visit the island and see it.

Identification Similar in size and shape to the other three *Catharus* thrushes on the British an Irish List. It is readily identifiable, however, by its rather bright orangey-brown upperparts and the rather limited area of diffuse orangey-brown streaking on the upper breast. Also of note are the virtual absence of an eye-ring and the long pink legs, a characteristic which this species shares with a number of other unrelated ground-dwelling forest birds. It can be aged as a first-winter by the buff tips to the greater coverts and by the pointed tips to the tail feathers (the latter are readily visible in photographs taken of it in the hand). It has a distinctive, slightly mournful *wi-er* or *quier* call, which allows easy detection. The name Veery comes from the downward-slurred fluty notes of its song (Allsopp, 1972).

EYEBROWED THRUSH
Turdus obscurus

Range Breeds in eastern Siberia from the Yenisey to the Pacific and south to Lake Baikal. It winters from north-eastern India through Southeast Asia to the Philippines and southern Japan.

Occurrences The Eyebrowed Thrush was first recorded as recently as 1964, when there were three records, but it is another Siberian vagrant which has increased significantly in recent years, with 16 up to 1995. Most have occurred in October but there have also been three in April–May. Since 1984, it has proved to be something of a Scilly speciality with a remarkable nine records, including perhaps as many as three in 1991.

Identification The bird in Plate 67.3 was a very confiding individual on St Mary's and St Agnes, Isles of Scilly, in October 1993. The Eyebrowed Thrush is most similar to the Redwing *T. iliacus* but shows a narrower supercilium, a whitish line below the eye, a whitish submoustachial stripe and unstreaked underparts. The breast and flanks are instead washed with a beautiful soft peach. The pale-tipped greater coverts show the 1993 bird to be a first-winter. The flight call suggests a thin, sibilant Redwing.

DUSKY AND NAUMANN'S THRUSHES
Turdus naumanni

Range Two distinct races occur and are sometimes treated as separate species, although their relationship is not fully understood. They breed in northern and central Siberia from the tree limit south to Lake Baikal and east to the Pacific. They winter in Japan, Korea, China and in small numbers to northern Myanmar (Burma) and Assam. The 'Dusky Thrush' (*eunomus*) occupies the northern part of the range, while the nominate 'Naumann's' (*naumanni*) occurs in the south, although there is much intergrading between the two.

Occurrences There have been eight late-autumn and winter records of the Dusky Thrush (up to 1987), but the bird in Plate 67.6 represented the first record of Naumann's. It was present at, of all places, Woodford Green, Chingford, Essex, from 19 January to 9 March 1990. This was another example of an extreme rarity – indeed a first for Britain – turning up at an unexpected locality. It was discovered by Ken Murray as he sat slumped in a kitchen chair with that 'morning-after-the-night-before' feeling. The thrush was feeding in an ivy hedge in his garden (Murray, 1990). News soon spread, and over the following weeks the bird became a celebrity in the national press.

Identification Naumann's Thrush is about the size of a Song Thrush *T. philomelos*, and the individual in Plate 67.6 shows mottled orangey underparts, a long buff supercilium, dark lores, a buff submoustachial stripe and a brown malar stripe. The pale fringes to the wing feathers are also distinctive, whilst orangey underwings and reddish outer tail feathers were obvious in flight. Naumann's Thrush is a variable form, some also appearing mottled with orange on the upperparts. The neatly pale-fringed greater coverts show this individual to be a first-winter. Svensson (1992) states that sexing may be difficult, although individuals without prominent dark streaks on the chin, throat and sides of the breast (like this one) should be males.

Plate 67.5 shows a Dusky/Naumann's Thrush, present at Firth, Shetland, in November 1975. Its superficial similarity to the Chingford Naumann's is readily apparent. The main difference is that the underparts are much whiter, with only light mottling, and there is a hint of a messy band of mottling across the breast. Also, the supercilium is both whiter and stronger and there is little chestnut in the upperparts, just small amounts on the scapulars. The fact that some of the sparse underpart mottling is rather orange would suggest that this bird is an intergrade. The pale fringes and tips to the greater coverts would indicate that it is a first-winter. Lewington *et al.*, (1989) give a number of calls, including a loud, very shrill, nasal *cheeh cheeh*, a harder *cha-cha-cha* and a hard *chack* alarm (the number of notes varies), as well as a shrill *shrree* flight call for the Dusky.

RED-THROATED THRUSH
Turdus ruficollis ruficollis

Range Breeds in southern Siberia, from the Altai Mountains northeast to the Lake Baikal area. It winters in Afghanistan eastwards through northern Pakistan and northern Kashmir to Assam and northern Myanmar (Burma), as well as in parts of western China.

Occurrence There is just one accepted record: a first-winter male at The Naze, Essex, from 29 September to 7 October 1994 (Plate 68.1). The Red-throated replaces the Black-throated Thrush *T. r. atrogularis* in the eastern part of their ranges. There are marked ecological differences between them: the Red-throated is a bird of the mountains, whereas Black-throated frequents various types of lowland forest and sparse dry woodlands in subalpine steppes, up to altitudes of 7,200 ft (2,200 m) in the south of its range (*BWP*). Differences between their songs, and possibly their calls, need to be clarified. Although the two forms are currently treated as conspecific and it is stated that intergrades are locally more numerous than typical forms, there is some evidence to suggest that intergrades are in fact unusual. It seems possible that they will one day be split.

Identification As Plate 68.1 shows, this is a beautiful thrush, readily identifiable in male plumage. It is about the size of a Song Thrush *T. philomelos*, pale grey above with a buff supercilium (tinged reddish-orange), and with a reddish-orange throat and breast which are clearly demarcated from the rest of the underparts (these are white, faintly streaked with grey). Pale tips to the breast feathers produce a mottled effect when fresh. The inner webs of the tail feathers are also reddish-orange, so the underside of the tail appears this colour. The upperside is a blackish colour, although reddish-orange may be visible at the base and sides. The underwing-coverts are a similar colour. Like the Black-throated Thrush, the wing feathers are prominently fringed pale grey. In the field, there was a contrast between the outer greater coverts (which were darker and clearly edged grey) and the inners (which were duller and more diffusely fringed); this showed it to be a first-winter, the inner greater coverts being newly acquired adult feathers. Like the Black-throated, it showed a yellow base to the lower mandible. Females are streakier below, but still show varying amounts of 'red'.

BLACK-THROATED THRUSH
Turdus ruficollis atrogularis

Range Breeds in western and central Siberia (just creeping into the Western Palearctic) with an outpost in the Caucasus. It winters from eastern Saudi Arabia eastwards through Iran and the Indian subcontinent to Myanmar (Burma) and south-western China. Some remain in Siberia in good berry years.

Occurrences There were 34 records up to 1995 (all but three since 1974), mainly in late autumn and winter, and these included two together on Fair Isle, Shetland, in October 1994. During a cold spell in January–February 1996, at least four were discovered amongst Fieldfares *T. pilaris* and Redwings *T. iliacus* which had moved into urban environments to take advantage of ornamental berry bushes. Another two were discovered later in the winter, bringing the total to 40. Considering the millions of thrushes which winter here, the Black-throateds found must surely represent the tip of an iceberg, and it seems likely that the species is becoming regular here in small numbers. It will be interesting to see if the upward trend continues.

Identification The Black-throated is similar to the Red-throated Thrush *T. r. ruficollis* (*see* page 124 for a discussion on its taxonomy) except that the red is replaced by black. Plate 68.4 shows a first-winter male present on a modern housing estate at Webheath, Redditch, Worcestershire, in January–February 1996, while Plate 68.3 shows a similar bird at Peterborough, Cambridgeshire, at the same time. The most striking feature is the black chin, throat and breast the individual feathers being fringed whitish, and this whole area is sharply demarcated from the whitish belly. Like the Red-throated, they also showed a prominent yellow base to the lower mandible and a narrow yellow eye-ring but the supercilium is weaker. The upperparts are similarly grey, with the wing feathers fringed pale grey. Like the Red-throated (*see* above), sharply pale-fringed juvenile outer greater coverts contrast with more

diffusely-fringed adult inners. Sharply pointed tail feathers also showed them to be first-winters. Orangey under-wing-coverts were visible in flight. Some males are less distinctive, and a less-advanced first-winter in Victoria Park, Bristol, in February 1996 still retained a breast which was largely streaked, although newly grown black-centred feathers on the sides of the breast clearly showed it to be a male. Plate 68.2 shows a female at Holkham Park, Norfolk, in March 1996. It resembles the male except that the upperparts are browner, and it shows dark malar stripes and a buff submoustachial stripe and throat. Where it differs most is in the underparts, which are heavily but diffusely lined with brown (strongest on the breast). In direct comparison with the Redwing, Black-throated is bigger, longer-bodied and longer-tailed. The Redditch bird was heard to give a chacking call, reminiscent of that of the Fieldfare but harder.

AMERICAN ROBIN
Turdus migratorius

Range Breeds across virtually the whole of North America, south into Mexico. It winters mainly in the southern states, Mexico, Guatemala, Cuba and the Bahamas. The extent of the migration is dependent on berry crops and the severity of the weather.

Occurrences Evans (1994) recognized 27 records, 19 since 1958 (to 1988). Most have occurred in late autumn and winter, although the species has also been recorded in spring and summer, including one at Edenberry, Co. Offaly, in June–July 1983. In recent years records have been few and far between – a first-winter male at Inverbervie, Kincardineshire, on 24–29 December 1988 (Plate 68.5) was the first recorded since 1984 and the first twitchable one since 1976. It was responsible for several abandoned Christmas dinners!

Identification The American Robin is a distinctive thrush which, in North America, occupies a similar niche to our Common Blackbird *T. merula*, being familiar in urban as well as rural environments. The male has a black head with a white chin and a prominent white eye-ring (this may extend towards the bright yellow bill), grey upperparts, a blackish tail (with white corners), brick-red underparts and white undertail-coverts. The female is similar but appears more 'washed out'. Looking at its plumage, the Inverbervie bird was clearly a male, and well-defined pale tips to browner outer greater coverts, contrasting with more diffusely fringed greyer inners, showed it to be a first-winter. The usual flight call is a thin *see-up* or *tzeee-up*, similar to that of the Redwing *T. iliacus* but more disyllabic. It also gives a thin, sibilant, slightly trilling *seeeep*.

PALLAS'S GRASSHOPPER WARBLER
Locustella certhiola

Range Breeds across much of Siberia, south into Mongolia and northern China. It winters from India through Southeast Asia to Indonesia.

Occurrences This species remains a major rarity, with just 18 records (up to 1996). Like the Lanceolated Warbler *L. lanceolata*, it too has a northerly pattern of occurrence, with 11 recorded in Shetland, nine of which have been on Fair Isle. Surprisingly, however, the first record was at the Rockabill Lighthouse, Dublin, on 28 September 1908, and there was a second in Ireland in 1990: on Cape Clear Island, Co. Cork, on 8 October. All have occurred in September and October.

Identification Plates 69.1 & 2 show one present on North Ronaldsay, Orkney, in September 1992. Fortuitously, it turned up just in time to be seen by a number of birders who had arrived from the south to twitch a Yellow-browed Bunting *Emberiza chrysophrys*. It is about ten per cent larger than a Grasshopper Warbler *L. naevia* and its sturdier appearance (particularly the bill) can be appreciated in the photographs. It can be distinguished from the Grasshopper by its obvious buff supercilium, stronger upperpart streaking on a rather dark rufousy-brown background, sharply defined dark centres to the wing coverts and tertials, and by the whitish tips to the dark tail, most obvious on the four outer feathers (shown well in Plate 69.2). It should be noted, however, that the latter can be difficult to see, particularly if the tail is held closed in flight; they may be best appreciated from below as the white tips contrast with the very dark underside of the tail. Note also the prominent white 'bulge' on the inner web of the tertial tips. In flight, it usually shows a strongly rufous rump (recalling the Sedge Warbler *Acrocephalus schoenobaenus*). Fresh wing feathers, the strong yellowish-buff tone to the underparts and spotting on the upper breast indicate a young bird; this plumage may in fact be juvenile, rather than first-winter. Migrants and winterers give a short, rolled *chirr* or *cher(k)*, sometimes doubled (*BWP*).

LANCEOLATED WARBLER
Locustella lanceolata

Range Breeds across Siberia, with westernmost populations extending into European Russia. It winters from northern India through Southeast Asia to the Philippines and parts of Indonesia.

Occurrences This was formerly an extremely rare vagrant but it has been almost annual since 1972 and,

by 1995, it had amassed a total of 67 records (with a peak of seven in 1994). It is a northern bird and it is still very much a Fair Isle speciality: 44 have been recorded there, mainly in September and early October. Its secretive nature undoubtedly mitigates against discovery elsewhere, and four out of six recent English records, including one as far south as Hampshire, were discovered in mist nets.

Identification The Lanceolated Warbler is similar to the Grasshopper Warbler *L. naevia* but is typically smaller, shorter tailed and more heavily streaked. Like all members of its genus, it is secretive but not necessarily shy, creeping around amongst vegetation and even running like a mouse at great speed across barer ground. When feeding, it constantly flicks its wings, like a Dunnock *Prunella modularis*. Once found, it may be possible to obtain extremely close-range views – there have even been cases of Fair Isle vagrants crawling over people's feet.

The first-winter in Plates 69.3 & 4 was on Fair Isle, Shetland, in September 1990. Compared with the Grasshopper Warbler, it shows: (1) a heavily streaked mantle (with the black mantle streaks extending to the feather tips); (2) a gorget of fine breast streaking; (3) a heavily streaked rump; and, perhaps most important, (4) neatly defined clear-cut brown fringes to the tertials, these contrasting with the black feather centres (on the Grasshopper, the fringes are broader, less clearly defined, and they merge into duller, browner centres; *see* Riddiford & Harvey, 1992, for a full discussion). The pattern of the undertail-coverts is also important; these may be rather gingery and show narrow and clear-cut brown shaft streaks (or spots) which reach neither the tip nor the base of the feather. On some, the longer undertail-coverts are plain, diffusely tipped whitish (the Grasshopper shows long, broad, diffuse central steaks on all these feathers, all of which reach the base of the feather). The breast streaking is also variable; the individual photographed is very much a 'classic' but some have very faint, diffuse streaking whilst others are heavily lined; the former are thought not to have body-moulted from their looser and fluffier juvenile plumage (Lewington *et al*, 1991). Fresh primaries also indicate a young bird. Autumn vagrants are silent.

RIVER WARBLER
Locustella fluviatilis

Range Breeds across mid-latitude Eastern Europe, apparently between the 17°C and 23°C (63°F and 73°F) isotherms, and forms the western counterpart to Gray's Grasshopper Warbler *L. fasciolata* (*BWP*). It winters in East Africa.

Occurrences The first British record was made in September 1961 on Fair Isle, Shetland (Davis 1962). There were then two in September 1969, and a further 19 between 1981 and 1995. There has been a distinct split in the records, 11 having occurred in spring and summer and 11 in late August and September. Six records have involved singing males in suitable breeding habitats in eastern England or Scotland. There were a further three singing males in 1996.

The recent upsurge and the presence of singing males can be related to a marked increase in northern Europe and a spread in the species' range. An earlier expansion at the beginning of the 20th century was followed by a retreat, but it has been spreading west again since the 1950s (*BWP*). In Sweden, for example, it was first recorded in 1937, and in 1988 there were a record 220 singing males, with the first confirmed breeding, followed by about 255 in 1993. There were also 31 singing males in Denmark in 1995 (*Brit. Birds* **83**: 228; **88**: 276; **89**: 40). It remains to be seen whether the species will ever gain a permanent toe-hold here.

Identification Plate 69.6 shows a singing male near Kielder Water, Northumberland, in June 1996. The River is quite a large warbler, similar in size and shape to Savi's *L. luscinioides*. Like all *Locustellas*, it has an obviously rounded tail and curved primaries, as well as a sloping forehead and a long neck, the overall shape recalling that of Common Nightingale *Luscinia megarhynchos*. It is rather a deep, dark oily brown above and dark greyish-buff below. What immediately distinguishes it from Savi's is that the throat is finely streaked and the breast is diffusely lined with dark brown, similar in shade to the mantle. It has a dull pink bill and is rather plain faced with a narrow, pale eye-ring and a very faint short supercilium over the eye (although the latter is variable). An important difference from Savi's is the pattern of the undertail-coverts, which have thick whitish crescent-shaped tips to the feathers (they are plain or lightly tipped on Savi's). It should be noted, however, that Normaja (1994) discovered considerable individual variation in River Warblers. Some are very white below, with indistinct breast streaking and white tips to the undertail-coverts that are so broad that the dark bases are difficult to detect. Conversely, some are so dark that the breast streaking forms an all-dark breast band, the undertail-covert tips can be pale brown and difficult to see, and they can show a virtually all-dark bill.

Summer males are usually detected by their amazing song, which is given with the bill fully open and often in full view. It is a high-pitched, pulsating, cicada-like *z-z-z-z-z-z*..., rising and falling in pitch as the bird turns its head from side to side. At the same time, it also gives a high-pitched metallic undertone. This is much more cricket-like and is reminiscent of the slow spinning of a bicycle wheel. The net effect is that it sounds like two insects, a big one and a little one, singing at the same time. Like all *Locustellas* it creeps around on long deep pink legs, frequently flicking its wings. When disturbed, it will scarper across bare ground like a mouse.

SAVI'S WARBLER
Locustella luscinioides

Range Breeds in North Africa and across middle and southern Europe, reaching as far east as Kazakhstan, apparently between the July isotherms of 18° and 32°C (64°F and 90°F; *BWP*). It winters in a narrow zone immediately south of the Sahara.

Occurrences Savi's Warbler has had a chequered history as a British breeding bird. It bred in small numbers in eastern England until the mid-19th century, when it became extinct. It then recolonized Kent in 1960 and subsequently spread. The population reached a peak level in 1978–80, with a possible maximum of 28–30 pairs, but it has since declined again (*BWP*). In 1993, the last year for which information has been published, about five pairs are thought to have bred in Suffolk, Kent and Sussex, and with another singing male in Norfolk (Ogilvie *et al.*, 1996).

Savi's fortunes here have been mirrored on the Continent. A moderate range expansion has occurred in northern and western parts during the last 30 years, but some areas, such as Belgium and the Netherlands, have recorded serious recent declines (*BWP*). Like many wetland species it has suffered generally from habitat destruction but to what extent recent sub-Saharan droughts may be implicated is not known.

Apart from the breeding records, Savi's is otherwise a fairly regular spring overshoot in small numbers, with a smaller peak in autumn (birds at this time of year are generally discovered only as a result of ringing activities).

Identification Plate 69.5 shows a singing male at Stanwick Gravel Pits, Northamptonshire, in July 1991. Savi's breeds in reed beds and, when singing, often climb to the top of the reeds or similar vegetation; otherwise, they are very secretive. Savi's is a large warbler and shows the typical *Locustella* shape, with rather a long, pointed bill, a wedge-shaped head profile, a small head and rather a scrawny, thin neck, curved primaries, long undertail-coverts, and a full and conspicuously rounded tail (often obvious in flight). Most of these features are visible in Plate 69.5. Plumage-wise, it is similar to a River Warbler *L. fluviatilis*, being dull brown above and a dingy buff below (whiter on the throat), and showing only a faint 'shadow' of a supercilium and a faint eye-ring. Where it differs most is that it is completely plain on the breast and shows plain cinnamon-buff undertail-coverts, with, at most, only faintly paler tips (*see* page 127 for a discussion of the variation in River Warblers). Savi's behaviour is typical of a *Locustella*, walking around at the base of reeds, or climbing up and down the stems, and this alone separates it from the Reed Warbler *Acrocephalus scirpaceus*. The song is a low pitched buzzing reel, lower pitched than a Grasshopper Warbler's *L. naevia*, and is sometimes preceded by the call: a quiet *tip tip*, reminiscent of that of the European Robin *Erithacus rubecula*.

AQUATIC WARBLER
Acrocephalus paludicola

Range Breeds from north-eastern Germany, Poland and Hungary eastwards through European Russia to the Urals, with isolated populations to the east. Its winter quarters are poorly known, but western populations apparently move to West Africa, south of the Sahara.

Occurrences This is an interesting species which has become very localized in eastern Europe, mainly as a result of land drainage. It breeds within the 18–26°C (64–79°F) July isotherms and nests in marshes, favouring low tracts of sedge and iris rather than reeds and willows. In Germany it has been reduced to two populations of 30–40 pairs in the north-east, while in Poland a survey conducted in 1992 revealed about 7,640 singing males, with the Biebrza Marshes being the main site (*Brit. Birds* **81**: 337; **86**: 289). In Hungary, 170–200 singing males at a single site is the only population to have shown a marked recent increase (*BWP*). In 1995, however, there was the exciting discovery of about 5,000–10,000 pairs in the Brest region of Belorussia (*Brit. Birds* **89**: 40).

The Aquatic Warbler's migration routes have been something of a mystery, but the western autumn route has been clarified by ringing in reed beds. From Eastern Europe, they initially head on a west–southwest course to reach staging-posts in Western Europe, thereafter heading south into north-west Africa via Iberia. This migration is carried out in a series of long loop flights, alternating with long stopovers at traditional sites (*BWP*).

The main autumn migration passes through Belgium and western France – the former recorded an exceptional influx of 200 birds in 1989 (*BWP*).

Despite being considered a rarity here, southern Britain is very much on its main migration route and annual totals have been as high as 83 (in 1976), but, that said, the numbers recorded largely reflect levels of ringing activity. What is particularly puzzling is that most occur in the South-west Peninsula and that occurrences are distinctly rare on the east coast. The largest numbers have been recorded at Radipole Lake, Dorset (22 in 1972), and at Poole Harbour, Dorset (21 in 1991), while Marazion Marsh, Cornwall, remains the favoured spot for actually seeing the species in the field. The peak time is the middle of August, but records span the period from late July to early November. Confirmation of the origin of British migrants was achieved in 1990 when two Polish individuals with consecutive ring numbers were trapped at Marazion and at Chew Valley Lake, Somerset.

Identification Some 93 per cent of Aquatic Warblers aged in this country have been juveniles (a complete post-juvenile moult does not take place until it reaches its winter quarters; *BWP*), and the individual in Plate 70.1, photographed on St Agnes, Isles of Scilly, in October 1990, is typical. Although superficially similar to the Sedge Warbler *A. schoenobaenus*, the photograph clearly shows that, if seen well, the Aquatic Warbler is very distinctive. It is a buffer looking bird than a juvenile Sedge, with prominently 'tiger striped' mantle and scapulars (this striping extends onto the rump and uppertail-coverts) and with sharply defined black centres to the wing coverts and tertials. The head is particularly distinctive, with pale lores (creating a more open-faced expression than on the Sedge), a curving buff supercilium, black lateral crown stripes and a thin but well-defined buff central crown stripe. The legs are noticeably pink and the tail feathers pointed. Its plumage pattern is, in fact, strangely reminiscent of a winter Bobolink *Dolichonyx oryzivorus* (*see* Plate 96.3). Plate 70.2 shows another juvenile trapped at Chew Valley Lake, Somerset, in August 1995, with a juvenile Sedge for comparison. Autumn adults are much more heavily worn and, consequently, darker.

PADDYFIELD WARBLER
Acrocephalus agricola

Range Breeds around the northern coast of the Black Sea eastwards through Kazakhstan to south-western Siberia, Mongolia and western China, as well as in Afghanistan and north-eastern Iran. It winters in the Indian subcontinent.

Occurrences The first British record was on Fair Isle, Shetland, on 1 October 1925, and there were a further four up to 1974. Since the 1980s there has been a marked upsurge, with 29 between 1981 and 1995, and a peak of nine in 1994. Most have occurred in the Northern Isles and down the east coast in late September and October. Since 1984 there have been four spring records in late May and early June, plus one on Holm, Orkney, on 18 July 1994. Two notably late occurrences which did not conform to the established pattern involved an individual photographed at Tring Reservoirs, Hertfordshire, on 9 November 1981, and another on the North Slob, Co. Wexford, on 3 December 1984, this being found dead the following day. Another interesting record involved a first-winter found on a fishing boat 254 miles (409 km) south-west of Ireland on 14 September 1993 (*see* page 14 for a further discussion).

As with several other east European passerine migrants, there have been signs of an increase and spread in the western part of its range. In the Crimea in the 1960s, for example, it increased and spread with the advent of rice cultivation (*BWP*). It bred for the first time in Finland in 1991 and has been breeding in Latvia since 1987 (*Brit. Birds* **86**: 44 and 289), well to the north-west of its traditional range. One trapped on Fair Isle in October 1996 had been ringed in Estonia.

Identification Plate 70.3 shows a first-winter from the 1994 influx at Quendale, Shetland, in October. Compared to the Reed Warbler *A. scirpaceus*, the Paddyfield has a finer and more pointed bill, a short primary projection and a rather long, mobile tail which is twitched in all directions. The tail appears square when closed but it is often flicked and held partly open, when it appears more rounded. The tail length is emphasized by proportionately shorter undertail-coverts. It is also easily distinguished from the Reed Warbler (and from the similar Marsh *A. palustris* and Blyth's Reed *A. dumetorum*) by the head pattern, which recalls that of a Sedge Warbler *A. schoenobaenus*: it shows a distinct narrow cream supercilium, flaring and then tapering at the rear, a dark eye-stripe and a diffuse dark lateral crown stripe. The grey-brown ear-coverts are clearly demarcated from the very white throat. The upperparts of a first-winter are a pale sandy-brown (with a hint of olive) and it shows obvious buff-brown fringes to the wing feathers. It may appear slightly chestnut on the rump. The underparts are a pale buffy-white, much whiter than those on the Reed Warbler. The combination of its pale plumage and its overall structure (particularly the long, mobile tail) may suggest a miniature babbler (Timaliidae). In flight, Paddyfields look very pale and quite long-tailed. The call is a throaty, squeaky *chjik*, (reminiscent of a 'soft' Sedge Warbler) or a rapid, chattering *ch-d-d-d*.

BLYTH'S REED WARBLER
Acrocephalus dumetorum

Range Breeds from Finland and the former Baltic republics east across Russia and western Siberia, with scattered breeding to the south of its main range. It winters in the Indian subcontinent.

Occurrences The first British record, on Fair Isle, Shetland, in September 1910, was followed by a remarkable influx of seven or eight in September–October 1912, including four or five on Fair Isle. There was another on Fair Isle in 1928 but we had to wait until 1969 for the next, since when there have been at least 24 (to 1996), with as many as seven in 1993. Most have occurred from late August to October, but there have also been five in late Spring. There can be little doubt that identification problems have clouded the species' true position, as evidenced by the fact that most have been discovered in mist nets.

As with the Paddyfield Warbler *A. agricola*, Blyth's Reed may well be on the increase here. In the last 100 years it has spread north from its main range, breeding for the first time in Estonia in 1890–93 (with 2,000 pairs in 1989), in Latvia in 1944 and in Finland in 1947 (a rapid expansion took place there, with 5,000 pairs in 1989; *BWP*). There has also been a slow increase in Sweden since the 1970s, with as many as 62 recorded in 1993 (*Brit. Birds* **88**: 276).

Identification Plates 70.4 & 5 show a singing male at Kergord, Shetland, in May 1994. As with many difficult species, a holistic approach to its identification is required. It is most similar to a Marsh Warbler *A. palustris* except that the primaries are rather short and bunched, more like those of the Reed Warbler *A. scirpaceus*. This bird was unusual in that it showed prominent whitish tips to the primaries (recalling a Marsh Warbler); they are usually distinctly plain in this area and they show little contrast between the centres and fringes of the tertials. Like the Marsh, Blyth's Reed is cold and pallid, rather pale olivey-brown above with a definite greyish tinge, and essentially white below with a slight buff wash that is strongest on the flanks and undertail-coverts. The chin and throat are noticeably white. There may be a faint rufous tint to the rump in fresher birds. The facial pattern looks relatively plain, almost *Hippolais*-like, with a very narrow dark line across the lores (often reduced to a small spot in front of the eye on first-winters), a creamy supercilium before the eye (this tends to be more subdued on first-winters) and a noticeable whitish eye-ring. Note that the bill is fine, pointed, and rather sharp and 'spiky'. The culmen is dark, but the lower mandible and cutting edge are rather pinkish right to the tip. Plate 70.4 shows a sloping forehead with a distinct peak above the eye. The legs are pinkish, but on autumn first-winters they are distinctly grey, sometimes with yellow-green feet.

For observers thoroughly familiar with the Reed Warbler, it should appear markedly different. Blyth's Reed is slightly smaller, daintier and perhaps more active, showing a fine bill and lacking any strong rufous tones (although Kennerley *et al.*, 1992, on which some of the above is based, indicate that the Blyth's Reed is more rufous in fresh plumage). It is rather white on the vent and undertail-coverts, whereas the Reed is quite strongly buff in this area. A useful behavioural difference is its habit of frequently and obviously cocking its tail, or jerking it upwards. In its winter quarters it inhabits drier habitats than the Reed Warbler, and it may be very vocal, giving a soft but penetrating *thik*, similar to the call of the Lesser Whitethroat *Sylvia curruca* but with an initial fricative (*BWP*). Ellis *et al.*, (1994) described the song of the Kergord bird as being slower than that of a Marsh Warbler, full of whistles and almost thrush-like at times, with mimicry of the Long-tailed Tit *Aegithalos caudatus*, European Goldfinch *Carduelis carduelis* and House Sparrow *Passer domesticus*. In full song it gives characteristic thin, high-pitched whistling phrases: *sit-EE-oo*, *soo-EE* and *si si sooee*.

GREAT REED WARBLER
Acrocephalus arundinaceus

Range Breeds in North Africa and much of continental Europe east through Asia to the Pacific. Western birds winter throughout much of tropical Africa, apparently migrating in one continuous flight from stopover areas in the Mediterranean, and migrants may pause in the northern tropics before continuing further south (*BWP*). Eastern birds, often split as the Eastern Great Reed Warbler *A. orientalis*, winter in Southeast Asia and Indonesia.

Occurrences Numbers have severely decreased in many parts of the Western Palearctic, and the species is now threatened with extinction in some areas (*BWP*). Needless to say, habitat destruction is the main culprit. In the Netherlands, however, its population is stable, with over 300 territories, while in Sweden it has shown a marked increase since the 1960s, with a record 395 singing males in 1993 (*Brit. Birds* **88**: 276). Here it occurs mainly as a spring overshoot in late May and early June (81 per cent of all records from 1958 to 1985 were in spring, with most in southern and south-eastern England; Dymond *et al.*, 1989). There is a minor secondary peak in late August and early September. It is still a very rare bird,

averaging four or five a year during 1983–94, and, as noted by Dymond *et al.*, its failure to increase in line with the increase in birdwatching must surely reflect the Continental decline.

Identification Similar in length to a Redwing *Turdus iliacus*, but about half its weight, the Great Reed Warbler is readily identifiable by size alone. Plate 71.1 shows a singing male present at Cley, Norfolk, in June 1994. It shows the brown eye-stripe and conspicuous buff supercilium (most obvious before the eye), as well as the pronounced white jowl and raised crown feathers, so typical of singing birds. The heavy, thrush-like bill, with its pale base to the lower mandible, is also distinctive. Note also its long primary projection with pale fringes to the individual feathers. Most are located by their loud and powerful song, which has hard, disjointed guttural notes (including a deep *ur ur* and a familiar *karra karra*) interspersed with squeaking phrases. It reveals a bright orange gape when singing. As befitting its size, it hops heavily and clumsily through the reeds, and even feeds on the ground. It flies low and direct between reed clumps, appearing rather like a plain Song Thrush *T. philomelos*.

OLIVACEOUS WARBLER
Hippolais pallida

Range Breeds in parts of Iberia, North Africa and the central Sahara, and from the former Yugoslavia eastwards through the Balkans, Asia Minor and parts of the Middle East to Turkestan. It occurs within the July isotherms of 22–32°C (72–90°F; *BWP*). The Iberian and north-west African race *opaca* winters in western Africa south of the Sahara. The smaller southeast European and Asian race *elaeica* winters in East and north-eastern Africa.

Occurrences Although 17 records were made between 1951 and 1995, the Rarities Committee has been reviewing the British records and it seems likely that some will not stand the test of time. Evans (1994) recognized only six in Britain (compared with the accepted 12). All have turned up from 12 August to 17 October, except for one on Fair Isle, Shetland, on 5–13 June 1995. The fact that a number of recent records have occurred in south-western England and Ireland may suggest that they involved the western race *opaca*. An individual on the Isle of May, Fife, in September 1967, however, was killed by a Great Grey Shrike *Lanius excubitor* and was identified as the eastern *elaeica*. Three other trapped individuals have also been assigned to *elaeica* on the basis of measurements, so it seems likely that we have received vagrants from both directions.

Identification Plate 71.3 shows the Fair Isle bird of June 1995 (probably *elaeica*), while Plate 71.2 shows one on St Mary's, Isles of Scilly, in October 1985. *Elaeica* is a large, pallid warbler, pale brownish-grey above and whitish below, with greyish fringes to all the wing feathers, those on the secondaries forming a slight panel. It has a long, pale pinkish or orangey bill and a sloping forehead (both typical of the genus). It sometimes raises its crown feathers or shows a slightly ragged effect to the rear crown. It also has a typically bland *Hippolais* facial pattern, with pale lores and a faint supercilium and eye-ring. The tail is full and square, and narrow whitish outer tail feathers are clearly visible in Plate 71.3. When feeding, it habitually tail-dips, rather like a Chiffchaff *Phylloscopus collybita* only in a more exaggerated manner. In many ways the Olivaceous suggests a Melodious Warbler *H. polyglotta* which is totally devoid of yellow or green coloration and, like that species, it has a short primary projection (about half or two-thirds the overlying tertial length). Unlike the Melodious, it is very vocal, persistently giving a soft, slightly sneezing *stt...stt*, easily imitated. This may suggest a soft Blackcap *Sylvia atricapilla*. The two races of Olivaceous differ principally in size and plumage tone: *opaca* is larger, slightly browner and also shows a broader-based bill.

BOOTED WARBLER
Hippolais caligata

Range Breeds in diverse habitats in European Russia, Kazakhstan and western Siberia, into western Mongolia and north-western China, and south to Iran and Pakistan. It has two races, the nominate *caligata* in Eastern Europe and central Asia, and the larger *rama* (or 'Sykes's Warbler') in south-western Asia. It winters in the Indian subcontinent.

Occurrences The Booted Warbler was formerly considered a very rare vagrant, with only nine records before 1977, six of which were made on Fair Isle, Shetland. By 1995, however, this total had risen to 62, with most occurring down the east coast as well as eight in the Isles of Scilly. There was a peak of 14 in 1993. Up to 1991, all had occurred in autumn, from late August to late October, but in 1992 there were three spring records, including a singing male at Spurn, Yorkshire, on 10–22 June (Plate 71.4). Another spring bird was recorded in Sussex in June 1994. These sightings reflect recent summer records in Finland, Estonia and Sweden (*Brit. Birds* **81**: 21; **83**: 228; **85**: 12) – perhaps indicated signs of a westward range expansion?

Identification Undoubtedly one of the reasons for the recent increase is a better understanding of the species' field characteristics. It is a somewhat nondescript bird and, although it has a distinctive character, it is a difficult species to get across on paper. This is certainly a classic case of a photograph speaking more than a thousand words.

The nominate race is small for a *Hippolais*, being not much bigger than a Chiffchaff *Phylloscopus collybita*. The main characteristics shown in Plate 71.4 are as follows: (1) it has a longer bill than, say, a Chiffchaff, and this is predominantly orangey-pink; (2) it has a sloping forehead more typical of a *Hippolais*; (3) it has a better marked head pattern than the other members of its genus, with a pronounced whitish supercilium, often a hint of a dark lateral crown stripe, and more of a dark line across the lores and through the eye, this bisecting a narrow pale eye-ring. This may impart a more *Acrocephalus-* or *Phylloscopus*-like appearance to the head; (4) it is a pale bird and, to repeat a well-used but nevertheless

Booted Warbler.

appropriate cliché, the upperparts are the colour of milky tea. The underparts are whitish, washed with buff; (5) there are pale fringes to the greater coverts, tertials and secondaries, the latter forming a pale panel in the wing; (6) the primary projection is short, only about half to two-thirds the overlying tertial length; (7) there is a distinct 'step' between the primaries and the tertials; (8) the legs are typically a rather nondescript horn or grey colour; and (9) the undertail-coverts are short, unlike those on an *Acrocephalus*. All these features are readily apparent in Plate 71.4. The photograph fails to show, however, the slightly warmer toned rump and rather square tail, the latter with narrow pale edges which may be difficult to detect in the field. The Booted Warbler feeds in low vegetation, particularly in weeds or crops, often flying up into low bushes to eat its prey. Unlike the Olivaceous *H. pallida*, it does not persistently tail-dip (indeed, it may flick its tail).

The south-west Asian race (*rama*) is larger, being closer in size to the smaller eastern race of the Olivaceous Warbler *H. pallida elaeica*, and is also rather paler. Its lack of persistent tail-dipping may be a useful clue to its distinction from *elaeica*. Plate 71.5 shows an individual trapped at Seafield, Lerwick, Shetland, in October–November 1993. The photograph shows a remarkably pale, sandy bird with rather a heavy bill, but the overall appearance, particularly the head pattern, is nevertheless indicative of a Booted. On examining plumage wear, the finders considered it to have been an adult. It was heard to call: a quiet *tac* or *tchak*, as well as a soft, low *tuc* (Osborn, 1993).

ICTERINE WARBLER
Hippolais icterina

Range Breeds in the upper and middle latitudes of continental Europe from northern Norway (within the Arctic Circle) south to northern France, and east across Eastern Europe and Russia into Kazakhstan. It occurs between the July isotherms of 15–25°C (60–77°F; *BWP*). As befitting such a long-winged species, it is a long-distance migrant, wintering in southern Africa.

Occurrences Given the close proximity of its breeding range, the Icterine Warbler's wide latitudinal tolerance and its abundance on the near Continent (35,000–55,000 pairs in the Netherlands and 10,000 pairs in Belgium; *BWP*), it seems astonishing that it does not breed in Britain. Instead, it is a regular migrant, occurring mainly in late May and early June, but with larger numbers from early August to mid-October. Inevitably, most occur in the Northern Isles and down the east coast, but the

south coast and southern Ireland also receive their fair share in autumn.

Dymond *et al.* (1989) recorded 1,990 between 1958 and 1985, and although numbers have risen in line with the increased popularity of birdwatching, recent increases in Sweden (and probably also in Finland and the Netherlands) may indicate that the upsurge here is to some extent genuine. Although records average 74 per year, annual totals inevitably vary according to the prevalence of easterly airstreams. The best year on record is 1992, and Evans (1993a) estimated a total of 321, including no less than 225 in a remarkable 'easterly' spring. In such years multiple arrivals may occur, and a total of 14 on North Ronaldsay, Orkney, on 28 May, was quite remarkable. Following on from that influx, the first successful British breeding occurred in Scotland (Ogilvie *et al.*, 1995).

Identification Plate 72.1 shows a first-winter on St Mary's, Isles of Scilly, in October 1990 (it can be aged by the fresh remiges). It is similar to the Melodious Warbler *H. polyglotta* in both structure (but is more attenuated), plumage (including the 'bland' facial pattern) and bill colour (*see* below). The best way to distinguish it is by the very long primary projection, which is approximately equal to the overlying tertial length (it is about half to two-thirds the length on the Melodious). As if to emphasize this, there is a noticeable whitish panel on the closed wing, caused by the fringes to the secondaries. First-winter Icterines are usually more 'washed out' than Melodious, appearing a greyer shade of green on the upperparts and whiter below, the primrose coloration being strongest on the chin and throat (but pale yellow is nevertheless still present right across the underparts). The legs are a noticeably bluer shade of grey. Narrow, pale outer webs to the outer tail feathers may be visible in the field. The long wings produce a noticeably more dashing, flycatcher-like flight and it has rather a more impetuous character than the Melodious. Like the Melodious, spring adults are yellower below and have a yellower wing panel. Migrants are usually silent, although they may give a soft *tec* (Grahame Walbridge, verbally).

MELODIOUS WARBLER
Hippolais polyglotta

Range Largely replaces the Icterine Warbler *H. icterina* in south-western Europe, breeding throughout France, Iberia, and parts of Italy and North Africa. It is a shorter-range migrant than the Icterine, wintering in West Africa.

Occurrences It is salutary to remember that when the *Handbook of British Birds* was published in

1938–41, there had been just three British Melodious records – it took the establishment of the bird observatory network in the 1950s to reveal the species' true status as a scarce but regularly occurring autumn migrant. Dymond *et al.*, (1989) recorded a total of 871 between 1958 and 1985, 44 per cent of the Icterine Warbler total. It thus averaged 32 per year, but with a steady increase during the period. Although related to an upsurge in observer activity, its appearances may also be connected to recent dramatic increases as it has spread northwards into Belgium and Germany (*BWP*). There has, however, been a suggestion in recent years of lower numbers at some traditional south coast localities.

Unlike the Icterine, the Melodious is very rare in spring, but there is a large peak from early August to mid-October. Reflecting its Continental breeding range, there is a strong south-westerly bias to the records, with the Isles of Scilly, Cornwall, Devon and Dorset accounting for most, but with a significant minority in southern Ireland and at the Irish Sea observatories. It remains remarkably rare in Scotland. Virtually all the autumn records involve first-winters, these having presumably dispersed northwards prior to their main southward migration.

Identification Plate 72.2 shows a classic first-winter on Tresco, Isles of Scilly, in October 1989. It is a large warbler with a long, pale orange bill, a sloping forehead, a peaked crown and a bland facial expression. The supercilium is faint (strongest before the eye), it has unmarked lores, a narrow eye-ring and only a faint eye-stripe behind the eye. The dull olive-green upperparts and soft primrose-yellow underparts, strongest on the throat and upper breast, are characteristic (spring adults are much yellower below). The key feature in its distinction from the Icterine is the short primary projection (about two-thirds of the overlying tertial length). The wings are fairly plain but, like many, this bird shows a faint wing panel produced by greeny-yellow fringes to the secondaries (not to be confused with the prominent whitish panel of the Icterine). Note also the greyish legs (often browner). The fresh plumage shows this individual to be a first-winter. It has a different character from Icterine, being less impetuous and more reserved in its movements, content to feed in one small area for a considerable time. Its shorter wings also give it a weaker flight. It is usually silent although individuals sometimes give a low, brief, sparrow-like chatter.

MARMORA'S WARBLER
Sylvia sarda

Range Breeds along the east coast of Spain, the Balearic Islands, Corsica, Sardinia and possibly Sicily.

The Balearic race *balearica* is largely resident, but the nominate winters in North Africa.

Occurrences The first British record concerned a singing male that was found on the sides of a steep moorland valley at Mickleden Clough, Langsett, Yorkshire, on 15 May 1982 (Lunn, 1985). To the delight of hundreds, it remained until 22 July and was seen display-flighting and even carrying nest material. At the time this was considered an astonishing one-off occurrence, and there were the inevitable rumours that it had escaped from captivity. Ten years later all residual doubt evaporated when another male was trapped at Spurn, Yorkshire, on 8–9 June 1992, followed by a third male at St Abb's Head, Berwickshire, on 23–27 May 1993 (Plate 72.4). Exactly what inspires a tiny short-range migrant to travel so far is not known, but one can only speculate that these individuals somehow failed to 'switch off' their migratory urge, stranding them 900 miles (1,440 km) out of range. The close geographical cluster of occurrences (all were found in the north-east) clearly suggests that the birds were on a very specific heading when they arrived in Britain. Coincidentally, the appearances here corresponded with the second to fifth mainland French records in 1987 and 1989, as well as one on the north-west Adriatic coast of Italy in 1991 (*Brit. Birds* **81**: 21; **83**: 15; **87**: 11).

Identification Marmora's Warbler is superficially similar to the Dartford Warbler *S. undata*, but has a rounded body and is slightly shorter tailed. The most obvious difference is that virtually the whole bird is completely grey, the only relief being a slightly browner cast to the back and worn brown wing feathers (the latter indicative of a first-summer). The bare-part colours are distinctive, with an orange-red orbital ring, a predominantly pale orange bill and (not really visible in the photograph) pale orange legs (sometimes bright). It is a skulking bird, usually found in low vegetation, and when flushed it flies off with a weak, jerky flight (similar to that of a Long-tailed Tit *Aegithalos caudatus*) before diving back into the centre of the next clump. Narrow smoky outer tail feathers may be visible in flight. The call is a quiet, soft *chrer* or *thick*, with a definite fricative.

SUBALPINE WARBLER
Sylvia cantillans

Range Breeds around the Mediterranean, from Morocco to Tunisia in the south and from Portugal to western Turkey in the north. It winters in Africa immediately south of the Sahara.

Occurrences The Subalpine Warbler is now an annual vagrant, mainly occurring from mid-April to June and with a smaller peak from August to early November. There were only 12 recorded prior to 1958 but, by the end of 1995, the total had risen to 371. Inevitably, numbers fluctuate from year to year but a steady increase has been apparent, with peaks of 32 in 1988 and 1995. There is a wide scatter of records from coastal localities but, surprisingly, the largest cluster has been in the Northern Isles, with smaller numbers down the east coast. Whilst many of the spring occurrences must involve overshoots of the nominate race from Iberia, it seems that later in the spring most are of the more contrasting eastern race *albistriata*, which produces the northern bias. One wonders whether the upsurge here reflects a so far undetected increase on the Continent.

Identification The Subalpine is a small, delicate *Sylvia*, with a rounded head, a fine bill and a medium-length tail. Males are easily identified by the deep pinkish-red throat (becoming paler and more salmon-coloured towards the flanks), grey upperparts and a thin white moustachial stripe. There is also a noticeable red or reddish orbital ring. Plate 72.5 shows a male at the Naze, Essex, present from 15 August to 2 September 1993. It is a stunning bird, and the brightness and freshness of its plumage, as well as the reddish eye and orbital ring, confirm that it is an adult male which has recently undergone a complete moult. Williamson (1968) stated, however, that first-winter males do not differ from adults except perhaps in the browner and more worn wing and tail feathers; they are also a duller pink below and show a creamier orbital ring. Young birds also lack pure white outer tail feathers (instead they are sullied with brown). Although there is individual variation, the eastern race *albistriata* has a deeper brick-red throat and upper breast, this coloration contrasting more abruptly with a whiter belly.

Plate 72.6 shows a female on North Ronaldsay, Orkney, in May 1990 and Plate 72.3 shows a first-winter female on St Agnes, Isles of Scilly, in October 1987. Plumage-wise, it is somewhat nondescript and most resembles a Lesser Whitethroat *S. curruca*. It is rather blue-grey above, browner on the mantle, and is sullied buff below. What immediately grabs the attention, however, is the prominent white eye-ring and the white throat, this being sharply demarcated from the ear-coverts. In the field, the legs appear orangey-brown. The usual calls are a soft *tac* or *chur*. The song is lively and sustained and, although it includes some harsh notes, it is rather sweet for a *Sylvia*.

Male Sardinian Warbler.

SARDINIAN WARBLER
Sylvia melanocephala

Range Breeds from the Canaries through Morocco and around much of the Mediterranean. It is both a resident and a partial migrant, with some movement south, chiefly into North Africa and the Sahara.

Occurrences The first British record was a male on Lundy, Devon, in May 1955. The species remained an extremely rare vagrant until the early 1980s, since when there has been a marked upsurge with 50 recorded by the end of 1995, 37 of which were males. There were peaks of eight in 1992 and seven in 1994. It is an abundant and familiar species in the Mediterranean and it has shown signs of spreading in Italy, Romania, Bulgaria and Cyprus, as well as in northern Spain (*BWP*; *Brit. Birds* **87**: 322; **88**: 40). One wonders whether the recent upsurge here may also reflect more general increases in the western part of the range, and, indeed, whether it has the potential to follow Cetti's Warbler *Cettia cetti* and the Fan-tailed Warbler *Cisticola juncidis* in spreading northwards up the Atlantic coast of France.

The records have been widely scattered from Scilly to Shetland, and there were two in Ireland in April 1993. Perhaps the most remarkable was a female trapped in Surbiton, London, in June 1992. Records have occurred from early March to late October, but with a distinct peak from April to June. As befitting a relatively sedentary species, some individuals have stayed for several months.

Identification Plate 73.1 shows a male at Holme, Norfolk, in May 1994. It is about the size of a Common Whitethroat *S. communis*, but rather robust and shorter tailed. The male is easily identifiable by a combination of the black head (which sharply contrasts with the white throat), a red orbital ring, grey upperparts and a black tail with prominent white outer feathers. The underparts are sullied grey. The individual in the photograph shows a brown eye, rather a dull black head with grey feathering in the crown, and it appears to show rather brownish wings. This would indicate a first-summer. Remarkably, what was presumably the same bird reappeared back at exactly the same site a year later. It was then an adult, with a jet-black head, a prominent bright red eye and orbital ring, and much greyer upperparts and flanks. Plate 73.2 shows another male on St Mary's, Isles of Scilly, in October 1985. Females lack the black head (it is grey instead), and are rather browner above and dull below, brownest on the flanks. As Plate 73.1 shows, they often raise their tail. It has a distinctive, rather explosive machine-gun call: *ch-ch-ch-ch-ch-ch-ch-ch*, usually the first indicator of its presence. It also gives a *chur, churk*, a scolding *chack-chack-chak-chak* and variations on these themes.

DESERT WARBLER
Sylvia nana

Range Has two populations. The nominate race breeds from the Caspian Sea eastwards in a narrow band to central Asia, and winters from north-eastern Africa through the Arabian Peninsula eastwards to the deserts of north-western India. Another race, *deserti*, breeds in north-western Africa and is much more sedentary. Another Asian race, '*theresae*', is not recognized by some authorities.

Occurrences The first record was made as recently as 1970 (at Portland, Dorset) but there have been a further nine since (to 1993), with three in 1991. All have been of the nominate Asian race, these occurring from mid-October to late December, and mainly on the east and south coasts of England. An exception was one at Blakeney Point, Norfolk, in May 1993. It was a male and, like a similar bird in Germany in 1991, it sang and built a nest (Plate 73.5)!

Identification Plate 73.6 was taken at Bembridge, Isle of Wight, in October–November 1991. This individual clearly shows the species' general pallor, being pale greyish-sandy above and off-white below, but the rump, uppertail-coverts and central tail feathers are more russet (and the outer tail feathers are white). Perhaps most significant are the bare-part colours: the irides are yellow, the base of the bill is

usually pale yellowish and the legs are creamy-yellow. Ageing is not easy in autumn, but it is probably safe to assume that this is a first-winter. The spring Norfolk bird is noticeably more worn, being particularly brown on the wings and quite a deep orange at the base of the tail. In contrast, the North African *deserti* is positively ethereal, being an even paler golden-sandy above (lacking grey tones), with a more orangey tail.

The Desert Warbler feeds in low vegetation and on the ground, and the tail is frequently flicked up once or twice and then lowered with a more deliberate action. As the tail is raised, the front of the bird is bobbed downwards, the whole action being very distinctive, particularly when observed from a distance. Clafton (1972) described the call of the Portland individual as a sharp *wee-churr*, with something of the rhythm of a Grey Partridge *Perdix perdix*.

RÜPPELL'S WARBLER
Sylvia rueppelli

Range Has a limited breeding distribution, almost the entire world population breeding in Crete, southern Greece and Turkey. It winters in Chad and the Sudan.

Occurrences Rüppell's Warbler was formerly admitted to the British List on the strength of a record of two males said to have been shot near Hastings, Sussex, in May 1914. These were rejected as part of the notorious 'Hastings Rarities' incident. It was another 63 years before the genuine article turned up: a male at Dunrossness, Mainland Shetland, from 13 August to 16 September 1977 (Plate 73.3; Martins, 1981). This was followed by a male on Lundy, Devon, in June 1979, a male on Whalsay, Shetland, in October 1990 and a heavily twitched individual at Holme, Norfolk, in August–September 1992.

Identification Plate 73.3 shows a very distinctive *Sylvia*. Its basically grey plumage and black head suggests a Sardinian Warbler *S. melanocephala*, but the black throat and prominent white moustachial stripe allow for instant recognition. Females and first-winters are far more subtle. The Norfolk individual (Plate 73.4) is a beautiful soft pale grey above, the head being sharply demarcated from the white throat, and it shows a brown eye and a narrow yellow orbital ring. Perhaps most distinctive are the thick off-white fringes to the wing feathers (although these become narrower when worn). Also of note is the rather long, fine bill which has a decurved upper mandible, this at times imparting a decurved impression to the whole bill. Compared to the Sardinian, Rüppell's is larger, more attenuated, and rather

Male Rüppell's Warbler.

slower and more deliberate in its movements. Lewington (1992) considered the Holme bird to be a fresh adult female that had recently undergone a complete moult. Martins (1981) described three calls for the one in Shetland: (1) a soft, subdued *tuc-tuc*; (2) a harsher, more strident *tac-tac* or *tchak-tchak*; and (3) a rapid series of harsh notes similar to the chatter of a Winter Wren *Troglodytes troglodytes*. The latter can be described as a fast, rattling *trrrrr*.

ORPHEAN WARBLER
Sylvia hortensis

Range Breeds in Morocco, Iberia and southern France through the Mediterranean, Asia Minor and parts of the Middle East into Turkestan and Iran. It winters from West Africa through the Sahel zone east to the Arabian Peninsula and the Indian subcontinent.

Occurrences There are just six British records (to 1991): one in May, another in July and four in September–October. Only one has been seen by more than a handful of people: a male on St Mary's, Isles of Scilly, on 16–22 October 1981 (Plate 74.1). Considering that it is a long-range migrant with an estimated 10,000 pairs as close as southern France (*BWP*), its rarity here is astonishing. Reasons for this enigma are not immediately apparent.

Identification At 6 in (15 cm) long, the Orphean is a large warbler with slow, heavy movements. It is reminiscent of a giant Lesser Whitethroat *S. curruca*, but with a heavy bill which is noticeably blue-grey at the base. Males have a black head (contrasting with a white throat), but females are grey in this area, sometimes darker on the ear-coverts. The most distinctive feature is the male's white eye, but this is sometimes dark, particularly in the east of its range. On the face of it, the St Mary's bird appears to have been an adult male, but the photograph shows brown wings and there is a contrast between the majority of greater coverts (which are also brown) and one or two grey adult outers. This would indicate that, despite its black head and white eye, it was actually a first-winter. The commonest call is a *tac tac*, similar to that of a Blackcap *S. atricapilla* but fuller, as well as a loud rattle in alarm: *trrrrr* (*BWP*). Interestingly, the western nominate has a simple song, two to four syllables, fairly coarse and deep (Jonsson, 1992), whereas the eastern *crassirostris* has a deep, melodic song which recalls a Common Nightingale *Luscinia megarhynchos*.

BARRED WARBLER
Sylvia nisoria

Range Breeds from central Europe east to western Siberia and winters in East Africa.

Occurrences Dymond *et al.*, (1989) were able to trace 2,933 autumn records between 1958 and 1985, an average of 109 a year. They occurred mainly from mid-August to October, with a peak at the end of August. Most occurred in the Northern Isles and down the east coast, with smaller numbers west to the Isles of Scilly. It is very rare elsewhere. Just why these birds occur here so regularly and in such numbers is not immediately apparent. All appear to be first-winters, so it would seem that pre-migratory dispersal would be the best explanation rather than true reversed migration. This theory gains credibility from the record of an individual ringed on Fair Isle and subsequently recovered in the former Yugoslavia (*BWP*), indicating correct re-orientation.

Perhaps the most remarkable aspect of the Barred Warbler's occurrence pattern is its rarity in spring. Dymond *et al.* could trace only seven at this time between 1958 and 1985. The relatively north–south orientation of the species' migration routes from East Africa to Eastern Europe would apparently render it unlikely to overshoot into Britain, a scenario similar to that shown by other species with a similar migration route – such as the Thrush Nightingale *Luscinia luscinia* and Collared Flycatcher *Ficedula albicollis.*

Identification Plate 74.3 shows a first-winter at Cley, Norfolk, in August 1985. It is a large, hefty warbler with rather a pronounced jowl, a domed head, a rounded back and strong, sturdy legs. It has something of a shrike-like jizz. It is quite heavy and sluggish when moving through vegetation. First-winters are pale grey above, with a faint supra-loral line and a slightly darker line through the eye. The darker wings show whitish feather fringes, the tips of the median and greater coverts forming two whitish wing bars. Dark bases to the median coverts may also stand out. It is white below, but with a buffer wash to the flanks and it has white only at the tips of the outer tail feathers. It has a thick-based, pointed bill which has a grey base, and the legs are also grey. Unlike adults, it shows a dark eye. Plate 74.2 shows another first-winter on St Mary's, Isles of Scilly, in October 1990. This bird is more advanced: the eye is blue-grey, the flanks are delicately barred and the wing feathers more worn. Migrants give a loud repeated chacking call.

SPECTACLED WARBLER
Sylvia conspicillata

Range Rather a localized species, breeding mainly around the western Mediterranean, extending through Morocco and out to the Canary and Cape Verde islands. It also breeds on Cyprus and in Israel and adjacent areas. Most move south to winter mainly in North Africa.

Occurrences The Spectacled Warbler has had a chequered history as a British bird. Three records were at one time accepted: Spurn, Yorkshire (October 1968); Porthgwarra, Cornwall (October 1969); and Fair Isle, Shetland (June 1979). The Spurn individual later was reidentified as a first-winter female Subalpine Warbler *S. cantillans*, but the Fair Isle record clocked up an amazing eight circulations of the

Rarities Committee before being marginally rejected (Rogers *et al.*, 1990). We had to wait until 1992 for the first fully acceptable record: a singing male at the Filey North Cliff Country Park, Yorkshire, (on 24–29 May; Plate 74.4).

Identification Superficially, the Spectacled resembles a small, brightly coloured Common Whitethroat *S. communis* and shows similar but brighter rufous fringes to the wing feathers (the whole wing looks rufous at a distance). The photographs show particularly well two key differences. First, as befitting a short-range migrant, the primary projection is very short: only about a third to half the overlying tertial length (on the longer-winged Common Whitethroat it is about two-thirds to three-quarters in length). Second, it shows a large dark area on the lores, which is usually a feature of spring males. The photograph also shows the clear-cut white eye-ring (but note that many Common Whitethroats are similar), extensive pale yellow at the base of the bill, and rather dark, orangey-pink underparts that contrast with the white throat. The legs may appear a dull pinky-horn colour in low light, but become bright orange when viewed in strong sunlight. The female is duller and paler, with browny-grey head and upperparts.

The Spectacled's character is perhaps more distinctive than its plumage. It usually feeds close to the ground, and its small size and active behaviour are distinctive. When flushed, it flies low and fast towards the next area of vegetation, its flight being obviously weaker than that of a Common Whitethroat. It looks small, slim and delicate in flight, and lacks the Common Whitethroat's full, mobile square-ended tail. Of particular importance is its loud, grating call – *trrrrr* - similar to that of a Winter Wren *Troglodytes troglodytes*. Although the Spectacled Warbler has a reputation for being tricky to distinguish from the Common Whitethroat, when one sees the genuine article the differences are in fact quite obvious. Unfortunately, it is not a species that comes across well on paper so the careful evaluation of the primary projection and a proper description of the call would be essential for acceptance.

GREENISH WARBLER
Phylloscopus trochiloides

Range Occurs in three forms that were, until recently, treated as full species. The Greenish Warbler *P. t. viridanus* and *P. t. trochiloides* breeds from the Baltic eastwards to western Siberia, the central and eastern Himalayas and central Asia. The Two-barred Greenish Warbler *P. t. plumbeitarsus* replaces it in central and eastern Siberia, while the Green Warbler *P. t. nitidus* breeds in northern Turkey, the Caucasus and west central Asia east to north-east Iran (Svensson, 1992). They winter in India and Southeast Asia.

Occurrences The Greenish Warbler is mainly an autumn visitor from August to October, with a pronounced peak at the end of August. Most occur in the Northern Isles and down the east coast. A secondary peak occurs in late spring, mainly in late May and June. It has increased markedly in recent years. There were just 13 records prior to 1958, but 261 had been recorded by the end of 1994, with a peak of 29 in 1992. That total included 15 in spring, eight of which were singing males, and this has led to speculation that it might eventually breed here. It has been spreading westwards since at least the second half of the 19th century, although this has taken the form of waves and the westernmost limits of the range have been constantly fluctuating. Invasion years have been linked to high May–June temperatures, but they alternate with years when the species is absent or scarce (*BWP*). Recent years have seen another push westwards, and the Greenish bred for the first time in Denmark and Germany in 1990, Norway in 1991 and the Czech Republic in 1992, while in Sweden there were five breeding records and 235 singing males in 1992 (*Brit. Birds* **83**: 228; **86**: 45 and 291; **87**: 11; **88**: 277). In 1995, about 40 were recorded in Britain and Ireland, including a remarkable influx of at least 32 in September.

The other two forms have occurred only once each, both first-winters in the Isles of Scilly: the Green Warbler was recorded on St Mary's from 26 September to 4 October 1984, and the Two-barred Greenish was recorded on Gugh from 21–27 October 1987 (another was seen in Norfolk in October 1996). The decision to lump the three forms has recently been supported by the discovery that the genetic differentiation between the Green and Greenish Warblers is intermediate between typical species and subspecies. Also, playback experiments indicate that the Green Warbler responds to the songs of other members of the Greenish Warbler complex (*Journal of Avian Biology* **26**: 139–153).

Identification Plate 75.3 shows a first-winter Greenish (*viridanus*) at Wells-next-the-Sea, Norfolk, and 75.4 shows another at Quendale, Shetland, both in September 1994 (adults do not moult their primaries until they reach their winter quarters and are thus very worn in autumn). It is a small, energetic warbler, feeding in a manner similar to that of a Yellow-browed *P. inornatus*, leaping around and tumbling through the vegetation. The wings are constantly flicked when feeding and the tail is also occasionally nervously dipped, but this is unlike the more consistent movement of the Chiffchaff *P. colly-*

bita. As the photographs show, it has a small bill and quite a rounded head. It is rather a dull olive-green above and whitish below, the latter often 'flashing' white at a distance. It has a prominent whitish supercilium, joining over the bill, and an olive-green eyestripe. There is a short, whitish wing bar, formed by tips to the greater coverts, and the remiges are evenly fringed with quite a bright green coloration (it lacks the contrastingly whiter fringes to the tertials shown by the Yellow-browed Warbler). The Quendale bird appears to have an all-dark bill but the lower mandible is usually orange (an important difference from the Chiffchaff) and the legs are rather dark (an important difference from the Arctic Warbler *P. borealis*). Spring males are often located by song, a thin jumble of notes, individual phrases sounding like *chi-chi-chi-chip d-d-d-dup*, perhaps suggesting a thin, fast distant Cetti's Warbler *Cettia cetti*. This readily separates it from the Arctic Warbler which gives a dry, one-noted trill. The call is a rather shrill, loud, penetrating and disyllabic *chee-wee* or *see-wee*, suggesting that of a Pied Wagtail *Motacilla alba* or a House Sparrow *Passer domesticus*.

Plates 75.1 & 2 show the Two-barred Greenish (*plumbeitarsus*) on Gugh in October 1987. It is practically identical to the Greenish but shows broad tips to all the greater coverts, these forming a solid white bar, and also a short white bar on the median coverts which the Greenish very rarely shows. The call is more trisyllabic than that of the Greenish.

ARCTIC WARBLER
Phylloscopus borealis

Range Breeds from northern Norway east across Siberia to western Alaska, and south to Japan. It winters in Southeast Asia, Indonesia and the Philippines.

Occurrences The Arctic Warbler is rarer here than the Greenish *P. trochiloides*, with 215 records to the end of 1995 (compared with at least 285 Greenish), and, unlike that species, it has shown no real signs of a recent increase. In fact, the Rarities Committee is currently reviewing the old British records, so it seems likely that the eventual total will be somewhat lower than it is at present. Arctics turn up mainly in the Northern Isles and down the east coast, as well as occasionally west to the Isles of Scilly. Most occur from mid-August to mid-October, with a peak in September – distinctly later than the Greenish. There are three 'spring' records: at Titchwell, Norfolk, on 5 July 1975; and on Fair Isle, Shetland, on 3 July 1982 and 27 June 1995. Since it is very late in arriving on its breeding grounds, the June/July occurrences are best treated as overshooting spring migrants rather than early autumn ones.

Identification Plate 75.5 shows a first-winter on St Agnes, Isles of Scilly, in October 1988, and Plate 75.6 shows another at Kenidjack, Cornwall, in October 1994. They can be aged in the same way as the Greenish Warbler but the adults' primaries are less prone to wear (Svensson, 1992). It is similar to the Greenish but is a larger, more attenuated, sturdier bird and it tends to look relatively front-heavy and short-tailed. The overall size and shape may suggest a Wood Warbler *P. sibilatrix*, particularly when it is seen from below. It has a lower forehead and a more wedge-shaped head profile than Greenish (this is partially due to its heftier, broad-based, more wedge-shaped bill). With its orange lower mandible it may suggest a *Hippolais*. It is longer winged and also shows a slightly longer primary projection (about three-quarters of the tertial length). Plumage-wise it is similar to a Greenish (*see* page 137) but shows a longer supercilium which does not extend across the forehead and which extends further back towards the rear crown, sometimes showing an upward kink at the rear. Also, the eye-stripe is stronger across the lores. It often, but not always, shows a second wing bar on the median coverts. The legs are distinctly paler, looking pale brown in dull conditions but orange in bright light. It is less mercurial than Greenish and its behaviour is similar to that of a Wood Warbler, being rather deliberate in its movements, although it will hover to pick prey off the vegetation. The call is diagnostic: a husky *djik*. Remarkably, an individual on St Mary's, Isles of Scilly, in September–October 1986, was flavistic.

PALLAS'S WARBLER
Phylloscopus proregulus

Range Breeds in southern Siberia, east from the Altai Mountains and south to northern Mongolia and Manchuria. It winters mainly in southern China and northern Indo-China.

Occurrences For many, Pallas's Warbler represents the ultimate rarity. It is a tiny bird, roughly the size of a Goldcrest *Regulus regulus*, brightly patterned and originating in a far-flung and magical part of the globe. That such a bird even gets here seems, on the face of it, extraordinary. In recent years it has occurred in numbers, and at the end of 1990 the unthinkable happened: it was actually removed from the Rarities List. Prior to 1958 there had been only three records, yet by the mid-1970s we were receiving up to 29 per year, this increase culminating in remarkable influxes of 123 in 1982 and at least 180 in 1994. Most have occurred in Shetland and down the east coast, with smaller numbers penetrating along the south coast and west to the Isles of Scilly, but it remains very rare in Ireland. It has occurred as early as 23 September,

but most arrive in October and November, with a tiny number through December. Intriguingly, there have been no real wintering records and only one in spring (in Sussex, on 14–23 March 1992; *Brit. Birds* **85**: 486). *BWP*, however, mentions a wintering record from the Netherlands, while there have been at least five March–May records on the Continent (Lewington *et al.*, 1991, and *Brit. Birds* **89**: 41).

Identification Pallas's Warbler is a beautiful little bird and as such is a great favourite amongst birdwatchers. It is most similar to the Yellow-browed Warbler *P. inornatus* but is smaller and always appears bull-necked and large-headed. Although rather variable in plumage tone, it is greener above and whiter below, with a long green eye-stripe, a long yellow supercilium and yellow wing bars. Like the Yellow-browed, it shows thick tertial fringes. The most obvious differences are a clear-cut but narrow yellow median crown stripe and a rectangular pale yellow rump patch, best seen when the bird is preening or hovering. It is an unobtrusive bird, moving quickly through the foliage and flicking its wings as it does so. Its call is soft, quick and squeaky: *djueet*, *ch-weet* or *t-weet*. Plate 76.1 shows an individual at Felixstowe, Suffolk, in November 1994.

YELLOW-BROWED WARBLER
Phylloscopus inornatus

Range Has a huge breeding range across Siberia, where it is one of the commonest birds, and it winters from the Persian Gulf eastwards through the Indian Subcontinent to Southeast Asia and southern China.

Occurrences This is the commonest Siberian vagrant to Western Europe, Dymond *et al.* (1989) recording 2,648 between 1958 and 1985, an average of 98 per year. Numbers fluctuate but it has increased considerably in recent years, culminating in a remarkable influx of at least 615 in 1985. The incidence of easterly winds in late autumn may be instrumental in pushing already westward-moving Yellow-broweds into Britain and Ireland, but it seems possible that annual population cycles could also be significant.

Most occur in the Northern Isles, along the east and south coasts, in the Isles of Scilly and in southern Ireland. They arrive from mid-September to early November, but with a marked peak in early October. They seem to arrive slightly earlier in the north and east than in the south-west, suggesting some onward movement.

What happens after the birds leave Britain and Ireland is a mystery. Very small numbers may winter here and, by following the great circle route from Siberia through Britain and beyond, it seems possible that some may end up in Iberia and north-western Africa. Such individuals may be responsible for our very occasional spring records from late March to early May. Unless an undiscovered wintering area comes to light, it seems likely that most of our autumn Yellow-broweds simply continue south-westwards and perish in the Atlantic.

Identification Plate 76.2 shows an individual on St Agnes, Isles of Scilly, in October 1989. As with Pallas's Warbler *P. proregulus*, ageing is not possible. It is a small, rather rotund, short-tailed warbler, with a rather large rounded head. It is olive-green above and yellowish-white below, and shows a prominent tapering yellowish supercilium and double wing bars. Some also show a diffuse pale line down the centre of the crown, this being much less obvious and less clear-cut than that of Pallas's. Obvious whitish fringes to the tertials are a clear difference from the Greenish Warbler *P. trochiloides*. Note also the orangey lower mandible and legs (*see also* Hume's Yellow-browed Warbler *P. humei* below). The Yellow-browed is an active feeder, constantly on the move and occasionally hovering. It can often be located by its distinctive, penetrating, high-pitched call, variously described as *suu-eet*, *stu-eet*, *sweet-eet* or *sueet-soo*.

HUME'S YELLOW-BROWED WARBLER
Phylloscopus humei

Range Occurs in montane habitats to the south of the range of the Yellow-browed Warbler *P. inornatus*, breeding from north-eastern Afghanistan through the Pamir, Tien Shan, Altai and Sayan mountains into western Mongolia. Another race, *mandelli*, breeds from the central Himalayas to central China (Svensson, 1992). The nominate winters in the western Himalayas and over much of peninsular India, while *mandelli* winters from eastern India to Thailand (Williamson, 1967).

Occurrences Detailed analysis of the records is hindered by the fact that until recently the species has never been dealt with by the Rarities Committee. Evans (1994), however, noted at least 23 between 1966 and 1993, with a further five in 1994. There has been a definite increase in recent years as the species' identification criteria have become more widely known. It occurs later than most Yellow-broweds, mainly from late October to early December, and at least four have wintered, including one at Great Yarmouth Cemetery, Norfolk, in January–April 1995.

Identification Plate 76.3 shows the Great Yarmouth bird in March 1995. Hume's Yellow-browed is

similar to the Yellow-browed but is distinctly duller: greenish above and greyish-white below. The supercilium is dull buff, lacking any yellow tones, and there is a faint, diffuse greyish crown-stripe. The wing bars are also dull buff but there are pale yellowy fringes to the tertials. The bill appears darker than Yellow-browed's, but there is a dull orange base to the lower mandible, and the legs are a dull browny-orange. It is best identified by its calls, which are obviously different from the Yellow-browed's. A wintering bird in Plymouth in 1992 gave a thin, penetrating *tuuee*, much more similar to the call of a Chiffchaff *P. collybita*. The 1995 Great Yarmouth bird also gave a *TU-eet*, again recalling a Chiffchaff but with a harder first syllable and more emphatic. The Plymouth bird gave a *sid-u sid-u* when mobbing a cat. The song is completely different from that of the Yellow-browed, being a remarkable buzzing wheeze that suggests the flight call of a Redwing *Turdus iliacus* (*BWP*). The Yellow-browed's song is a penetrating *see-soo seueet sueet*, like an elaborated version of its call.

RADDE'S WARBLER
Phylloscopus schwarzi

Range Breeds from west-central Siberia eastwards in a rather narrow band to the Pacific. It winters in Southeast Asia.

Occurrences There was just one record prior to 1958, and even up to the mid-1970s Radde's Warbler was considered an extreme vagrant. Since then it has been virtually annual, with peaks of 14 in 1982, and 24 in both 1988 and 1991. By the end of 1995, there had been 157 records. Most have occurred down the east coast and in the Isles of Scilly, where it was annual from 1984 to 1991, with 27 records in total. No doubt reflecting its breeding range, it is decidedly rarer in the north; Fair Isle, Shetland, had its first record as recently as 1987. Virtually all have occurred in October, with a few in late September and early November.

Identification Plate 76.5 shows an individual, presumably a first-winter, on St Agnes, Isles of Scilly, in October 1986. Plate 76.4 shows another on St Mary's, Isles of Scilly, in October 1994. It is a large, heavy, thick-set, robust *Phylloscopus*, with sturdy legs and a rather thick, almost tit-like bill. It is olive-green above and pale yellowy-buff below, whiter on the throat and slightly darker on the sides of the breast. More distinctively, it is darker on the undertail-coverts, some being yellower but others more orangey. It shows a striking, long yellowy supercilium which curves up at the rear (but does not reach the bill) and a long, thick, green eye-stripe. The primaries are short, rather rounded and bunched. It has a pale lower mandible and, more distinctively, pale legs which vary from pale grey-brown (with yellow feet), through horn-yellow and pale yellow to bright orangey. It feeds close to the ground and often holds up, jinks and constantly flicks its mobile tail; the tail and whole rear end are jinked from side to side when the bird is nervous. It also constantly flicks open its wings like a Dunnock *Prunella modularis*. It has an unobtrusive yet distinctive call, variously described as a low *cluk*, or *chuk...chuk...*, and a soft *qulip*, distinctly softer than that of a Dusky Warbler *P. fuscatus*.

DUSKY WARBLER
Phylloscopus fuscatus

Range Unlike Radde's Warbler *P. schwarzi*, the Dusky Warbler has a large breeding range over much of Siberia and south to the eastern Himalayas. It winters from Nepal and northern India east to southern China and Southeast Asia.

Occurrences Like Radde's Warbler there was just one record prior to 1958, and it too has shown a marked upsurge since the mid-1970s. By the end of 1995, there had been 164 records, seven more than Radde's. The peak numbers were 17 in 1987, 19 in 1990 and 21 in 1994. It tends to occur slightly later than Radde's, with a peak in late October and early November, and there has been a larger northerly component to the records.

Unlike Radde's, there have been three spring records. One of these, trapped on the Calf of Man, Isle of Man, on 3 May 1970, was subsequently found dying near Limerick on 5 December 1970. It is generally suggested that this individual spent the intervening summer somewhere in Western Europe, but it seems more likely that when it was originally trapped on the Calf of Man, it was on its spring migration, having wintered in Ireland. It then seems likely that it went back to Siberia for the summer, only to return westwards the following autumn winter again in western Ireland. The orientation of its migration route would certainly tie in with this theory (*see* page 18). That the species will winter here is confirmed by two wintering records in 1994/95 in Bude, Cornwall, and Bideford, Devon, both being last seen on 1 May (note the coincidence in date between their departure and the Calf of Man record).

Identification Plate 77.1 shows the one at Bideford, no doubt a first-winter, in January 1995. Compared with Radde's Warbler *P. schwarzi*, it is structurally much more similar to a Chiffchaff *P. collybita*, although it is dumpier and shorter tailed. It has rather a more pointed head/bill profile than the Chiffchaff, this caused by the more wedge-shaped bill

(note that the bill is finer and more pointed than Radde's). Unlike the Chiffchaff, the tail tip is rounded. It completely lacks the green and yellow tones of Radde's. Instead, the upperparts are predominantly dull grey but with a brown or olive tint, the strength of which is light-dependent. The wings are rather uniform. The underparts vary from buff-brown to a cold greyish-white, but the flanks and undertail-coverts are buff, often with an orange tinge. There is a prominent short buff or white supercilium, a narrow pale eye-ring and a thick greyish line through the eye. The bill shows a pale lower mandible, and the legs are duller and darker than Radde's, varying from dark brownish through horn, pale yellow and dull orange to even quite a pale orange, sometimes with obviously yellow feet.

Like Radde's, the Dusky Warbler feeds low and constantly flicks its wings, but its tail is much less mobile although it will also jink its rear end from side to side when nervous. It calls frequently, and this is an abrupt, hard, dry *tic*, *twik*, *tac* or *tchuk*, easily imitated. Although softer versions of the call may be given, it is nevertheless readily distinguishable from the softer 'clucking' calls of Radde's. The Dusky's call suggests a Winter Wren *Troglodytes troglodytes*, Lesser Whitethroat *Sylvia curruca* or Sedge Warbler *Acrocephalus schoenobaenus*.

WESTERN BONELLI'S WARBLER
Phylloscopus bonelli

Range Breeds from Morocco to Tunisia, and from Iberia and much of France through Switzerland, Austria and south into Italy. It winters in a narrow band immediately south of the Sahara.

Occurrences Bonelli's Warbler was first recorded in Britain as 'recently' as August 1948 on Skokholm,

Western Bonelli's Warbler.

Pembrokeshire. The observers at the time were so unsure of the bird's identity that they decided to kill it and send it to the Yorkshire Museum (Conder & Keighley, 1949)! It remained very rare until the early 1970s, since when there has been an upsurge, with 134 recorded by the end of 1995. Whilst this increase has been due largely to increased observer coverage, it has been spreading north in France since the middle of this century, breeding for the first time in Belgium in 1967 and in the Netherlands in 1976 (*BWP*).

Considering that the species breeds as close as France (where there are 100,000–1 million pairs; *BWP*) and that it is a long-range migrant, it is surprising that it is not more common. To illustrate this point, the total number of records of 134 compares with 164 Dusky *P. fuscatus* and 157 Radde's Warblers *P. schwarzi*, neither of which breeds any closer than western Siberia! Most have occurred at well-watched coastal localities, mainly in the southern half of Britain and Ireland, although there have been several records in the Northern Isles. It remains surprisingly rare in spring (late April and May), but is more common in autumn (mid-August to early November).

Identification Plate 77.2 shows a first-winter at Sumburgh Head, Shetland, in September 1995. Bonelli's is closely related to the Wood Warbler *P. sibilatrix*, and there is much in its character and sleek appearance which suggests that species, although it is proportionately shorter winged and longer tailed. It is grey-brown above, some being greener than others, and silky-white below, and shows prominent lime-green fringes to the remiges and rectrices. The fresh fringes show it to be a first-winter; adults are more worn as they do not moult these feathers until they reach their winter quarters. The rump is rather yellowy, but this can be frustratingly difficult to detect in the field even though the coloration extends down onto the sides of the vent. Although it has a subdued narrow, pale supercilium and a browner line through the eye, it has a bland facial expression in which the dark eye stands out (emphasized by a pale eye-ring), making it look beady-eyed. The relatively plain face and the strong, spiky, almost dagger-like orangey bill may suggest a *Hippolais*. The legs are a dark blackish-brown, sometimes appearing more orangey. The call resembles that of a Willow Warbler *P. trochilus*, but is slower and perhaps thinner and more piercing: *poo-weet*. It should be noted that there have been several examples of pale grey and white Wood Warblers which have resembled Bonelli's superficially. They have nevertheless retained the strong supercilium and eye-stripe of the Wood Warbler, and have given the characteristic loud *pew* call.

EASTERN BONELLI'S WARBLER
Phylloscopus orientalis

Range Breeds in central and southern parts of the former Yugoslavia, east through Greece into Turkey. It winters immediately south of the Sahara.

Occurrences Although there were 136 records of 'Bonelli's Warblers' (up to 1995), only two are known to have given the characteristic call of an Eastern Bonelli's. The first was on St Mary's, Isles of Scilly, in September–October 1987. Unfortunately, the descriptions mention that it also gave the *poo-weet* call of the Western *P. bonelli*, and so the record was deemed unacceptable. Other observers, however, are adamant that it gave only the *chip* of the Eastern (Lee Evans, Chris Heard and Brian Small, verbally). A less-controversial individual turned up on 20–29 September 1995, at Whitley Bay Cemetery, Northumberland (Plate 77.3). Given the presumably north–south orientation of the Eastern's migration route, it seems likely that it may prove to be genuinely rare here.

Identification The Eastern Bonelli's is similar to the Western but is on average larger, and duller, being greyer above, and usually with paler yellow under-wing-coverts and perhaps a stronger supercilium. These plumage differences are not to be relied upon, however, and the diagnostic difference is its call: an abrupt *chip*, reminiscent of that of the Common Crossbill *Loxia curvirostra*.

RED-BREASTED FLYCATCHER
Ficedula parva

Range Breeds from southern Sweden south to northern Greece, and right across Eastern Europe and Siberia to the Pacific. It winters in the Indian subcontinent and in Southeast Asia.

Occurrences The Red-breasted Flycatcher is a regular autumn vagrant from mid-August to mid-November, with a peak in early October. Most occur in the Northern Isles, down the east coast and in the Isles of Scilly, with fewer along the south coast, in southern Ireland and at the Irish Sea observatories. Very small numbers occur as spring overshoots from mid-April to mid-June. There have also been two intriguing winter records: in Caithness on 6 January 1981; and in Montgomeryshire from 31 January to 3 February 1983.

Dymond *et al.* (1989) noted 2,141 records during 1958–85, an average of 79 a year. Numbers have increased in recent years in line with the rise in the popularity of birdwatching, and the peak annual total was 200 in 1984. It should be noted, however, that there has been a recent westward spread, and that the species bred for the first time in Sweden in 1944 and in Norway in 1982 (*BWP*). Whilst some of the autumn records could perhaps relate to dispersing first-winters prior to their real migration, it seems likely that most are true reversed migrants and, as such, their origins may lie well to the east. That being the case, it may be possible that we are receiving examples of the Eastern Palearctic race *albicilla*, which has an entirely different song from the nominate. It has even been suggested that this race could be split as the 'Red-throated Flycatcher'.

Four records from the Canary Islands, one in Morocco in December 1992 and one on a fishing boat 12 miles (20 km) off Terciera, the Azores, in November 1995 (*Brit. Birds* **86**: 291; *Birding World* **9**: 31) may indicate what happens to reverse migrating Red-breasted Flycatchers (at least the lucky ones) after they leave Western Europe.

Identification Plate 77.4 shows a first-winter on St Mary's, Isles of Scilly, in October 1994 (the small buff tips to the greater coverts indicate its age). The photograph shows the bird in classic pose, with the full, square tail held slightly cocked and the wings drooped. The former is constantly flicked. The Red-breasted is a small flycatcher with rather a stubby bill, a rounded head and a large dark eye which is emphasized by a pale eye-ring. Both the bill and legs are black, the former with a slightly paler base to the lower mandible. First-winters are a cold buffy-brown above and vary from pale buff to uniform deep orangey-buff below, becoming whiter on the undertail-coverts (these are often fluffed out around the sides of the tail). The latter is diagnostic, being black with large white patches at the base. These may be practically invisible at rest but are often prominent when the bird is flycatching. Very occasionally red-breasted males are recorded in autumn, such as the one in Plate 77.5, taken at Spurn, Yorkshire, in October 1992. It is a beautiful bird with an orangey-red throat, bordered with bluish, it has an obvious whitish eye-ring and a greyish head, and the underparts are colder and whiter than the usual autumn first-winters.

The call is variously described as a very quiet *stip stip*, a dry *tip*, or an abrupt *tup* or *tp*, and is sometimes strung together two or three times. It also gives a low *trrrrr*, recalling a low-pitched Winter Wren *Troglodytes troglodytes* but not as harsh. The Red-throated Flycatcher *F. (p). albicilla* has browner upperparts and blacker uppertail-coverts. The adult male has a smaller red patch and this is completely bordered with grey (including the lower part). Females and first-winters have a whiter throat and the breast is more grey-brown (*BWP*).

MUGIMAKI FLYCATCHER
Ficedula mugimaki

Range Breeds in eastern Siberia from the north-eastern Altai Mountains to the Pacific, its range being similar to that of Pallas's Warbler *Phylloscopus proregulus*. It has been expanding westwards in recent years (Rogacheva, 1992). It winters in Southeast Asia and western Indonesia.

Occurrence There is one record: a first-winter male present in a wood at Stone Creek, Yorkshire, on 16 and 17 November 1991 (Parrish, 1991). It unfortunately departed prior to the main twitch on 18th. Given its breeding range and the presumed orientation of its migration routes, the Mugimaki must be a prime candidate for vagrancy to Western Europe; the time of year and the north-east coastal locality combine to make a wild origin extremely likely for the Stone Creek bird. Indeed, Leader (1995) showed that there is a distinct peak in Hong Kong between 16 and 23 November which ties in exactly with the Yorkshire record. It should be borne in mind that our bird would have been coming to the end of its long autumn migration (albeit in reverse) like those moving through Hong Kong, so the above information is significant. There was also an earlier European record from Treviso, Italy, on 29 October 1957, although this has not been admitted to the Italian List. The BOURC decided to place the record in Category D1 as there were several advertisements for the species in the cage bird press in 1989 and 1990 (Parkin & Shaw, 1994). Given the circumstances of the record, however, this was not a popular decision.

Identification Plate 77.6 shows the Stone Creek bird. Although it is only a record shot, the bird shows a peaked head, grey-brown upperparts, an orange throat and upper breast, a pale supercilium drooping back from the eye and double cream wing bars. In the field, it was larger than a Red-breasted Flycatcher *F. parva* and more similar in shape to a Pied Flycatcher *F. hypoleuca*, appearing rather elongated and with the wings extending about two-thirds of the way down the tail. Two small white patches at the base of the tail were sometimes visible. Its short bill and the legs were black. Unlike the Red-breasted, it did not cock its tail, but at rest the wings were occasionally flicked and the crown feathers raised to give it its dome-headed appearance. When feeding, it would hover to pick insects from the undersides of the leaves (Parrish, 1991). Adult males retain their black, white and orange plumage all year and are thus readily distinguishable from first-year males. First-winter females lack both the prominent supercilium and the white in the base of the tail, and are also a paler orange below.

ASIAN BROWN FLYCATCHER
Muscicapa dauurica

Range The migratory nominate race breeds from southern Siberia east to Japan (and also in India), and winters in India, Sri Lanka and Southeast Asia.

Occurrence There is just one confirmed British Record: a first-summer on Fair Isle, Shetland, on 1 and 2 July 1992 (Plate 78.1; which was taken in a Heligoland trap). Two earlier European records, from Denmark in 1959 and from Sweden in 1986, both occurred in late September, and so the date of the Fair Isle bird is clearly not typical of a Far Eastern vagrant, the vast majority of which occur in late autumn. It seems possible, however, that this individual arrived as a spring 'overshoot', its route out of Siberia being similar to that shown by autumn reversed migrants. To support this theory, there have been Fair Isle records of both the Arctic Warbler *Phylloscopus borealis* and Yellow-breasted Bunting *Emberiza aureola* in early July. Although there is no evidence that the species occurs in captivity, the BOURC placed the record in category D1 of the British List, pending further investigations into the species' captive status. The main worry is that importations of 'female flycatchers' to the Continent may include this species, and that such birds could subsequently escape, head north and end up in northern Europe. It may be noted that the bird in Plate 78.1 shows a certain amount of damage to the tail, but this presumably occurred in the trap. It was also quite abraded but, surprisingly, museum searches discovered that this is not incompatible with a year-old bird in worn plumage.

Identification Despite being devoid of obvious plumage characteristics, the Asian Brown Flycatcher is nevertheless distinctive. It is a small bird, about the size of a Red-breasted Flycatcher *Ficedula parva*, with a large head, a very large black eye and a very broad 'boat-shaped' bill (when seen from below), with an orange base to the lower mandible. It has rather a short tail and behaves more like a Pied Flycatcher *F. hypoleuca* than a Red-breasted, not cocking its tail like the latter. It has a pale eye-ring, but the only other notable plumage features are the fine fringes to the wing feathers. The Fair Isle individual was aged in the hand as a first-summer, mainly by the fact that some juvenile greater coverts and probably also some juvenile uppertail-coverts were retained (Harvey, 1992).

The separation of the Asian Brown Flycatcher from the three regularly occurring British species is straightforward, but there are two other flycatchers in eastern Asia that also need to be taken into account: the Grey-streaked *M. griseisticta* and Siberian *M. sibirica*. As its name suggests, the former has heavy streaking down the underparts, this being even more pronounced than on the Spotted Flycatcher *M. striata*, but the Siberian is more similar. The latter's main features include a dark 'vest' across the breast and down the flanks, a bill which generally appears all dark in the field, and very long primaries that extend about three-quarters of the way down the tail (*see* Bradshaw *et al.* (1991) for further discussion). Finders of unusual flycatchers would also do well to bear in mind the possibility of escaped tropical species which are being imported.

COLLARED FLYCATCHER
Ficedula albicollis

Range Breeds from eastern France, Switzerland and Italy through eastern Europe into European Russia. It winters mainly in east-central Africa.

Occurrences Considering the closeness of its breeding range and the fact that it is a long-range migrant, the Collared Flycatcher is remarkably rare in Britain, with just 19 records to the end of 1995. Most of these have occurred in late spring, mainly down the east coast and in the Northern Isles. There have been just two in autumn but no doubt it is to some extent overlooked at this time of year. The orientation of its migration route is likely to be the reason for its rarity here. It migrates on a basically north–south axis to and from its wintering grounds in East Africa, so any overshooting spring migrants and any autumn reversed migrants would be unlikely to hit Britain. Contrast this situation with that of the Red-breasted Flycatcher *F. parva*, which also breeds in eastern Europe but which migrates in a completely different direction (south-east towards India). That species amassed a remarkable 2,141 records between 1958 and 1985 (Dymond *et al.*, 1989).

Identification Plates 78.2 & 3 show a first-summer male which was present at Lowestoft, Suffolk, on 13 and 14 May 1985. Although not completely sharp, the photographs nevertheless show the salient features of a spring male: the large white forehead, the large area of white in the wing, the paler upper rump and the striking white collar. All these readily distinguish it from the more familiar Pied Flycatcher *F. hypoleuca*. The rather brown primaries (just detectable in the photographs) and the relatively small white patch at their base show it to be a first-summer. The identification of females and autumn first-winters remains difficult, and would-be finders should consult detailed texts such as Mild (1994).

RED-BREASTED NUTHATCH
Sitta canadensis

Range Breeds mainly in coniferous forests across southern Canada and northern USA, south through the Rockies to California and east into Texas. It is an irruptive migrant, wintering within the breeding range and south to northern Mexico and the Gulf coast.

Occurrence The only record was of a first-winter male at Holkham, Norfolk, from 13 October 1989 to 6 May 1990 (Aley & Aley, 1995). In view of its east coast location, it seems likely that this individual was ship-assisted (indeed, the species has been recorded on ships in the western Atlantic; *Brit. Birds* **88**: 152). The species' irruptive movements apparently relate to the abundance of pine seeds and show a one to two year cycle which synchronizes with that of the Mealy Redpoll *Carduelis flammea* and the Pine Siskin *C. pinus* (*BWP*). The Norfolk occurrence correlated with such an invasion in North America: there were as many as 350 on Seal Island, off the coast of Nova Scotia, on 8 October 1989 (*Brit. Birds* **88**: 152). There is one other Western Palearctic record: an individual in Iceland in May 1970.

The initial twitch of the Holkham bird will be remembered as an horrendous experience, with a couple of thousand birders rampaging through the wood in an attempt to see the bird which moved around with the local tit flock. Tempers became so fraught that at one point a fight broke out! It was ironic that it then stayed for the best part of seven months.

Identification The Red-breasted Nuthatch is a small bird, readily distinguished from our own European Nuthatch *S. europaea* by its striking head pattern: a black crown, a long white supercilium and a long black eye-stripe. In this respect it is similar to the endemic Corsican Nuthatch *S. whiteheadi*, but shows distinctive orangey-red underparts, the coloration strongest on the flanks and undertail-coverts. Pyle (1995) was able to age and sex the Holkham individual as a first-winter male. The slight contrast between the wing-coverts and the back/scapulars indicated a first-winter and, given its age, the black crown and eye-stripe indicated a male (females are greyer). It was best located by its characteristic quiet nasal call: *neh-neh*, reminiscent of that of a Zebra Finch *Poephila castanotis*.

WALLCREEPER
Tichodroma muraria

Range Breeds in the mountain chains of Europe and Asia, from the Cantabrians and Pyrenees through the Alps, the Apennines and the Carpathians, south-east through the Balkans, Turkey and the Caucasus, and east to the Himalayas. In winter, it is generally an altitudinal and short-distance migrant.

Occurrences The Wallcreeper is an extremely rare vagrant, with just ten records between 1792 and 1985. Only five of these records have occurred since 1938, including the famous male which wintered in a quarry near Cheddar, Somerset, in the winters of 1976/77 and 1977/78. News of this individual was suppressed in the first-winter, but it was twitched by hundreds in the second thanks to the very tolerant employees of the then Central Electricity Generating Board, who allowed access onto a balcony high above

Summer male Wallcreeper.

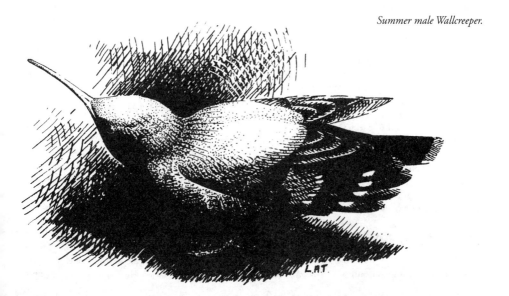

the quarry floor. On one memorable occasion, about 50 birders were huddled on the balcony when a worker hollered up from the quarry below to say that it had been designed to take only ten! The ensuing scramble for safety was as comical as it was hair-raising. The bird proved to be highly mobile, visiting other quarries in the area as well as the nearby Cheddar Gorge.

The Cheddar bird is not the only case of a Wall-creeper returning to the same site in successive winters, as another famous individual wintered at the Amsterdam Free University in the winters of 1989/90 and 1990/91. The other recent British records involved a male at Worth Matravers, Dorset, in the winter of 1969/70, one near Hastings, Sussex, in April 1977, and another at St Catherine's Point, Isle of Wight, in May 1985. It is currently one of the most wanted species on the British List.

Identification Plate 78.5 shows the summer-plumaged male at Hastings in April 1977. Although a record shot, the photograph nevertheless shows one of the most stunning birds on the British List. The Wallcreeper has a long, curved bill, and is pale grey above and much darker below, being darkest on the belly. The throat is white in winter but in males it turns black by the beginning of April. It shows three or four whitish crescents on the undertail-coverts and a white tip to the tail. What makes it so stunning are its long, broad, rounded wings, these showing brilliant flashes of red, mainly on the wing coverts, and large white spots on the primaries. In flight it resembles a Hoopoe *Upupa epops* or a huge Red Admiral butterfly *Vanessa atalanta*, its fluttering flight and swooping actions being very distinctive, even when seen from a distance. It feeds on ledges, slopes and broken rock, tending to avoid sheer rock faces. It moves around rather like a European Nuthatch *Sitta europaea*, with an excitable, bounding hop, frequently flitting up to pounce on insects or to inspect small holes and cracks. It does not use its wings or tail for support but the former are constantly flicked open while feeding, the purpose apparently being to flash the white primary spots, perhaps as some kind of mechanism to assist feeding. The Cheddar bird started to sing before it left, giving a variety of song types, a quick, weak, rising, throaty *wee woo weeoo* being most frequent. The more usual song type, however, seems to be a high-pitched whistling, rising up the scale: *wee-wee wee-wee wee-wee wee-wee wee-weet.*

SHORT-TOED TREECREEPER
Certhia brachydactyla

Range Breeds throughout much of Western, central and southern Europe, east into Turkey and the Caucasus, as well as in north-western Africa.

Occurrences Despite the fact that it breeds just across the English Channel in France, the Short-toed Treecreeper is extremely rare here, with just 18 recorded since the first in 1969, and all but three of these occurring in Kent (to 1994). Its rarity is undoubtedly due to two reasons: it is very sedentary and it is extremely difficult to identify.

Identification The bird in Plate 78.6 resided at Dungeness, Kent, from October 1990 to January 1991. As the ring indicates, it was identified in the hand. This and the Common Treecreeper *C. familiaris* undoubtedly represent one of the most difficult 'species pairs' on the British List. The photograph shows the Short-toed to be a rather duller, greyer bird than the Common, with brownish flanks and a dull supercilium. Daunicht (1991) described fine but apparently consistent differences in the pattern of the wing (*see* Svensson, 1992, for a summary of this). Plate 78.6 appears to show: (1) a virtually continuous narrow white border to the alula; (2) angled as opposed to truncated distal tips on the pale bar across the primaries; and (3) the 8th–11th primaries (visible on the opposite wing) have distinct diamond-shaped tips, whereas on the Common the whole tip and inner web is diffusely tipped whitish. Reference to the diagrams in the aforementioned texts will be the best way to appreciate these subtle variations.

Differences in the call are particularly helpful, the Short-toed consistently giving calls which are louder and more ringing than those of the Common, the quality of which often recalls a Coal Tit *Parus ater*. These include a loud, descending *tsui tsui tsui tsui tsui tsui tsui*. The flight call is louder and harder. The song, at least in northern France, is a *tui tui too-te-too-tee*, the first two syllables quick and the last part ringing. This is quite different from the more trilling *swee swee see-see-see-see-see-seet STOO-EET* of the Common.

PENDULINE TIT
Remiz pendulinus

Range Breeds across much of the Western Palearctic from Iberia to eastern Asia. It is migratory in the north of its range, resident in the south, with intermediate populations partially migratory. European breeders migrate in a direction that lies mainly between south and west to winter in south-west and southern Europe.

Occurrences First recorded in Britain in October 1966, the Penduline Tit has become much more frequent in recent years, with some 98 recorded up to

Penduline Tit.

the end of 1995. It has been annual since 1986, with peaks of at least 13 in 1993 and 18 in 1994, and with most occurring in late autumn. The reason for the increase is that its range has expanded north, west and south-west. Since about 1930 it has spread across Poland, the former Czechoslovakia and Germany, and has bred for the first time in Switzerland, Estonia, Finland, Sweden, Norway, Denmark and Belgium. Oddly, it has recently shown a major decrease again in Sweden (*Brit. Birds* **89**: 42). In the Netherlands it first bred in 1968, but the main colonization took place from 1981 so that by 1990, there were 100–150 pairs (*BWP*). It seems likely that we can look forward to the first breeding records in Britain, particularly since a male built a nest in east Kent in 1990. Penduline Tits ringed in southern Sweden have been recovered in southern Portugal, and a female ringed at Pett Level, Sussex, on 15 October 1988, was retrapped in central-southern Sweden in early May 1989. This interesting recovery reveals the origins of at least some of our vagrants and no doubt this bird too had headed south-west during the intervening winter.

Identification The Penduline Tit occurs mainly in mixed reeds and other tall herbage, tamarisk, willow and poplars. It can thus be difficult to locate and its thin, plaintive, mournful *seeeu* call (resembling the bird of prey alarm of the Common Blackbird *Turdus merula* or European Robin *Erithacus rubecula* or perhaps even a 'thin' Reed Bunting *Emberiza schoeniclus*

is often the first indication of its presence. The high-pitched call is very difficult to locate and often the would-be observer is unsure whether to look high in the sky or down on the ground! Once seen, it resembles a miniature male Red-backed Shrike *Lanius collurio*, with its black mask, grey head and chestnut back. The individual in Plate 79.1 was present at Titchwell, Norfolk, in April 1993, and the rather brownish mask, hardly extending over the forehead, the lack of deep rufous on the mantle and the lack of rufous flecking on the breast would indicate that it was a female (Svensson, 1992). The individual in Plate 79.2 was seen on St Agnes, Isles of Scilly, in October 1988. Its complete lack of a mask suggests that it was a first-winter female (*BWP*).

GOLDEN ORIOLE
Oriolus oriolus

Range Breeds in North Africa and across much of continental Europe, mainly south of the Baltic, and eastwards into western Siberia and south into northern India. It winters in Africa, mainly south of the equator, and in the Indian subcontinent.

Occurrences The species spread north into Denmark in the 19th century and into southern Sweden in the 1930s, and its range has expanded in Finland after earlier contraction. There have, however, been declines in other areas, such as in parts of Germany. It probably bred in East Anglia and in Kent in the mid- to late 19th century, but it subsequently became only a spring overshoot during the first part of the 20th century. Dymond *et al.* (1989) noted 1,311 during 1958–85, with a large peak in late May and early June. Most of these occurred along the south and east coasts of England and in the Northern Isles. Numbers increased during the 1950s and 1960s, with irregular breeding. From the mid-1960s it colonized the East Anglian Fenland, centred mainly on a large plantation of hybrid black poplars *Populus* × *canadensis* at Lakenheath, Suffolk. The plantation was owned by the Bryant & May Company who had planted the trees for matchstick-making, and, inevitably, by the late 1970s the trees were being felled. Consequently, the orioles have once again declined. In 1987 it was estimated that there were some 30 pairs in Fenland (Dagley, 1994), and since then pairs have become less concentrated (Allsop and Mason, 1993). A 1994 census found only six confirmed breeding pairs, many fewer than expected, but they were observed during the breeding season at 43 sites (*BTO News* **199**: 15). Breeding has occurred elsewhere in south-east England and even in central Scotland (Ogilvie *et al.*, 1996).

Identification Plates 80.1 & 2 show a breeding pair in East Anglia in June 1993. These stunning photographs illustrate not only the beauty of the birds themselves but also their remarkable nest, suspended under a fork in a branch. The physical beauty of the Golden Oriole is enhanced by its remarkably atmospheric song: a clear, fluty *wheelu-wheeloo* (or variations thereof), although it also gives a rather more unprepossessing loud, harsh cat-like *kerraa*, recalling that of a Eurasian Jay *Garrulus glandarius*. The usual view of orioles is as they fly through the tree canopy or high across open ground from one belt to another, often chasing each other as they do so. In flight they look rather thrush-like in shape, but with long wings and a powerful dashing flight, swooping up into the canopy when alighting. It should be noted that first-summer males resemble females, whilst some adult females resemble adult males (*see* Svensson (1992) for further details).

BROWN SHRIKE
Lanius cristatus

Range Breeds from central Siberia east to Kamchatka and south into China and Japan. It winters from India through Southeast Asia to Borneo and the Philippines.

Occurrence The Brown Shrike was officially split from the Red-backed *L. collurio* and Isabelline Shrikes *L. isabellinus* in 1980. The only accepted British record occurred five years later: at Grutness, Sumburgh, Shetland, from 30 September to 2 October 1985 (Hume, 1993; Plate 79.3).

Identification The Brown Shrike is superficially similar to the Isabelline Shrike but, as its name

suggests, it is browner above. Most importantly, the tail is also typically browner (rather than reddish) and is concolorous with the mantle, although it is duller than the bright orange-rufescent rump. Unlike most Isabellines, it lacks any white at the base of the primaries. Structurally, the bill is thick and the head is rather large. The tail is more graduated and is rather long and narrow, although its width is unfortunately not apparent in the photograph. Most of these differences are readily apparent in comparison with the Isabelline Shrike pictured in Plates 79.4 & 5. The combination of the black bill, the strong black mask (including the lores), the strong supercilium (which extends across the forehead), the apparently plain wing coverts and a lack of dark chevrons below indicate that it was, remarkably, an adult, and was almost certainly a male.

ISABELLINE SHRIKE
Lanius isabellinus

Range As its pallid coloration suggests, Isabelline Shrike is mainly a bird of desert scrub, breeding in south-central Asia from Iran in the west to Mongolia in the east. It winters in southern and south-western Asia and in north-east Africa (Voous 1979).

Occurrences The Isabelline Shrike has had a chequered history as a British bird due entirely to early disagreement concerning its taxonomic position. Since 1980, however, the BOURC has recognized it as a distinct species that forms a species group with the Red-backed *L. collurio* and Brown Shrikes *L. cristatus*. Early confusion over its taxonomic status and appearance meant that there were just four records up to 1974, but since then it has been

Male Isabelline Shrike.

virtually annual in late autumn. By 1995, there had been 43 records, with as many as seven in 1988, but it has still to be recorded in Ireland. There have been records as early as late August, but most have occurred from late September to early November, mainly in the Northern Isles, down the east coast and in the South-west Peninsula. There have, however, been four spring records of males: on Fair Isle, Shetland, in May 1960; remarkably, one at Siddlesham, Sussex, in March–April 1975; one found dead in Richmond, Surrey, in March 1994, and one at Snettisham, Norfolk, in May 1995. It seems likely that these were spring migrants starting to move back the way they had come.

Identification Virtually all the British records have related to first-winters, and the bird in Plates 79.4 & 5 was a typical example, present at Minehead, Somerset, in September 1989. It can be aged by the dark subterminal tips to the greater coverts and tertials. Superficially similar to a first-winter Red-backed Shrike, it shows *uniformly* pale, sandy-brown upperparts and whitish underparts, with inconspicuous delicate scalloping confined to the crown, breast sides and flanks. The most distinctive feature is the orangey-red tail, which contrasts with the pallid upperparts to create an impression reminiscent of a subdued female Common Redstart *Phoenicurus phoenicurus*. Most show a small pale patch at the base of the primaries. Compared with the Red-backed and Brown Shrikes, the Isabelline's stubby bill is noticeably pale, with a distinct pink component. Most British records probably relate to the western race *phoenicuroides*, but subspecific identification is best left to adult males.

LESSER GREY SHRIKE
Lanius minor

Range Breeds thinly from northern Spain across southern and eastern Europe, through Asia Minor and across southern Russia into the steppes. It winters in southern Africa.

Occurrences The Lesser Grey Shrike occurs mainly in late spring and summer with smaller numbers in autumn. Its temporal and geographical occurrence patterns are similar to those of the European Roller *Coracias garrulus*, a species which has a similar distribution. Like the roller, it has shown a worrying decline over much of its European range. This has been occurring since the mid-19th century and has been linked to climatic change, particularly lower summer temperatures and heavy rainfall (*BWP*). In Germany, for example, it last bred in 1987, having declined from 1,000 pairs in 1950 (*BWP*; *Brit. Birds*

87: 12). Although it is still virtually annual in Britain, it has shown signs of becoming less frequent and, in view of its decline in Europe, one wonders whether its regular occurrences will continue.

Identification The bird in Plate 81.1 was an adult male present at Abersoch and Aberdaron, Caernarfonshire, in October–November 1986. Compared with the Great Grey Shrike *L. excubitor*, it has: (1) a stubbier bill; (2) a large black mask which extends over the forehead and forecrown; (3) a pink wash to the underparts (which contrasts with the white throat); (4) little white in the scapulars; (5) a larger white patch at the base of the primaries; (6) a longer primary projection (as long as the tertials); and (7) a broader-tipped tail with noticeable white patches at the base. The depth and blackness of the mask across the forehead indicates its age and sex. Plate 81.2 shows a first-winter at Rudston, Yorkshire, in September 1989. It shows barring on the scapulars, rump and breast sides, white tips to the greater coverts and it lacks black on the forehead. Structural differences, particularly the thick black bill, the long primaries and the medium-length tail, readily separate it from the Great Grey Shrike (but *see also* the Steppe Grey Shrike *L. meridionalis pallidirostris* below).

STEPPE GREY SHRIKE
Lanius meridionalis pallidirostris

Range The Southern Grey Shrike breeds from Iberia and the south of France across North Africa and the Sahara, through the Middle East and the Arabian Peninsula to India. North of the main range is the race *pallidirostris*, or 'Steppe Grey Shrike', which breeds from the Caspian Sea, north-eastern and eastern Iran and Afghanistan east to southern Mongolia and north-western China. It is partially migratory, wintering to the south of its breeding range and as far as north-eastern Africa, the Arabian Peninsula, Iraq and east to western Pakistan. Although now treated as a race of the Southern Grey Shrike, there is an argument for giving it specific status in its own right.

Occurrences There have been 11 British records (1956–94), all from mid-September to early December, with the exception of one at Cape Cornwall and Kenidjack Carn, Cornwall, on 21–23 April 1992. There were as many as four in 1994.

Identification With greater interest in this form and a clearer understanding of its identification features, it seems likely that it will be recorded more frequently. Plate 81.3 shows a first-winter which was initially picked up injured and eventually released at

Rodbourne Sewage Works, Swindon, Wiltshire, in September 1993. It can be aged by the retained juvenile greater and primary coverts, which are a dull brown and noticeably fringed with white (they are black, finely tipped white on the adult). It is similar to the Great Grey Shrike *L. excubitor* but can be separated by a combination: of (1) its pale-based bill; (2) the pale lores (although its face is unfortunately rather messy); (3) a larger white patch at the base of the primaries; and (4) a much longer primary projection which is approximately equal to the tertial length. As its scientific name suggests, its overall plumage tone is much paler than that of the Great Grey.

With its long primary projection and large white primary patch, the Steppe Grey Shrike may resemble a first-winter Lesser Grey *L. minor*. The latter is darker grey above, lacks a supercilium, shows dark lores and has a darker, thicker bill (*see* Plate 81.2). For a more detailed discussion of the subject, refer to Clement (1995), on which much of the above is based.

WOODCHAT SHRIKE
Lanius senator

Range Breeds across much of southern Europe, north into Germany and Poland, and east through the Balkans and Asia Minor into Iran, as well as in North Africa. It winters in a broad band south of the Sahara.

Occurrences The Woodchat Shrike is an annual spring and autumn visitor, those in spring relating to overshooting adults and first-years, and those in autumn being mainly dispersing juveniles. They occur mostly from mid-April to early June, with a secondary peak from mid-August to early October. In 1990 there was a remarkably early influx with seven recorded during 17–22 March in Dorset, Devon and southern Ireland. As to be expected of a southerly species, most occur in the southern half of Britain and Ireland, particularly in the South-west Peninsula. The species was removed from the Rarities List at the end of 1990, by which time there had been 586 records. Between 1958 and 1990, it was averaging 15 per year. It will be interesting to see if it can maintain this occurrence rate since, in common with other shrikes, it has shown alarming decreases in the northern part of its range (for example, there were only 30–40 pairs in Germany in the early 1990s; *Brit. Birds* **87**: 13).

Identification Plate 81.5 shows a male on Gugh, Isles of Scilly, in May 1989. With its black and white plumage and the large chestnut patch on the crown and nape, it is unmistakable. The solidly black forehead and ear-coverts show it to be a male (these are usually a mixture of black, brown and buffish-grey on the female; Svensson, 1992). Plate 81.4 shows a

juvenile/first-winter near Polgigga, Cornwall, in September 1992. Superficially similar to a first-winter Red-backed Shrike *S. collurio*, it can be separated by its cold, buffy-grey plumage tones (the Red-backed is rusty), its lack of a supercilium, dark scalloping over the crown, and, most importantly, by the white-based scapulars and by the prominent whitish patch at the base of the primaries. Not visible in the photograph are a whitish rump and uppertail-coverts (scalloped black), this area being noticeable in flight. Post-juvenile moult is complicated. It starts in the breeding areas, so that on leaving, about 70–90 per cent of the juvenile's head, body and lesser and median coverts are new, although some individuals (no doubt later hatching birds) remain much less advanced at this time (*BWP*). The bird in Plate 81.4 has acquired some plain adult mantle feathers and shows some distinctly rufous feathering in the nape.

SPOTTED NUTCRACKER
Nucifraga caryocatactes

Range The thick-billed nominate race breeds in the mountain chains of central and south-eastern Europe, Scandinavia, Finland and Russia, where it is largely resident. The slender-billed *macrorhynchus* breeds from north-eastern Russia east to the Pacific coast. Following the 1968 irruption (*see* below) this subspecies became established as close as the Ardennes in Belgium, where there were at least 60 pairs in 1989–91 (*BWP*).

Occurrences The Spotted Nutcracker is traditionally a very rare vagrant, usually occurring in winter, and it has never been seen in Ireland. Only three were recorded during the whole of the 1980s, all occurring in October–November 1985 (Dymond *et al.*, 1989). The slender-billed form periodically irrupts into western Europe from Siberia. It is a very specialized feeder and numbers fluctuate according to the cone crop of the Arolla Pine *Pinus cembra*. An irruption occurs whenever an abundant crop is followed by a poor one. The most spectacular example of this took place in 1968 when some 315 were reported in Britain, mostly in east coast counties from Norfolk to Kent. The first occurred as early as 6 August, with a second, heavier wave arriving from 21 August. It seems that the premature onset of cold weather in Siberia and a vast area of high pressure over Europe contributed to the scale of the influx (Hollyer, 1970).

Although it is generally a specialized feeder, the 1968 nutcrackers fed on a wide variety of food, from insects, seeds and fruit to House Mice *Mus musculus*, Brown Rats *Rattus norvegicus* and even House Sparrows *Passer domesticus*! A well-watched bird at Westleton, Suffolk, in 1985, (Plate 82.1) fed exclusively on apples, to the point where it seems to have died of an overdose. Unfortunately, it seems that the lack of Arolla Pine seeds eventually proves detrimental, and hence their irruptions have been aptly described as 'death-wanderings' (Hollyer, 1970).

Identification As the photograph shows, the Spotted Nutcracker is pretty well unmistakable, although because it is sometimes claimed by non-birdwatchers, it suffers from a surprisingly high rejection rate. In the field, it showed narrow white tips across the greater coverts and small white tips to the primary coverts, indicating that it was a first-winter. They can sometimes be located by a far-carrying, rather high-pitched, rasping *kraak* or *kreak* (*BWP*).

HOUSE CROW
Corvus splendens

Range Breeds from south-eastern Iran through Pakistan into India and Nepal, and east into Myanmar (Burma). Ship-assisted birds have been spread widely to ports around the Arabian Peninsula, the Red Sea and East Africa. There were as many as 800–850 at Suez, Egypt, in 1981, and 32 at Eilat, Israel, in 1990 (*BWP*), the latter being well known to many British and Irish birders.

Occurrence Two were discovered at the Hook of Holland, the Netherlands, in April 1994, and they were still present at the end of 1995, by which time a third had been discovered at Renesse (*Birding World* **7**: 214; **8**: 413). The species has reached Japan, Australia and even the USA, but these individuals were thought to be the first records for north-western Europe. Following the publication of the above information, it transpired that a House Crow had been seen and photographed at the fishing harbour of Dunmore East, Co. Waterford, on 3 November 1974 (Plate 82.2). Since ship-assistance is no longer a barrier to admission to the British and Irish List (as long as the bird has not been artificially maintained by man), there would seem to be no reason why the House Crow should not be admitted to Category A.

Identification The House Crow is ten per cent smaller than a Carrion Crow *Corvus corone corone* but has a very large bill which is both deeper, longer and shows a more curved upper mandible. The head is more domed, and it shows a greyish shawl over the nape and a greyish lower breast, demarcated from the black head and upper breast. In flight it looks long and slim with a long, slender tail. The call is quieter and generally higher pitched than that of the Carrion Crow (*BWP*).

ROSE-COLOURED STARLING
Sturnus roseus

Range Breeds from the Balkans and the Black Sea eastwards through south-western and central Asia to Afghanistan, and north to the Kirghizian steppes and the Altai. It winters mainly in the Indian subcontinent.

Occurrences There are two distinct waves of Rose-coloured Starlings in Britain and Ireland, involving adults and first-years in May–August and juveniles in September–October, some of which may remain to winter. Summer adults are widely distributed, but autumn juveniles tend to be concentrated in south-western Britain. There is a remarkable cluster of records in the Isles of Scilly, where the 'Pink Stink' is virtually annual and very much taken for granted.

Autumn juveniles are undoubtedly reversed migrants which have set off at 180° to their normal south-easterly heading towards India. Records of summer adults are related to the species' remarkably nomadic and irruptive lifestyle. It is basically a bird of the steppes, relying on grasshoppers, beetles and locusts, and huge numbers may irrupt westwards into

Juvenile Rose-coloured Starling.

south-eastern Europe in years when locusts swarm across the Mediterranean from North Africa. With more effective locust control, however, its invasions are on a smaller scale than in former times. In 1925 some 15,000 pairs were reported in Hungary, and one bird ringed there was recovered 11 years later 2,200 miles (3,520 km) to the south-east in eastern Uzbekistan (Ferguson-Lees, 1969). It is equally nomadic in the east of its range, with large numbers sometimes irrupting into southern Siberia.

It is in irruption years that we see the largest numbers penetrating into Western Europe. In 1994, the largest irruption since 1961 led to 550–600 pairs breeding in Hungary, and a roost of more than 3,000 was discovered in Bulgaria (*Brit. Birds* **88**: 43 and 278). Not surprisingly, a record total of 29 was recorded in Britain and Ireland in the same year. The following year, there were 1,600–1,700 pairs in Hungary (*Brit. Birds* **89**: 42) and at least 28 in Britain. It averaged about 11 a year between 1958 and 1995, and had accumulated 456 records by the end of that period. The former more cynical view that many of our vagrants were simply escapes from captivity has lost credibility in recent times.

Identification Plate 82.3 shows an adult at Bradfield, Essex, in June 1992. With its black and pink plumage, its relatively stubby pink bill and (not visible in the photograph) its shaggy crest, it is unmistakable. Plate 82.4 shows a juvenile on St Mary's, Isles of Scilly, in October 1986. It is much paler and sandier than a juvenile Common Starling *S. vulgaris* – although some are darker than others – with darker wings, the feathers narrowly fringed with buff. The most obvious difference from the Common Starling is the thicker bill, which has a more decurved culmen and which is predominantly yellow with a variably pink tip. It has a distinctly bland, open-faced expression, with a prominent dark eye. By the time juvenile Rose-coloured Starlings appear (late August onwards), most young Common Starlings will have started to acquire their adult-like first-winter plumage.

SPANISH SPARROW
Passer hispaniolensis

Range Breeds in the Canaries, north-western Africa and Iberia, then eastwards from Greece through Asia Minor into the Middle East, Turkestan and Afghanistan. Although some populations occur alongside man and occupy the niche that would otherwise be filled by the House Sparrow *P. domesticus*, the species is more usually associated with desert or dry steppe, often in areas of cultivation. There is some movement in winter to the south of its breeding range. In Italy and Tunisia, intermediate populations occur, such as the so-called 'Italian Sparrow'.

Occurrences With just six British records (to 1996), the nine-day stay of an individual on North Ronaldsay, Orkney, in August 1993, induced a large number of twitchers to make the expensive journey northwards. Those who resisted this temptation were rewarded in July 1996 when another long-stayer took up residence in Waterside, Cumberland (Plate 82.5) (to at least November 1996). Two of the previous records had occurred in spring (Lundy, Devon, and Martin's Haven, Pembrokeshire), while two others, both in the Isles of Scilly, were seen in late October. In view of the westerly bias, it would seem likely that our vagrants originated from the south rather than from the east, although eastern populations are more migratory. The appearance of two apparent hybrid Spanish × House Sparrows at Portland Bill, Dorset, in May 1984 (personal observation) may suggest that they had been bred locally, in which case it seems likely that another occurrence, possibly of a female, was overlooked! On the north coast of France, four males and two females in Antifer Harbour, Seine-Maritime, in May 1995 (*Brit. Birds* **89**: 43) were considered to have been ship-assisted, and it is possible that some of our vagrants may have arrived by the same method.

Identification Owing to the difficulties of picking out and identifying females, it is not surprising that all the British records have related to males. Despite being 'just a sparrow', the Spanish Sparrow is in fact an extremely attractive bird. Plate 82.5 shows all the features to good effect: (1) a chestnut-brown crown; (2) a well-defined narrow white line over the lores and behind the eye; (3) a very white cheek patch; (4) extensive black streaking across the breast and down the flanks; and (5) heavily streaked, predominantly blackish back and scapulars, showing two buff 'tramlines' down the mantle. The Cumberland bird, being present prior to its late-summer moult, was particularly well-marked and striking. When fresh, the patterning is greatly subdued as much of the body plumage is then obscured by pale feather fringes. The upperparts are browner and the underpart streaking is more restricted and less obvious, particularly on the flanks. The male's calls are thinner, more musical and more 'silvery' than those of a House Sparrow; the 'song' is a distinctive, musical *cheeoowee*, rising on the last syllable. Females are very similar to female House Sparrows, but some show fine blackish streaking across the breast and down the flanks, as well as a more prominent supercilium, a better-defined narrow white median covert bar and a somewhat heavier bill, with the gape line reaching the eye, and a more contrasting whitish patch at the base of the primaries.

YELLOW-THROATED VIREO
Vireo flavifrons

Range Breeds across much of the eastern USA, just creeping into southern Canada, and it winters mainly in Central America and northern South America.

Occurrence The sole Western Palearctic record concerns an individual at Kenidjack, Cornwall, on 20–27 September 1990 (Birch, 1994; Plates 83.1 & 2). It undoubtedly made an unaided transatlantic crossing, its occurrence coinciding with two Red-eyed Vireos *V. olivaceus* and an Ovenbird *Seiurus aurocapillus*, all found in Cornwall or south-western Ireland.

Identification Although the vireos tend to be overshadowed by the more colourful North American wood-warblers, the photograph shows that the Yellow-throated Vireo is a strikingly beautiful bird. The green upperparts and the bright yellow supra-loral line, spectacle and throat provide smart contrast to the brilliant white underparts and the crisp white wing bars and fringes to the remiges. In turn, all this is contrasted with the blue-grey scapulars. The typically thick vireo bill and the blue-grey legs and feet are also shown to good effect.

PHILADELPHIA VIREO
Vireo philadelphicus

Range Breeds in a wide band across southern Canada, mainly from Alberta to Newfoundland, and just creeps into the northern states of the USA. It winters from Guatemala south to Panama and north-western Colombia.

Occurrences There are just two records: at Galley Head, Co. Cork, on 12–17 October 1985 (Dowdall, 1995); and on Tresco, Isles of Scilly, on 10–13 October 1987. The Tresco individual occurred after a series of particularly fast-moving Atlantic depressions (Good, 1991). Given that this is not a particularly abundant species in North America, it was not highly rated as a potential vagrant to Western Europe.

Identification Plate 83.3 shows the Tresco bird. It is smaller than the Red-eyed Vireo *V. olivaceus*, rather large-headed and front-heavy with a shortish tail. It is dome-headed and weaker billed, lacking the more dagger-like profile of the Red-eyed. It has a matt greyish-blue crown and forehead, a distinctive pale yellow supercilium which curves over the eye and with a pale crescent below it. A dark eye-stripe is similar in shade to the crown. It is grey-green above but, unlike the Red-eyed, it is pale yellow below, being yellowest on the throat and undertail-coverts. Like the Red-eyed, it is a slow, purposeful feeder, but occasionally hanging upside down and also flycatching.

RED-EYED VIREO
Vireo olivaceus

Range Breeds right across northern and eastern North America, where it is one of the commonest birds of deciduous woodland. It winters in South America, south to Argentina.

Occurrences Its abundance, coupled with its huge migration, explains why the Red-eyed Vireo is the commonest North American passerine in Britain and Ireland, with 79 records up to 1994. Autumn migrants can clearly put on sufficient fat to facilitate an unassisted transatlantic crossing, and the occurrence pattern, with most in south-western England and south-western Ireland in late September and October, must surely confirm this. Its distribution is distinctly southerly, Scotland's first record being made as recently as October 1985, and with only four subsequent records. It is interesting to note that the species has never been recorded in Shetland. It has, however, penetrated to several sites along the English east coast, as well as to the Netherlands, France and, remarkably, Malta, where one was ringed in October 1983 (*Brit. Birds* 77: 242).

Identification The Red-eyed Vireo is a big, sluggish warbler-like bird with a thick, hook-tipped bill that is typical of the genus. Although not as instantly striking as the American wood-warblers, it is nevertheless

Red-eyed Vireo.

attractive, being bright green above and silky white below, this offset by a beautiful blue-grey crown, a dark eye-stripe and lateral crown stripe, and a white supercilium. The thick, blue-grey legs are also distinctive. Despite its name, the eye is usually dark in autumn, but, as with the Yellow-throated *V. flavifrons* and Philadelphia Vireos *P. philadelphicus*, ageing at this time of year, either by this or other features, is inadvisable (Pyle *et al.*, 1987). Despite this, it seems probable that all our autumn vagrants are first-winters. The bird in Plate 83.4 was photographed at Trevilley, Cornwall, in October 1995. There was an unprecedented fall in late September/October 1995, with at least 24 reported; one can only hazard a guess at the number that actually turned up. The photograph shows to good effect the reddish eye, the distinctive bill and the head pattern.

EUROPEAN SERIN
Serinus serinus

Range Breeds across much of mainland Europe south of the Baltic and east to a line from the Baltic to the Black Sea, as well as in Turkey and North Africa. Northern populations winter mainly in the southern part of the breeding range in countries bordering the Mediterranean.

Occurrences The European Serin was dropped from the Rarities List at the end of 1982. Dymond *et al.* (1989) noted 70 records prior to 1958 and 492 in 1958–85, an average of 18 per year. There was an obvious increase during the period, and in 1986–92 the average increased to 46 per year, with as many as 68 in 1990, 60 in 1991 (Fraser & Ryan, 1992), 64 in 1992 and a record 99 in 1993 (Evans, 1994). Coupled with this increase has been a number of breeding records, the first being in Dorset in 1967 (Ferguson-Lees, 1968).

The increase here is linked to a dramatic spread on the Continent. At the beginning of the 19th century the species was confined to the Mediterranean, but from the middle of that century there was a northward spread into Germany and west through France. It reached the Netherlands in 1922, and by 1925 it was breeding across virtually the whole of France as well as in eastern Germany and Poland. By 1942 it had reached Sweden, and by 1950 it had reached the Channel coast of France. By 1967 it had even bred in Finland (Olsson, 1971). That it has not properly colonized Britain has been a great disappointment but this is perhaps not surprising in view of the torrid state of our own arable farmland birds.

Serins have been recorded throughout the year, but there is a large peak from mid-April to early June and a smaller one from mid-October to late November.

Not surprisingly, most occur along the English Channel coasts, although it has been recorded as far north as Fair Isle, Shetland.

Identification Plates 84.1 & 2 show a male at Southwold, Suffolk, in April 1994. It is a small, dumpy, round-headed finch with a stubby bill. The most obvious feature is the bright yellow forehead, supercilium and ear-covert surround, extending onto the chin, throat and breast. The belly and flanks are white, the latter showing dark streaking. Note also the yellow crescent below the eye and the yellow spot in the middle of the ear-coverts. Its upperparts are fresh and rather greyish, streaked brown, and, unlike the Eurasian Siskin *Carduelis spinus*, it shows two whitish wing bars and lacks the yellow 'flash' in the secondaries and primaries. The short tail shows whitish fringing to the feathers, lacking the siskin's yellow patches at the base. It shows pinkish legs (they are blackish on the siskin). The female in Plate 84.3 was present at Ramsgate, Kent, in March 1994. She resembles the male but is totally lacking in yellow, being rather brown overall. In flight, the male shows a clear-cut bright yellow rectangular rump patch, but this is buffer on the female. The flight is light and jerky, and the commonest flight call is a distinctive, high-pitched, dry, fast *tillillit* (or variations thereof). The male has a high-pitched, speeded-up jangling song which is given with the bill open, the head jinked from side to side, and often with the tail cocked. This song is also given in display flights, when the bird flies with slow wingbeats, similar to that of a European Greenfinch *C. chloris*.

ARCTIC REDPOLL
Carduelis hornemanni

Range Has a circumpolar breeding distribution in the high Arctic tundras. It moves short distances to the south in winter, but the extent of the movements varies from year to year.

Occurrences Although by the end of 1994 there had been some 303 records, the Arctic Redpoll has had a tortuous history in Britain and Ireland as a result of perceived identification problems. Indeed, many authorities have considered it to be conspecific with the Mealy Redpoll *C. flammea flammea*, and the occurrence of so-called intermediates was cited as evidence that the two formed a 'hybrid swarm'. Recent thinking recognizes that the two are good species and that the so-called intermediates are, on the whole, simply immature Arctics which are browner than the adult 'frosty snowballs'. In Britain and Ireland, the position became even clearer following the publication of an excellent identification paper in February

1991 (Lansdown *et al.*, 1991), much of which was based on work carried out on the Continent by, amongst others, Molau (1985).

The Arctic Redpoll has traditionally been regarded as a rare and irregular vagrant, mainly to the Northern Isles, and for a long period records were accepted only if the birds were trapped. There were, however, marked influxes in the winters of 1961/62, 1972/73 and 1975/76. Increased observer confidence enabled the identification of about 43 in the winter of 1984/85, but this was totally eclipsed by some 84 in the winter of 1990/91. These included two notable flocks in Norfolk of at least 12 at Holkham Meals and 20 at Mousehold Heath, Norwich. It remains rare away from the Northern Isles and the east coast. The vast majority have been of the race *exilipes*, which originates in northern Scandinavia and Russia. Examples of the larger nominate race from Greenland and north-east Canada are much rarer.

In the winter of 1995/96, we experienced an unprecedented irruption of Arctic Redpolls, with a provisional total of perhaps 500, mainly in Scotland and down the east coast, but even inland as far south as Dorset. Most have occurred with Mealy Redpolls, and as many as 48 have been seen together. It seems likely that we will have to re-evaluate our ideas about the species' status here; it may well be that it is a fairly regular irruptive winter visitor.

Identification The Arctic Redpoll's separation from the Mealy Redpoll is complicated and has been covered in detail by Lansdown *et al.* (1991), Czaplak (1995) and Millington (1996), and summarized by Steele (1996). Plates 84.4 & 5 show two fairly straightforward examples. Plate 84.4 is of an adult at Carnoustie, Angus, in January 1989. This is a stunning 'frosty snowball' and should present no identification problems. It shows no brown in the plumage, with the exception of a faint wash to the ear-coverts and sides of the throat. Rounded tips to its tail feathers confirm its age as an adult. Plate 84.5 shows a first-winter at Langham, Norfolk, in February 1996 (if in doubt, first-winters can be aged by their pointed tail feathers). It shows the jizz of the species to good effect. Note in particular that it has a short bill and a steep forehead, producing a squashed-up face which makes it look as though it has flown into a wall!

On average, the Arctic is larger, bulkier and less compact than a Mealy and, as befitting a bird of the high Arctic, the plumage is rather loose and fluffy, the flank and belly feathering all but covering its legs and feet. Plumage-wise, the face is rather plain and it is hardly streaked below, with just a few wispy black lines on the sides of the breast and flanks. Two key features are: (1) it shows a broad white rump which is typically unstreaked for at least 0.4 in (10 mm), often over 0.8 in (20 mm; Svensson, 1992) – this is shown well in Plate 84.5; as to be expected, adult males tend to show the best rumps, immature females the poorest; and (2) the longest undertail-coverts are completely white, with at best a fine dark hairline shaft streak, or (rarely) a longer narrow central line (Mealies show much broader, more wedge-shaped dark centres). The undertail-coverts should always be carefully checked and are best viewed from below. The call is similar to the Mealy's *chi-chi-chi*, but is perceptibly harder.

TWO-BARRED CROSSBILL
Loxia leucoptera

Range Has a circumpolar breeding distribution in the boreal forests of North America and Eurasia, where it breeds further north than the Common Crossbill *L. curvirostra*. In the old world, it breeds mainly in forests dominated by the Siberian Larch *Larix sibirica* or Dahurian Larch *L. dahurica* (Newton, 1972). It does not normally breed in Scandinavia, so our vagrants originate from further east.

Occurrences Like other crossbills, the Two-barred may irrupt in response to food shortages within its breeding range, and in Scandinavia large irruptions seem to occur every seven years (Lewington *et al.*, 1991). Most of the British records have involved singles which have appeared with Common Crossbill irruptions, but a genuine Two-barred invasion in August 1987 involved at least 21 in Orkney and Shetland, all but one being juveniles. Another invasion in 1990 produced a further 18, but these were more widely scattered and included more adults. The pair in Plates 85.1 & 2 was present on Fair Isle, Shetland, in July 1990.

Identification The birds in the photographs are so distinctive that it is difficult to believe that there could be an identification problem with this species. Common Crossbills, however, can occasionally show narrow wing bars and it is this that has sometimes led to the rejection of individuals which have been poorly described. The Two-barred is typically slightly smaller and thinner billed than the Common (although there is overlap), with a proportionately longer tail. The male's plumage is typically pinker, but there is variation. Some are very bright but others, presumably younger males, are very pale and washed out. Males may also be quite black on the scapulars (less so on the mantle and undertail-coverts) and also show an obvious dark ear-covert surround. On adults, the wing bars are 0.2–0.5 in (5–12 mm) wide and squarely cut off to form two thick bars, the one on the greater coverts bulging on the inner feathers and tapering onto the outers. Unless worn, thick white tips to the tertials are also prominent. On juveniles, the wing bars are narrower and less well-defined, as are the tertial tips, but these are still usually thicker and more prominent than on the Common Crossbill (Svensson, 1992). It is becoming increasingly obvious that the risk of confusion with wing-barred Common Crossbills has been exaggerated, although worn juvenile Two-barreds may be the most problematical. The Two-barred has a softer higher-pitched call than Common, a dry, slightly metallic *tyip tyip*, but the differences are subtle to the untrained ear. Some give very subdued versions of this. Begging juveniles give a persistent *dyi-dyip dyi-dyip*, strongly reminiscent of young European Goldfinches *Carduelis carduelis*. Delin & Svensson (1990) also mention a *tweeht* from feeding flocks, reminiscent of a Canary *Serinus canaria*.

PARROT CROSSBILL
Loxia pytyopsittacus

Range Breeds in Fenno-Scandia east to northern Russia, and sporadically south to the Baltic States, Poland, Germany and, occasionally, Denmark.

Occurrences There were 13 records (18 individuals) prior to the winter of 1962/63, when there was an irruption involving at least 85, 61 of which occurred on Fair Isle, Shetland. There were only four records in the next 20 years, but another irruption in the winter of 1982/83 produced 104. Leftovers from that influx hung around for some time and, in 1984 and 1985, a pair bred in Wells Wood, Norfolk, whilst another pair in Suffolk almost certainly did so. A third irruption in 1990/91 produced about 264, including flocks of up to 44 in Lincolnshire and 47 in the former Cleveland. In all the invasions a pattern emerged, with the initial arrivals being in the Northern Isles and down the east coast, but with wintering flocks developing inland. They arrive later than irrupting Common Crossbills *L. curvirostra*, mainly from late September to mid-November, with some remaining until the following spring (Catley & Hursthouse, 1985).

In their native areas, Parrot Crossbills feed mainly on pine seeds. As the pine has a more consistent cone crop than the spruce (the preferred food of the Common Crossbill), Parrots usually adjust to local food shortages by making smaller migratory movements. In 1982, however, there was an almost total failure of the pine cone crop in Norway, and that year's irruption is thought to have originated in northern Scandinavia and was centred on southern Sweden, Denmark, the Netherlands and Britain (loc. cit.).

Identification Plates 85.3–5 show the historic breeding birds in Norfolk in April 1985. They are very similar to the Common Crossbill but are larger, heavier, larger-headed more bull-necked and rather front-heavy. The most obvious difference is the size and shape of the bill, although this is least obvious in the juvenile. In the adults the bill is indeed rather parrot-like, being obviously deeper at the base, and having strongly arched mandibles and a less obviously crossed tip. Note also how the bill seems to merge with the head, showing a rather flat forehead (although the crown feathers are sometimes raised to produced rather a dome-headed appearance). Plumage differences from the Common are minimal, although the Parrot is on average duller, with greyish tones to the head, neck and mantle, while pale ivory cutting edges to the bill may be more obvious. The calls are lower and deeper than those of the Common and include a deep *choop choop*.

TRUMPETER FINCH
Bucanetes githagineus

Range Breeds from the Canaries and Morocco across the Sahara to the Middle East and east to Afghanistan and Pakistan. It is considered resident, dispersive or nomadic.

Occurrences There have been just seven records between 1971 and 1992, five of which have occurred in late May and early June. Remarkably, three of these have been in the north of Scotland. The most heavily twitched was an individual at Church Norton, Sussex, on 19–23 May 1984, when it was unfortunately killed by a Eurasian Sparrow Hawk *Accipiter nisus* (James, 1986). At the time of the first occurrences, the Trumpeter Finch was not a predicted vagrant, but investigations revealed that it had spread north into south-eastern Spain since the early 1960s and, by the end of that decade, it was abundant in Almeria (Wallace *et al.*, 1977). By the mid-1980s, it had spread west towards Malaga (*Brit. Birds* **81**: 22). The coincidence of the first British records (and others in France and Germany) combined with the spread across the Mediterranean allowed the species to be added to Category A of the British List.

Identification Plate 86.1 is very much a record shot of the Church Norton bird. It is similar in size to a Common Linnet *Carduelis cannabina* but much bulkier and bull-necked, with a stubby, conical bill. The bill is in fact the most distinctive feature, being dull yellowy-orange (with greyish feathering around base). The plumage is sandy and the small, beady eye stands out. The rump was pale orangey-pink and the tail was also tinged with this colour. The legs were a noticeably pale yellowy-orange. It was in active primary moult but, since juveniles may occur as early as February and may undergo a complete moult by May (*BWP*), the ageing of this bird was considered uncertain.

Breeding males are far more attractive, with a bright carmine bill, a grey head, a carmine forehead, rump, uppertail-coverts and sides of the tail, and pink fringes to the wing feathers. As its name suggests, it has a distinctive nasal call: *nee* or *eeep*, sometimes likened to the sound of a child's trumpet. Other calls include a lower *zoop* and a hard *chick chick chick*.

COMMON ROSEFINCH
Carpodacus erythrinus

Range Breeds from the Netherlands right across Europe and Asia to the Pacific, south to the Himalayas and west into Turkey. It winters in India, Southeast Asia and southern China.

Occurrences The Common Rosefinch is traditionally a spring and autumn migrant, with most records coming from the Northern Isles, the east coast and the Isles of Scilly. Annual totals have increased steadily since the mid-1960s and it was dropped from the Rarities List in 1982. It is particularly interesting to note that there was only one spring record prior to 1958, but it has been annual at this time of year since 1963. In 1992, there was a major spring influx of at least 157, this culminating in at least two pairs breeding at Flamborough Head, Yorkshire, and two pairs in Suffolk (Evans, 1993a). These were the first breeding attempts since an isolated occurrence in Scotland in 1982, and followed a large increase and westward range expansion on the Continent. It first bred in the Netherlands in 1987 and in France in 1993 (*Brit. Birds* **81**: 338; **87**: 13), and it seems likely that we can look forward to a consolidation of its breeding status in the future. One wintered in Pembrokeshire from December 1991 to January 1992, feeding on peanuts in a garden, and one wonders if the species adapted more widely to food provided by man, whether it could perhaps emulate the success of the closely related House Finch *C. mexicanus*, which is a common garden bird in North America.

Identification Plate 86.2 shows a male on North Ronaldsay, Orkney, in May 1990. Its bright carmine-red crown, throat and upper breast and, not visible in the photograph, its rump, are distinctive. Most male Common Rosefinches do not acquire this red plumage until their second summer. Older males are even redder on the mantle, wing coverts and tail, and pinker on the belly. Plate 86.3 shows an individual in its more familiar brown plumage. This is either a female or a first-summer male, photographed in June 1995 on Fetlar, Shetland. It is a rather plain and non-

descript bird, rather bull-necked and dome-headed, with a thick, conical bill, and a noticeably forked tail. It is lightly streaked on the crown, mantle and breast. The two most obvious features are the beady black eye, which stands out from the bland face, and the double wing bar, the white tips to the median coverts being most prominent. Autumn migrants are almost invariably juveniles (note that the post-juvenile moult does not take place until it reaches its winter quarters). They can be separated from adult females at this time by the neater, fresher, more immaculate plumage, which is more olive in tone. The typical call is a thin, high-pitched, slightly buzzy *zoo-eet*, rising on the second syllable. The song is very distinctive: a loud, thin, cheerful whistling, usually transcribed as a 'pleased to SEE you'. The number of notes, the speed of delivery and the emphasis are, however, individually variable. Hence, some sing 'pleased to see YOOUU', 'pleased to see you too', 'to-see-YOOU' and so on.

PINE GROSBEAK
Pinicola enucleator

Range Has a circumpolar distribution which extends from northern Scandinavia eastwards in a narrow belt straddling the Arctic Circle, but it is more widespread in Siberia and North America, where the range extends southwards down the Rockies and Cascades into Colorado and California (Newton 1972).

Occurrences The Pine Grosbeak is mainly resident but like many inhabitants of the coniferous forest zone, it is occasionally irruptive. Southward movements in Finland have been correlated with the rowan crop, the grosbeaks moving south when it fails. In years of severe food shortage they may move much further south into Europe. In mid-November 1976, for example, at Toro, Sweden, as many as 17,400 flew west in just two days (*Brit. Birds* **70**: 219). It seems that these larger irruptions originate further east as the Fenno-Scandian population is too small to account for the numbers involved (Newton, 1972). Despite the size of some of these movements, the species is no more than an extremely rare vagrant to Britain, with just ten records (to 1992). The individual in Plate 86.4 was present at Lerwick, Shetland, from 25 March to 25 April 1992, enabling it to be appreciated by over 200 twitchers (Harrop, 1992). As is usually the case, it was very tame.

Identification At 8 in (20 cm) in length, the Pine Grosbeak is the largest European finch. The longish tail, the swollen bill (with a slight hook), the double white wing bars and the white fringes to the remiges are distinctive. The male is rose-red on a blue-grey background, whereas the adult female has the red replaced by a bronze or greenish colour. The Shetland bird, with its combination of reddish-orange plumage and pointed tail feathers, was a first-year male. In flight, it is long-tailed and heavy. Its commonest call is a whistled, trisyllabic *tee-tee-tew* (*BWP*).

BLACK-AND-WHITE WARBLER
Mniotilta varia

Range Breeds from north-western Canada across southern Canada and south through the eastern half of the USA to the Gulf states. It winters from the Gulf states south through the West Indies and Central America to northern Peru, Ecuador, Colombia and northern Venezuela (Godfrey, 1966, Curson *et al.*, 1994).

Occurrences There are 16 records: one found dead in Shetland in October 1936, ten between 1975 and 1987 and, remarkably, five in 1996. All but four were in south-western England and Ireland. All have occurred from early September to mid-October apart from three notable exceptions: one at Tavistock, Devon, on 3 March 1978; a first-winter male at How Hill, Ludham, Norfolk, on 3–15 December 1985 (Plate 87.1); and one in Norwich, Norfolk in November 1996.

Identification As the photograph reveals, the Black-and-white Warbler is quite simply unmistakable. The combination of the white chin and throat and the heavy black striping down the sides identify it as a first-winter male. Adult males have solidly black ear-coverts and a solidly black throat in summer, this being mottled in winter. Females are streaked only lightly with grey below, and first-winter females are washed buff over the entire face and underparts (Curson *et al.*,1994). Almost as distinctive as its appearance is its behaviour. It is an active, lively bird, creeping and flitting up and down tree trunks and under branches, carefully and inquisitively inspecting bark and twigs in an almost nuthatch-like manner. Characteristically, the Norfolk bird fed with a large flock of tits.

GOLDEN-WINGED WARBLER
Vermivora chrysoptera

Range A scarce breeding species in a relatively limited area of the north-eastern USA, south of the Great Lakes and down the Appalachians (it just creeps into southern Canada). It is increasing in the north of its range but declining in the south, where there is inter-breeding with and replacement by the Blue-winged Warbler *V. pinus*. It winters mainly from Guatemala to Panama, with some reaching Colombia and Venezuela (Curson *et al.*, 1994).

Occurrence Being a relatively scarce breeding bird, and with a range much further south than most of our other North American vagrants, the Golden-winged Warbler had never been considered a potential vagrant to Europe. On 7 February 1989, however, Paul Doherty made one of the most extraordinary discoveries in British birdwatching history.

On the way to post a letter on the Lunsford Park Estate, Larkfield, Kent, Doherty came across a small, brightly coloured bird feeding in a cotoneaster bush. He did not have his binoculars with him and, having dismissed from his mind all the North American wood-warblers on the British and Irish List, he understandably began to wonder whether he had seen an escaped cagebird. On returning home, he consulted the National Geographic Society's *Field Guide to the Birds of North America* and was astonished to discover that he had found a first for the Western Palearctic: a male Golden-winged Warbler. The following afternoon, he rediscovered the bird in some bushes bordering, of all places, a supermarket car park, and his confirmation that he hadn't been hallucinating set in train Britain's biggest-ever twitch (Doherty, 1989, 1992). On the following Saturday, a minimum of 2,000 people turned up, with a further 600 on the Sunday. Birdwatching had reached football-crowd proportions! The national press ran stories on their front pages and it made the radio and television news. Some of the stories from the twitchers themselves were quite bizarre. One concerned a double-decker bus which became stuck in the crowd; some quick-witted birders, seizing an opportunity, boarded the bus and went upstairs, where they were able to view the bird which had been feeding out of sight in a garden! It subsequently transpired that it had originally been seen by a local resident on 24 January, but its remarkable occurrence on a housing estate, inland, in Kent and in mid-winter, seemed to confirm the old adage that anything can turn up, any time, any place.

Needless to say, there was the inevitable debate about the bird's origin, but the BOURC accepted it as a genuinely wild vagrant. Their decision was helped by the fact that there had been several other North American passerines recorded down the east coast during the previous autumn. Whether it reached these shores unaided or was ship-assisted, is another matter. Interestingly though, the first record for Newfoundland occurred only the previous year, on 15 September 1988 (*Brit. Birds* **85**: 600), and it seems likely that our bird was a reversed migrant out across the Atlantic. It subsequently transpired that another North American wood-warbler, a first-winter male Common Yellowthroat *Geothlypis trichas*, was also wintering in Kent at the time just 18 miles (25 km) from the Golden-winged Warbler. A first-winter female Baltimore Oriole *Icterus galbula* in

Pembrokeshire completed a remarkable trio of over-wintering North American passerines. All three remained until April, the Golden-winged Warbler being last seen on 10th.

Identification As Plate 87.2 shows, the Kent bird was quite simply unmistakable!

TENNESSEE WARBLER
Vermivora peregrina

Range Breeds across much of southern Canada, creeping into the northern states of the USA. Its numbers show cyclical fluctuations, correlating with outbreaks of the Spruce Budworm *Choristoneura fumiferana*. It winters from southern Mexico and Guatemala south to Colombia and northern parts of Ecuador and Venezuela (Curson *et al.*, 1994).

Occurrences There are just four records. Two first-winters were trapped on Fair Isle, Shetland, in September 1975 (Broad, 1981), and another first-winter was trapped on Holm, Orkney, in September 1982 (Meek 1984). The fourth was one present on St Kilda, Western Isles, in September 1995. It is remarkable that all four – plus others in Iceland and the Faeroes (the latter in September 1984) – have occurred in September and so far to the north, suggesting that reversed migration is the primary reason for their presence. Since eastern birds move down the Atlantic coast to Florida and through the West Indies to northern South America (Curson *et al.*, 1994), any reversed migrant would be likely to hit northern Britain (*see* page 22).

Identification Although the Tennessee Warbler is one of the less colourful American wood-warblers, it is nevertheless much brighter than our own *Phylloscopus* warblers. It is stockier than a Willow Warbler *P. trochilus* and proportionately shorter tailed. It is bright olive-green above, with a yellow tinge, and varies from bright yellow to pale yellow on the breast, becoming paler further down and with white undertail-coverts. First-winters lack the blue-grey head of a spring male but show a slightly darker line through the eye, a subdued short yellow supercilium and eye-ring, and an indistinct narrow whitish wing bar. The rump is brighter and, perhaps most distinctive, first-winters show clear-cut green fringes to the black primaries and secondaries, while white crescents on the tips of the primaries produce a white 'ladder'. The legs are dark grey. Plate 87.3 shows the first Fair Isle bird in September 1975; it can be aged as a first-winter by its pointed tail feathers. It gives a *zit zit* call, reminiscent of that of the Firecrest *Regulus ignicapillus* but perhaps more penetrating (Broad, 1981).

NORTHERN PARULA
Parula americana

Range Breeds in the eastern half of North America, from southern Canada to the Gulf coast. In the north it is associated with the *Unsea* lichen Old Man's Beard, and in the south with Spanish Moss (*Tillansia*; Curson *et al.*, 1994). It winters from Mexico south to Nicaragua and from southern Florida south through the West Indies.

Occurrences There were 16 records between 1966 and 1995, all occurring in late September to early November except for a very late individual at St Ives, Cornwall, on 26 November 1967. Their late occurrence here is surprising since, at Cape May, New Jersey (which is on a similar latitude to Lisbon), the peak migration is in early to mid-September. All have occurred in south-western England and southern Ireland except for one found moribund at, of all places, the Wigan Infirmary, Lancashire, on 2 November 1982.

Identification The Northern Parula is a small, vivid bird, arguably one of the most attractive American wood-warblers. Plates 88.1 & 2 show a male on the Garrison, St Mary's, Isles of Scilly, in October 1985. It is easily identifiable. The upperparts are blue-grey with a large patch of bright green on the mantle. The throat and breast are brilliant yellow, giving way to a gleaming white belly, flanks and long undertail-coverts. It has a fine, pointed, predominantly orange bill, an incomplete white eye-ring, two white wing bars, whitish, greenish and bluish fringes to the remiges and dark legs with orangey feet. When viewed from below, the rather short tail shows white spots towards the tip. It can be sexed by the presence of chestnut feathering across the upper breast and a chestnut patch on the sides of the breast. Plate 88.3 shows a female in the Cot Valley, Cornwall, in October 1988. Its sheer vividness comes over well in this photograph. Unlike the male, it is greener on the crown and lacks any chestnut in the breast. Vagrants are usually seen actively gleaning insects off leaves and twigs, occasionally giving a soft *sit* call.

YELLOW WARBLER
Dendroica petechia

Range The *aestiva* group of races breeds from Alaska right across southern Canada, the bulk of the United States and south to central Mexico. It winters in Central and South America (south to central Peru and northern Bolivia) and in the West Indies. Other forms occur in the West Indies, coastal Central America and northern South America, and these are perhaps best split as the 'Mangrove Warbler' (Curson *et al.*, 1994).

It is one of the commonest warblers over much of North America.

Occurrences There are five records. The first was a first-winter male trapped on Bardsey, Caernarfonshire, on the early date of 29 August 1964. It was roosted overnight but died the following morning, and this rather unhappy episode generated an infamous exchange of correspondence in *British Birds* (**59**: 316–317). The second occurred surprisingly late, a first-winter male at Helendale, Lerwick, Shetland, on 3–4 November 1990 (Plates 88.5 & 6), followed by a first-winter male trapped on North Ronaldsay, Orkney, on 24 August 1992, again an early date. There were then two in Ireland in October 1995: a first-winter male at Brownstown Head, Co. Waterford; and a first-winter female at Kilbaha, Loop Head, Co. Mayo. The latter stayed for nearly three weeks, enabling a number of twitchers to catch up with it.

Identification Plates 88.5 & 6 show rather a featureless bird but, as its name suggests, the sheer brightness of its yellow plumage is striking. Indeed, the finders of the Bardsey individual wondered at first whether they had a flavistic *Phylloscopus* warbler (Evans, 1965). Its face is rather bland but shows a prominent dark eye, a faint supra-loral line and a pale eye-ring. The lack of a supercilium and eye-stripe may even suggest a *Hippolais* warbler, and the bill is longer and slightly more spiky than that of a *Phylloscopus*. The neat yellow fringing to the wing feathers, with white tips to the primaries, and the yellow inner webs to the tail feathers are all typical. In the field, faint orange streaks on the sides of the breast showed it to be a male (Suddaby, 1990). This feature is shown to greater effect by adult males, which are very yellow. In autumn, the intensity of the yellow is variable but the Shetland bird showed pointed tips to the tail feathers indicative of a first-winter (the adult's are more truncated). The call is a *zit* or a high, buzzy *zzee*, given in flight (Curson *et al.*, 1994).

YELLOW-RUMPED WARBLER
Dendroica coronata

Range Has a huge breeding range, from Alaska south to northern Mexico, and across southern Canada east to Newfoundland and the north-eastern USA. It is an 'early and late' migrant in North America, and it winters further north than other wood-warblers, from British Columbia in the west and from Nova Scotia in the east, south to the West Indies and through Central America to Panama.

Occurrences As befitting such a hardy species, the first British and Irish record occurred in winter: a

male visiting a bird table at Newton St Cyres, Devon, from 4 January to 10 February 1955, when it was found dead (Smith, 1955). It is interesting to note that at least 60 people went to see it, some of whom had travelled considerable distances! Since then, there have been a further 21 in October–November (to 1995), mostly in south-west England and southern Ireland. There have also been two spring records which, as to be expected, were in the northern half of the country: on Fair Isle, Shetland, on 18 May 1987, and on the Calf of Man, Isle of Man, on 30 May 1985. Inevitably, all the records have been of the northern and eastern nominate 'Myrtle Warbler'.

Identification Plate 88.4 shows what was probably a first-winter male on Ramsey Island, Pembrokeshire, in November 1994. It appears almost pipit-like, except for the deep yellow patches at the sides of the breast and the brilliant yellow rump patch. It otherwise has a faint supercilium, an obvious white eye-ring, a streaked mantle, two narrow buffy-white wing bars and a streaked breast and flanks. Both the bill and the legs are blackish. When seen from below, it has large white patches on the undersides of the tail; in flight these appear as large white tips to the outer tail feathers, further enhancing its pipit-like appearance. It has large black centres to the uppertail-coverts, indicative of a male (Pyle *et al.*, 1987). It is a hyperactive feeder, rarely keeping still, and it calls frequently: a soft, rather liquid *tlip* or *tip*. When first found, an individual on St Mary's, Isles of Scilly, in October 1985, fed in a grassy field amongst Meadow Pipits *Anthus pratensis*.

BAY-BREASTED WARBLER
Dendroica castanea

Range Has rather a narrow breeding range across southern Canada from the south-western Northwest Territories and eastern British Columbia, east to southern Newfoundland and Nova Scotia, and just creeping south into the USA, principally in northern New England. It winters from Panama to western Colombia and north-western Venezuela. Its numbers fluctuate in response to the Spruce Budworm *Choristoneura fumiferana* (Curson *et al.*, 1994).

Occurrence The only Western Palearctic record concerns an individual that was fortuitously video-recorded by David Ferguson at a windswept Land's End, Cornwall, on 1 October 1995 (Plate 89.1, which is a still from the video). This was the highlight of a classic autumn for American passerines.

Identification The Bay-breasted Warbler is most similar to a Blackpoll Warbler *D. striata*, but it is quite a large, sturdy, bull-necked warbler with rather clumsy, heavy movements. Plumage-wise, the bird in the photograph is a relatively plain yellowish olive-green on the upperparts and unstreaked buffish below with a white throat (yellow throat and breast on the Blackpoll). Like the Blackpoll, it shows two prominent white wing bars and even more contrasting white-fringed tertials, and it also has a faint supercilium and a noticeable yellow eye-ring. An important difference is its blackish legs and feet (the Blackpoll has brown legs and orange feet). Its rather plain upperparts would suggest that it was a first-winter female. It is an arboreal species but, clearly newly arrived, the Cornish bird was found hopping around on short grass and lichen-covered rocks. The call is a high-pitched *sip* or *see*, often quite loud and buzzing (Curson *et al.*, 1994).

BLACKPOLL WARBLER
Dendroica striata

Range Breeds from Alaska through the northern Canadian coniferous forest belt east to Newfoundland and south into the north-eastern corner of the USA. It is a very long-range migrant, wintering in South America from Colombia to southern Peru, northern Bolivia and western Brazil, occasionally even further south (Godfrey, 1966; Curson *et al.*, 1994).

Occurrences Surprisingly, the Blackpoll Warbler was first recorded only as recently as 1968, but since then it has become the most numerous North American wood-warbler, with 34 records up to 1995. All except one have occurred from late September to late October, mainly in southern Ireland and south-western England, including a staggering 19 in the Isles of Scilly. The latter included what can only be described as a fall of at least seven in October 1976.

In autumn, eastern Blackpoll Warblers move down the Atlantic coast to Florida and the West Indies, and then on to South America. Some swing out into the Atlantic to make a huge transoceanic crossing from the USA direct to the West Indies and northern South America, picking up the north-easterly trade winds in the latter stages of their journey. Although this route is well documented, whether it is regularly used is still disputed (Curson *et al.*, 1994). Whatever the answer, Blackpoll Warblers clearly accumulate sufficient amounts of fat to facilitate a transatlantic crossing. Their distinctly southerly occurrence pattern is compatible with them being swept across the Atlantic in rapidly moving depressions. The species is very rare in the north, with only three records from Scotland, all in Shetland since 1985. An exception to the pattern involved one at Bewl Water, Sussex, on 10–20

December 1994. This was undoubtedly another example of attempted over-wintering by an American wood-warbler, but it seems likely that it did not survive a cold spell just before Christmas

Identification Plate 89.2 shows an individual on St Mary's, Isles of Scilly, in October 1990. It is olive-green above, faintly lined with black. This merges into primrose-yellow on the throat and breast, with faint streaking on the breast sides and flanks (this may not be apparent at certain angles). The belly, vent and undertail-coverts are whiter. It shows a pale yellow supercilium, a similarly coloured eye-ring, two prominent white wing bars and white fringes to all the remiges, the thick white tertial fringes being particularly prominent. Of particular significance is the leg colour, which varies from brown to dull orange, but with obviously brighter orange feet. From below, it shows large white patches on the inner webs of the tail feathers and, in flight, these are occasionally visible from above.

The Blackpoll is rather a bulky warbler, with slow movements through the vegetation. As with the Yellow-rumped Warbler *D. coronata*, it has something of a pipit-like feel to it, and an individual on St. Agnes, Isles of Scilly, in October 1995 actually spent several hours feeding in a grass field with a flock of Meadow Pipits *Anthus pratensis* – and one Red-throated Pipit *A. cervinus*. The Blackpoll was surprisingly difficult to pick out in a cursory scan. The call is a thin *zit* with a definite 'z' in it.

AMERICAN REDSTART
Setophaga ruticilla

Range Breeds from north-western British Columbia, southern Yukon and south-western Northwest Territories east across southern Canada to Newfoundland, across the northern USA and more locally south-east to the Gulf states. Its numbers have recently declined, although it is possible that this may be a cyclical fluctuation. It winters from Mexico, Cuba and Puerto Rico to northern South America, and from there east to Surinam and south to southern Peru (Godfrey, 1966; Curson *et al.*, 1994).

Occurrences There have been just seven records, all between 1967 and 1985. Four occurred in traditional American passerine localities in Cornwall and Co. Cork, but the others were found in Argyllshire, Hampshire and, surprisingly, Lincolnshire, where a heavily twitched first-winter (probably a male) was present at Gibraltar Point from 7 November to 5 December 1982. All the others have occurred between 13 October and 1 November, over a month later than the peak passage at Cape May, New Jersey.

Identification Plate 87.4 shows a first-winter at Kenidjack, Cornwall, in October 1983. It is a distinctive and beautiful bird, with a greyish head and noticeable white eye-ring, brownish upperparts and white underparts. It has a long tail with huge yellow flashes at the base. Equally distinctive is the rich yellow patch on the sides of the breast (this is more orangey on first-winter males). Some show a bright yellow wing bar across the base of the primaries and secondaries, and the virtual absence of this feature (plus the yellow tone to the breast-sides) indicates that this individual is a first-winter female.

American Redstarts tend to feed in the canopy where they are active, agile and mobile, frequently fluttering through the branches and making sallies after insects in an acrobatic, flycatcher-like manner. The tail is continually cocked and spread to reveal the diagnostic basal patches, and is also jinked from side to side for maximum effect. Its feeding behaviour, combined with its tail patches, reminds one of a Red-breasted Flycatcher *Ficedula parva*. The call is an explosive, metallic *psit*, vaguely recalling that of a Winter Wren *Troglodytes troglodytes*.

OVENBIRD
Seiurus aurocapillus

Range Breeds in Canada from eastern British Columbia and Alberta east to Newfoundland, and in the USA south locally to Colorado in the west and to Oklahoma and South Carolina in the east. It winters from Florida and the Gulf coast to Panama and the West Indies, and occasionally south to northern Colombia and Venezuela (Curson *et al.*, 1994).

Occurrences There have been five records, although only two of these birds have been seen alive. The first record related to a wing found on the beach at Formby, Lancashire, on the odd date of 4 January 1969; such a record should reside in Category D3 of the British List. The first Category A occurrence was an individual found on the Out Skerries, Shetland, on 7–8 October 1973 (Robertson, 1975). This was then followed by dead ones in Co. Mayo in December 1977 and in Devon in October 1985, and by another live one on Dursey Island, Co. Cork, on 24–25 September 1990 (Plate 89.4). As with many North American songbirds, the Ovenbird has shown some worrying decreases in many parts of its range, so it seems unlikely that it will become any more frequent here.

In February 1995, an individual was reported wintering inside the atrium of a hotel in Chicago, where it had been living for several months (*Winging It 7*, Number 3). Maybe we've been checking the wrong habitat!

Identification Although it lacks the bright colours of many of the North American wood-warblers, the Ovenbird is nevertheless a great favourite. The plumage resembles a miniature thrush, with rather olive-brown upperparts and heavily streaked white underparts. The most distinctive features are the large black eye, which is surrounded by a striking white eye-ring, and a dark orange crown stripe bordered with black. The head pattern is thus similar to that of a giant Goldcrest *Regulus regulus*. As its large eye suggests, it is a bird of the forest floor and, in common with many such birds, it has strikingly pale pink legs (and a similarly coloured bill). It walks around on the ground, searching the leaf litter while constantly bobbing its head and flicking up its tail. Its calls are a sharp, dry *chip* and a thin, high-pitched *see*, given in flight (Curson *et al.*, 1994).

NORTHERN WATERTHRUSH
Seiurus noveboracensis

Range Breeds from Alaska across Canada to Nova Scotia, creeping into the northern states of the USA. It winters from southern Florida, Cuba and Mexico south to Ecuador, north-eastern Peru and northern Brazil (Godfrey, 1966; Curson *et al.*, 1994).

Occurrences There were just seven records between 1958 and 1996, four in Scilly, one on Cape Clear Island, Co. Cork, one at Gibraltar Point, Lincolnshire, and another at Portland, Dorset. Arrival dates have ranged from 29 August to 22 October. Two on St Agnes both obligingly fed along the seashore, but others have been more typically elusive.

Identification Plate 89.3 shows a first-winter on St Agnes, Isles of Scilly, in August 1989. It can be aged by its pointed tail feathers. It resembles a small pipit, with its brown upperparts, heavily streaked underparts, long buff supercilium and brown eye-stripe. It has a hesitating walk, continually wagging its short tail, which is slightly spread. In comparison with the Louisiana Waterthrush *S. motacilla*, the following features should be noted: (1) it has obviously dull buff tones to the supercilium and underparts (eastern birds only); (2) the legs are a dull, reddish-brown or pinky-brown; and (3) the bill is darker and shorter. The Northern has an incisive, metallic *stick* or *tip* call, perhaps recalling a White-throated Dipper *Cinclus cinclus*. The Louisiana Waterthrush is an early autumn migrant, leaving its breeding grounds in late July and August. This, coupled with the fact that it has a southerly breeding range, makes it an unlikely candidate for vagrancy to Britain or Ireland. The Louisiana is not difficult to distinguish. It is larger and more elongated, it has a longer, more dagger-like bill, a longer white supercilium (which may curve down to the base of the neck), an unstreaked throat, and it is less heavily streaked and much whiter below (although buffy on the rear flanks). Particularly obvious are its long, pale, bubblegum-pink legs.

COMMON YELLOWTHROAT
Geothlypis trichas

Range Breeds across southern Canada, the USA and northern Mexico, and winters in the southern USA, the West Indies and Central America, although some may remain well to the north of their usual winter range.

Occurrences There are five British records, the male in Plate 89.5 being present on Fetlar, Shetland, on 7–11 June 1984. In addition, there are three autumn records, from Lundy, Devon, in November 1954, from Bryher, Isles of Scilly, in October 1984, and from Bardsey, Caernarfonshire, in October 1996, while another was present at Murston Gravel Pits, Kent, from January to April 1989, at the same time as the Golden-winged Warbler (page 158).

Identification The Common Yellowthroat is an abundant inhabitant of North American swamps and marshes, although it also occurs to some extent in drier habitats. Its loud *witchity witchity witchity* song is one of the most familiar and easily learned of North American bird songs. Unlike most North American wood-warblers, it keeps low in the vegetation and moves rather like an *Acrocephalus* warbler but with a nervous wing- and tail-flicking. As Plate 89.5 shows, it has something of a front-heavy, wren-like shape, with a dumpy body, short wings, a short primary projection, and a short rounded tail which is often cocked and flicked up when excited. The male is distinctive, with its black facial mask (bordered above with white), olive upperparts and yellow throat. Females are much more nondescript, lacking the black mask and appearing plain-headed, apart from a variable incomplete eye-ring and a line of demarcation between the ear-coverts and the throat, this giving something of a hooded impression. Both sexes show noticeably dull pink legs. First-winter males show variable amounts of black feathering on the lores and ear-coverts, this being initially obscured by grey feather tips. They can readily be located by a distinctive low, dry *djip* call, which starts with a definite fricative.

WILSON'S WARBLER
Wilsonia pusilla

Range Breeds from Alaska south through the Rockies to southern California and northern New Mexico and east across Canada to Newfoundland and Nova

Scotia, as well as in some of the bordering states of the USA. It is commoner in the west although it is also one of the five most abundant breeding wood-warblers in Newfoundland (Smaldon, 1990). It winters mainly from northern Mexico south to western Panama (Curson *et al.*, 1994).

Occurrence There is just one Western Palearctic record: a male at Rame Head, Cornwall, on 13 October 1985 (Plate 89.6; Smaldon, 1990). Its south coast location may suggest that it was ship-assisted.

Identification Wilson's Warbler is a small, rather rounded, plump-looking warbler with short wings and a shortish, slightly rounded tail. Its plain body plumage is olive-green above and brilliant yellow below, right down to the undertail-coverts. The male is readily recognizable by its prominent black skull cap and its large black eye. The female is similar but duller and usually has a reduced patchy black cap (sometimes appearing greyish in the field), although this is lacking in first-years. Despite the prominent black cap, the Rame Head bird was most likely a first-winter as an adult-like plumage is acquired after the late-summer post-juvenile moult. It is an active feeder, often drooping its wings and flicking its tail. The Rame bird gave a loud, rather liquid *twick*, as well as a series of *kick-kick-kick* calls that resembled those of the Red-breasted Flycatcher *Ficedula parva* (Smaldon, 1990).

SUMMER TANAGER
Piranga rubra

Range Breeds across the southern two-thirds of the eastern USA (north to southern New Jersey), and then west to southern California and northern Mexico. It winters from south-central Mexico south to Bolivia and Brazil.

Occurrence The sole Western Palearctic record involved a first-winter male trapped on Bardsey, Caernarfonshire, on 11–25 September 1957 (Arthur, 1963). In view of its rather southerly breeding range, this is one of the more surprising North American passerines to have occurred here. It seems that reversed migration was the most likely cause of vagrancy, although ship-assistance may also have been at least partly responsible.

Identification The Bardsey individual is shown in Plates 90.1 & 2. Being in black and white, the photographs show a rather nondescript bird, but perhaps the most obvious feature is the thick, pointed pale-coloured bill. This is, in fact, longer than that of the Scarlet Tanager *P. olivacea*. In real life, it was large –

approaching a Redwing *Turdus iliacus* in size – with a steep forehead and rather short dark legs. It was yellow-green above and deep yellow below (the Summer is more orangey-yellow below than the Scarlet). It was readily identifiable as a first-winter male by the presence of reddish or orange feathers scattered throughout its plumage. Adult males are completely red all year, whereas adult male Scarlets moult into a green and yellow winter plumage (but retain their distinctive black wings and scapulars). Once its sex was established, the lack of black scapulars and wing coverts were an immediate distinction from a first-winter male Scarlet (*see* Plate 90.3). The Bardsey bird perched in the open with rather an upright, shrike-like manner, occasionally making flycatcher-like sallies, but it fed mainly on blackberries. It occasionally flicked its wings, cocked its tail and raised its crown feathers, and was heard to give a *chic* or *chic chic* note when disturbed (loc. cit.).

SCARLET TANAGER
Piranga olivacea

Range Breeds in the eastern USA and adjacent parts of Canada, south to north-eastern Texas, central Alabama and northern Georgia. Winters mainly in north-western South America, from Colombia to north-western Bolivia (*BWP*; Price *et al.*, 1995).

Occurrences There were seven records between 1963 and 1985, all of these individuals arriving between 28 September and 18 October. Apart from the original record in Co. Down, all have occurred in Co. Cork or in the Isles of Scilly and Cornwall.

Identification The adult male Scarlet Tanager, with its intense scarlet plumage and black wings, is one of the most stunning North American birds. Inevitably, the individuals that turn up here are much less eye-catching. Plate 90.3 shows a first-winter male which was present on Tresco, Isles of Scilly, in September–October 1975. It is a bulky bird, larger than a European Greenfinch *Carduelis chloris* and has a noticeably stout, conical pale bill. The round head and bland facial expression (relieved only by a yellow eye-ring) give it rather a pleasant character. In autumn, both sexes are bright lime-green above, this merging imperceptibly into pale yellow underparts which fade on the belly and flanks before turning yellow again on the undertail-coverts. Both adult and first-winter males at this time have solidly black scapulars and inner wing-coverts (they are green on females). The entire wing on adult males is a glossy black, whereas first-winters, like the Tresco bird, have blackish-brown primary coverts and remiges, whose feathers are prominently fringed a yellowish-green

(Pyle *et al.*, 1987). Adult males in autumn may also show an orangey-red tint to the rump, vent and undertail-coverts. The Scarlet Tanager is often rather slow and lethargic in its movements, but it also makes agile flycatching sallies. The call is a low, toneless, hoarse or rasping *chip-burr* or *keep-back* (*BWP*).

LARK SPARROW
Chondestes grammacus

Range Breeds over much of the USA west of the Mississippi, and just creeps into southern Canada. Isolated breeding pockets have also been discovered to the east of its normal range in North Carolina (Brown, 1991). It winters in the southern USA, and south into Mexico and Central America.

Occurrences The Lark Sparrow enjoys the dubious distinction of being one of the most controversial species on the British List. The first occurred at Landguard Point, Suffolk, from 30 June to 8 July 1981 (Charlton, 1995), and, despite the fact that container ships from the USA regularly dock at nearby Felixstowe, it was placed in Category D1 on the grounds that it may have escaped from captivity. This created such widespread dissatisfaction amongst the twitching fraternity that the BOURC eventually reassessed the record. In April 1993, it was finally promoted to Category A, a decision that was perhaps inevitable following the appearance of a second Lark Sparrow at Waxham, Norfolk, on 15–17 May 1991 (Plates 90.4 & 5). A White-throated Sparrow *Zonotrichia albicollis* at Felixstowe in May-June 1992 (Plate 91.3) confirmed the area's potential to produce records of American sparrows.

There can be little doubt that all these birds were ship-assisted. Although the Lark Sparrow does not traditionally breed on the North American east coast, it does occasionally turn up there as a vagrant, and records from Newfoundland and Sable Island, Novia Scotia, clearly indicate that it has the potential to fly out over the western Atlantic. Once this point is established, the possibility of ship-assistance is inevitable.

Identification As Plates 90.4 & 5 clearly show, the Lark Sparrow is one of the most stunning North American sparrows. The head pattern is particularly striking, but it also shows a double black spot in the centre of the breast (not clearly visible in these photographs), double buff wing bars and contrasting white corners to the end of the full, rounded, black tail (these may be particularly prominent in flight). Its call is a high-pitched *seee* or a soft, muffled, barely audible *sic*.

SAVANNAH SPARROW
Passerculus sandwichensis

Range Breeds across virtually the whole of Canada and the northern USA and south down the west coast to Baja California, southern Mexico and Guatemala. It winters mainly from the southern USA through Mexico to Costa Rica, as well as in the West Indies.

Occurrences There are two records. The first was a male at Portland Bill, Dorset, on 11–16 April 1982 (Broyd, 1985), which was, remarkably, of the race *princeps*, formerly split as a separate species known as the 'Ipswich Sparrow'. *Princeps* breeds on Sable Island, described by Godfrey (1966) as 'a desolate, treeless stretch of shifting sand in the Atlantic Ocean, ninety miles [east of] Nova Scotia'. Its entire world population is estimated to be only 2,000–3,000 birds, and it seems that the sub-species is doomed since the island itself is unlikely to last more than a few hundred years (Brown, 1971). It winters from Nova Scotia south to southern Georgia. In spring it migrates up the eastern seaboard during the first two weeks of April, two weeks earlier than the other races of Savannah Sparrow. It then has to head out to reach a tiny fog-shrouded dot in the ocean. Such a migration leaves no room for error, and it would appear that the Portland bird either missed or overshot the island and then continued east across the Atlantic. The orientation of this flight suggests that it could have arrived under its own steam, but ship-assistance is perhaps more likely.

The second record was found at the opposite end of the country and in a different season: a first-winter on Fair Isle, Shetland, on 30 September and 1 October 1987 (Ellis & Riddiford, 1992). This individual was not racially identified although, geographically, it was most likely to have been either *labradorius* or *savanna* from north-eastern Canada (it clearly was not *princeps*). Its occurrence was likely to have been the result of reversed migration across the North Atlantic.

Identification Plate 90.7 shows the Portland Ipswich Sparrow. The pale, greyish plumage is related to its habitat of beaches and dunes. The whole plumage is covered with a confusion of brown streaking and, as such, the bird is somewhat nondescript. The head shows a pale crown stripe, a pale eye-ring, a dark eye-stripe behind the eye, and thin dark moustachial and malar stripes, yet none of these catches the eye. The only feature which really stands out is a noticeably pale yellow fore-supercilium. In comparison with a Song Sparrow *Melospiza melodia*, the Ipswich Sparrow's shape is quite distinctive. It is a bulkier and stockier bird with a large head, a neckless appearance and rather a short tail (the Song is a longer

and slimmer bird). The thick, pointed bill (which has a straight culmen) merges with the head and there is little in the way of a forehead. An important difference from the Song Sparrow is that it has a noticeable cleft in its tail and that the tips of the tail feathers are pointed (the Song has a proportionately longer, slightly rounded tail). The legs are long and orangey-pink, looking very orange in sunlight. It half walks, half hops, and even runs. It feeds rather like a pipit, and it digs around in the grass for grubs and caterpillars. The Portland bird occasionally burst into song, throwing back its head and emitting a high-pitched insect-like buzz, suggesting a speeded-up Corn Bunting *Miliaria calandra* song. It also gave a faint *sip* and a harder *tup*.

Plate 90.6 shows the Fair Isle bird in September 1987. As can clearly be seen, it is much darker and browner, showing blacker streaking and positively chestnut fringes to most of the wing feathers. The fore-supercilium was strikingly lemon-yellow in the field (Ellis & Riddiford, 1992), but it should be noted that, frustratingly, some individuals fail to show this feature. Also in the field, it showed a clumping of the breast streaking to form a central spot (this was much less apparent on the Portland bird), as well as slightly paler outer tail feathers. It was aged in the hand as a first-winter by the shape and amount of wear on the tail feathers (they were more worn and more pointed than those on an adult).

Incidentally, the species is named after the town in Georgia, while the Ipswich Sparrow gets its name from a specimen collected near Ipswich, Massachusetts.

SONG SPARROW
Melospiza melodia

Range Breeds across much of southern Canada and the northern United States, down the Rockies and into Mexico. It winters in the southern part of its range, and in the southern USA and northern Mexico.

Occurrences There were seven records between 1959 and 1994, all in the period April to June with the exception of a heavily twitched individual at Seaforth Docks, Lancashire, in October 1995. As is likely with other North American sparrows, at least some crossed the Atlantic on board ship. Interestingly, five were found on offshore islands, including three on Fair Isle, Shetland.

Identification The bird in Plate 91.2 was present on Fair Isle in April 1989. It is a short-winged, long-tailed sparrow but, plumage-wise, it is rather nondescript, distinctive only for its streakiness. It is perhaps most reminiscent of a Reed Bunting *Emberiza schoeniclus* but, in the field, its lack of white outer tail feathers would be indicative of an American sparrow (note also that the long rufous tail is slightly rounded). Compared with the Reed Bunting, its head markings and the heavy body streaking are far more rufous and the underparts are whiter. Although not apparent in the photograph, most show a dark blotch in the centre of the breast. Note also the grey crown stripe, supercilium and ear-covert surround, and the grey centre to the ear-coverts. In the field, it shows narrow pale tips to the greater coverts and contrasting black centres to the tertials.

It is a furtive, ground-loving species and, in a brief encounter, it may remind one of a Dunnock *Prunella modularis*. Unlike the Reed Bunting, it half hops and half runs, and it may even run at some speed across open ground like a small rodent. Its call is a barely audible *sip*. The Song Sparrow may be confused with the Savannah Sparrow *Passerculus sandwichensis* (Plates 90.6 & 7; *see* page 165 for a discussion of the differences).

WHITE-CROWNED SPARROW
Zonotrichia leucophrys

Range Breeds across northern Canada from Alaska to Newfoundland, and south down the Rockies to California, Arizona and New Mexico. It winters from British Columbia down the west coast, across most of the southern states, up to the Great Lakes and across to North Carolina, as well as south into northern Mexico (Byers *et al.*, 1995).

Occurrences Remarkably, there were two recorded within eight days of each other in the spring of 1977: one trapped on Fair Isle, Shetland, on 15–16 May; and another seen at Horsey Mere, Yorkshire, on 22 May (Broad & Hawley, 1980). They no doubt overshot across the North Atlantic, their arrival coinciding with a Yellow-rumped Warbler *Dendroica coronata* on Fair Isle on the 18th, a Dark-eyed Junco *Junco hyemalis* in Inverness-shire, on the 19th and a Cape May Warbler *D. tigrina* in Renfrewshire on 17 June, but it seems possible that they may have been ship-assisted for at least part of the journey. A third record concerned a widely appreciated first-winter at Seaforth Docks, Lancashire, on 2 October 1995, which had undoubtedly hitched a ride.

Identification The summer adult is most similar to a 'white-striped' White-throated Sparrow *Z. albicollis* (Plate 91.3) but lacks the white throat patch, yellow fore-supercilium and dark grey bill. It shows a sharply defined white supercilium and crown stripe and in the nominate north-eastern race, to which the

British records relate, the black eye-stripe and lateral crown stripe meet in the supra-loral region, the lores themselves being grey. Also, the bill of this race is pinkish (*see* Dunn *et al.*, 1995). The plumage is otherwise similar to that of the White-throated Sparrow.

Plate 91.1 shows the first-winter at Seaforth Docks. It resembles the adult but is browner on the face and shows a brown, as opposed to black, eye-stripe and lateral crown stripe. Like the 1977 adults, the stripes merge in the supra-loral region (again indicating the nominate *leucophrys*). The pink bill is prominent, as is a clear-cut broken double white wing bar. The most frequent call is a sharp *pink* note, and also a thin *see* (Dunn *et al.*, 1995).

WHITE-THROATED SPARROW
Zonotrichia albicollis

Range Breeds mainly across the southern half of Canada (extending into north-eastern USA) and winters mainly in eastern and southern USA and northern Mexico (Byers *et al.*, 1995).

Occurrences Like most North American sparrows, the White-throated occurs here mainly in spring (14 records), particularly in May and early June. There have, however, been seven records in late September– December, with two over-wintering (up to the end of 1996). It is generally accepted that most, if not all, cross the Atlantic on board ship. In addition to these, Evans (1994) noted records in Yorkshire in January 1893 and at least six others which arrived in Southampton on board ship between 1958 and 1962. The individual in Plate 91.3 was photographed at Trimley St Mary, Suffolk, where it was present from 31 May to 8 June 1992. The site is adjacent to Felixstowe Docks, where ships from Montreal and New York had arrived in the two days prior to its discovery (Brame, 1992).

Identification Plate 91.3 shows how distinctive and unmistakable the Suffolk bird was, the striped head, yellow fore-supercilium and large white throat patch grabbing the attention. It should be noted, however, that White-throated Sparrows occur in two distinct plumage types: the so-called 'white-striped', like this bird, and the 'tan-striped', which is altogether duller, browner and far less impressive. The two phases are unrelated to age or sex, although all first-winters resemble the 'tan-striped' (*see* Brewer, 1990). Plate 91.4 shows such a bird, at Willingham, Lincolnshire, in December 1992. The apparently dark (as opposed to reddish-brown) eye would indicate that this is in fact a first-winter (Byers *et al.*, 1995). Its buff crown stripe and supercilium, brown ear-coverts and streaked breast are in marked contrast to the smart plumage of the Suffolk bird. The white throat is much smaller and is reduced by a narrow malar stripe; also, it shows only a small area of yellow on the fore-supercilium. The two forms are otherwise similar, sharing a prominent white greater covert bar, a greyish rump, and a chunky body and long-tailed silhouette.

Rather surprisingly, the White-throated's beautiful, clear, whistling song, variously described as 'Old Sam Peabody, Peabody, Peabody' or 'Pure Sweet Canada, Canada, Canada' (depending, presumably, on which side of the border you originate) is one of the most evocative of North American bird songs. Its calls are far less impressive, a soft *sss* or *sssp*.

DARK-EYED JUNCO
Junco hyemalis

Range Breeds in mixed and coniferous woodland across a large area of northern North America and down the Rockies into northern Mexico. There are 15 races, these formerly having been split into four species: the 'Slate-coloured Junco' in the north; and the 'White-winged', 'Oregon' and 'Grey-headed' Juncos in the west. It moves south to winter in the southern part of its breeding range, in the southern states of the USA and in northern Mexico.

Occurrences There have been 18 widely scattered records to 1995, all but one occurring since 1960 (plus two in 1996). Evans (1994) also traced an additional individual on board the RMS *Mauretania* in Southampton in October 1962. Like the other American sparrows, most have occurred in spring, with a peak in late April and May, but there have also been five arrivals in winter. It seems likely that most, if not all, have been ship-assisted. The species shows a marked predilection for gardens; the individual in Plate 91.5, present at Weston, Portland, Dorset, from December 1989 to April 1990, was discovered by Grahame Walbridge as he was washing up. At the same time, another was discovered at Church Crookham, Hampshire, also in gardens (Plate 91.6). What was remarkable about the latter individual was that it had originally been seen there as a first-summer in May and June 1987. It reappeared in May 1988 and in February 1989, before its more protracted stay from December 1989 to March 1990. This is the only known case of an American passerine returning to the same area in successive years.

Identification With its slate-grey plumage, white belly, sharply pointed pink bill and brilliant white outer tail feathers (obvious in flight), the male Dark-eyed Junco is not difficult to identify. The brown feathering on the crown, back and scapulars, and the

pale brown fringes to the dark brown flight feathers clearly show the Portland bird to be a first-winter. The concurrent Church Crookham individual, being an adult, was altogether greyer and more immaculate. The call is a hard *stt* and a softer *ssp*. In December, the Portland bird was also heard to give sub-song, and by spring it was giving the full song, which is a dry, rising trill, falling in pitch at the end.

PINE BUNTING
Emberiza leucocephalos

Range Breeds right across Siberia from the Urals to the Pacific. It winters from Iran, across northern India to China. Small numbers have also been recorded wintering in Israel and, remarkably, in Italy, where one flock of 45–50 was recorded in 1995/96 (Corso, 1996), with another flock of 20 elsewhere.

Occurrences There were 32 records up to 1995; of these, 21 occurred in the Northern Isles. The peak time is October and early November. The species has, however, also occurred in winter, while four March/April records no doubt related to birds that had wintered further south.

The bird in Plate 92.1 was present at Dagenham Chase, Essex, in February-March 1992, where it was seen by over 2,000 people (Harrap, 1992). It was one of two Pine Buntings recorded that winter, the other being found at Cresswell, Northumberland. The Essex bird echoed a record of a female found dead at

Male Pine Bunting.

the roadside at Ewhurst, Surrey, in January 1989, and strongly suggests that the species winters here more frequently than the handful of records indicates.

Identification The Pine Bunting is very much the eastern equivalent of the Yellowhammer *E. citrinella,* but as that species occurs as far east as Lake Baikal there is a large area of overlap. The species are closely related and hybridization is sometimes recorded, apparently as a result of a recent human-induced breakdown in the ecological barrier between them. A controversial bird at Sizewell, Suffolk, in April 1982 – the notorious 'Sizewell Bunting' – was eventually identified as a hybrid (Lansdown & Charlton, 1990).

Fortunately the Dagenham bird was untainted with such problems. The Pine Bunting is identical in shape and structure to the Yellowhammer and has very similar calls. Plate 92.1 shows it to be very distinctive, with its pale median crown stripe, its chestnut supercilium and throat, and the white patch on the ear-coverts. The plumage shows this individual to be a male, the pale tips to the chestnut head feathering wearing off towards spring. Like the Yellowhammers with which it consorted, it had a chestnut rump and uppertail-coverts but, unlike that species, the rest of its plumage was totally devoid of yellow, the predominant tones being pinkish-buff and white. Sharply pointed tail feathers showed it to be a first-winter. The first step to take when identifying a female Pine Bunting would be to establish a complete lack of yellow, particularly on the fringes to the remiges (in the hand, the Pine should also lack yellow on the underwing-coverts). The identification of females is, of course, complicated by the occurrence of hybrids and by the possibility of female Yellowhammers of the race *erythrogenys* (Russia, east to Siberia) lacking yellow. This is a complex subject and would-be finders should consult detailed texts such as Shirihai *et al.* (1995).

ORTOLAN BUNTING
Emberiza hortulana

Range Breeds in Fenno-Scandia and across much of continental Europe, extending east to Iran in the south and north-western Mongolia in the north. It winters in Africa, along the southern edge of the Sahara, and probably also in the southern part of the Arabian Peninsula (Harrison, 1982).

Occurrences Dymond *et al.* (1989) noted 1,320 during 1958–85, an average of 49 per year. Of these, 30 per cent occurred in spring from mid-April to mid-June, with a peak in early May. The rest occurred in autumn from mid-August to early November, with a peak in September. Spring records were mainly found in Shetland, with smaller numbers down the east coast, but in autumn most occurred in the Southwest Peninsula. It seems likely that spring occurrences relate mainly to displaced Scandinavian migrants, whereas those in autumn are mainly dispersing individuals from the south.

Despite the recent increase in observer numbers, there has been no associated increase in Ortolans, and this is indicative of a real decline in the numbers turning up. There have been worrying population crashes across much of northern Europe, largely related to changes in agricultural practices. In the Netherlands, for example, the species became extinct in 1994 (*Brit. Birds* **88**: 44). Such changes in Britain itself have also affected the numbers recorded; for example, at Portland, Dorset, Britain's premier autumn site, there has been an almost total switch from arable to pastoral farming. Evans (1993a) could trace only 37 British records in 1990 and 38 in 1991, but 81 in 1992 were the product of an excellent 'eastern' spring. These totals are in marked contrast to the numbers that occurred in the 1950s and 1960s, when there were remarkable falls of at least 100 on Bryher, Isles of Scilly, on 25 September 1956, and 32 on Fair Isle, Shetland, on 3 May 1969.

Identification The male in Plate 92.2 was photographed at Minsmere, Suffolk, in May 1990. It is a sleek, compact bunting, with a low forehead and a pointed bill. It is streamlined and in flight it looks almost like a blunt-headed pipit. It is easily identifiable by its grey head and prominent white eye-ring, its yellow submoustachial stripe and throat, and by its pointed pink bill and double white wing bars. A front view would also show a grey breast, demarcated from orange underparts, and pinkish legs. Plate 92.3 shows a very confiding first-winter on Tresco, Isles of Scilly, in October 1988 (in the field it could be aged by its pointed and abraded tail feathers). It differs from the spring male in that it is much browner, particularly about the head, and it shows fine streaking across the crown, breast and flanks. It still shows the yellowish submoustachial stripe and throat, albeit subdued, whilst the underparts are distinctly orangey-buff. An unobtrusive soft, liquid *plip* call (sometimes sounding more of a *plink, tlip* or *tswip*) is often the first indication of the presence of an Ortolan. This call is often given as birds are flushed from autumn stubble fields.

CRETZSCHMAR'S BUNTING
Emberiza caesia

Range Breeds in Greece, Cyprus and southern Turkey, and south into northern Israel and Jordan. It winters almost exclusively in the Sudan.

Occurrences There are just two records, both of males on Fair Isle, Shetland: on 10–20 June 1967 (Dennis, 1969) and 9–10 June 1979 (Oddie, 1981). Both can be attributed to long-range overshooting.

Identification Plates 92.4 & 5 show the 1967 Fair Isle bird. It is similar to the Ortolan Bunting *E. hortulana* but is smaller, shorter billed and shorter tailed (not as 'long and sleek'). The male is easily separated by its blue-grey head, its orange submoustachial stripe and throat, and in dark orange underparts (the Ortolan has a greeny-grey head, yellow submoustachial stripe and throat, and is paler below). Some males completely lack the grey malar stripe, so that the whole throat area appears as a large orange patch. On others, such as the individual in the photographs, the malar stripe is faint and inconspicuous (although its obviousness is dependent on the angle at which it is viewed). The orange extends onto the lores and even the forehead. The female is buffer in tone, with a buff throat and submoustachial stripe, browner ear-coverts, and with light streaking on the crown and breast. Its calls are harder, more abrupt, more metallic, more explosive and less liquid than those of the Ortolan: a *stlip*, *plik*, *tchlip* or *tchlik*. Flocks may even sound somewhat crossbill-like. A quieter *plip* may also be given, but this is rather softer and less liquid than the unusual call of the Ortolan.

YELLOW-BROWED BUNTING
Emberiza chrysophrys

Range Breeds in a relatively restricted area of south-eastern Siberia to the north and east of Lake Baikal, but the full extent of its breeding range is not known. It winters in eastern China.

Occurrences There have been four records: at Holkham, Norfolk, in October 1975; on Fair Isle, Shetland in October 1980; on North Ronaldsay, Orkney, in September 1992; and on St Agnes, Isles of Scilly, in October 1994. Needless to say, the St Agnes bird was appreciated by hundreds. If our knowledge of the breeding range is reliable, then this is one of the most easterly breeding passerines to have occurred in Britain.

Identification Plate 93.1 shows the St Agnes bird. It is a rather bulky, thick-set, heavy billed bunting, most easily identified by its striking head pattern. It shows a clear-cut narrow white crown stripe, blackish lateral crown stripes, and a prominent white supercilium with yellow before and over the eye, the intensity of which shows individual variation from faint to bright. There is a blackish eye-stripe and lower border to the ear-coverts, with a brown centre and a white spot at the rear. A white submoustachial stripe curves up under the ear-coverts and a dark malar stripe broadens on the throat. The whole head pattern is perhaps reminiscent of that of a first-winter Rose-breasted Grosbeak *Pheucticus ludovicianus*. Also distinctive is the presence of profuse but fine streaking right across the white underparts, including the belly and flanks. It otherwise shows a pink bill, with a dark culmen and tip, noticeably pink legs, and two narrow white wing bars. The Fair Isle bird gave a *tic* call, probably indistinguishable from that of a Little Bunting *E. pusilla* (Kitson & Robertson 1983).

RUSTIC BUNTING
Emberiza rustica

Range Breeds in the boreal zone from Scandinavia eastwards across northern Eurasia to the Pacific. It winters mainly in eastern China, Korea and Japan. Small numbers also winter in southern Kazhakstan and in western China (Byers *et al.*, 1995).

Occurrences The Rustic Bunting is principally a late-spring and late-autumn vagrant, with most occurring in the Northern Isles, down the British east coast and in the Isles of Scilly. It remains extremely rare in Ireland (only ten records during 1958–94). Several March records and four recent winter ones indicate that small numbers overwinter in Western Europe but, inevitably, it must be largely overlooked at this time of year. Autumn occurrences no doubt relate mainly to reversed migrants, while those in early spring are probably northward-returning reversed migrants which have wintered further south. Those occurring in late spring are more likely to be mainly Scandinavian-bound birds which have drifted across the North Sea on easterly winds. A record of an individual ringed on Fair Isle, Shetland, on 12 June 1963 and recovered on Chios, Greece, on 15 October the same year clearly indicates that spring drift migrants are to some extent capable of subsequent reorientation. The species averaged six or seven a year from 1958 to 1992 but has increased in recent years, with a remarkable 50 in 1993. Its increase here can be linked to a large increase and westward spread in Fenno-Scandia. For example, although it was first recorded breeding in Sweden only in 1897, there were 50,000 pairs by the 1970s (*BWP*).

Identification The bird in Plate 93.4 was present on Fair Isle in October 1987. Autumn individuals are often difficult to age and sex, but the apparently pointed tail feathers would indicate a first-winter, whilst the rather brownish head markings and poorly marked breast suggest a female. The Rustic Bunting is superficially similar to a Reed Bunting

E. schoeniclus but is colder and less buff, the ground colour of the underparts being noticeably whiter. It can be distinguished from the Reed by the following features: (1) a distinctly crested effect; (2) a prominent creamy-buff supercilium from the eye back (mirrored below the ear-coverts by a prominent buff sub-moustachial stripe); (3) a pale crown stripe, which is most obvious as it runs down the nape (just visible in the photograph); (4) a small buff spot at the rear of the ear-coverts; (5) heavy but diffuse rufous-brown streaking across the breast and down the flanks; and (6) more prominent and more clearly defined whitish wing bars. Plate 93.3 shows another first-winter, on Tresco, Isles of Scilly, in October 1994. Its pointed tail feathers confirm its age, and thick black centres to the crown feathers (with narrow pale fringes), a dark border to the ear-coverts and obvious rufous in the nape, scapulars and breast streaking suggest that it is a male. Plate 93.2 shows a male at Arthog Bog, Caernarfonshire, in April 1991 (this record has never been submitted to the Rarities Committee). It resembles the first-winter in shape and patterning, but the browns on the head are replaced with black. It shows a stunning white supercilium, and the rump, uppertail-coverts, nape, scapulars and underpart streaking are rusty. The latter forms a striking contrast with the pure white background colour. The call is a hard *tsik*, quite unlike the familiar *shwee* of a Reed Bunting.

LITTLE BUNTING
Emberiza pusilla

Range Breeds from Scandinavia east across northern Siberia to the Pacific. It winters from Nepal and north-eastern India to southern China and parts of Southeast Asia.

Occurrences There were 93 records prior to 1958 and 522 between 1958 and 1993, an average of 15 per year. The species has recently shown a marked upsurge, and there were as many as 50 in 1989. As a consequence, it was dropped from the Rarities List at the end of 1993. The increase can be linked to a westward spread into Fenno-Scandia that started in the 1930s (the species first bred in Finland in 1935, and there were about 1,000 pairs in 1988; *BWP*). It is traditionally an autumn migrant, occurring from September to November and with a peak in early October. Most records have come from the Northern Isles, with smaller numbers down the east coast and in Scilly, but it can turn up almost anywhere. There has been a marked upsurge in winter and spring records in recent years, and many of these have been found inland amongst finch and bunting flocks. Those found must inevitably represent the tip of an

iceberg. It seems likely that most of our early spring migrants have moved north after wintering further south, presumably in France and Iberia. The bird in Plate 93.5 was present in a garden in Chippenham, Wiltshire, in March–April 1991.

Identification The Little Bunting is a small, compact bunting, superficially similar to a female Reed Bunting *E. schoeniclus* but readily identifiable given a reasonable view. It has an open-faced expression, this being caused by a prominent buff eye-ring and the lack of a dark loral line and moustachial stripe. Although plumage tone varies between individuals, much of the face is chestnut (adult males in spring are brightest) with a buff spot at the rear. The bill is small and pointed and shows a straight culmen, it has quite a rich buff supercilium and crown stripe, the upperparts are often rather a rich rufous (but sometimes quite grey), and the underparts are neatly streaked across the breast and down the flanks. The wing bars are better defined and more contrasting than on the Reed (the median covert bar is often whiter). Its call also readily distinguishes it from the Reed Bunting: a soft *stic*, similar to the call of a Song Thrush *Turdus philomelos*, or a harder, more emphatic *tic*, more reminiscent of a European Robin *Erithacus rubecula*. Although vagrants are usually associated with weedy fields, spring birds may feed on newly emerging insects right up in the tops of trees.

YELLOW-BREASTED BUNTING
Emberiza aureola

Range Breeds from Finland eastwards across Asia to Kamchatka and Japan. It winters from north-eastern India throughout much of Southeast Asia.

Occurrences Although practically annual in Britain, the Yellow-breasted Bunting is very much a bird of the Northern Isles. Dymond *et al.* (1989) noted that no less than 71 per cent of the records made between 1958 and 1985 were of birds on Fair Isle, Shetland. One must assume that the species' rarity in the south is due to the fact that those which reach this country are reversed migrants on a very precise heading out of north-eastern Europe, one that cuts across only northern Britain (*see* page 15). To illustrate its rarity in the south, there have been only three recorded in the Isles of Scilly (to 1994) and only four in Ireland. It is very much a September bird – and thus earlier than true Siberian vagrants – although early individuals appear at the end of August. There have been five 'spring' records in June–July, presumably involving overshoots (plus another in May 1996). There were only ten records prior to 1958 but it has averaged about four a year from 1958 to 1994, with a peak of ten in 1977. It has spread westwards in recent times, having first bred in Finland in the 1920s, where a recent estimate stands at about 300 pairs (*BWP*). It has, however, shown signs of a decline in recent years so it will be interesting to see how the trend continues.

Identification The individual in Plates 94.1 & 2 was seen as far south as Portland, Dorset, in September 1993. It shows what is, in many ways, a rather nondescript bunting. The underparts are slightly yellow, and it shows a pale crown stripe, a pale supercilium and a 'hollow' centre to the ear-coverts, a double wing bar, and a lightly streaked breast and flanks. Pale 'tramlines' down the mantle are also visible. Some individuals appear to retain at least some juvenile body feathering during their southward migration, thus appearing more heavily streaked on the breast. They also vary in plumage tone, some being yellower than others, although the intensity of the yellow is light-dependent. Adults of the nominate race leave the breeding grounds before moulting and have a complete moult on a stopover in central China (*BWP*). The Portland bird, like all autumn Yellow-breasted Buntings in this country, is in fresh and immaculate first-winter plumage. Plate 94.3 shows a spring male at Sumburgh, Shetland, in May 1996. Its rufous upperparts, black face, chestnut breast band and white median and lower lesser coverts are distinctive. Some of its feathers retained buffish fringes. First-summer males are variable. Whilst some acquire obvious male characters, others are very female-like, retaining a pale crown stripe and supercilium. Such birds should, however, show at least a partial chestnut breast band and some chestnut on the nape. As indicated in Plate 94.1, it often walks rather than hops when feeding, rather like a Lapland Bunting *Calcarius lapponicus*. In the field, a quiet *tsip* or *twik* call may initially attract attention, although this is sometimes a harder *tick*, like the call of a European Robin *Erithacus rubecula*.

BLACK-FACED BUNTING
Emberiza spodocephala

Range The nominate race breeds in eastern Siberia, northern Mongolia and north-eastern China, east from about 90°E to the Pacific. Other races breed in Japan and in central China. It winters in southern Japan, and from eastern Nepal to southern China and Southeast Asia (Bradshaw, 1992).

Occurrence The only record concerns a first-winter male trapped at Pennington Flash Country Park, Lancashire, from 8 March to 24 April 1994. It was feeding on seed put down to attract finches and buntings

for ringing purposes, and it was seen by several thousand people during its protracted stay. The species has occurred several times before in Europe: on Heligoland, Germany, in November 1910 and May 1980; in Finland in November 1981; and first-winter males in the Netherlands in November 1986 and October 1993 (*Brit. Birds* 77: 591; 87: 324).

Identification Plate 94.4 is a fine portrait of the Pennington Flash bird. It could be aged by the pointed tail feathers. With its predominantly grey head and breast, streaked body and double wing bars, it is strongly suggestive of a thick-billed Dunnock *Prunella modularis*. Most distinctive are the pale pink base to the bill and the area of black on the lores and throat. The grey head and pale, washed-out yellow belly are indicative of the Siberian nominate race. The yellow becomes more intense towards the east of the range, with a sharper demarcation from the grey of the breast. Yellower eastern birds have been treated as an additional race '*extremiorientis*' (Byers *et al.*, 1995). The other eastern races, *sordida* and *personata*, are also much yellower below.

The female is a horribly nondescript bird with a pale supercilium, plain face, dark malar stripe and a finely streaked breast and flanks. It is a pale, grey-brown-looking bird, with faint yellowish shading confined to the supercilium and throat. From behind, it may suggest a female House Sparrow *Passer domesticus*.

The Black-faced Bunting feeds unobtrusively, rather like a Little Bunting *E. pusilla*. It sometimes raises its crown feathers to form a distinct crest, and it flicks open its tail when nervous. The call is usually slightly softer than that of a Little Bunting: a *twsik*, *tsik* or *swick*.

PALLAS'S REED BUNTING
Emberiza pallasi

Range Breeds over a large area of central and eastern Siberia, Mongolia, north-western and (probably) north-eastern China. Its range is divided between the tundra in the north and mountains and steppe in the south, with its distribution between being imperfectly known. It winters in northern and eastern China, Korea, Ussuriland and Japan (Byers *et al.*, 1995).

Occurrences There are three records: an adult female on Fair Isle, Shetland, in September–October 1976 (Broad & Oddie, 1980); a juvenile at the same location in September 1981; and a first-winter male trapped at Icklesham, Sussex, in October 1990. As a breeding species, Pallas's Reed Bunting just creeps into the Western Palearctic in the Polar Ural area, and it is thought to be expanding westwards and increasing (Green & Overfield, 1995). Perhaps we can look forward to further records.

Identification Plate 94.5 shows the juvenile on Fair Isle in September 1981. It is similar to a Reed Bunting *E. schoeniclus* but smaller, with something of a sparrow-like jizz. It is a colder-looking bird, its large, pale whitish-grey rump probably being the feature that would initially grab the attention; this may be virtually unstreaked. On some, however, the rump is warm buff, streaked darker (Riddiford & Broome, 1983). The head pattern is markedly different from that of a fresh Reed, having a plain crown, being lightly streaked (and lacking a significant lateral crown stripe), and having a variable creamy-buff supercilium and plain brown ear-coverts (sometimes tinged cinnamon). It lacks a significant dark eye-stripe along the upper edge of the ear-coverts but shows a slight to obvious dark lower border. The overall facial pattern is, therefore, rather plain, and the beady black eye stands out. The malar stripes are often heavy and rather triangular in shape. It shows a greyer nape, upperparts which are heavily streaked black and grey-buff (with two pale 'tramlines' obvious in the field), two whitish wing bars, and rustier fringes to the tertials and secondaries. In a good view, the lesser coverts would appear pale grey (they are chestnut-brown on the Reed). Adult females and first-winters are an almost completely plain sandy-grey below (largely unstreaked) but, as the 1981 Fair Isle bird was quite heavily streaked below, this showed that it had not yet moulted out of juvenile plumage (a minority migrate before moulting; Alström & Olsson 1994). Note also that Pallas's has a straighter culmen than the Reed, whilst the lower mandible is usually contrastingly pale pink (darker in breeding adults). It looks small and compact in flight and the pale rump is obvious; the flight itself is like that of a Reed Bunting. An important difference from the Reed is the call, which is a soft, quiet, sparrow-like *cheeup* or *chleeup*.

A summer male Pallas's Reed Bunting is colder and paler than a male Reed, with a whitish rump and blue-grey lesser coverts. It should be noted that some eastern races of the Reed Bunting are also pale, and one such bird on Tresco, Isles of Scilly, in October 1987, caused considerable interest. It was strikingly pale, only faintly streaked below, and showed a fairly plain, buffy rump. The size, shape, head pattern and chestnut-brown lesser coverts clinched the identification. The call would also have been important had it been heard.

RED-HEADED BUNTING
Emberiza bruniceps

Range Breeds in steppes, semi-deserts and deserts from the northern end of the Caspian Sea east through Kazakhstan into Mongolia and north-western China, and south into Iran, Afghanistan and Pakistan. It winters in Pakistan and India in similar habitats to the Black-headed Bunting *E. melanocephala* (*BWP*, Byers *et al.*, 1995).

Occurrences The occurrence of this species in Britain and Ireland has always been the subject of controversy. It was accepted onto the British List on the basis of a record on North Ronaldsay, Orkney, in June 1931 but, following a protracted debate in the pages of *British Birds* (**60**: 344–347 and 423–426; **61**: 41–43), it was removed from the list in 1968. At that time, very large numbers were being imported from India, not only into Britain but also into the Low Countries. Dennis (1968) described how four of 21 seen on Fair Isle between 1950 and 1967 showed evidence of having been in captivity; one even bore an avicultural ring. It is thought that these birds had escaped on the Continent and had headed north-west in response to their normal migratory urges.

Current records continue to be treated with derision, but are we correct to perpetuate this negative view? Evans (1994) discovered no less than 291 records in Britain up to 1990, the occurrence patterns mirroring very closely those of the Black-headed Bunting, most of which are now accepted as being wild. Large numbers of cagebirds are apparently no longer exported from India, and it seems clear that the Red-headed Bunting is now much less numerous in captivity. Despite this, small numbers continue to turn up. Given the orientation of the species' migration route, it would be astonishing if it *hadn't* occurred here as a spring overshoot and, by treating all records as escapes, there can be little doubt that we have thrown out the baby with the bath water. Perhaps the time has come to re-evaluate the situation.

Identification The male in Plate 95.1 was present in an urban garden in Ipswich, Suffolk, in May 1993. It is immediately distinguishable from the closely related Black-headed Bunting by its reddish head, throat and breast, by its streaked yellowish back and scapulars, and by its yellow rump. Vagrants/escapes have been heard to give a soft, quiet *chlick*.

Plate 95.2 shows a controversial first-winter which was present on Tresco, St Martin's and St Mary's, Isles of Scilly, in October 1994. It can be aged as a first-winter by fine streaking on the breast (visible in the field) and by clear-cut, contrasting creamy-buff fringes to all the remiges, which were quite fresh (note that adults do not complete their moult until they reach their winter quarters). First-winter Red-headed and Black-headed Buntings are notoriously difficult to separate. Both are basically pale sandy-brown above, lack strong head markings and are buff below, becoming yellow on the undertail-coverts. Neither shows white outer tail feathers (although the Scilly bird was greyish-white on the outer web and on the distal half of the inner web). Byers *et al.* (1995) note that, on average, first-winter Red-headed is slightly smaller, with a shorter, more conical bill, the ear-coverts contrast less with the throat, the mantle is more distinctly streaked and the back (as opposed to the mantle) is sandy-brown, never showing a rufous tint. All these features held true for the Scilly bird. There was a strong feeling that, in the field, its jizz did not look right for Black-headed, being rather small, small-billed and round-headed, lacking the long-billed 'weaver-like' feel of the Black-headed. It gave various calls: a throaty *tulip tulip* when at rest, and a soft *wip* or *chip* in flight. Whilst it can perhaps be said that the Scilly bird failed to show any positive Black-headed features, on present knowledge it is best left unidentified.

BLACK-HEADED BUNTING
Emberiza melanocephala

Range Breeds from Italy, former Yugoslavia and the Balkans east through Asia Minor to Iran, as well as between the Black and Caspian seas. It winters in western and central India.

Occurrences The Black-headed Bunting is mainly an overshooting spring migrant, with a peak in May, although it has occurred right through to October. There were 123 records up to 1995, scattered from Shetland to Scilly. Surprisingly, it has a tendency to occur on the west coast, although there have been only four in Ireland (Millington, 1995). Occurrences have been traditionally tainted with the escape problem. Whilst it is likely that escapes have occurred, it is now generally accepted that most, particularly those in late spring, relate to genuine vagrants. This theory is backed by the fact that it has shown no sign of a decrease here, despite the fact that imports have apparently been banned since 1984 (Evans, 1994).

Identification The Black-headed is a large, rather weaver-like bunting, showing a large, long bill (recalling that of a tanager, *Piranga*), a flat forehead and only dull off-white coloration in the outer tail feathers. The vast majority of records have related to spring males, which are very striking and easily identified, – like the one in Plate 95.4, taken on St Martin's, Isles of Scilly, in May 1992. It seems that first-summers are duller, retaining pale tips to their body feathers, rather like the bird in Plate 95.5, which was present at Fishguard, Pembrokeshire, in

May 1995. Following a variable late-summer body moult, at least some of the spring finery of autumn males is partially concealed by pale feather fringes. Spring females are a different kettle of fish since they are dull, nondescript and difficult to distinguish from the closely related Red-headed Bunting *E. bruniceps*. Would-be observers should consult more detailed texts such as Byers *et al.* (1995). Plate 95.3 shows such a bird at Birling Gap, Sussex, in June 1994. Fairbank (1994) considered that it was probably a Black-headed, based on the fact that it had a large and long bill, streaked forecrown, pure white tips to the median coverts, rufous scapular fringes and diffusely brown-streaked mantle. Also, the primary projection looked quite long. Some show rufous in the mantle and a 'ghost' of the male's dark crown; these are more easily identified. The separation of first-winters is discussed above. The usual flight call is a soft, metallic *tlip*, or a liquid *quilip*. Other calls include a brief, ringing *pitoop* (vaguely reminiscent of that of the European Goldfinch *Carduelis carduelis*), a quick, musical *pleet-up* and a deep *djup*.

ROSE-BREASTED GROSBEAK
Pheucticus ludovicianus

Range Breeds from north-eastern British Columbia east across southern Canada to Nova Scotia, as well as in the north-eastern quarter of the USA. It winters from central Mexico south to Ecuador, Colombia and Venezuela (Godfrey, 1966).

Occurrences There were 24 recorded between 1962 and 1995, all except one occurring in late September to early November. There is a distinct southwesterly bias to the records, with most in Co. Cork and, particularly, in the Isles of Scilly, where there have been ten. All have been first-winters, 15 of them males and nine females. The exception to the pattern was a first-winter male at Leigh-on-Sea, Essex, from 20 December 1975 to 4 January 1976.

Identification The Rose-breasted Grosbeak is a large, finch-like bird, about the size of a Corn Bunting *Miliaria calandra*, with a large head and a massive dark pink bill. The plumage of first-winters is similarly striking, with an ill-defined pale brown crown stripe, a long white supercilium (sometimes upcurved at the rear), a white crescent immediately below the eye, and a broad swathe of white curving from the throat under the ear-coverts to the sides of the neck. The upperparts are brown, streaked black, and on the wing there is a thick white bar across the median coverts, thick white tips to the greater coverts, white spots at the tips of the tertials and a white patch at the base of the primaries. The underparts of first-winter males are yellowy-buff, lightly streaked, and they show a variable rose-pink patch in the centre of the breast. First-winter females are less yellow below and lack the pink patch. When they take to the air, first-winters are readily sexed: males flash brilliant red underwing-coverts, females yellow.

Vagrants are usually found sitting unobtrusively in brambles munching blackberries, and this often leads to bill and facial staining. They will also eat elderberries and other fruit, while an individual on Tresco, Isles of Scilly, spent much of its time picking aphids off the bottoms of Sycamore *Acer pseudoplatanus* leaves (Plate 96.1). When feeding more actively, their movements are heavy and almost clumsy. They look large and heavy in flight, and have an abrupt, loud, thick, high-pitched, squeaky *seep* or *chip*.

INDIGO BUNTING
Passerina cyanea

Range Breeds in the eastern USA and in adjacent parts of southern Canada. Since the 1940s, its range has also expanded south-westwards into Utah, New Mexico, Arizona and south-eastern California. It winters in southern Florida, the West Indies and from central Mexico to Panama, with a few in Colombia and north-western Venezuela.

Occurrences The only record accepted into Category A of the British and Irish List was a first-winter on Cape Clear Island, Co. Cork, from 9–19 October 1985, its arrival coinciding with a record influx of North American landbirds, found mainly in south-western England and southern Ireland. Two October records from Iceland, including one in 1985, support the acceptance of the Irish bird. Two British records also have good credentials: an adult male at Holkham, Norfolk, from 21 October to 2 November 1988, and a female or first-winter male on Ramsey Island, Pembrokeshire, from 18–26 October 1996. Four other records are more contentious. A male on Fair Isle, Shetland, in August 1964, a male at The Naze, Essex, in September 1973, a female on Fair Isle in May 1974, and a male at Flamborough Head, Yorkshire, in May 1989. Simpson (1990) suggested that the species is now rare in captivity. Its increase and spread in North America is thought to be related to forest clearance in its winter quarters in Mexico and Central America (Guadagno, 1995). Perhaps we can look forward to more on this side of the Atlantic.

Identification The summer adult male is readily identifiable by its electric blue plumage which 'shimmers jewel-like in the sun' (Manry, 1995). First-

summer males acquire variable amounts of blue but always retain brown primary coverts and inner remiges (Pyle *et al.*, 1987). Females are a nondescript brown above and buffy below, sometimes rather gingery. They have a conical bill with a grey lower mandible, a faint pale eye-ring, indistinct wing bars, and sometimes a tint of blue in the wings, rump and tail. The tail is often dipped and swished. The calls include a harsh but thin *skier* and an abrupt *tip*.

Plate 96.2 shows the adult male at Holkham in October 1988. As is usual, its plumage is a patchy mixture of brown and blue. It can be aged by the blue fringes to the primaries and secondaries. An advanced first-year would show blue fringes to only the outer four to six primaries, these contrasting with the brown-fringed inner primaries, secondaries and primary coverts (Pyle *et al.*, 1987; Curson, 1990).

BOBOLINK
Dolichonyx oryzivorus

Range Breeds in fields and meadows across a wide band of southern Canada and the northern United States. In autumn, it migrates down the eastern seaboard to winter in the pampas of eastern Bolivia, western Brazil, Paraguay and northern Argentina.

Occurrences There were 19 records from 1962 to 1996, with 11 of these occurring in the Isles of Scilly. Surprisingly, there have been only two mainland records, the first as recent as 1991. All the records have occurred in autumn, from mid-September to mid-October. Unlike many other transatlantic passerine vagrants, records of this species are untainted with arguments concerning ship-assistance. This is due to the fact that the Bobolink is an extremely long-range migrant, its annual 12,000-mile (19,000 km) travels being longer than those of any other North American passerine. Although the species has spread westwards in historical times, the entire population moves east in autumn to follow a traditional path through the eastern and south-eastern United States and then across the Gulf of Mexico to South America. Bobolinks put on huge amounts of fat before migration – they can more than double their weight to around 2 oz (50 g) – and calculations have revealed that they are capable of travelling for a staggering 80 hours and covering 3,000 miles (4,800 km) without stopping. In Jamaica, where they are sometimes killed for food, they are still known as 'Butterbirds' because of the amount of fat on their bodies (Parslow, 1971).

In North America, the species spread considerably with the increase of agriculture, and when rice was grown in the south-eastern United States migrant

Bobolink.

Bobolinks became a serious agricultural pest in both spring and autumn. They were then slaughtered in immense numbers until earlier in the 20th century, when the rice-growing area shifted westwards to Louisiana and Texas, a region where Bobolinks do not normally occur on migration (loc. cit.).

Identification The individual in Plate 96.3 was photographed at East Soar, Devon, in September 1991. The tapered ends of the tail feathers show that it is a first-winter as, no doubt, are all our vagrant Bobolinks. (Adults have more truncated tail feathers, although the tips themselves are still pointed.) The Bobolink is a largish bird, about the size of a Corn Bunting *Miliaria calandra*, with a pointed, conical bill that merges with the forehead to form a flat head profile. Photographs seldom do these birds justice, but the immaculately patterned plumage and the gentle, open-faced expression make the Bobolink a great favourite amongst birders. Its overall appearance is similar to that of a giant Aquatic Warbler *Acrocephalus paludicola*, with its orangey-brown crown stripe, blackish lateral crown stripes, prominent orangey-buff supercilium, blackish eye-stripe and plain, pale grey lores. The underparts, unfortunately not visible in the photograph, are a beautiful plain yellowy-buff, with streaking confined to the sides of the breast and flanks; in good light they may appear appreciably yellower than anticipated. The long primary projection, the pointed tail feathers and the lack of white outer tail feathers immediately distinguish it from the superficially similar Yellow-breasted Bunting *Emberiza aureola* (*see* Plates 94.1 & 2). Vagrants can be surprisingly elusive, feeding in long grass and in weedy fields, where they often walk around catching craneflies. They have even been seen flying up from the ground to catch flying ants. In flight, they look sleek and yellow, the flight itself being slightly undulating. They often draw attention to themselves by a distinctive soft *wink* or *wick* call.

YELLOW-HEADED BLACKBIRD
Xanthocephalus xanthocephalus

Range Breeds predominantly in western North America, from British Columbia east to western Ontario and north-western Ohio, and south-west to northern Texas and northern Baja California. It winters from southern California, New Mexico and Texas south to southern Mexico (Godfrey, 1966).

Occurrences There have been five British records, but the first three – Leighton Moss, Lancashire (August 1964), Seaton Burn, Northumberland (July 1965) and Sandbach, Cheshire (September 1970) – are likely to have escaped from captivity, given their dates of occurrence and the fact that the species was imported from Mexico at that time. Two recent records on Unst and Yell, Shetland, on 10–13 May 1987, and on Fair Isle, Shetland, on 26–30 April 1990, are more interesting. The first occurred at the same time and in the same place as a White-throated Sparrow *Zonotrichia albicollis* (on 13–15 May), while the second coincided with above-average numbers of Yellow-headed Blackbirds in the north-eastern USA.

As the species has a relatively westerly breeding range it may seem an unlikely candidate for natural vagrancy to Britain, but it is conceivable that spring migrants heading north-east from Mexico or the south-western USA towards the Great Lakes may overshoot and keep going until they reach northern Britain. Records of males from Iceland (July 1983) and Norway (May 1979), and also from Greenland, would tie in with this theory, the northerly occurrence patterns correlating with other spring records of North American overshoots. The species has even been noted at sea in the western Atlantic (including a flock of 30 observed 350 miles, or 560 km, north-east of New York), so its occurrence here may not be as unlikely as it at first appears. It is disappointing to note, however, that the species was observed in the

Antwerp bird markets as recently as 1989, so there is the more mundane possibility that the Shetland individuals had escaped on the Continent and headed north in spring across the North Sea.

Identification Plate 96.4 shows the male on Fair Isle in April 1990. With its thick, pointed bill, yellow head and upper breast, black body and large white wing patches, it is quite unmistakable. It appears to be a first-summer: the tail feather tips appear to be pointed (apart from one still-growing adult-type feather), the yellow is rather dull, and it shows brown on the crown and nape, dull brownish-black body plumage, dull remiges and faint pale tips to the remiges, greater coverts and tertials. Unfortunately, it had lost its right eye. The female is brown with a dull yellow supercilium, throat and breast 'like leftover paint from a dried-out brush' (De Vore, 1992). Its voice is described as harsh and rasping, with guttural notes and a low, monosyllabic *krack* or *kack* (*BWP*).

BALTIMORE ORIOLE
Icterus galbula

Range Breeds east of the Rockies from Alberta across southern Canada to Nova Scotia, and in the eastern half of the USA south to northern Texas and Louisiana. It winters mainly from Mexico to north-western South America. Hybridization with Bullock's Oriole *I. bullockii*, occurs in the Great Plains, but this has been exacerbated by the planting of trees which

has enabled both species to spread into areas in which neither formerly occurred. The hybrid zone seems to have remained stable and the two forms have elsewhere remained distinct (Jackson, 1993). They are now once again split as two separate species (DeBenedictis, 1996).

Occurrences There were 19 acceptable records up to 1996. The peak time has been late September to early October, and no less than seven occurred in the three years 1966–68. There have been two spring records and, remarkably, three in winter. The bird in Plate 96.5 was a first-winter female present at Roch, Pembrokeshire, in January–April 1989. Its survival depended on the generous provision of suitable food, such as sugared water and fruit. A first-winter male at Westcliff-on-Sea, Essex, in the winter of 1991/92, survived in the same way. This behaviour is not unique to this side of the Atlantic as some in North America winter at feeding stations as far north as New York (Jackson, 1993).

Identification Plate 96.5 is somewhat unusual in that it depicts this essential arboreal species hopping around on the ground. In a British context, the combination of the hefty, sharply pointed pale grey bill, the deep orange-yellow head, underparts and tail, the grey mantle and rump and the conspicuous double white wing bars render the species unmistakable. An adult female would have shown black mottling on the crown and back. A thick, musical, sparrow-like *chowee* or *chu-it* may initially attract attention.

APPENDIX

Species for which no photographs of the live wild birds that were seen in Britain and Ireland exist or can be traced.

B = Category B species (not seen since at least 31 December 1957).

I = Recorded only in Ireland.

Soft-plumaged Petrel species *Pterodroma feae/-madeira/mollis*
Capped Petrel *P. hasitata* (B)
Bulwer's Petrel *Bulweria bulwerii*
White-faced Storm-petrel *Pelagodroma marina* (B)
Madeiran Storm-petrel *Oceanodroma castro* (B)
Magnificent Frigatebird *Fregata magnificens* (B)
Barrow's Goldeneye *Bucephala islandica*
Hooded Merganser *Lophodytes cucullatus* (B)
Egyptian Vulture *Neophron percnopterus*
Griffon Vulture *Gyps fulvus* (B)
Spotted Eagle *Aquila clanga* (B)
Eleonora's Falcon *Falco eleonorae*
Allen's Gallinule *Porphyrula alleni* (B)
American Purple Gallinule *P. martinica*
Short-billed Dowitcher *Limnodromus griseus* (I)
Eskimo Curlew *Numenius borealis* (B)
Great Black-headed Gull *Larus ichthyaetus* (B)

Royal Tern *Sterna maxima*
Least Tern *S. antillarum*
Red-necked Nightjar *Caprimulgus ruficollis* (B)
Egyptian Nightjar *C. aegyptius*
Northern Flicker *Colaptes auratus* (I)
Eastern Phoebe *Sayornis phoebe*
White-winged Lark *Melanocorypha leucoptera*
Lesser Short-toed Lark *Calandrella rufescens*
Crested Lark *Galerida cristata*
Crag Martin *Ptyonoprogne rupestris*
Grey Catbird *Dumetella carolinensis* (I)
Blue Rock Thrush *Monticola solitarius*
Wood Thrush *Hylocichla mustelina*
Fan-tailed Warbler *Cisticola juncidis*
Moustached Warbler *Acrocephalus melanopogon*
Thick-billed Warbler *A. aedon*
Rock Sparrow *Petronia petronia*
Evening Grosbeak *Hesperiphona vespertina*
Chestnut-sided Warbler *Dendroica pensylvanica*
Blackburnian Warbler *D. fusca*
Cape May Warbler *D. tigrina*
Magnolia Warbler *D. magnolia*
Hooded Warbler *Wilsonia citrina*
Eastern Towhee *Pipilo erythrophthalmus*
Fox Sparrow *Passerella iliaca* (I)
Rock Bunting *Emberiza cia*
Brown-headed Cowbird *Molothrus ater*

Male Barrow's Goldeneyes.

BIBLIOGRAPHY

GENERAL REFERENCES

BB = *British Birds*
BW = *Birding World*

CRAMP, S. (ed.). 1977–94. *Handbook of the Birds of Europe, the Middle East and North Africa. The Birds of the Western Palearctic.* Oxford University Press. Oxford. 9 vols. (= *BWP*)

DYMOND, J. N., FRASER, P. A. & GANTLETT, S. J. M. 1989. *Rare Birds in Britain and Ireland.* T. & A. D. Poyser. Calton.

EVANS, L. G. R. 1994. *Rare Birds in Britain 1800–1990.* Privately published.

HARRISON, P. 1983. *Seabirds – An Identification Guide.* Croom Helm. London.

LEWINGTON, I., ALSTRÖM, P. & COLSTON, P. 1991. *A Field Guide to the Rare Birds of Britain and Europe.* Harper Collins. London.

MADGE, S. & BURN, H. 1988. *Wildfowl: an Identification Guide to the Ducks, Geese and Swans of the World.* Helm. Bromley.

SVENSSON, L. 1992. *Identification Guide to European Passerines.* 4th edn. Stockholm.

Also the annual 'Reports on Rare Birds in Britain' in *BB.*

SPECIFIC REFERENCES

ALEY, J. & ALEY, R. 1995. Red-breasted Nuthatch in Norfolk: new to Britain and Ireland. *BB* **88**: 150–153.

ALISON, R. 1993. Decline of the American Black Duck. Hybridization with Mallards threatens Black Ducks as a pure species. *Wild Bird* (April 1993): 42–43.

ALLPORT, A. M. & CARROLL, D. 1989. Little Bitterns breeding in South Yorkshire. *BB* **82**: 442–446.

ALLSOPP, E. M. P. 1972. Veery in Cornwall: a species new to Britain and Ireland. *BB* **65**: 45–49.

ALLSOPP, J. & MASON, P. 1993. in GIBBONS, D. W., REID J. B. & CHAPMAN, R. A. (Eds) *The New Atlas of Breeding Birds in Britain and Ireland: 1988–1991.* BTO. London.

ALSTRÖM, P. & OLSSON, U. 1994. Identification of Pallas's Reed Bunting. *BW* **7**: 15–20.

ARTHUR, R. W. 1963. Summer Tanager in Caernarvonshire: a species new to Great Britain and Ireland *BB* **56**: 49–51.

BARRETT, M. 1992. Moussier's Redstart: new to Britain and Ireland. *BB* **85**: 108–111.

BECKER, P. 1995. Identification of Water Rail and *Porzana* crakes in Europe. *Dutch Birding* **17**: 181–211.

BIRCH, A. 1994. Yellow-throated Vireo: new to Britain and Ireland. *BB* **87**: 362–365.

BLICK, M. 1989. Double-crested Cormorant – a new Western Palearctic bird. *BW* **2**: 53–57.

BRADSHAW, C. 1992. Field identification of Black-faced Bunting. *BB* **85**: 653–665.

BRADSHAW, C. 1993. Separating juvenile Little and Baillon's Crakes in the field. *BB* **86**: 303–311.

BRADSHAW, C., on behalf of the Rarities Committee. 1994. Blyth's Pipit identification. *BB* **87**: 136–142.

BRADSHAW, C., JEPSON, P. J. & LINDSEY, N. J. 1991. Identification of brown flycatchers. *BB* **84**: 527–542.

BRAME, W. 1992. The White-throated Sparrow in Suffolk. *BW* **5**: 218–219.

BREWER, D. 1990. Ageing of White-throated Sparrows. *BB* **83**: 289–291.

BROAD, R. A. 1979. Hermit Thrush: new to Britain and Ireland. *BB* **72**: 414–417.

BROAD, R. A. 1981. Tennessee Warblers: new to Britain and Ireland. *BB* **74**: 90–94.

BROAD, R. A. & HAWLEY, R. G. 1980. White-crowned Sparrows: new to Britain and Ireland. *BB* **73**: 466–470.

BROAD, R. A. & ODDIE, W. E. 1980. Pallas's Reed Bunting: new to Britain and Ireland. *BB* **73**: 402–408.

BROOME, A. 1995. Ruddy Shelducks in Cheshire and Wirral. *Cheshire and Wirral Bird Report 1994.*

BROWN, B. J. 1986. White-crowned Black Wheatear: new to Britain and Ireland. *BB* **79**: 221–227.

BROWN, B. J. 1991. Lark Sparrow distribution changes. *BW* **4**: 212–213.

BROWN, R. G. B. 1971. Ipswich and Savannah Sparrows. In Gooders, J. (Ed) *Birds of the World.* Vol 8. London. IPC Magazines.

BROYD, S. J. 1985. Savannah Sparrow: new to the Western Palaearctic. *BB* **78**: 647–656.

BURNS, D. W. 1993. Oriental Pratincole: new to the Western Palearctic. *BB* **86**: 115–120.

BUTTLE, C. 1995. The Olivaceous Warbler in Suffolk. *BW* **8**: 293–294.

BYERS, C., OLSSON, U. & CURSON, J. 1995. *Buntings and Sparrows. A Guide to the Buntings and North American Sparrows.* Pica Press. East Sussex.

CAMPEY, R. & MORTIMER, K. 1990. Ancient Murrelet on Lundy – a new Western Palearctic bird. *BW* **3**: 211–212.

CAREY, C. J. 1993. Hybrid male Wigeon in east Asia. *Hong Kong Bird Report 1992:* 160–166.

CATLEY, G. P. & HURSTHOUSE, D. 1995. Parrot Crossbills in Britain. *BB* 78: 482–505.

CAVE, B. 1982. Forster's Tern: new to Britain and Ireland. *BB* 75: 55–61.

CHARLTON, T. D. 1995. Lark Sparrow in Suffolk: new to the Western Palearctic. *BB* 88: 395–400.

CLAFTON, F. R. 1972. Desert Warbler in Dorset: a species new to Britain and Ireland. *BB* 65: 460–464.

CLEMENT, P. 1987. Field identification of west Palearctic wheatears. *BB* 80: 137–157 and 187–238.

CLEMENT, P. 1995. Southern and eastern races of Great Grey Shrikes in northwest Europe. *BW* 8: 300–309.

CONDER, P. J. & KEIGHLEY, J. 1949. Bonelli's Warbler in Pembrokeshire: a species new to Great Britain and Ireland. *BB* 42: 215–216.

CONNIFF, R. 1991. Why catfish farmers want to throttle the crow of the sea. *Smithsonian* 22: 44–55.

CORSO, A. 1996. The Pine Buntings in Italy. *BW* 9: 14.

COX, S. & INSKIPP, T. P. 1978. Male Citrine Wagtail feeding young wagtails in Essex. *BB* 71: 209–213.

CRANSWICK, P. A., KIRBY, J. S. & WATERS, R. J. 1992. *Wildfowl and Wader Counts 1991–92.* Wildfowl and Wetlands Trust. Slimbridge.

CROSBY, M. J. 1988. Cliff Swallow: new to Britain and Ireland. *BB* 81: 449–452.

CUBITT, M. G. 1995. Swinhoe's Storm-petrels at Tynemouth: new to Britain and Ireland. *BB* 88: 342–348.

CURSON, J., QUINN, D. & BEADLE, D. 1994. *New World Warblers.* Christopher Helm. London.

CZAPLAK, D. 1995. Identifying Common and Hoary Redpolls in winter. *Birding* 27: 446–457.

DAGLEY, J. R. 1994. Golden Orioles in East Anglia and their conservation. *BB* 87: 205–219.

DAUNICHT, W. D. 1991. Unterscheidungsmerkmale in Grossgefieder von Wald – *Certhia familiaris* und Gartenbaumläuter *C. brachydactyla*. *Limicola* 5: 49–64.

DAVIS, P. 1962. River Warbler in Shetland: a species new to Great Britain and Ireland. *BB* 55: 137–138.

DAVIS, P. 1966. The great immigration of early September 1965. *BB* 59: 353–376.

DAWSON, J. 1994. Ageing and sexing of King Eiders. *BB* 87: 37–40.

DEAN, A. R., FORTEY, J. E. & PHILLIPS, E. G. 1977. White-tailed Plover: new to Britain and Ireland. *BB* 70: 465–471.

DEBENEDICTIS, P. A. 1996. Fortieth Supplement to the *AOU Checklist. Birding* 3: 228–231.

DELIN, H. & SVENSSON, L. 1990. *Photographic Guide to the Birds of Britain and Europe* (Revised edn). Hamlyn. London.

DEL NEVO, A. 1994. White-throated Robin in the Isle of Man: new to Britain and Ireland. *BB* 87: 63–86.

DENNIS, R. H. 1967. Olive-backed Pipits on Fair Isle: a species new to Britain and Ireland. *BB* 60: 161–166.

DENNIS, R. H. 1968. Red-headed Buntings on Fair Isle during 1950–76. *BB* 61: 41–43.

DENNIS, R. H. 1969. Cretzschmar's Bunting on Fair Isle: new to Britain and Ireland. *BB* 74: 532–533.

DE VORE, S. 1992. Cattail Copperhead. *Birders' World* (April 1992): 12–15.

DIXEY, A. E., FERGUSON, A., HEYWOOD, R. & TAYLOR, A. R. 1981. Aleutian Tern: new to the Western Palearctic. *BB* 74: 411–416.

DOHERTY, P. 1989. Golden-winged Warbler in Kent. A new Western Palearctic Bird. *BW* 2: 48–52.

DOHERTY, P. 1992. Golden-winged Warbler: new to the Western Palearctic. *BB* 85: 595–600.

DOWDALL, J. F. 1995. Philadelphia Vireo: new to the Western Palearctic. *BB* 88: 474–477.

DUBOIS, P. J. 1991. Identification forum: Royal, Lesser Crested and Elegant Terns. *BW* 4: 120–123.

DUBOIS, P. & C. H. N. 1990. Les Observations d'espèces soumises à homologation nationale en 1989. *Alauda* 58: 245–266.

DUKES, P. A. 1980. Semipalmated Plover: new to Britain and Ireland. *BB* 73: 458–464.

DUNN, J. L. 1979. Black, Vaux's and Chimney Swifts. *Western Tanager* (June 1979): 11.

DUNN, J. L. 1993. Identification of Semipalmated and Common Ringed Plovers in alternate plumage. *Birding* 25: 238–243.

DUNN, J. L., GARRETT, K. L. & ALDEFER, J. K. 1995. White-crowned Sparrow subspecies: identification and distribution. *Birding* 27: 182–200.

DUNNETT, J. B. 1992. Long-toed Stint: new to Britain and Ireland. *BB* 85: 429–436.

EBELS, E. B. & VAN DER LAAN, J. 1994. Occurrence of Blue-cheeked Bee-eater in Europe. *Dutch Birding* 16: 95–101.

ELDRIDGE, M. & HARROP, A. 1992. Identification and status of Baikal Teal. *BW* 5: 417–423.

ELLIS, P. M. 1992. Great Knot: new to Britain and Ireland. *BB* 85: 426–428.

ELLIS, P. M. & RIDDIFORD, N. J. 1992. Savannah Sparrow in Shetland: second record for the Western Palearctic. *BB* 85: 561–564.

ELLIS, P. M., JACKSON, W. & SUDDABY, D. 1994. The Blyth's Reed Warbler in Shetland. *BW* 7: 227–230.

ELMBERG, J. 1992. Arctic Norway: spectacular and accessible winter birding. *BW* 5: 17–23.

EVANS, G. H. 1965. Yellow Warbler on Bardsey Island. *BB* 58: 457–461.

EVANS, L. G. R. 1992. *Rare Birds in Britain in 1991.* Privately published.

EVANS, L. G. R. 1993a. *Rare Birds in Britain in 1992.* Privately published.

EVANS, L. G. R. 1993b. The Isles of Scilly Blyth's Pipit. *BW* 6: 398–400.

FAIRBANK, R. 1994. Black-headed Bunting identification. *BW* 7: 319.

FAIRCLOUGH, K. 1995. The Pallid Harrier in Orkney. *BW* 8: 253–255.

FERGUSON-LEES, I. J. 1968. Serins breeding in southern England. *BB* 51: 87–88.

FERGUSON-LEES, I. J. 1969a. Studies of less familiar birds. 153. Red-throated Pipit. *BB* 62: 110–115.

FERGUSON-LEES, I. J. 1969b. Rose-coloured Starling. In Gooders, J. (Ed.) *Birds of the World.* Vol 9. London. IPC Magazines.

FLOWER, G. 1983. Hybrid Coot × Moorhen in North Yorkshire. *BB* 76: 409–410.

FORSMAN, D. 1995. Field identification of female and juvenile Montagu's and Pallid Harriers. *Dutch Birding* 17: 41–54.

FRANSSON, T. & STOLT, B.-O. 1993. Is there an autumn migration of Continental Blackcaps (*Sylvia atricapilla*) into northern Europe? *Die Vogelwarte* 37: 89–95.

FRASER, P. A. & RYAN, J. F. 1992. Scarce migrants in Britain and Ireland. Part 1. Numbers during 1986–90: seabirds to waders. *BB* 85: 631–635.

FRASER, P. A. & RYAN, J. F. 1994. Scarce migrants in Britain and Ireland. Part 2. Numbers during 1986–92: gulls to passerines. *BB* 87: 605–612.

GODFREY, W. E. 1966. *The Birds of Canada.* Ottawa.

GOOD, J. B. 1991. Philadelphia Vireo in Scilly: new to Britain and Ireland. *BB* 84: 572–574.

GOODERS, J. (Ed.). 1969. *Birds of the World.* London. IPC Magazines.

GORMAN, G. 1996. Red-breasted Geese wintering in Europe. *BW* 9: 15–17.

GRANT, P. J. 1986. *Gulls: a Guide to Identification.* 2nd edition. T. & A. D. Poyser. Calton.

GREEN, I. & OVERFIELD, J. 1983. Birding the Polar Ural-Western Palearctic Siberia. *BW* 7: 15–20.

GREENWOOD, J. J. D. 1968. Bluethroat nesting in Scotland. *BB* 61: 524–525.

GREIJ, E. 1993. Prairie Birds... *Birders' World* (October 1993): 6.

GRIEVE, A. 1987. Hudsonian Godwit: new to the Western Palearctic. *BB* 80: 466–473.

GUADANGO, J. R. 1995. Bunting bonanza. *Birders' World* (August 1995): 8–9.

GUTIÉRREZ, R. 1995. Vagrancy likelihood of the Welsh Monk Vulture. *BB* 88: 607–608.

HAMPSHIRE ORNITHOLOGICAL SOCIETY. 1993. *Birds of Hampshire.* Privately published.

HANCOCK, J. & KUSHLAN, J. 1984. *The Herons Handbook.* Croom Helm. London & Sydney.

HANEY, J. C. 1993. A closer look: Ivory Gull. *Birding* 25: 330–338.

HARBER, D. D. 1982. Slender-billed Gull in East Sussex. In Sharrock, J. T. R. & GRANT, P. J. (Eds) *Birds New to Britain and Ireland.* T. & A. D. Poyser. Calton.

HARRAP, S. 1992. 1992: A review of the birding year. *BW* 5: 461–479.

HARRIS, A. 1988. Identification of adult Sooty and Bridled Terns. *BB* 81: 525–530.

HARRISON, C. 1982. *An Atlas of the Birds of the Western Palearctic.* Collins. London.

HARRISON, J. M. & HARRISON, J. G. 1966. Hybrid Grey Lag × Canada Goose suggesting influence of Giant Canada Goose in Britain. *BB* 59: 547–550.

HARRISON, J. M. & HARRISON, J. G. 1968. Wigeon × Chilöe Wigeon resembling American Wigeon. *BB* 61: 169–171.

HARROP, H. 1992. The Pine Grosbeak in Shetland. *BW* 5: 133–137.

HARROP, H. 1994. Albatrosses in the Western Palearctic. *BW* 7: 241–245.

HARVEY, P. 1992. The Brown Flycatcher on Fair Isle – a new British bird. *BW* 5: 252–254.

HARVEY, W. G. 1981. Pallid Swift: new to Britain and Ireland. *BB* 74: 170–178.

HAYMAN, P., MARCHANT, J. & PRATER, A. 1986. *Shorebirds – an Identification Guide to the Waders of the World.* Croom Helm. London and Sydney.

HEARD, C. D. R. 1990. Blyth's Pipit in Cornwall. *BW* 3: 375–378.

HIRST, P. & PROCTER, R. 1995. Identification of Wandering and Grey-tailed Tattlers. *BW* 8: 91–97.

HIRST, P. & STENNING, J. 1994. The Grey-tailed Tattler in Grampian – the second Western Palearctic record. *BW* 7: 469–472.

HOGG, A. 1991. The Thayer's-type Gull at Ayr. *BW* 4: 82–83.

HOLIAN, J. J. & FORTEY, J. E. 1992. Lesser Scaup: new to the Western Palearctic. *BB* 85: 370–376.

HOLLOM, P. A. D. 1960. *The Popular Handbook of Rarer British Birds.* H. F. & G. Witherby. London.

HOLLYER, J. N. 1970. The Invasion of Nutcrackers in autumn 1968. *BB* 63: 353–373.

HOOGENDOORN, W. & STREINHAUS, G. H. 1990. Nearctic gulls in the Western Palearctic. *Dutch Birding* 12: 109–164.

HOUGH, J. 1992. Snowy Owl Plumages. *BW:* 5: 96–97.

HUDSON, R. 1972. Green Heron in Cornwall in 1889. *BB* 65: 424–427.

HUME, R. A. 1973. Ring-billed Gull in Glamorgan: a species new to Britain and Ireland. *BB* 66: 509–512.

HUME, R. A., on behalf of the British Birds Rarities Committee. 1993. Brown Shrike in Shetland: new to Britain and Ireland. *BB* 86: 600–604.

HUME, R. A. & CHRISTIE, D. A. 1989. Sabine's Gulls and other seabirds after the October 1987 storm. *BB* 82: 191–208.

HUNT, D. B. 1979. Yellow-bellied Sapsucker: new to Britain and Ireland. *BB* 72: 410–414.

HURFORD, C. 1989. Lesser Crested Tern: new to Britain and Ireland. *BB* 82: 396–398.

HUTCHINSON, C. D., KELLY, T. C. & O'SUL-LIVAN, K. 1984. American Coot: new to Britain and Ireland. *BB* 77: 12–16.

INCLEDON, C. S. L. 1968. Brown Thrasher in Dorset: a species new to Britain and Ireland. *BB* 61: 550–553.

JACKSON, J. A. 1992. Red-capped Sap-tapper. *Birders' World* (December 1992): 24–27.

JACKSON, J. A. 1993. Lord Baltimore's Oriole. *Birders' World* (April 1993): 12–15.

JAMES, P. 1986. Trumpeter Finch in West Sussex. *BB* 79: 299–300.

JAMES, P. C. 1986. Little Shearwaters in Britain and Ireland. *BB* 79: 28–33.

JARAMILLO, A. & HENSHAW, B. 1995. Identification of breeding plumaged Long- and Short-billed Dowitchers. *BW* 8: 221–228.

JOHNS, R. J. 1991. From the archives: setting the scene. *BW* 4: 315–317.

JONES, M. 1965. Bimaculated Lark on Lundy: a bird new to Great Britain and Ireland. *BB* 58: 309–312.

JONSSON, L. 1992. *Birds of Europe with North Africa and the Middle East.* Christopher Helm. London.

JONSSON, L. & GRANT, P. J. 1984. Identification of stints and peeps. *BB* 77: 293–315.

KAUFMAN, K. 1995. April quiz answers: quiz photo B. *Birding* 27: 220–221.

KENNERLEY, P. R. & LEADER, P. J. 1992. The identification, status and distribution of small *Acrocephalus* warblers in eastern China. *Hong Kong Bird Report 1991*: 143–187.

KENNERLEY, P. R., LEADER, P. J. & LEVEN, R. 1993. Aleutian Tern: the first records for Hong Kong. *Hong Kong Bird Report 1992*: 107–113.

KILBANE, T. 1989. Thayer's Gull in Galway – A New Western Palearctic Bird. *BW* 2: 125–129.

KING, J. M. B. 1990. Veery in Devon. *BB* 83: 284–287.

KING, J. & MINGUEZ, E. 1994. Swinhoe's Petrel: the first Mediterranean record. *BW* 7: 271–273.

KITSON, A. R., MARR, B. A. E. & PORTER, R. F. 1980. Greater Sand Plover: new to Britain and Ireland. *BB* 73: 568–573.

KITSON, A. R. & ROBERTSON, I. S. 1983. Yellow-browed Bunting: new to Britain and Ireland. *BB* 76: 217–225.

KNOX, A. 1988. Taxonomy of the Rock/Water Pipit superspecies *Anthus petrosus, spinoletta* and *rubescens*. *BB* 81: 206–211.

KNOX, A. 1996. Grey-cheeked and Bicknell's Thrushes: taxonomy, identification and the British and Irish records. *BB* 89: 1–9.

LABUTIN, Y. V., LEONOVITCH, V. V. & YEPRINSTEV, B. N. 1982. The Little Curlew *Numenius minimus* in Siberia. *Ibis* 124: 302–319.

LANCTOT, R. B. 1995. A closer look: Buff-breasted Sandpiper. *Birding* 27: 384–390.

LANE, B. A. 1987. *Shorebirds in Australia.* Melbourne.

LANSDOWN, P. 1995. Age of Great Spotted Cuckoos in Britain and Ireland. *BB* 88: 141–149.

LANSDOWN, P. & CHARLTON, T. D. 1990. 'The Sizewell Bunting': a hybrid Pine Bunting × Yellowhammer. *BB* 83: 240–242.

LANSDOWN, P., RIDDIFORD, N. & KNOX, A. K. 1991. Identification of Arctic Redpoll *Carduelis hornemanni exilipes*. *BB* 84: 41–56.

LEADER, P. 1995. Status of Mugimaki Flycatcher. *BW* 8: 428–429.

LEHMAN, P. 1994. Franklin's vs Laughing Gulls. A 'new' problem arises. *Birding* 26: 126–127.

LEITCH, A. 1993. The Blyth's Pipit on Fair Isle. *BW* 6: 435–436.

LEWINGTON, I. 1992. Ageing and sexing of Rüppell's Warbler. *BW* 5: 339–340.

LOWE, A. R. 1979. Siberian Rubythroat: new to Britain and Ireland. *BB* 72: 89–94.

LUNN, J. 1985. Marmora's Warbler: new to Britain and Ireland. *BB* 78: 478–481.

McGEEHAN, A. & MULLARNEY, K. 1995. A little help. *Birdwatch* (September 1995): 38–42.

McKAY, C. R. 1994. Brown-headed Cowbird in Strathclyde: new to Britain and Ireland. *BB* 87: 284–288.

McKEE, N. 1993. The White's Thrush in Co. Down. *BW* 6: 143–144.

McLAREN, I. A. 1995. Field identification and taxonomy of Bicknell's Thrush. *Birding* 27: 358–366.

MADGE, S. C., HEARL, G. C., HUTCHINS, S. C. & WILLIAMS, L. P. 1990. Varied Thrush: new to the Western Palearctic. *BB* 83: 187–195.

MANRY, D. E. 1995. Singing the same tune. The importance of song learning in the complex social life of the Indigo Bunting. *Birders' World* (June 1995): 26–30.

MARSH, N. & ODIN, N. 1994. The Blyth's Pipit in Suffolk. *BW* 7: 473–475.

MARTINS, R. P. 1981. Rüppell's Warbler: new to Britain and Ireland. *BB* 74: 279–283.

MEEK, E. R. 1984. Tennessee Warbler in Orkney. *BB* 77: 160–164.

MEININGER, P. L., P.A. WOLF, D.A. HADOUD and M.F.A. ESSGHAIER. 1994.Rediscovery of Lesser Crested Terns breeding in Libya. *BB* 87:160–170.

MEININGER, P. L. & SØRENSEN, U. G. 1993. Egypt as a major wintering area of Little Gulls. *BB* 86: 407–410.

MELLOW, B. K. & MAKER, P. A. 1981. American Kestrel in Cornwall. *BB* 74: 227.

MILD, K. 1994. Field identification of Pied, Collared and Semi-collared Flycatchers. *BW* 7: 139–151, 231–240 and 325–334.

MILLINGTON, R. 1995. Black-headed Buntings in spring. *BW* 8: 215.

MILLINGTON, R. 1996. Identification forum: Arctic Redpoll revisited. *BW* 9: 65–69.

MILSON, G. R. & AUSTIN-SMITH, P. J. 1983. Changes in abundance and distribution of Double-crested (*Phalacrocorax auritus*) and Great Cormorants (*P. carbo*) in Nova Scotia. *Colonial Waterbirds* 6: 130–138.

MOLAU, U. 1985. Gråsiskkomplexet i Sverige. *Vår Fågelv.* 44: 5–20.

MOON, S. J. 1983. Little Whimbrel: new to Britain and Ireland. *BB* 76: 438–445.

MOORE, D. R. & PIOTROWSKI, S. H. 1983. Hybrid Coot × Moorhen resembling American Coot in Suffolk. *BB* 76: 407–409.

MULLARNEY, K. 1981. Belted Kingfisher: new to Britain and Ireland. *BB* 74: 242–245.

MULLARNEY, K. 1991. Identification of Semipalmated Plover: a new feature. *BW* 4: 254–258.

MULLARNEY, K. 1992. The Western Sandpiper in County Wexford. *BW* 5: 341–343.

MURRAY, K. 1990. Naumann's Thrush in London – a British first. *BW* 3: 50–53.

NEWELL, R. G. 1968. Influx of Great Shearwaters in autumn 1965. *BB* 61: 145–159.

NEWTON, I. 1972. *Finches.* Collins. London.

NIGHTINGALE, B. & ALLSOPP, K. 1994. Invasion of Red-footed Falcons in spring 1992. *BB* 87: 223–231.

NORMAJA, J. 1994. Plumage variation in River Warblers. *BW* 7: 192–193.

ODDIE, W. E. 1981. Cretzschmar's Bunting in Shetland. *BB* 74: 532–533.

OGILVIE, M. & the RARE BREEDING BIRDS PANEL. 1995. Rare breeding birds in the United Kingdom in 1992. *BB* 88: 67–93.

OGILVIE, M. & the RARE BREEDING BIRDS PANEL. 1996. Rare breeding birds in the United Kingdom in 1993. *BB* 89: 61–91.

OLSSON, V. 1991. Studies of less familiar birds 165. Serin. *BB* 64: 213–223.

OSBORN, K. 1993. The Shetland *Hippolais* warbler. *BW* 6: 437–438.

OUELLET, H. 1993. Bicknell's Thrush. Taxonomic status and distribution. *Wilson Bulletin* 105: 545–571.

PALMER, P. 1990. I should be so lucky... *BW* 3: 213.

PARKER, M. 1990. Pacific Swift: new to the Western Palearctic. *BB* 83: 43–46.

PARKIN, D. T. & SHAW, K. D., on behalf of the British Ornithologists' Union Records Committee.

1994. Asian Brown Flycatcher, Mugimaki Flycatcher and Pallas's Rosefinch. Three recent decisions of the British Ornithologists' Union Records Committee. *BB* 87: 247–252.

PARRISH, R. 1991. The Mugimaki Flycatcher in Humberside – a new Western Palearctic bird. *BW* 4: 392–395.

PARSLOW, J. 1971. Bobolink. In Gooders, J. (Ed.) *Birds of the World.* Vol 8. London. IPC Magazines.

PRICE, J., DROEGE, S. & PRICE, A. 1995. *The Summer Atlas of North American Birds.* Academic Press Inc. San Diego.

PROCTER, R. 1991. The Ross's Goose in Grampian. *BW* 4: 137–139.

PYLE, P. 1995. Age of Norfolk Red-breasted Nuthatch. *BB* 88: 611.

PYLE, P., HOWELL, S. N. G., YUNICK, R. P. & DE SANTE, D. F. 1987. *Identification Guide to North American Passerines.* Bolinas, California.

RAJASÄRKKÄ, A. 1996. Taigan tuulahdus sin iryrstö. *Linnut* 3: 20–28.

REDSHAW, K. 1972. Slender-billed Gull in Kent. *BB* 65: 395–397.

RICHARDS, B. 1989. Red-necked Stint: new to Britain and Ireland. *BB* 82: 391–395.

RIDDIFORD, N. & BROOME, A. 1983. Identification of first-winter Pallas's Reed Bunting. *BB* 76: 174–182.

RIDDIFORD, N. & HARVEY, P. V. 1992. Identification of Lanceolated Warbler. *BB* 85: 62–78.

RIEGNER, M. 1993. Thunder Pumper. *Birders' World* (June 1993): 12–15.

ROBBINS, C. S. 1980. Predictions of future Nearctic landbird vagrants to Europe. *BB* 73: 448–457.

ROBERTS, P. J. 1984. Identification and ageing of a Sora Rail. *BB* 77: 108–112.

ROBERTSON, I. S. 1975. Ovenbird in Shetland: a species new to Britain and Ireland. *BB* 68: 453–455.

ROBERTSON, I. S. 1977. Identification and European status of eastern Stonechats. *BB* 70: 237–245.

ROGACHEVA, H. 1992. *The Birds of Central Siberia.* Husum.

ROGERS, M. J. 1982. Ruddy Shelducks in Britain in 1965–79. *BB* 75: 446–453.

ROGERS, M. J. & THE RARITIES COMMITTEE. 1992. Report on rare birds in Great Britain in 1991. *BB* 85: 507–554.

ROGERS, M. J. & THE RARITIES COMMITTEE. 1990. Report on rare birds in Great Britain in 1989. *BB* 83: 439–496.

ROUND, P. D. 1996. Long-toed Stint in Cornwall: the first record for the Western Palearctic. *BB* 89: 12–24.

SAPSFORD, A. 1996. Mourning Dove in the Isle of Man: new to the Western Palearctic Bird. *BB* 89: 157–161.

SCOTT, M. 1995. The status and identification of Snow Goose and Ross's Goose. *BW* 8: 56–63.

SHARROCK, J. T. R. 1968. Little Swift in Co. Cork: a species new to Britain and Ireland. *BB* 61: 160–162.

SHAW, K. & WEBB, A. 1991. The Greater Sand Plover on the Don Estuary, Grampian. *BW* 4: 396–398.

SHIRIHAI, H., CHRISTIE, D. A. & HARRIS, A. 1995. Field identification of Pine Bunting. *BB* 88: 621–626.

SIMPSON, R. E. 1990. Indigo Bunting status. *BW* 3: 314–315.

SMALDON, R. 1990. Wilson's Warbler: new to the Western Palearctic. *BB* 83: 404–408.

SMALL, B. 1995. Field identification of Red-footed Falcon. *BB* 88: 181–189.

SMITH, F. R. 1955. Myrtle Warbler in Devon: a species new to Great Britain and Ireland. *BB* 48: 204–207.

SPENCER, R. & THE RARE BREEDING BIRDS PANEL. 1991. Rare breeding birds in the United Kingdom in 1989. *BB* 84: 349–370, 379–392.

STALLCUP, R. 1982. Cormorants. *Point Reyes Bird Observatory Newsletter* 57.

STEELE, J. 1996. Rump stakes. *Birdwatch* (March 1996): 26–31.

STODDART, A. 1992. Identification of Siberian Stonechat. *BW* 5: 348–356.

SUDDABY, D. 1990. Yellow Warbler in Shetland. *BW* 3: 381–382.

SUDDABY, D., SHAW, K. D., ELLIS P. M. & BROCKIE, K., on behalf of the Rarities Committee. King Eiders in Britain and Ireland in 1958–90: occurrences and ageing. *BB* 87: 418–430.

TAYLOR, A. M. 1981. American Kestrel in Cornwall. *BB* 74: 199–203.

THORPE, R. I. 1995. Grey-tailed Tattler in Wales: new to Britain and Ireland. *BB* 88: 255–262.

TOMKOVITCH, P. S. 1992. Breeding range and population changes of waders in the former Soviet Union. *BB* 85: 344–365.

TULLOCH, R. J. 1968. Snowy Owls breeding in Shetland in 1967. *BB* 61: 119–132.

VAN DEN BERG, A. B., LAMBECK, R. H. D. & MULLARNEY, K. 1984. The Occurrence of the 'Black Brant' in Europe. *BB* 77: 458–465.

VINICOMBE, K. E. 1994. Common Teals showing mixed characters of the Eurasian and North American races. *BB* 87: 88–89.

VINICOMBE, K. E., on behalf of the British Ornithologists' Union Records Committee. 1994. The Welsh Monk Vulture. *BB* 87: 613–622.

VOOUS, K. H. 1979. Capricious taxonomic history of Isabelline Shrike. *BB* 72: 573–578.

WALDON, J. 1994. Ancient Murrelet in Devon: new to the Western Palaearctic. *BB* 87: 307–310.

WALLACE, D. I. M. 1970. Identification of Spotted Sandpipers out of breeding plumage. *BB* 63: 168–173.

WALLACE, D. I. M. 1980. Possible future Palearctic passerine vagrants to Britain. *BB* 73: 388–397.

WALLACE, D. I. M., COBB, F. K. & TUBBS, C. R. 1977. Trumpeter Finches: new to Britain and Ireland. *BB* 70: 45–49.

WATERSTONE, G. 1968. Black-browed Albatross on the Bass Rock. *BB* 61: 22–27.

WEBB, R. 1988. Puna Ibis – a potential identification pitfall. *BW* 1: 57–58.

WILLIAMS, L. P. 1986. Chimney Swift: new to the Western Palaearctic. *BB* 79: 423–426.

WILLIAMS, T. J. 1996. Double-crested Cormorant: new to the Western Palaearctic. *BB* 89: 162–170.

WILLIAMSON, K. 1967. *Identification for Ringers. The Genus* Phylloscopus. (Revised edn). British Trust for Ornithology. Tring.

WILLIAMSON, K. 1968. *Identification for Ringers. The Genus* Sylvia. (2nd edn). British Trust for Ornithology. Tring.

WILSON, G. E. 1976. Spotted Sandpipers nesting in Scotland. *BB* 69: 288–292.

WOODBRIDGE, D. 1992. The Siberian Thrush on Orkney. *BW* 5: 377–379.

WRIGHT, G. 1987. Hudsonian Godwit in Devon. *BB* 80: 492–494.

ZIMMER, K. J. 1991. Plumage variation in 'Kumlien's' Iceland Gull. *Birding* 23: 254–268.

INDEX